DEADMAN
DARK MANSION OF FORBIDDEN LOVE

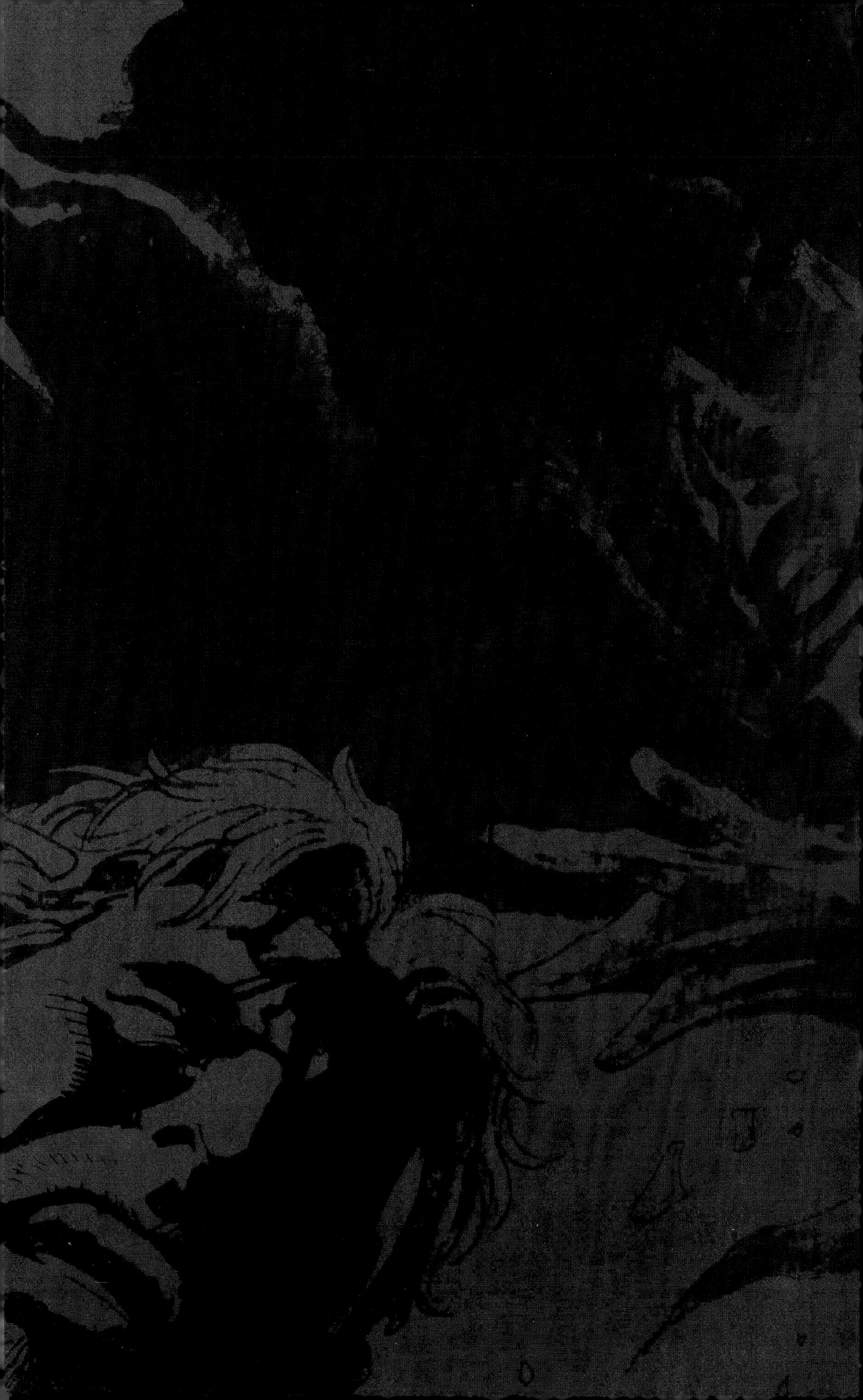

DEADMAN
DARK MANSION OF FORBIDDEN LOVE

SARAH VAUGHN writer LAN MEDINA & PHIL HESTER illustrators JOSÉ VILLARRUBIA colorist

JANICE CHIANG letterer STEPHANIE HANS original series and collection cover artist DEADMAN created by ARNOLD DRAKE

ALEX ANTONE Editor – Original Series
BRITTANY HOLZHERR Assistant Editor – Original Series
JEB WOODARD Group Editor – Collected Editions
ERIKA ROTHBERG Editor – Collected Edition
STEVE COOK Design Director – Books
LOUIS PRANDI Publication Design

BOB HARRAS Senior VP – Editor-in-Chief, DC Comics

DIANE NELSON President
DAN DiDIO Publisher
JIM LEE Publisher
GEOFF JOHNS President & Chief Creative Officer
AMIT DESAI Executive VP – Business & Marketing Strategy, Direct to Consumer & Global Franchise Management
SAM ADES Senior VP – Direct to Consumer
BOBBIE CHASE VP – Talent Development
MARK CHIARELLO Senior VP – Art, Design & Collected Editions
JOHN CUNNINGHAM Senior VP – Sales & Trade Marketing
ANNE DePIES Senior VP – Business Strategy, Finance & Administration
DON FALLETTI VP – Manufacturing Operations
LAWRENCE GANEM VP – Editorial Administration & Talent Relations
ALISON GILL Senior VP – Manufacturing & Operations
HANK KANALZ Senior VP – Editorial Strategy & Administration
JAY KOGAN VP – Legal Affairs
THOMAS LOFTUS VP – Business Affairs
JACK MAHAN VP – Business Affairs
NICK J. NAPOLITANO VP – Manufacturing Administration
EDDIE SCANNELL VP – Consumer Marketing
COURTNEY SIMMONS Senior VP – Publicity & Communications
JIM (SKI) SOKOLOWSKI VP – Comic Book Specialty Sales & Trade Marketing
NANCY SPEARS VP – Mass, Book, Digital Sales & Trade Marketing

DEADMAN: DARK MANSION OF FORBIDDEN LOVE
Published by DC Comics.

DC Comics, 2900 West Alameda Ave., Burbank, CA 91505
Printed by Vanguard Graphics, LLC, Ithaca, NY, USA. 4/28/17. First Printing.
ISBN: 978-1-4012-6841-1

Library of Congress Cataloging-in-Publication Data is available.

FSC www.fsc.org MIX Paper from responsible sources FSC® C016956

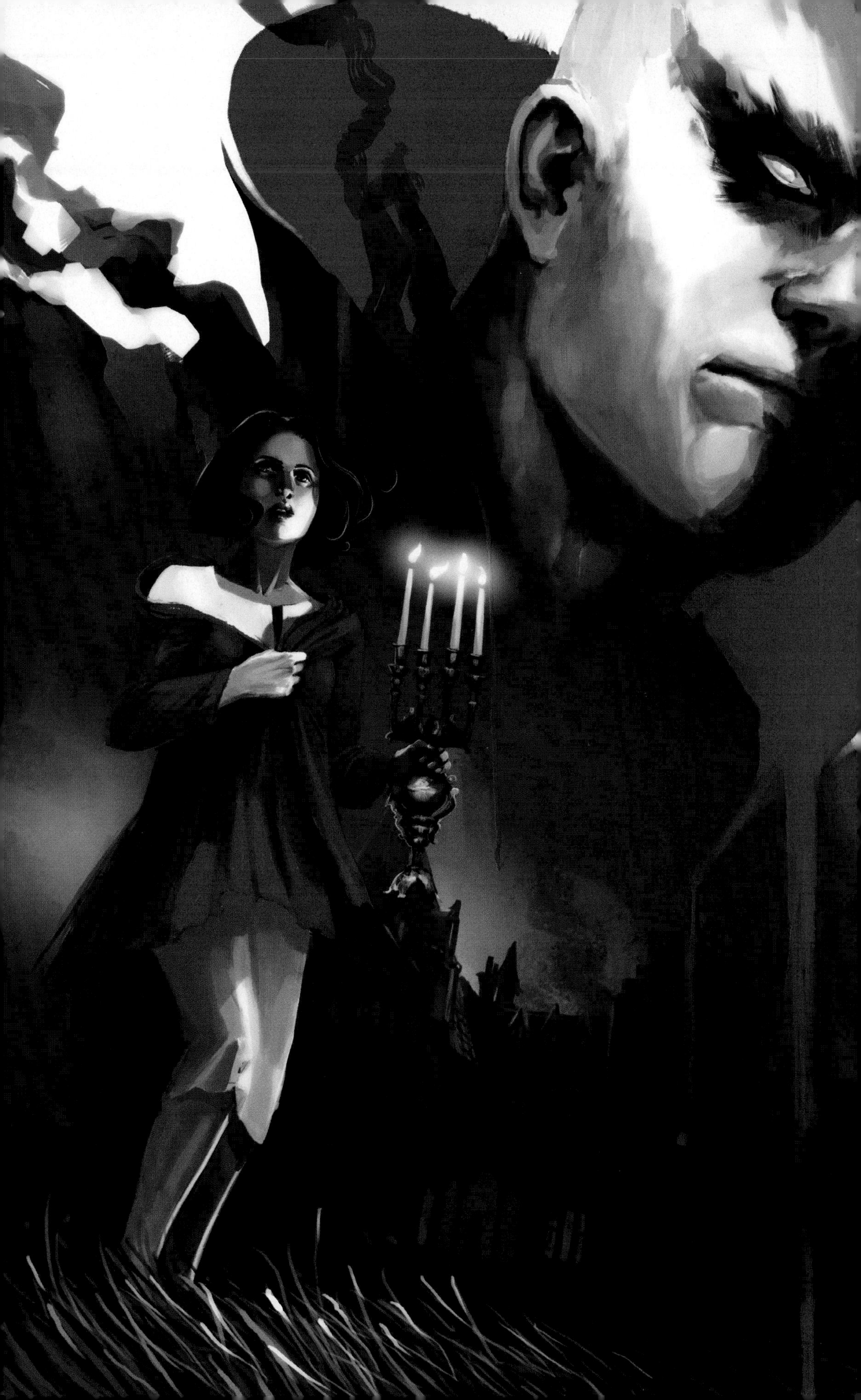

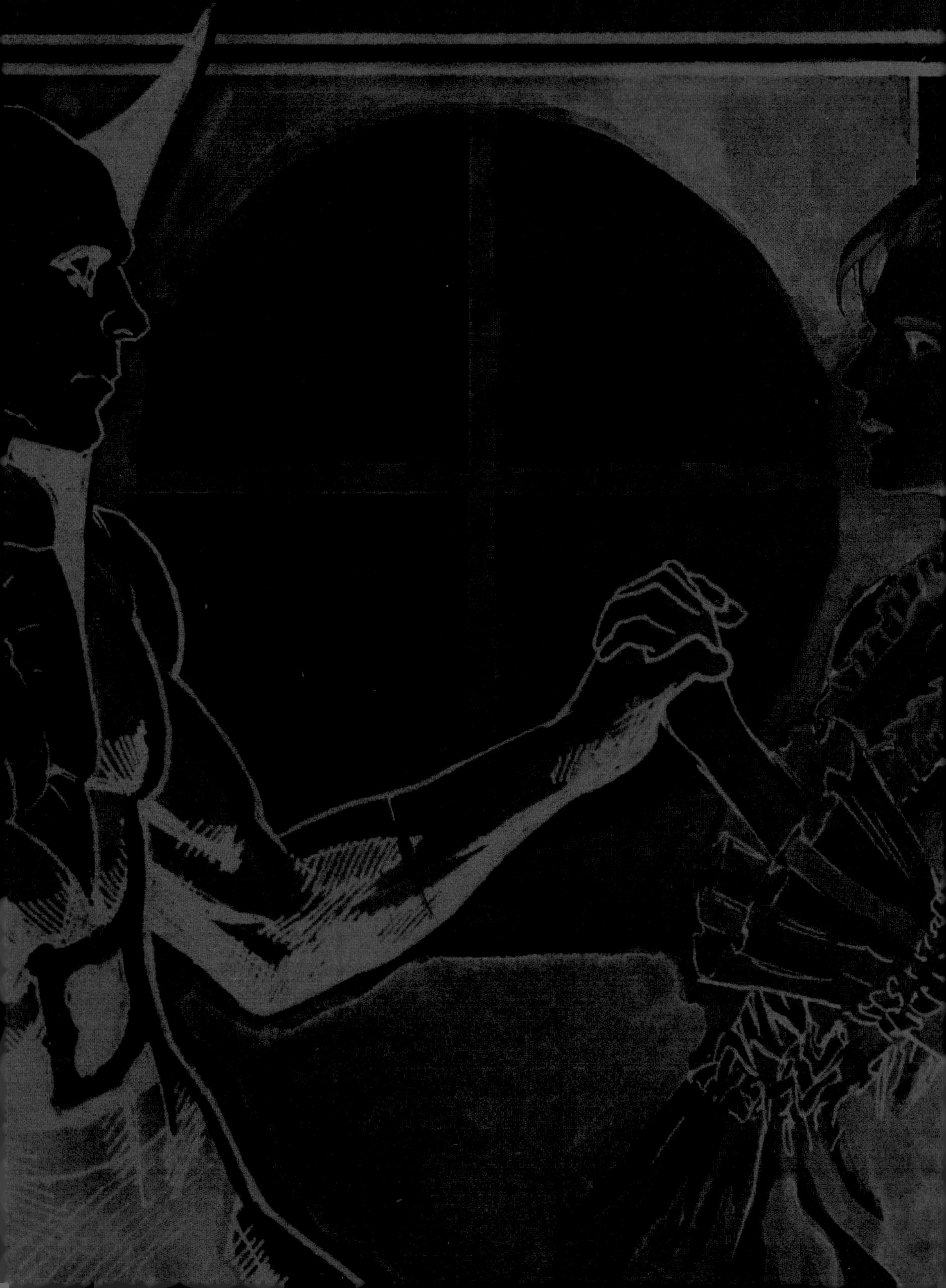

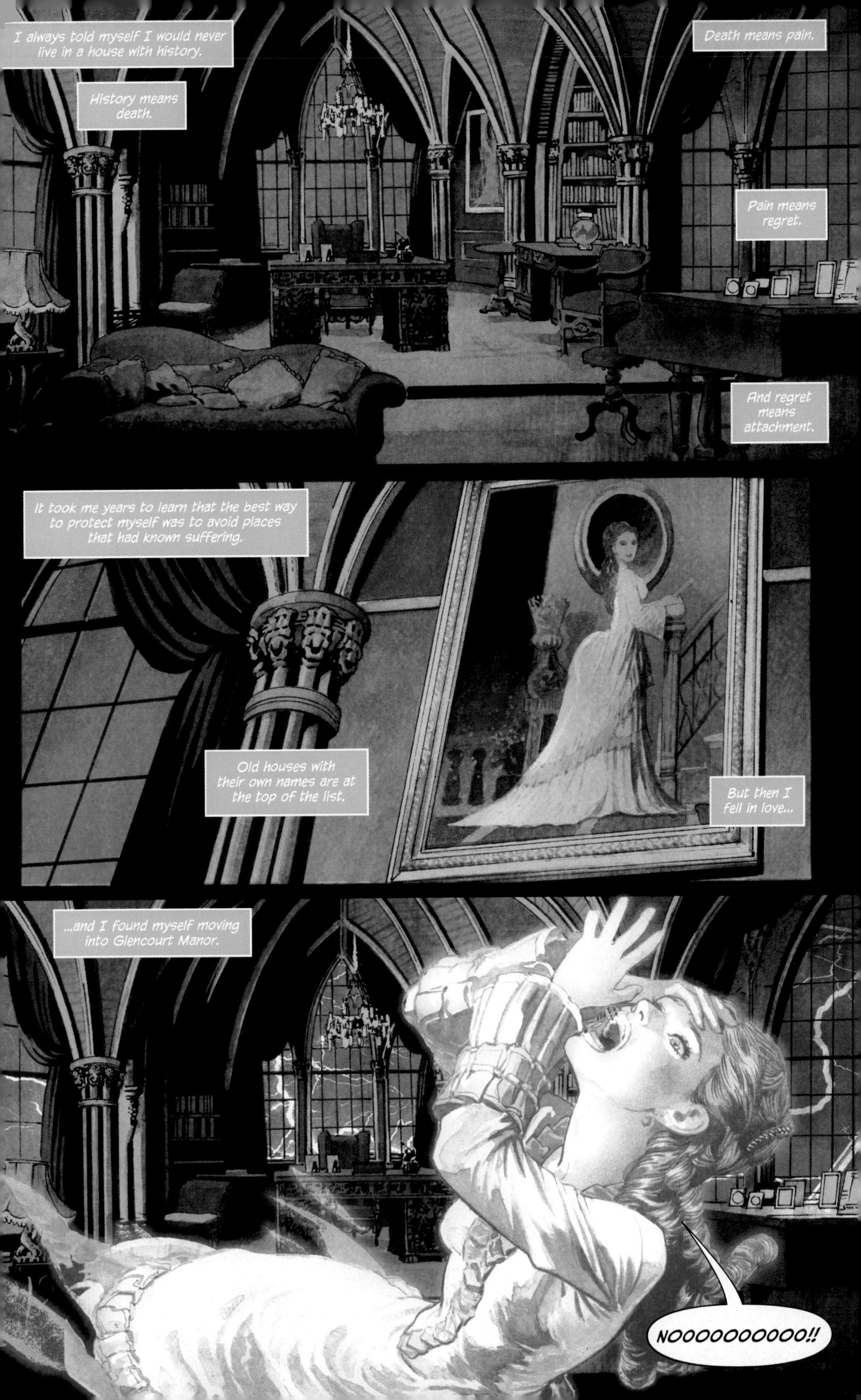
I always told myself I would never live in a house with history.
History means death.
Death means pain.
Pain means regret.
And regret means attachment.
It took me years to learn that the best way to protect myself was to avoid places that had known suffering.
Old houses with their own names are at the top of the list.
But then I fell in love...
...and I found myself moving into Glencourt Manor.
NOOOOOOOOOO!!

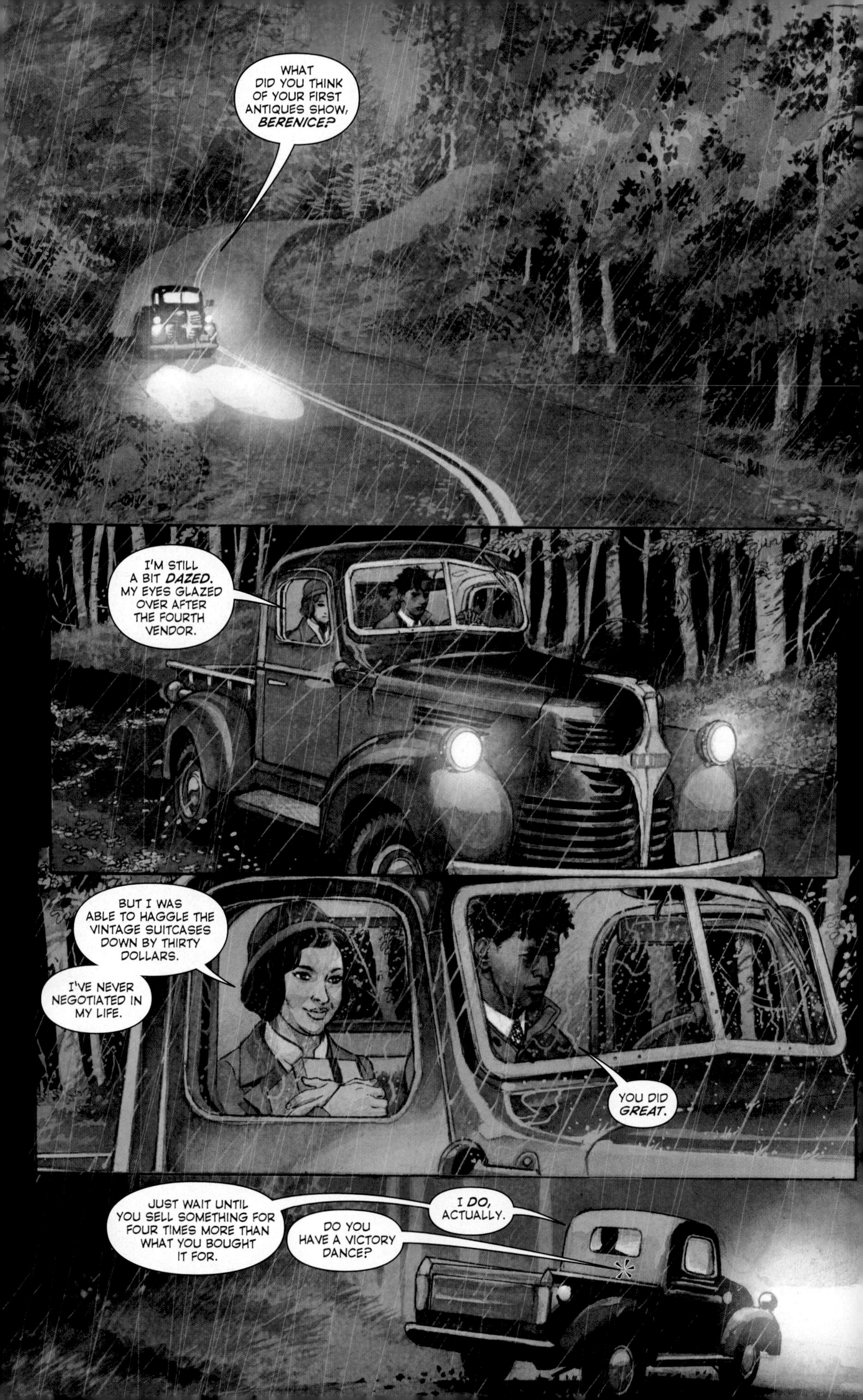
WHAT DID YOU THINK OF YOUR FIRST ANTIQUES SHOW, *BERENICE?*
I'M STILL A BIT *DAZED*. MY EYES GLAZED OVER AFTER THE FOURTH VENDOR.
BUT I WAS ABLE TO HAGGLE THE VINTAGE SUITCASES DOWN BY THIRTY DOLLARS.
I'VE NEVER NEGOTIATED IN MY LIFE.
YOU DID *GREAT*.
JUST WAIT UNTIL YOU SELL SOMETHING FOR FOUR TIMES MORE THAN WHAT YOU BOUGHT IT FOR.
DO YOU HAVE A VICTORY DANCE?
I *DO*, ACTUALLY.

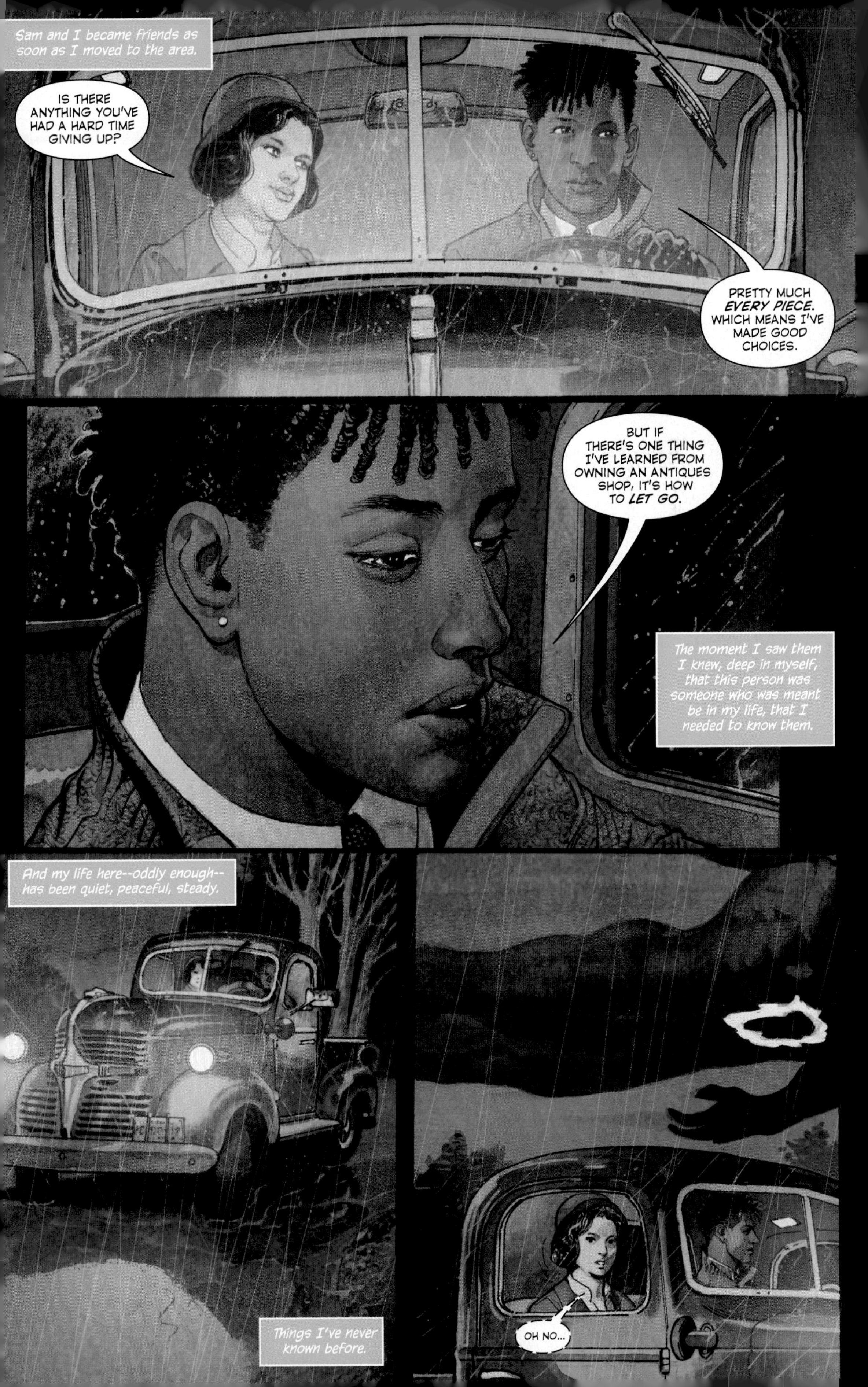

Sam and I became friends as soon as I moved to the area.
IS THERE ANYTHING YOU'VE HAD A HARD TIME GIVING UP?
PRETTY MUCH *EVERY PIECE.* WHICH MEANS I'VE MADE GOOD CHOICES.
BUT IF THERE'S ONE THING I'VE LEARNED FROM OWNING AN ANTIQUES SHOP, IT'S HOW TO *LET GO.*
The moment I saw them I knew, deep in myself, that this person was someone who was meant be in my life, that I needed to know them.
And my life here--oddly enough--has been quiet, peaceful, steady.
Things I've never known before.
OH NO...

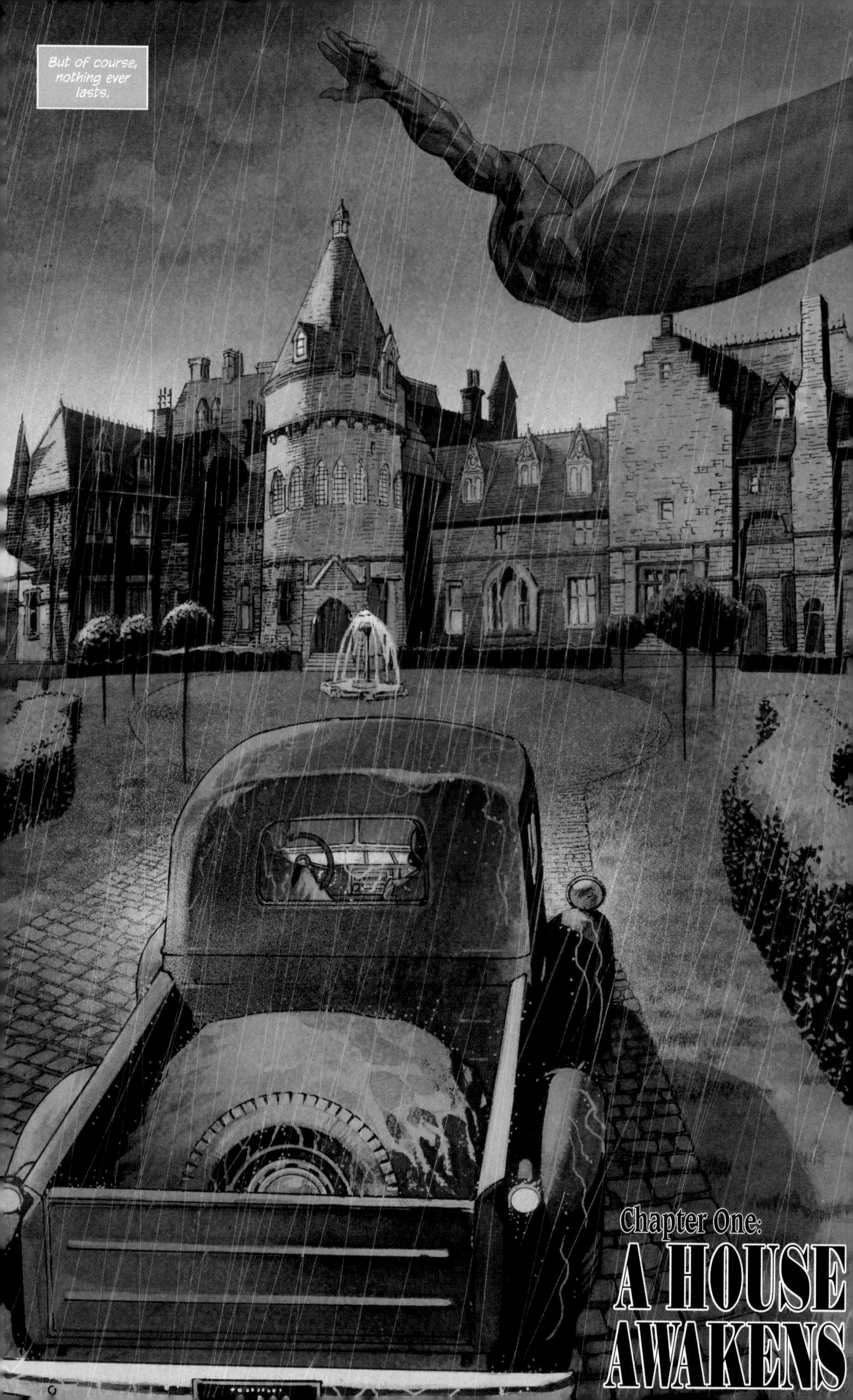
But of course, nothing ever lasts.
Chapter One:
A HOUSE AWAKENS

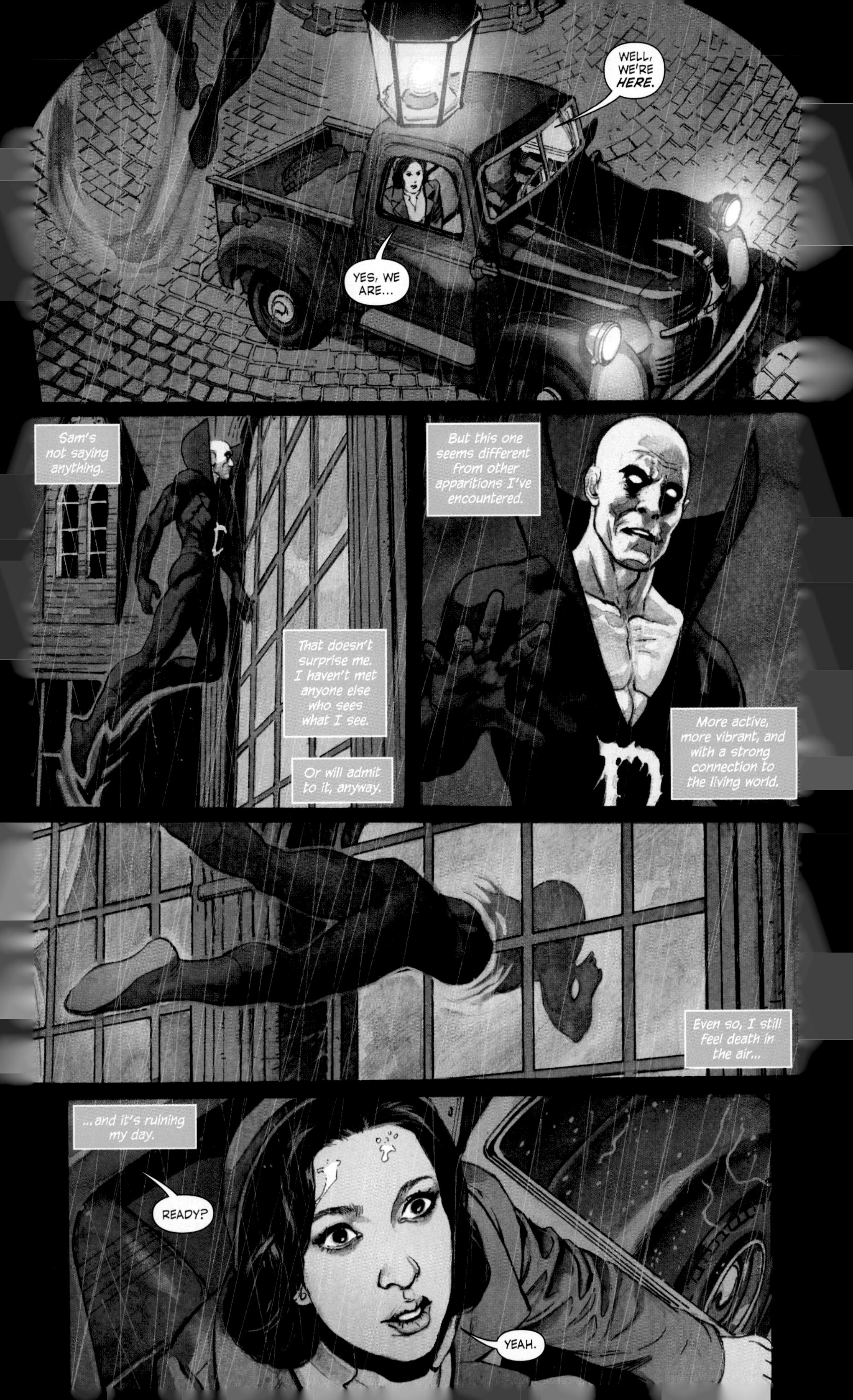
WELL, WE'RE HERE.
YES, WE ARE...
Sam's not saying anything.
That doesn't surprise me. I haven't met anyone else who sees what I see.
Or will admit to it, anyway.
But this one seems different from other apparitions I've encountered.
More active, more vibrant, and with a strong connection to the living world.
Even so, I still feel death in the air...
...and it's ruining my day.
READY?
YEAH.

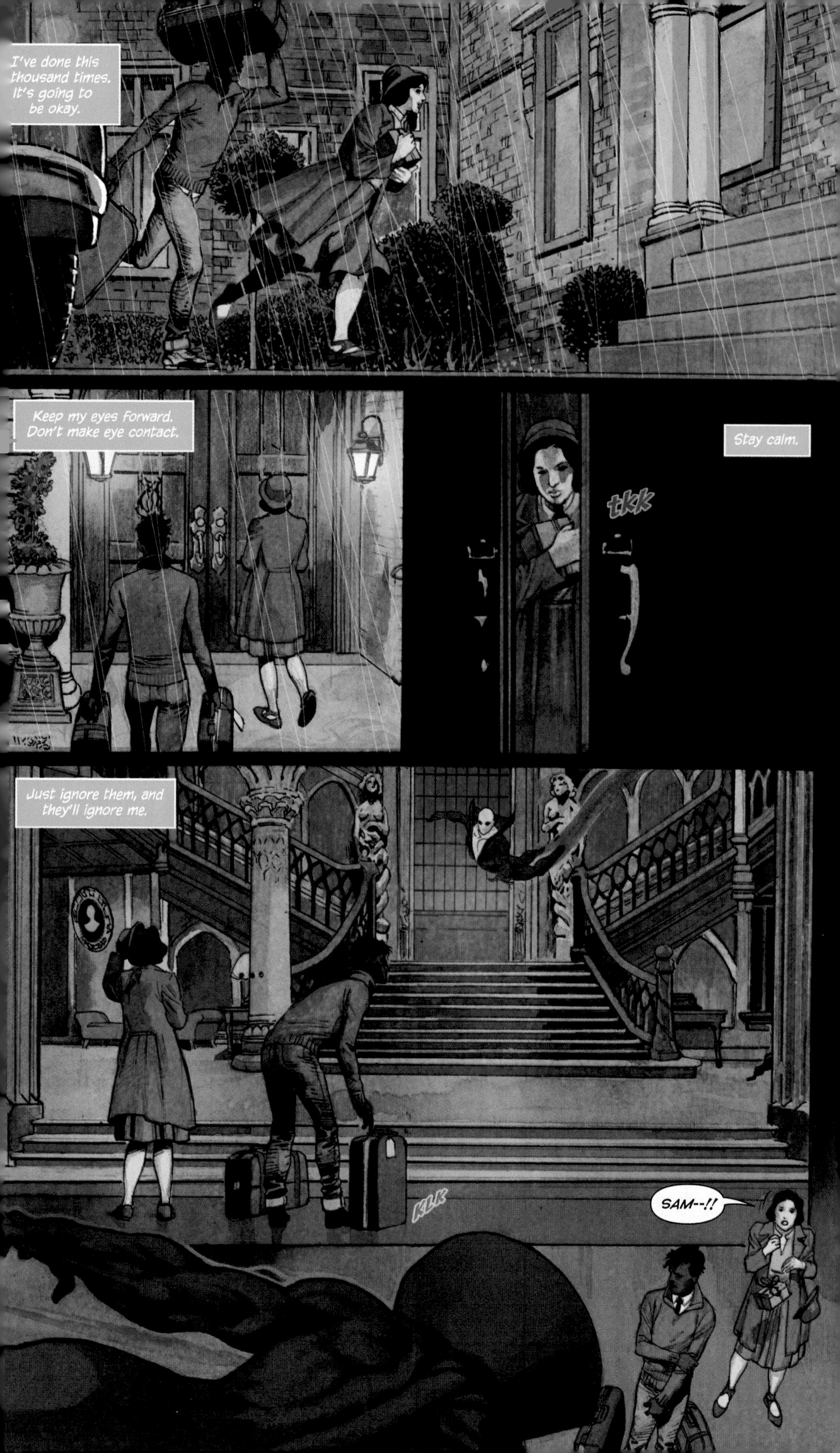

I've done this thousand times. It's going to be okay.
Keep my eyes forward. Don't make eye contact.
Stay calm.
tkk
Just ignore them, and they'll ignore me.
KLIK
SAM--!!

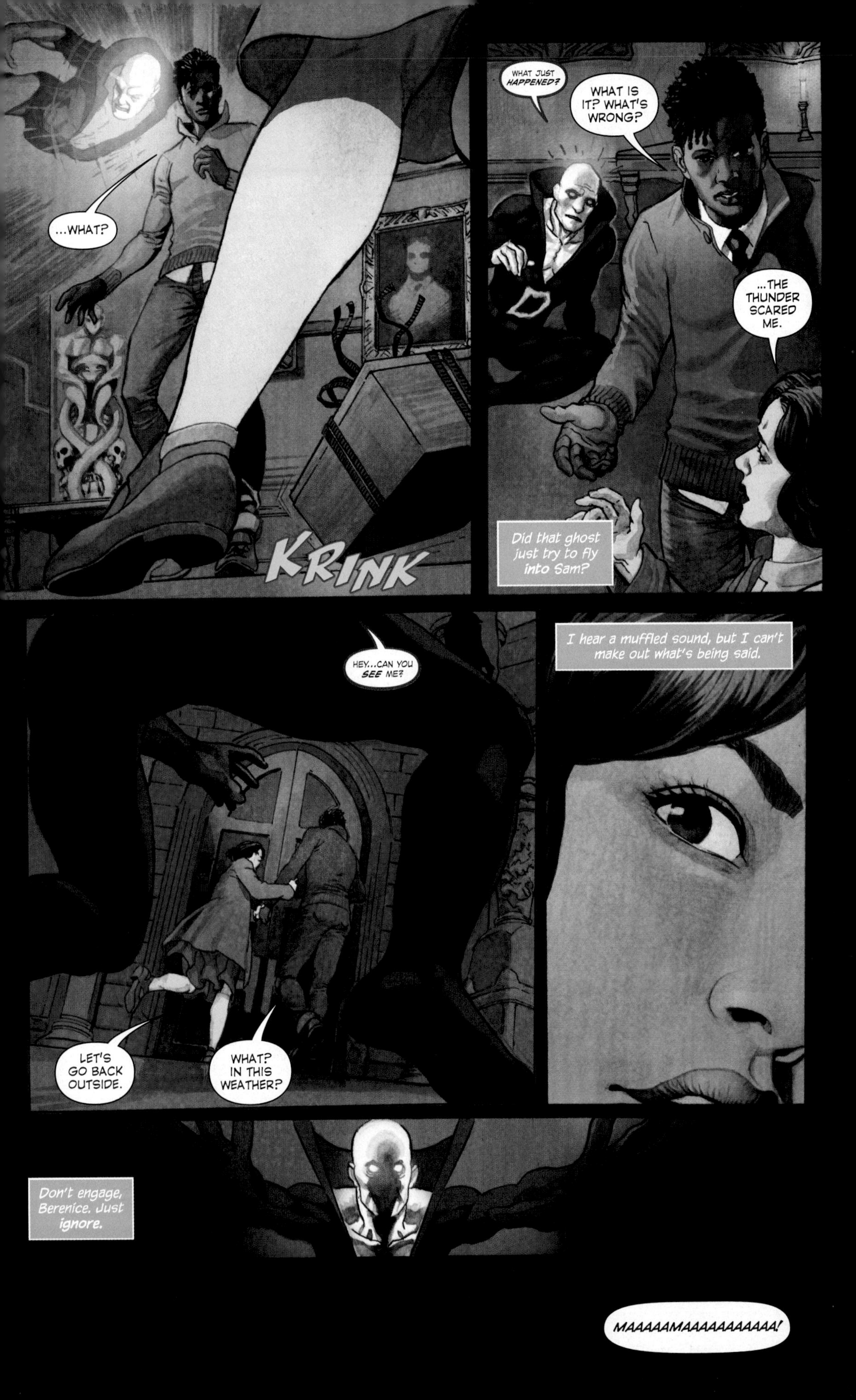

...WHAT?
KRINK
WHAT JUST HAPPENED?
WHAT IS IT? WHAT'S WRONG?
...THE THUNDER SCARED ME.
Did that ghost just try to fly into Sam?
HEY...CAN YOU SEE ME?
LET'S GO BACK OUTSIDE.
WHAT? IN THIS WEATHER?
I hear a muffled sound, but I can't make out what's being said.
Don't engage, Berenice. Just ignore.
MAAAAAMAAAAAAAAAAAA!

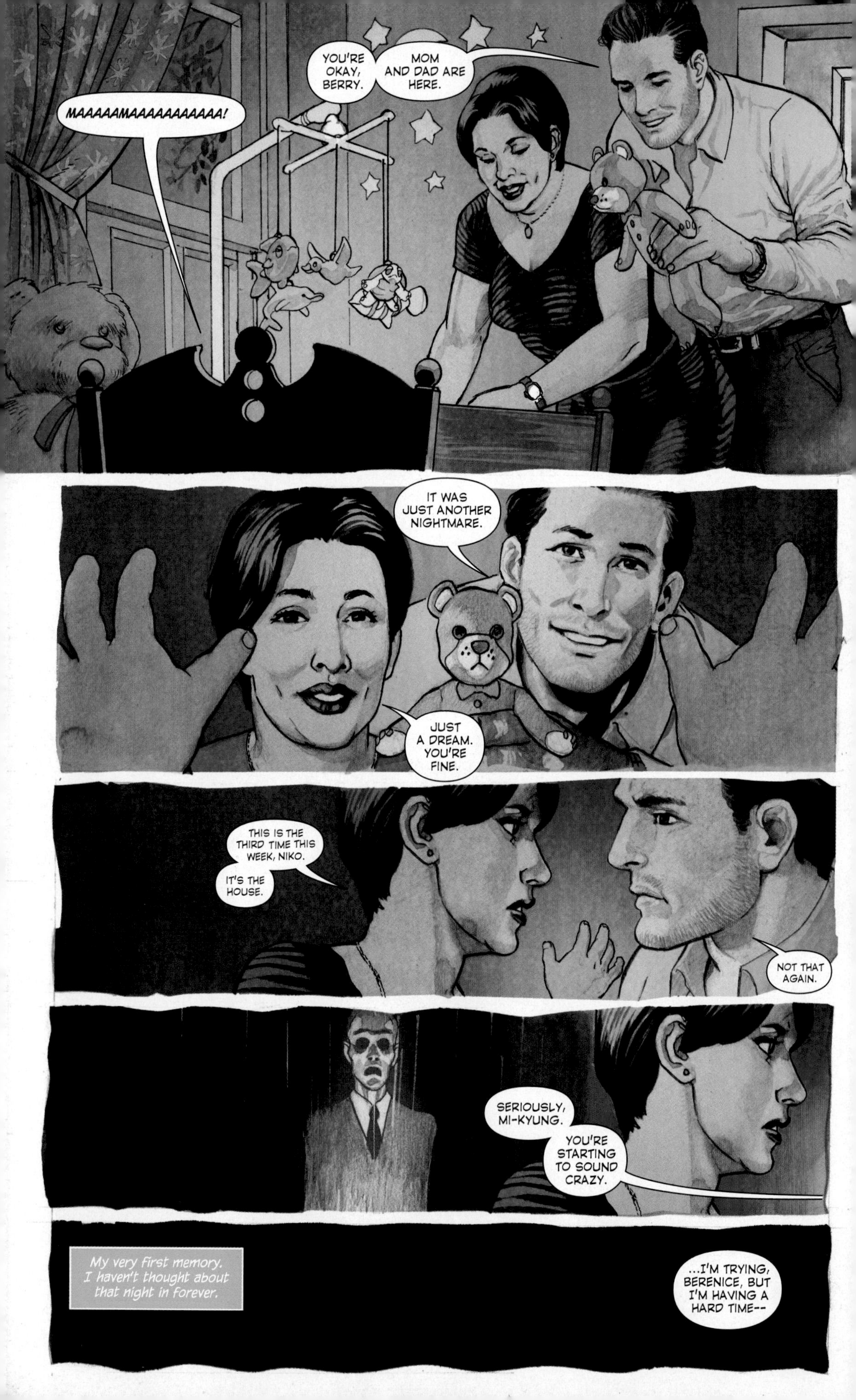
MAAAAAMAAAAAAAAAAAA!
YOU'RE OKAY, BERRY.
MOM AND DAD ARE HERE.
IT WAS JUST ANOTHER NIGHTMARE.
JUST A DREAM. YOU'RE FINE.
THIS IS THE THIRD TIME THIS WEEK, NIKO.
IT'S THE HOUSE.
NOT THAT AGAIN.
SERIOUSLY, MI-KYUNG.
YOU'RE STARTING TO SOUND CRAZY.
My very first memory. I haven't thought about that night in forever.
...I'M TRYING, BERENICE, BUT I'M HAVING A HARD TIME--

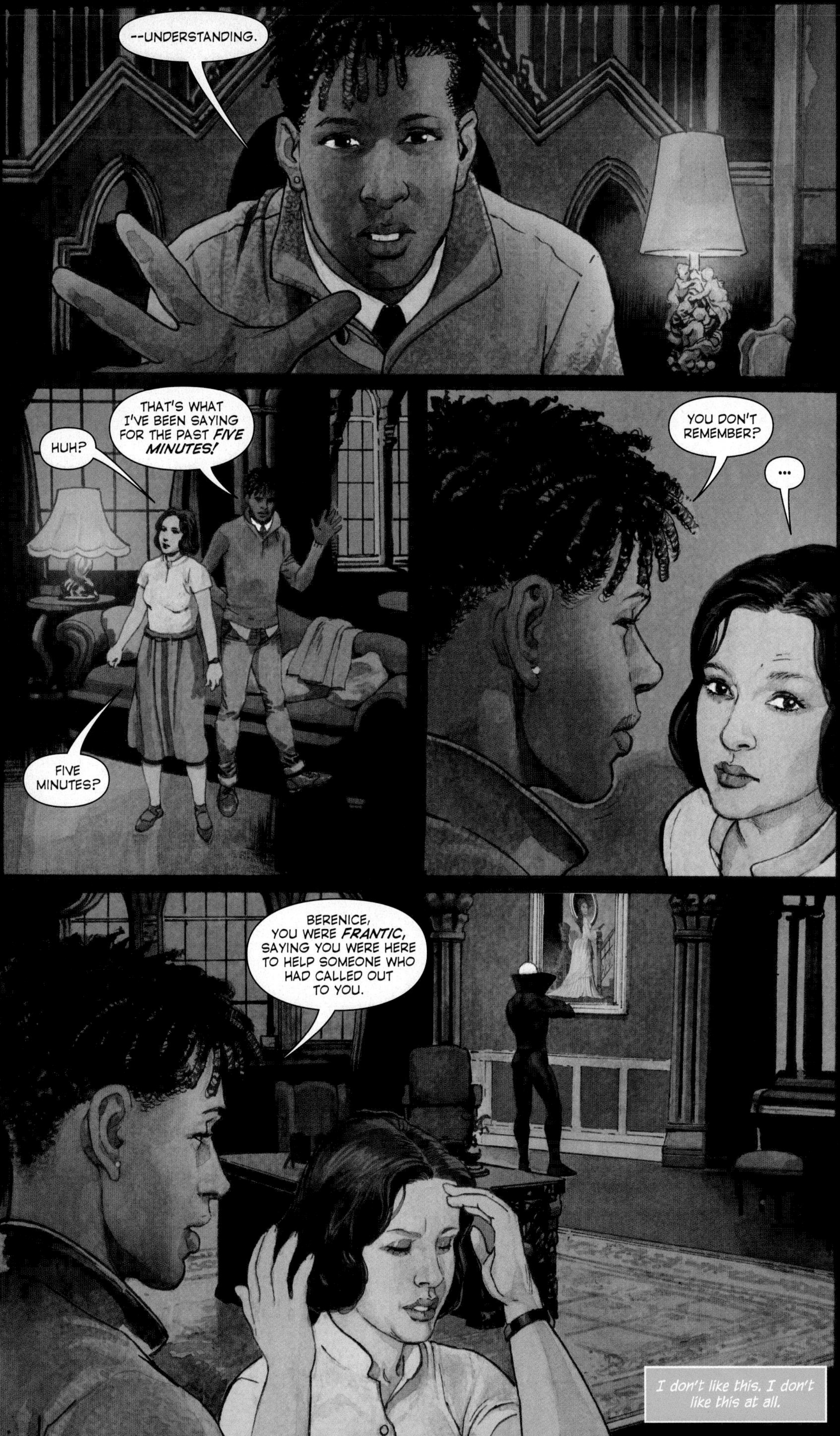
--UNDERSTANDING.
HUH?
THAT'S WHAT I'VE BEEN SAYING FOR THE PAST *FIVE MINUTES!*
FIVE MINUTES?
YOU DON'T REMEMBER?
...
BERENICE, YOU WERE *FRANTIC*, SAYING YOU WERE HERE TO HELP SOMEONE WHO HAD CALLED OUT TO YOU.
I don't like this. I don't like this at all.

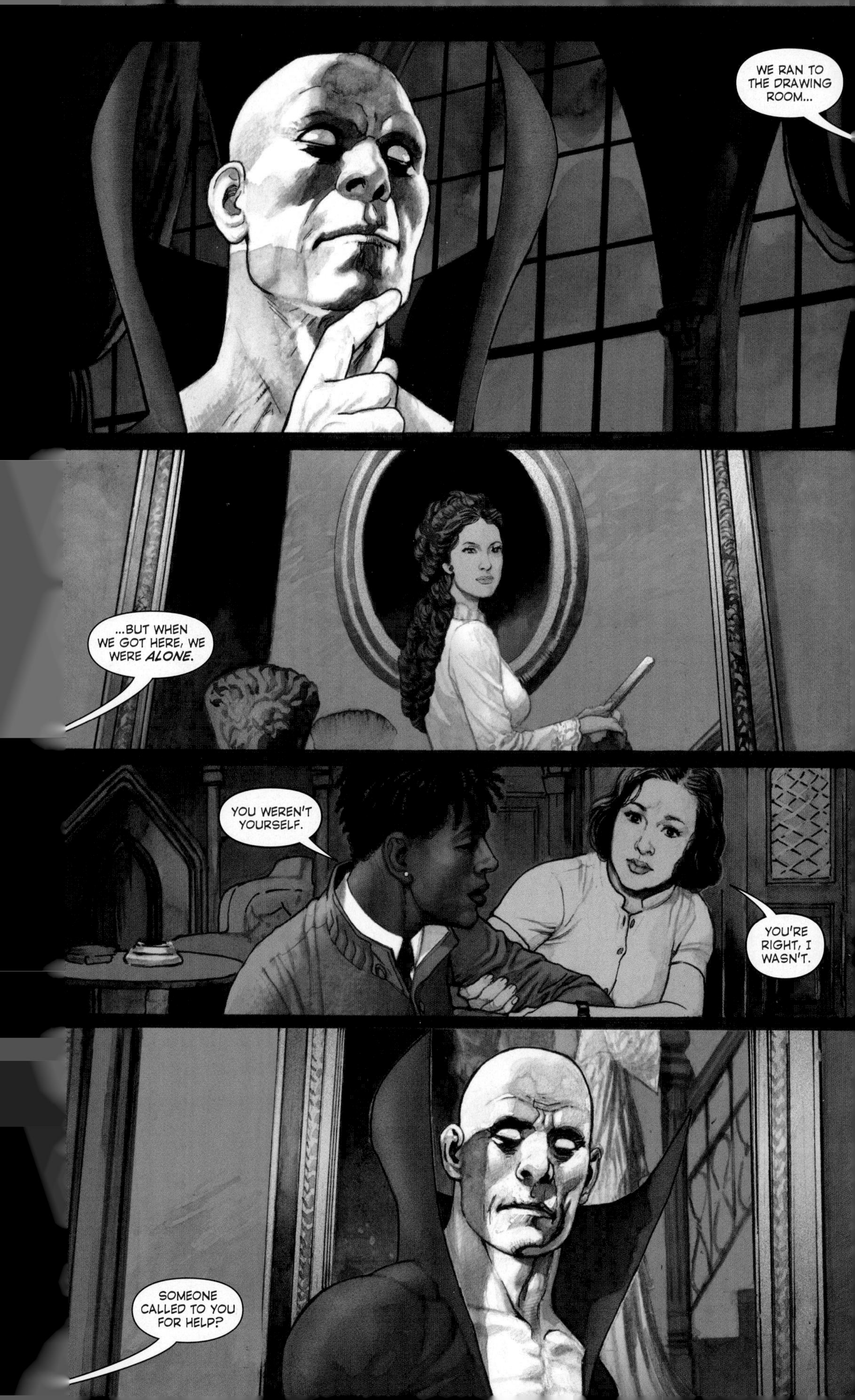

WE RAN TO THE DRAWING ROOM...
...BUT WHEN WE GOT HERE, WE WERE *ALONE*.
YOU WEREN'T YOURSELF.
YOU'RE RIGHT, I WASN'T.
SOMEONE CALLED TO YOU FOR HELP?

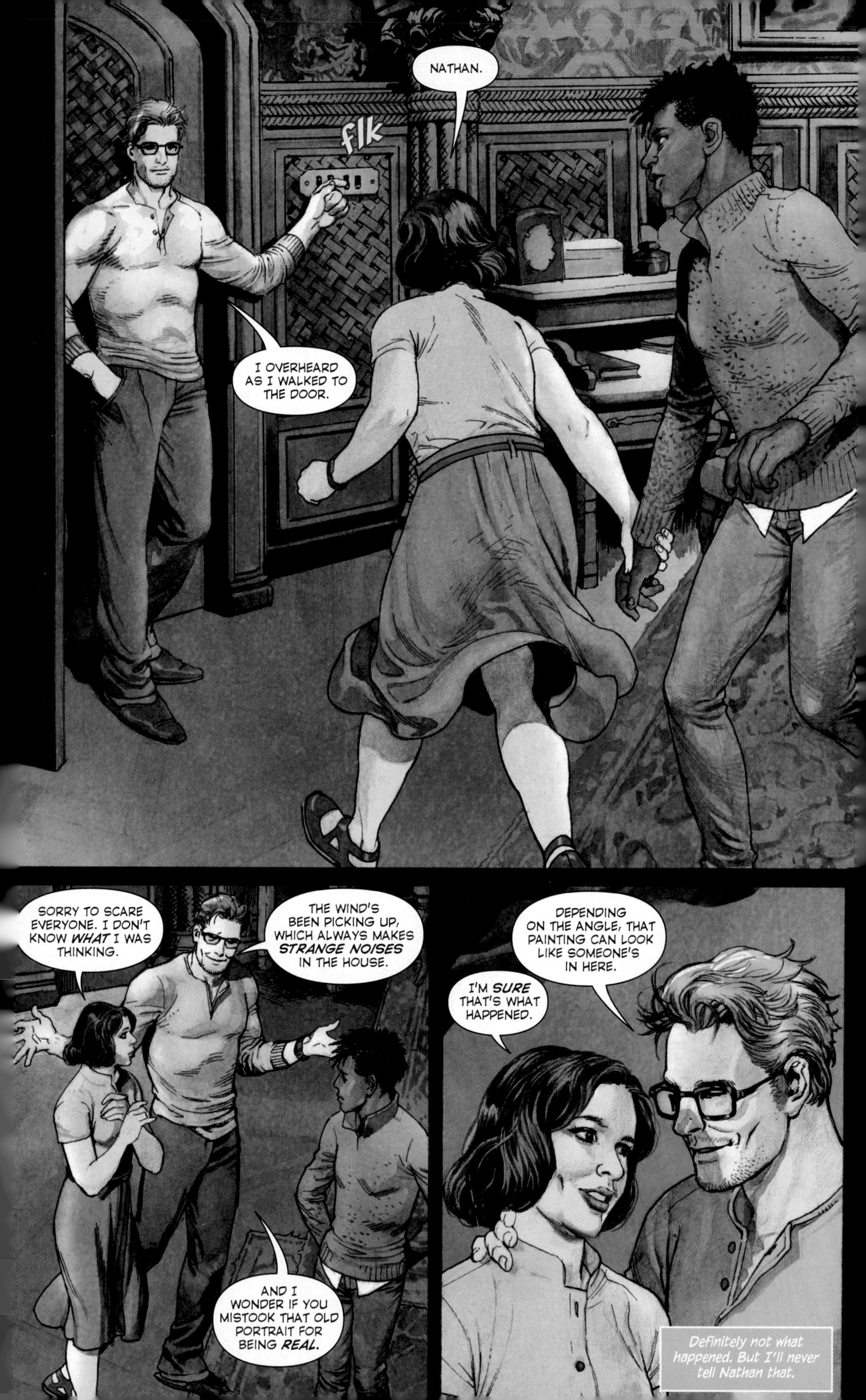
NATHAN.
flk
I OVERHEARD AS I WALKED TO THE DOOR.
SORRY TO SCARE EVERYONE. I DON'T KNOW ***WHAT*** I WAS THINKING.
THE WIND'S BEEN PICKING UP, WHICH ALWAYS MAKES ***STRANGE NOISES*** IN THE HOUSE.
AND I WONDER IF YOU MISTOOK THAT OLD PORTRAIT FOR BEING ***REAL***.
DEPENDING ON THE ANGLE, THAT PAINTING CAN LOOK LIKE SOMEONE'S IN HERE.
I'M ***SURE*** THAT'S WHAT HAPPENED.
Definitely not what happened. But I'll never tell Nathan that.

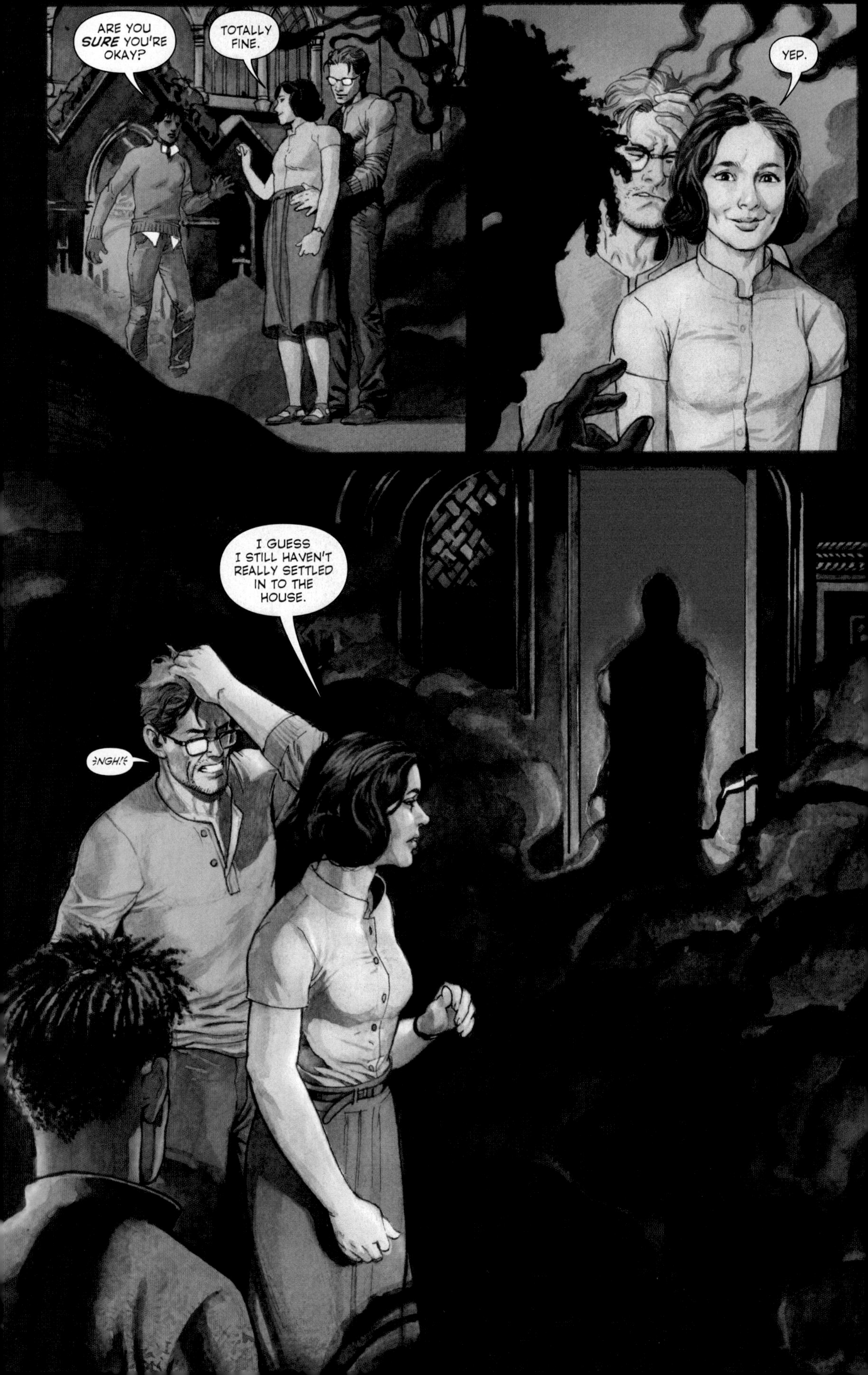
ARE YOU *SURE* YOU'RE OKAY?
TOTALLY FINE.
YEP.
I GUESS I STILL HAVEN'T REALLY SETTLED IN TO THE HOUSE.
NGH!

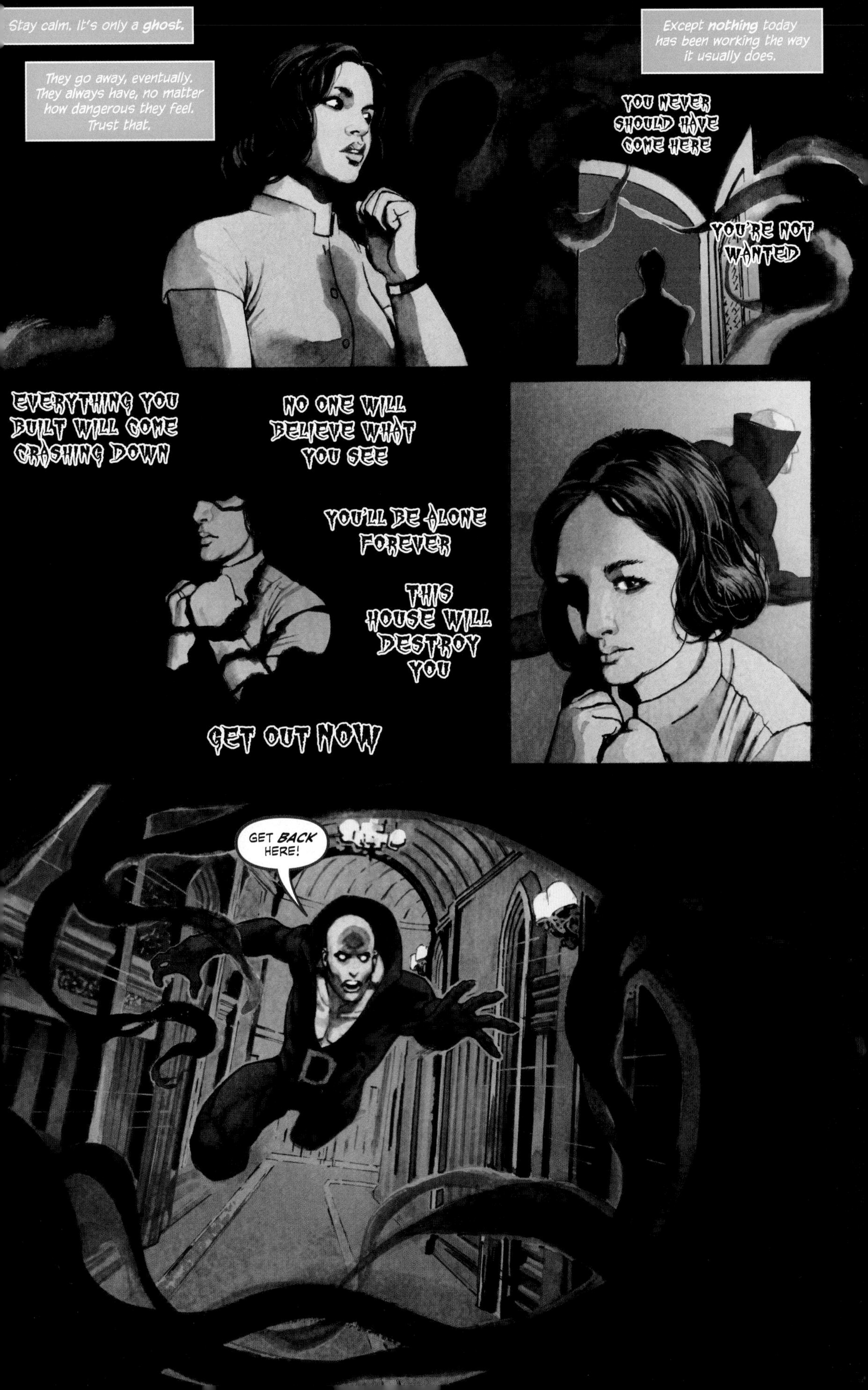
Stay calm. It's only a **ghost.**
They go away, eventually. They always have, no matter how dangerous they feel. Trust that.
Except **nothing** today has been working the way it usually does.
YOU NEVER SHOULD HAVE COME HERE
YOU'RE NOT WANTED
EVERYTHING YOU BUILT WILL COME CRASHING DOWN
NO ONE WILL BELIEVE WHAT YOU SEE
YOU'LL BE ALONE FOREVER
THIS HOUSE WILL DESTROY YOU
GET OUT NOW
GET *BACK* HERE!

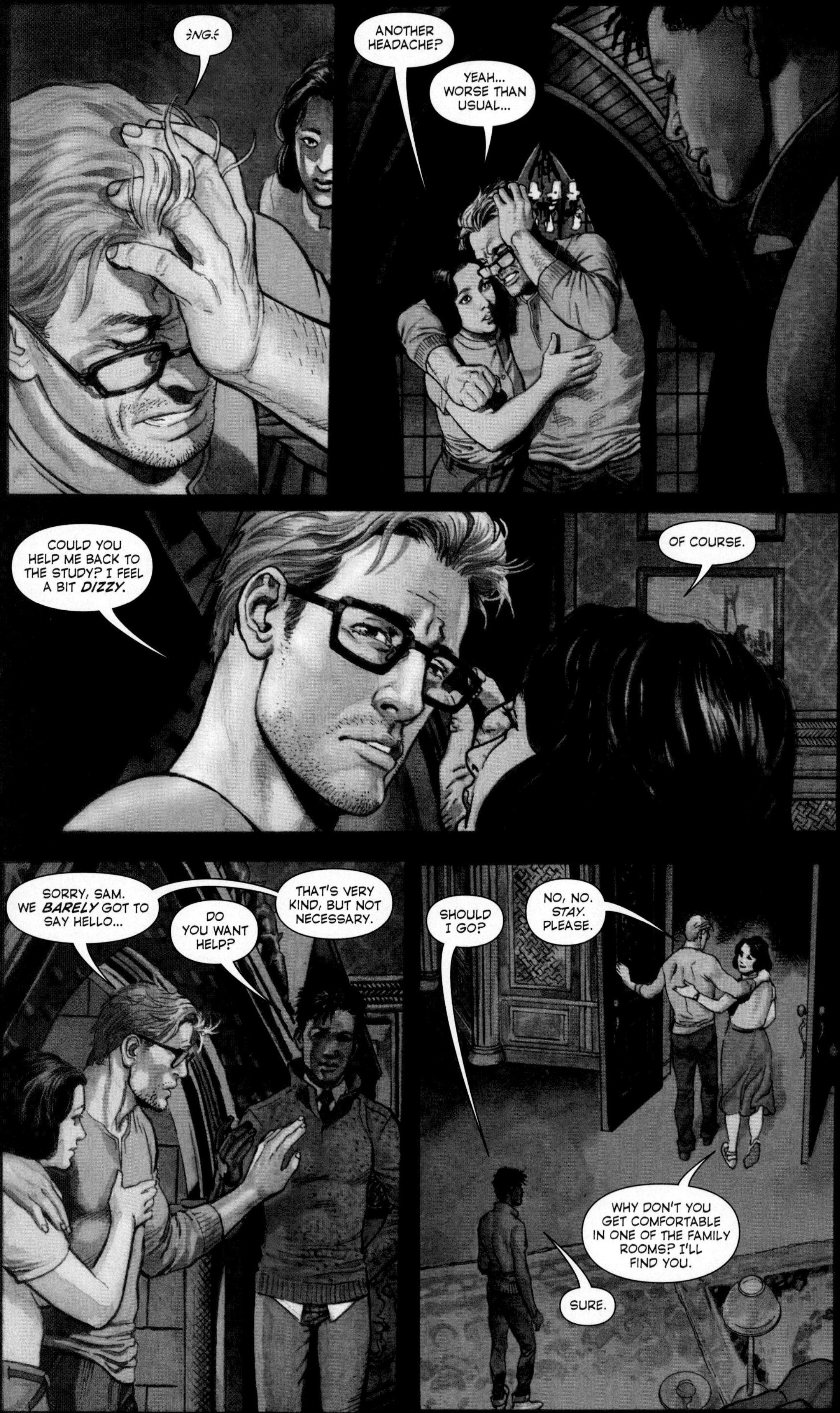
NG.
ANOTHER HEADACHE?
YEAH... WORSE THAN USUAL...
COULD YOU HELP ME BACK TO THE STUDY? I FEEL A BIT *DIZZY*.
OF COURSE.
SORRY, SAM. WE ***BARELY*** GOT TO SAY HELLO...
DO YOU WANT HELP?
THAT'S VERY KIND, BUT NOT NECESSARY.
SHOULD I GO?
NO, NO. *STAY*. PLEASE.
WHY DON'T YOU GET COMFORTABLE IN ONE OF THE FAMILY ROOMS? I'LL FIND YOU.
SURE.

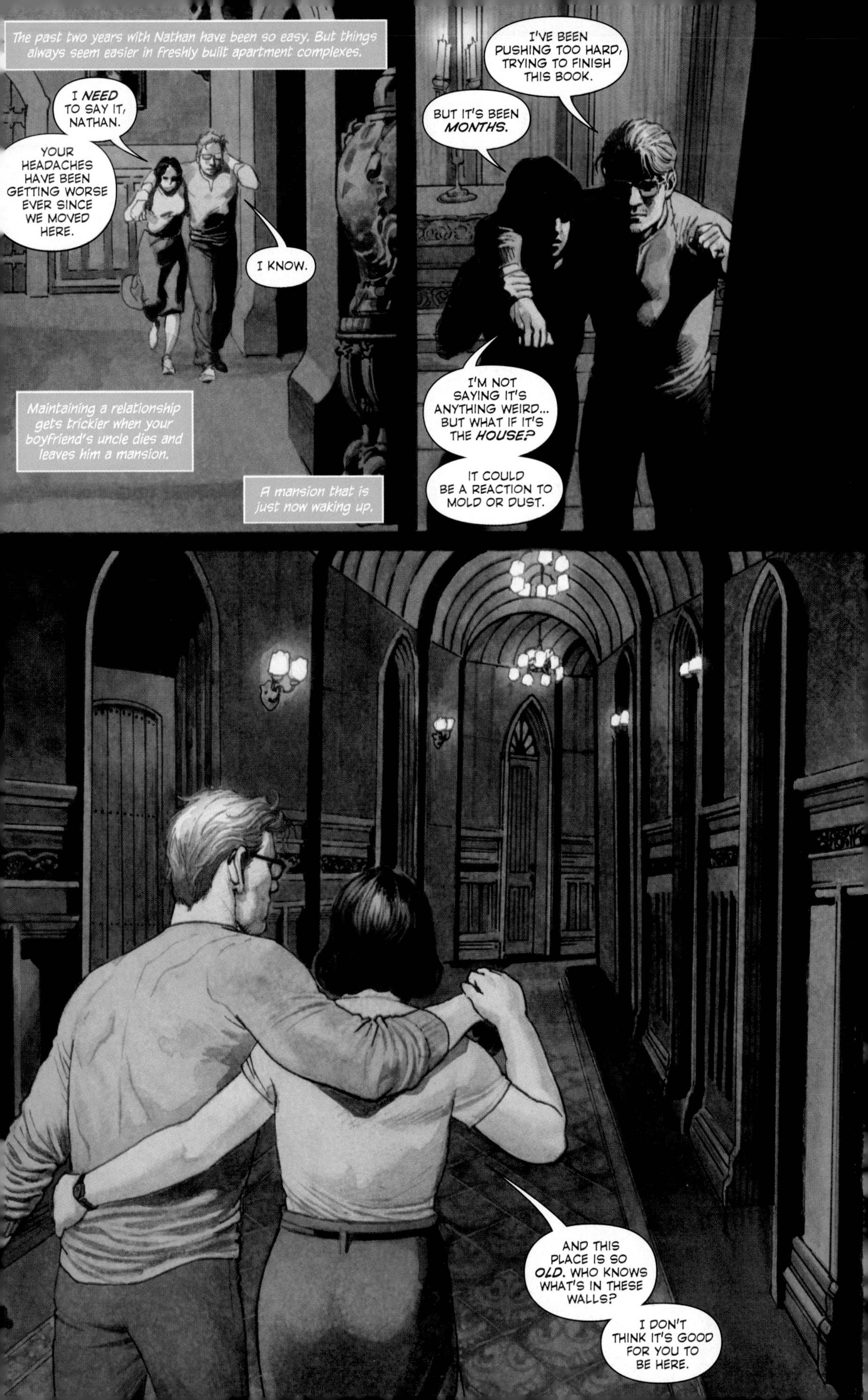
The past two years with Nathan have been so easy. But things always seem easier in freshly built apartment complexes.
I NEED TO SAY IT, NATHAN.
YOUR HEADACHES HAVE BEEN GETTING WORSE EVER SINCE WE MOVED HERE.
I KNOW.
Maintaining a relationship gets trickier when your boyfriend's uncle dies and leaves him a mansion.
A mansion that is just now waking up.
I'VE BEEN PUSHING TOO HARD, TRYING TO FINISH THIS BOOK.
BUT IT'S BEEN MONTHS.
I'M NOT SAYING IT'S ANYTHING WEIRD... BUT WHAT IF IT'S THE HOUSE?
IT COULD BE A REACTION TO MOLD OR DUST.
AND THIS PLACE IS SO OLD. WHO KNOWS WHAT'S IN THESE WALLS?
I DON'T THINK IT'S GOOD FOR YOU TO BE HERE.

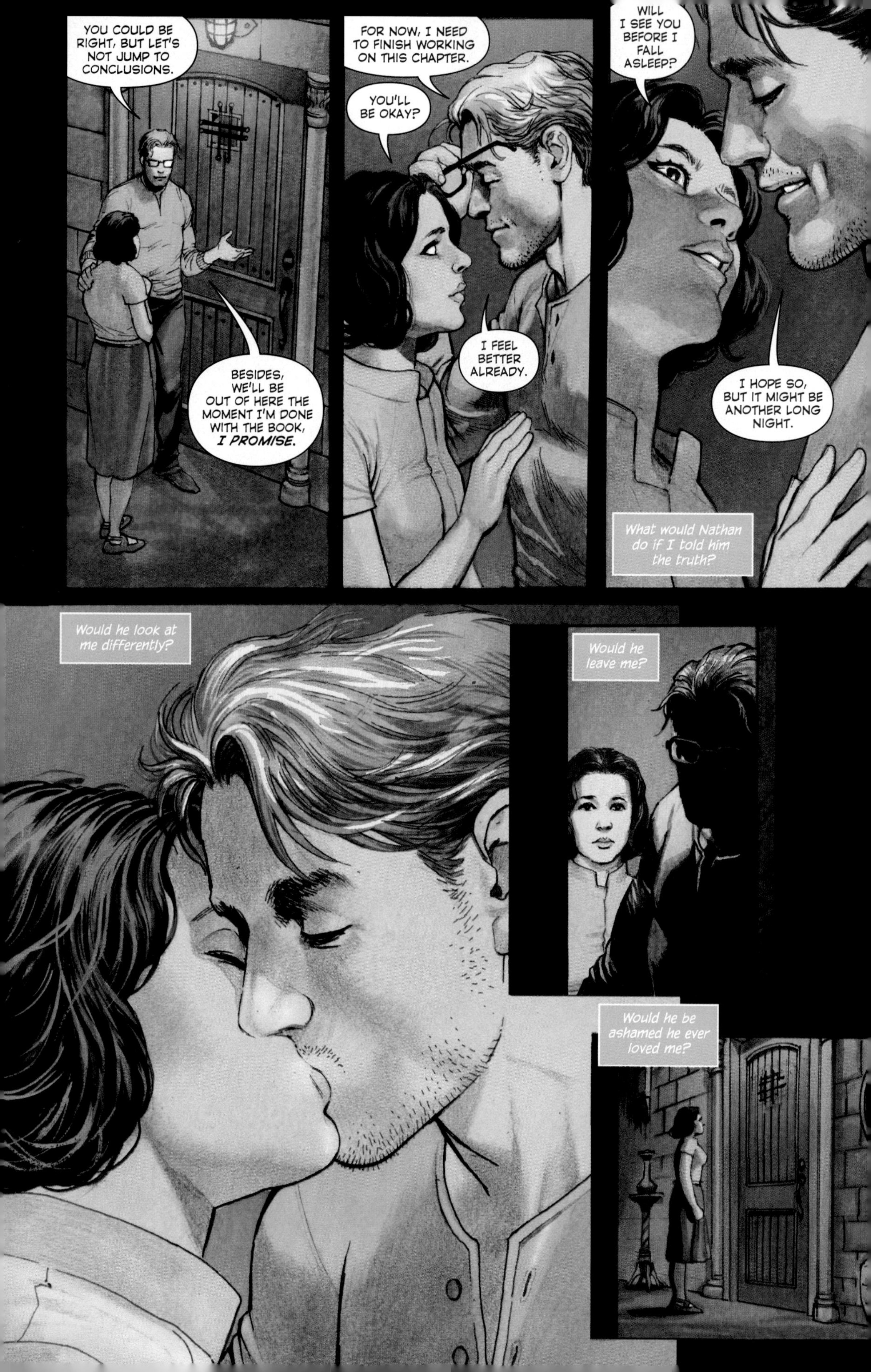
YOU COULD BE RIGHT, BUT LET'S NOT JUMP TO CONCLUSIONS.
BESIDES, WE'LL BE OUT OF HERE THE MOMENT I'M DONE WITH THE BOOK, I PROMISE.
FOR NOW, I NEED TO FINISH WORKING ON THIS CHAPTER.
YOU'LL BE OKAY?
I FEEL BETTER ALREADY.
WILL I SEE YOU BEFORE I FALL ASLEEP?
I HOPE SO, BUT IT MIGHT BE ANOTHER LONG NIGHT.
What would Nathan do if I told him the truth?
Would he look at me differently?
Would he leave me?
Would he be ashamed he ever loved me?

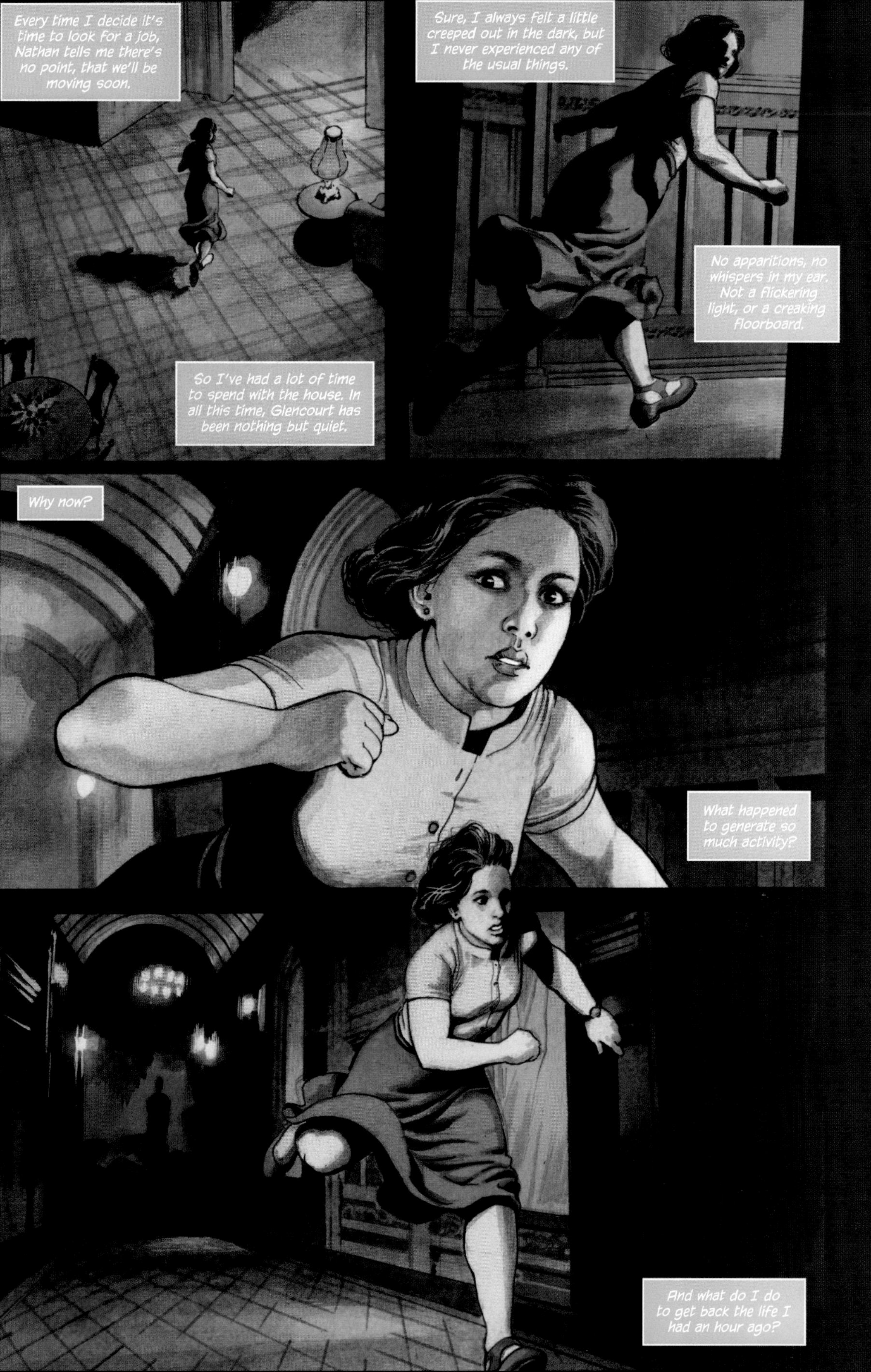
Every time I decide it's time to look for a job, Nathan tells me there's no point, that we'll be moving soon.
So I've had a lot of time to spend with the house. In all this time, Glencourt has been nothing but quiet.
Sure, I always felt a little creeped out in the dark, but I never experienced any of the usual things.
No apparitions, no whispers in my ear. Not a flickering light, or a creaking floorboard.
Why now?
What happened to generate so much activity?
And what do I do to get back the life I had an hour ago?

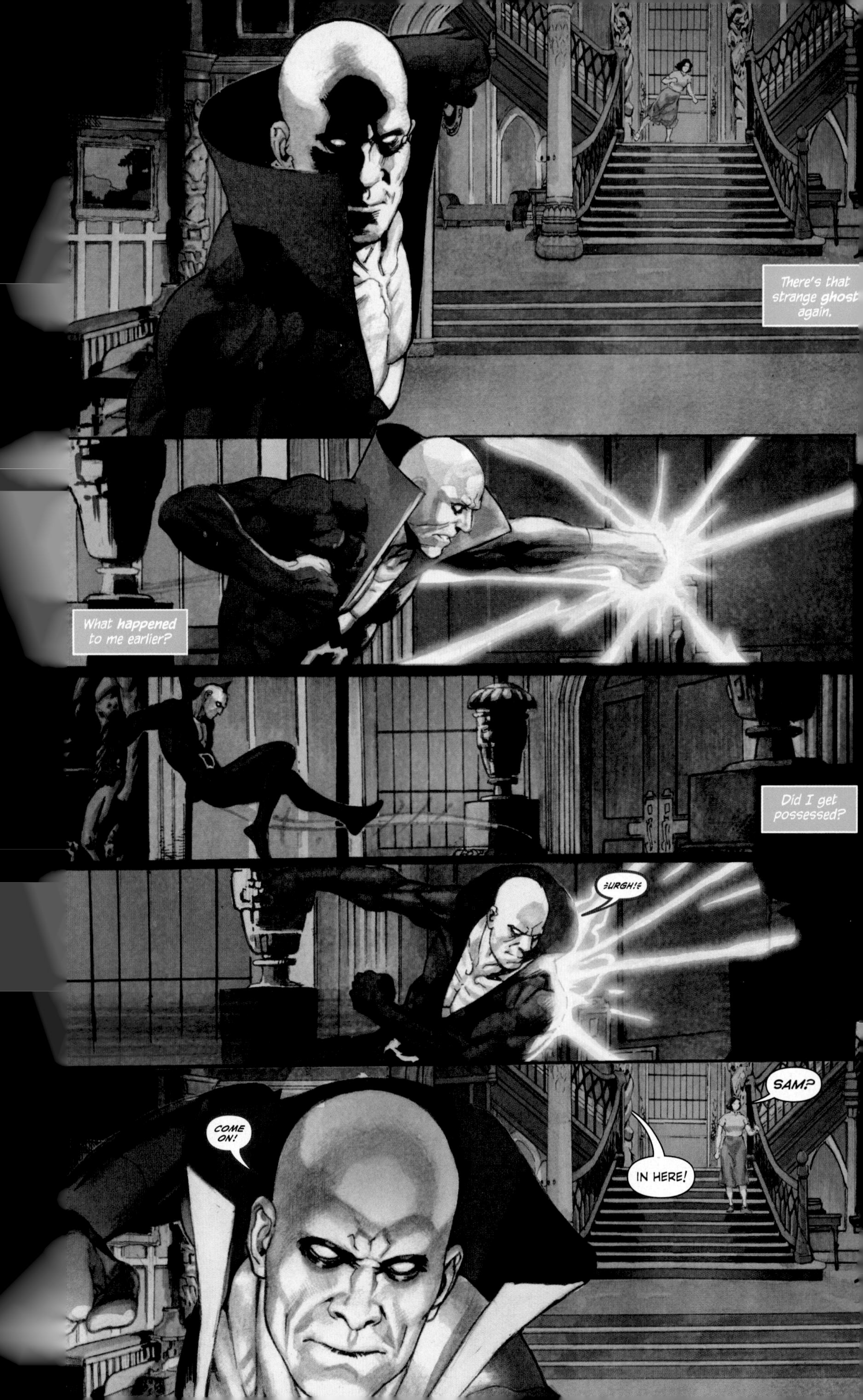

There's that strange ghost again.
What happened to me earlier?
Did I get possessed?
URGH!
SAM?
IN HERE!
COME ON!

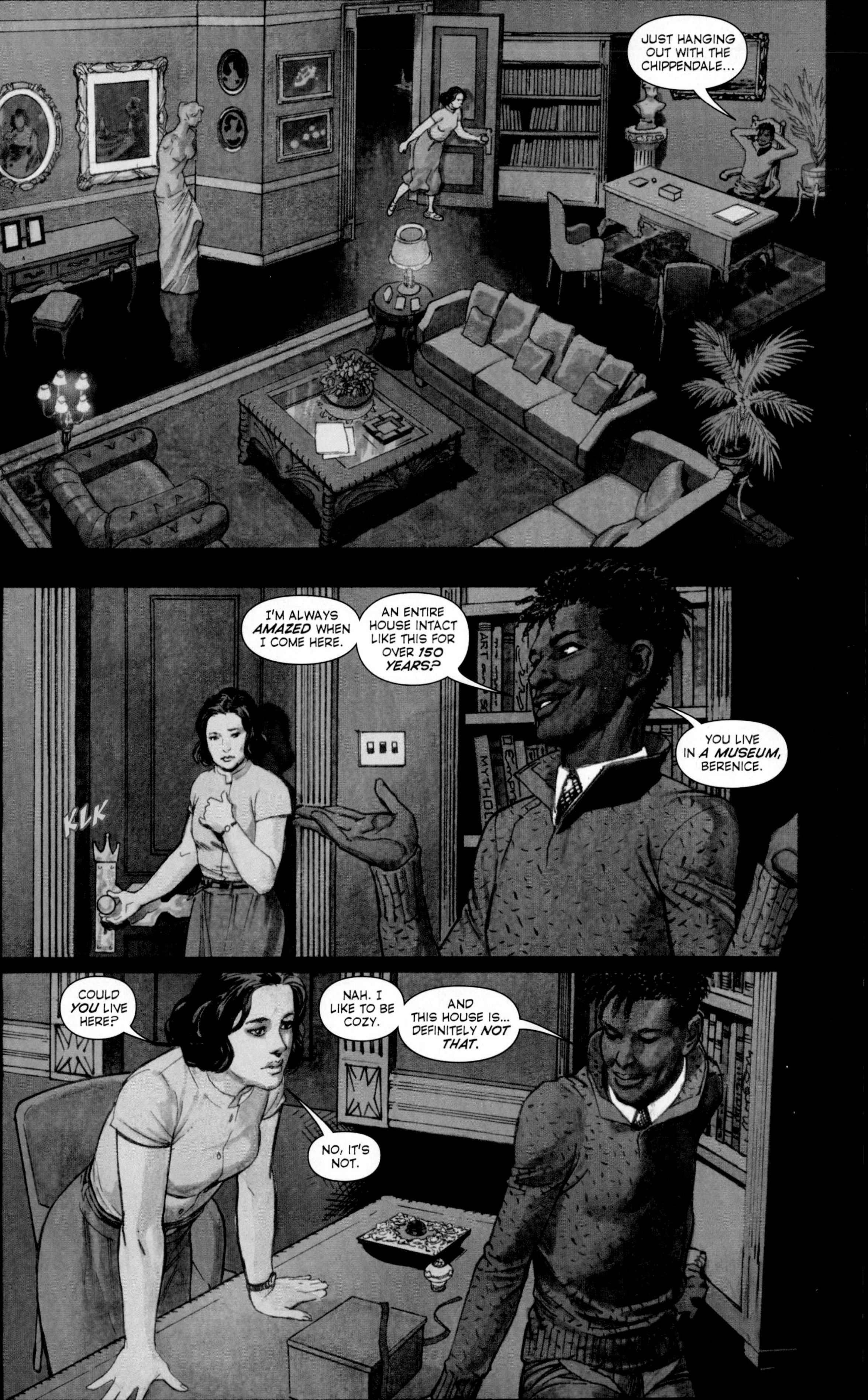
JUST HANGING OUT WITH THE CHIPPENDALE...
I'M ALWAYS AMAZED WHEN I COME HERE.
AN ENTIRE HOUSE INTACT LIKE THIS FOR OVER 150 YEARS?
YOU LIVE IN A MUSEUM, BERENICE.
KLK
COULD YOU LIVE HERE?
NAH. I LIKE TO BE COZY.
AND THIS HOUSE IS... DEFINITELY NOT THAT.
NO, IT'S NOT.

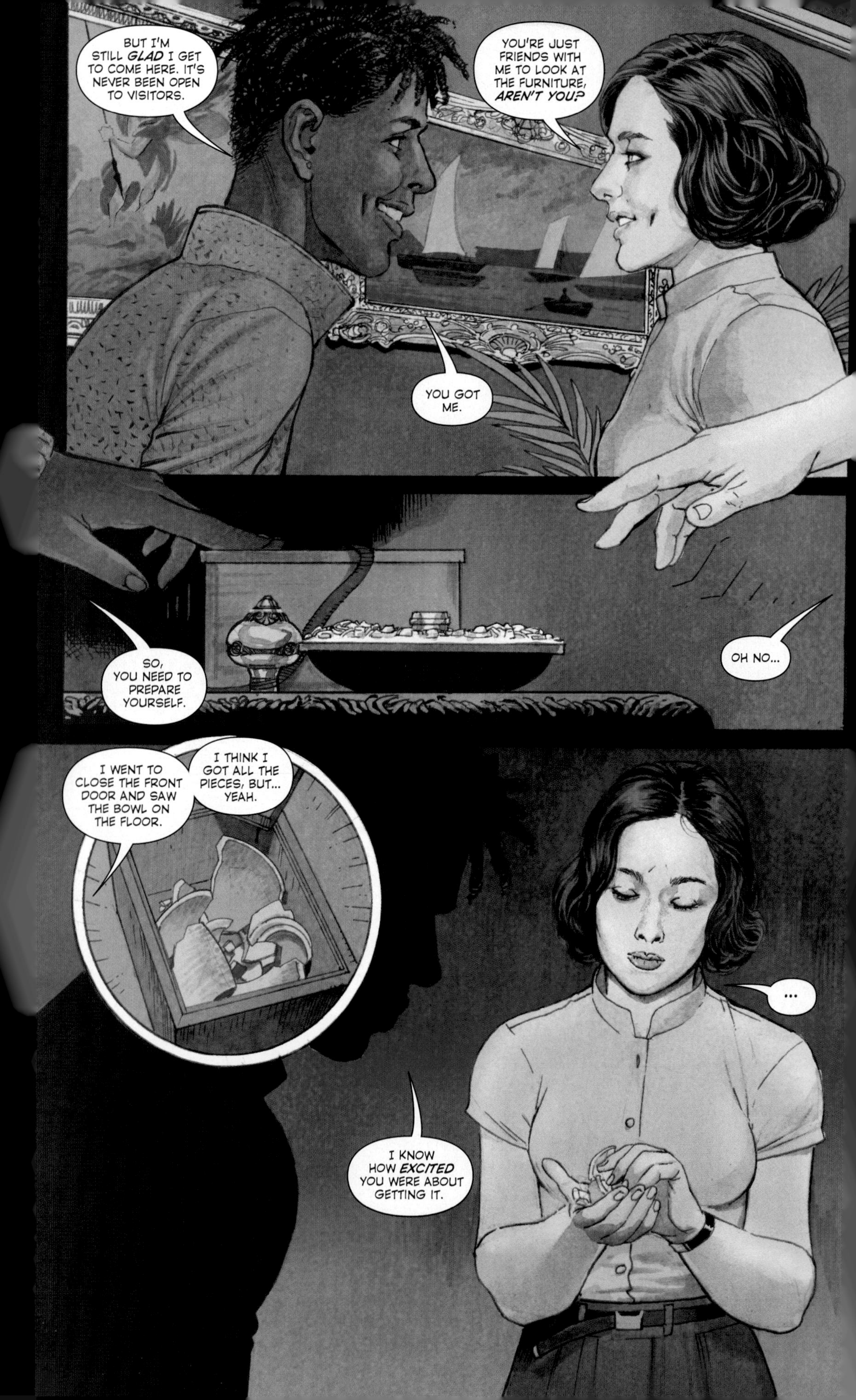
BUT I'M STILL GLAD I GET TO COME HERE. IT'S NEVER BEEN OPEN TO VISITORS.
YOU'RE JUST FRIENDS WITH ME TO LOOK AT THE FURNITURE, AREN'T YOU?
YOU GOT ME.
SO, YOU NEED TO PREPARE YOURSELF.
OH NO...
I WENT TO CLOSE THE FRONT DOOR AND SAW THE BOWL ON THE FLOOR.
I THINK I GOT ALL THE PIECES, BUT... YEAH.
...
I KNOW HOW EXCITED YOU WERE ABOUT GETTING IT.

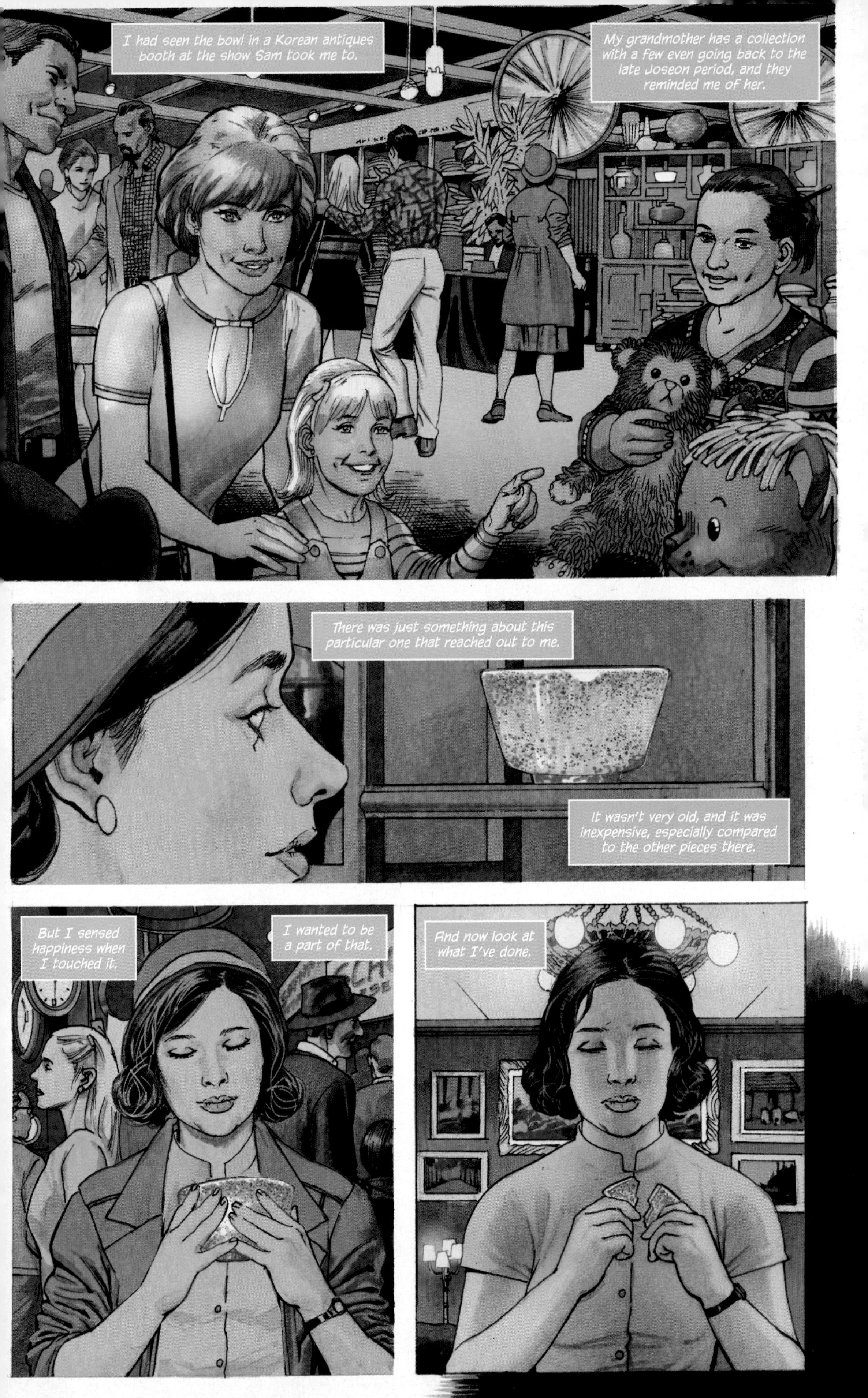

I had seen the bowl in a Korean antiques booth at the show Sam took me to.
My grandmother has a collection with a few even going back to the late Joseon period, and they reminded me of her.
There was just something about this particular one that reached out to me.
It wasn't very old, and it was inexpensive, especially compared to the other pieces there.
But I sensed happiness when I touched it.
I wanted to be a part of that.
And now look at what I've done.

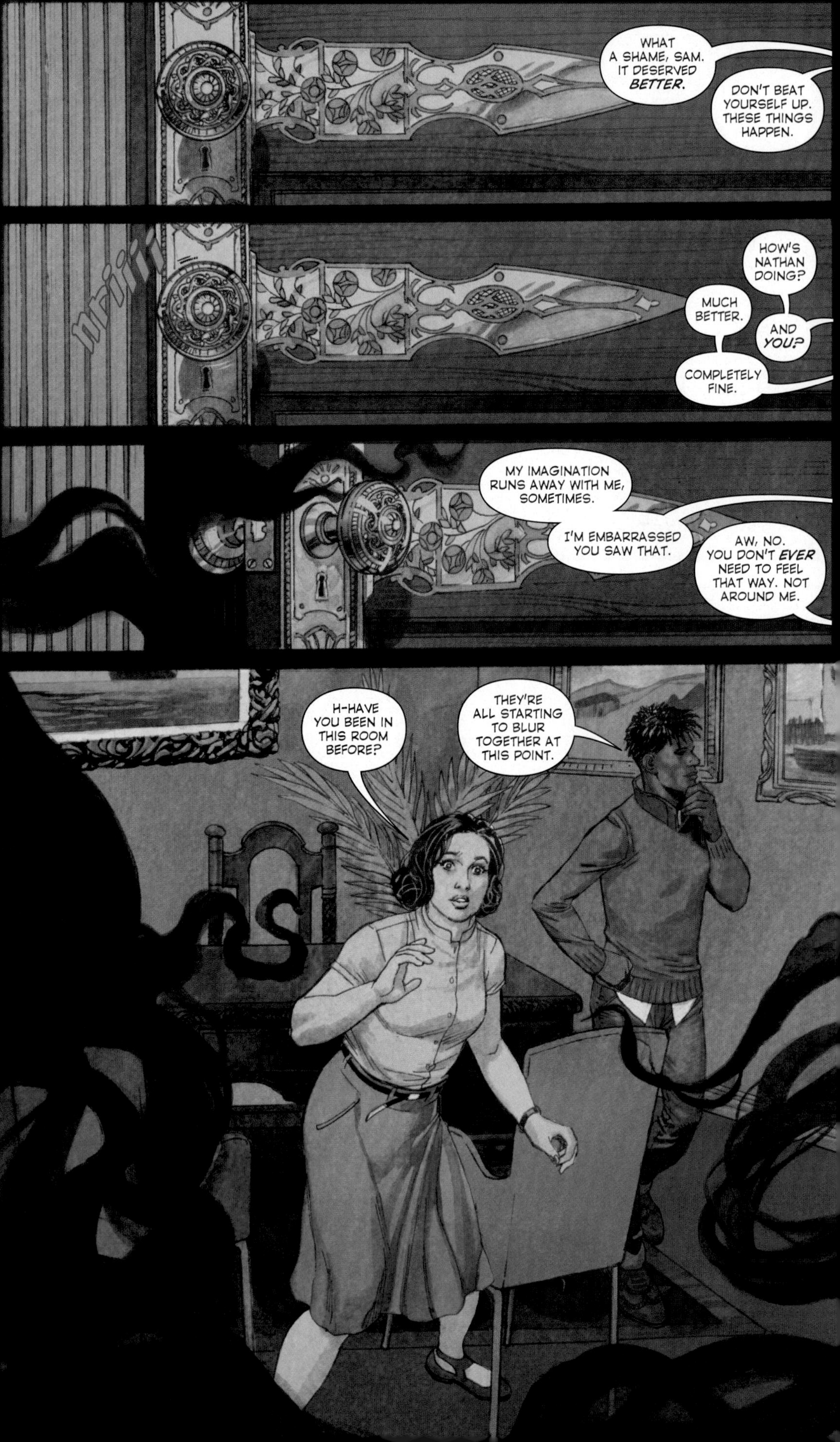
WHAT A SHAME, SAM. IT DESERVED **BETTER.**
DON'T BEAT YOURSELF UP. THESE THINGS HAPPEN.
HOW'S NATHAN DOING?
MUCH BETTER.
AND ***YOU?***
COMPLETELY FINE.
MY IMAGINATION RUNS AWAY WITH ME, SOMETIMES.
I'M EMBARRASSED YOU SAW THAT.
AW, NO. YOU DON'T ***EVER*** NEED TO FEEL THAT WAY. NOT AROUND ME.
H-HAVE YOU BEEN IN THIS ROOM BEFORE?
THEY'RE ALL STARTING TO BLUR TOGETHER AT THIS POINT.

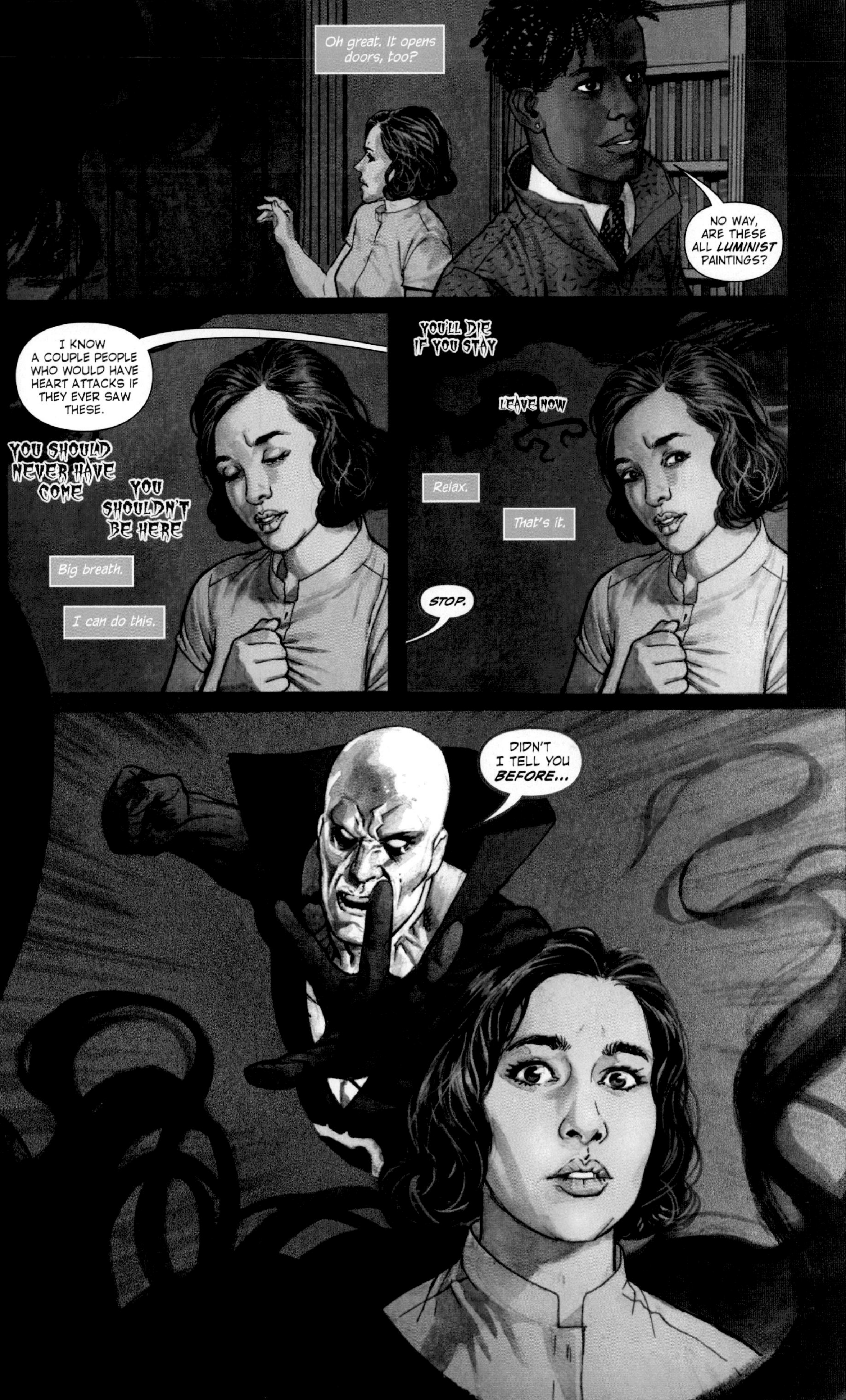
Oh great. It opens doors, too?
NO WAY, ARE THESE ALL *LUMINIST* PAINTINGS?
I KNOW A COUPLE PEOPLE WHO WOULD HAVE HEART ATTACKS IF THEY EVER SAW THESE.
YOU SHOULD NEVER HAVE COME
YOU SHOULDN'T BE HERE
Big breath.
I can do this.
YOU'LL DIE IF YOU STAY
LEAVE NOW
Relax.
That's it.
STOP.
DIDN'T I TELL YOU *BEFORE*...

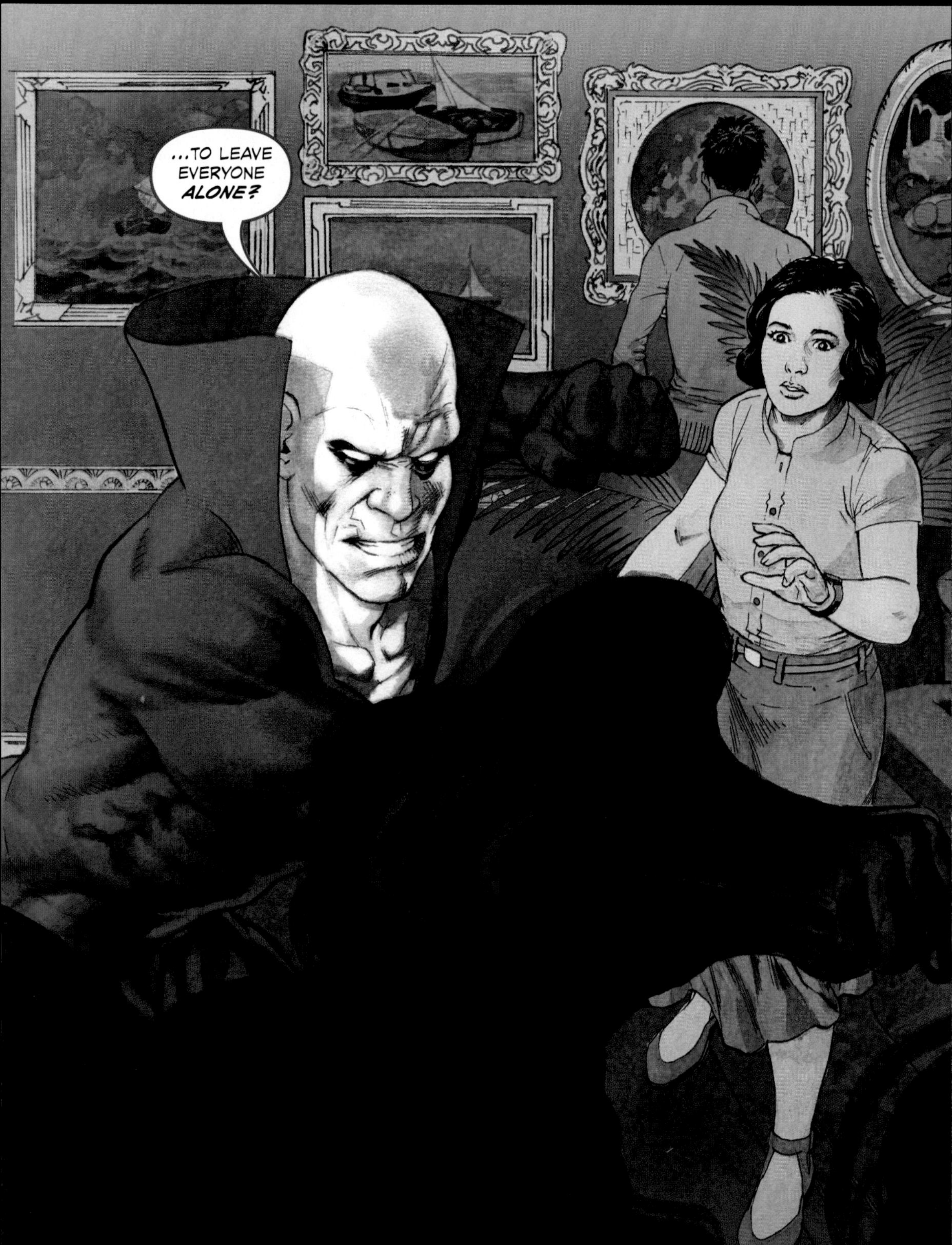
...TO LEAVE EVERYONE *ALONE?*

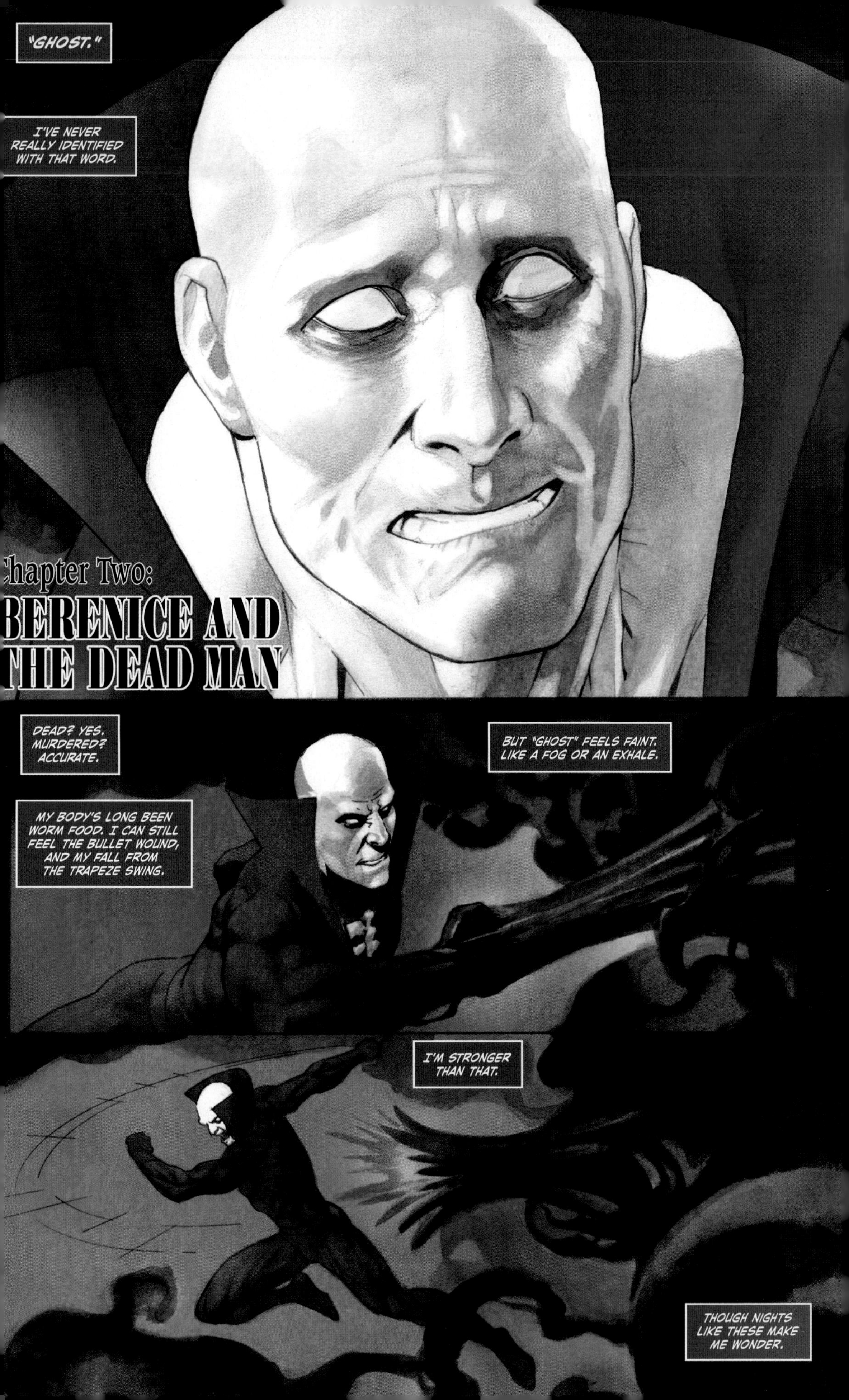
"GHOST."
I'VE NEVER REALLY IDENTIFIED WITH THAT WORD.
Chapter Two:
BERENICE AND THE DEAD MAN
DEAD? YES. MURDERED? ACCURATE.
MY BODY'S LONG BEEN WORM FOOD. I CAN STILL FEEL THE BULLET WOUND, AND MY FALL FROM THE TRAPEZE SWING.
BUT "GHOST" FEELS FAINT. LIKE A FOG OR AN EXHALE.
I'M STRONGER THAN THAT.
THOUGH NIGHTS LIKE THESE MAKE ME WONDER.

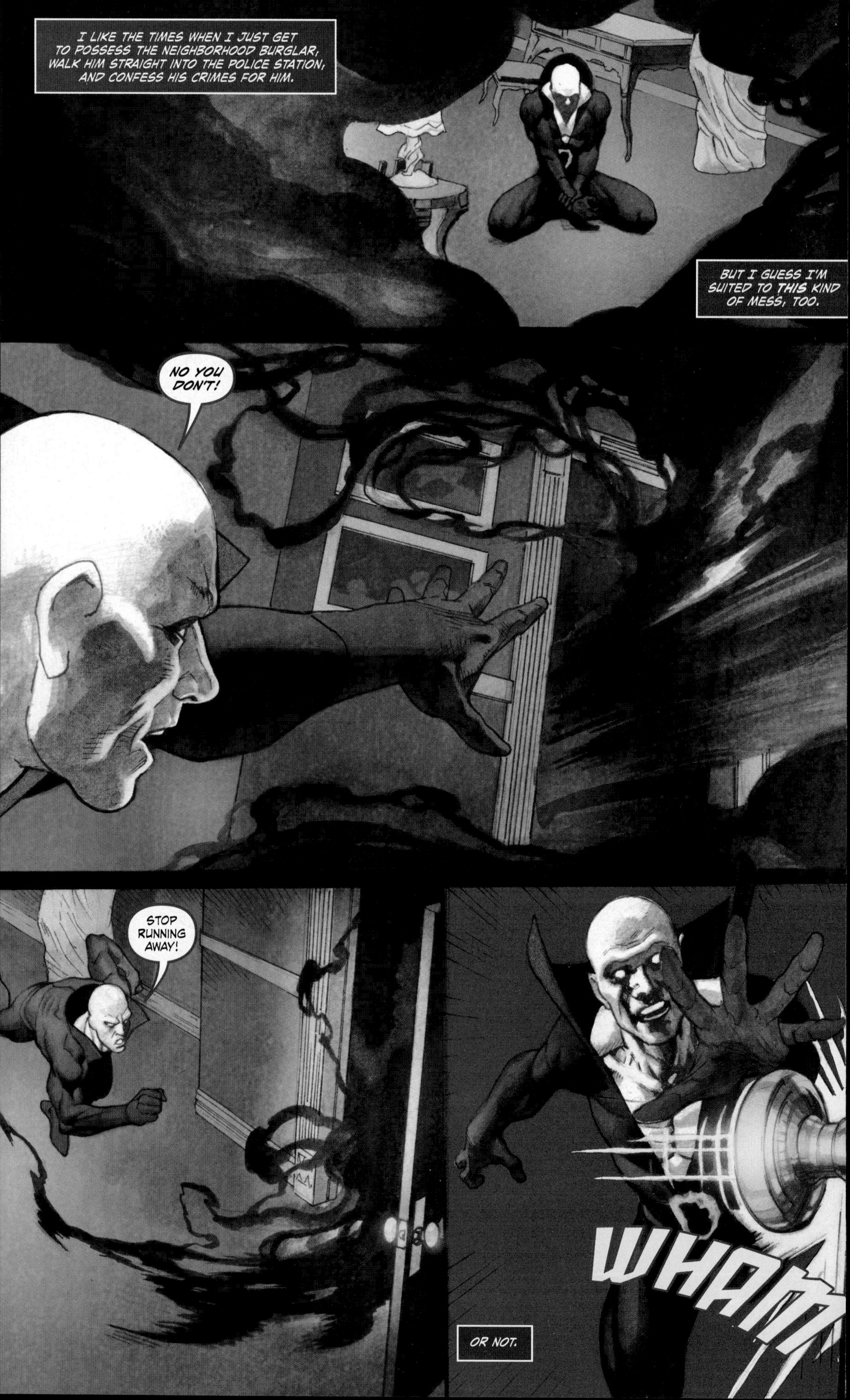
I LIKE THE TIMES WHEN I JUST GET TO POSSESS THE NEIGHBORHOOD BURGLAR, WALK HIM STRAIGHT INTO THE POLICE STATION, AND CONFESS HIS CRIMES FOR HIM.
BUT I GUESS I'M SUITED TO THIS KIND OF MESS, TOO.
NO YOU DON'T!
STOP RUNNING AWAY!
WHAM
OR NOT.

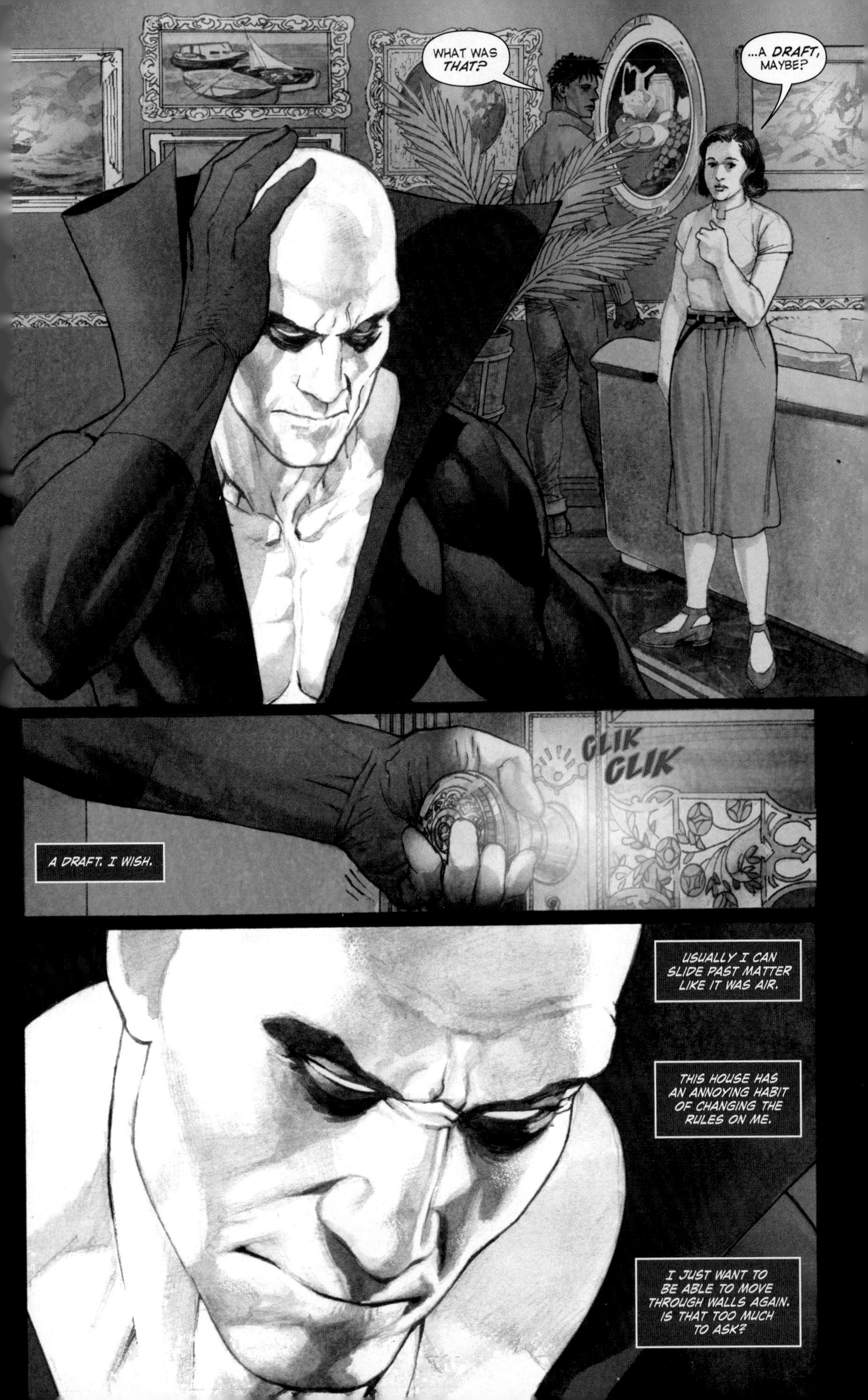
WHAT WAS *THAT?*
...A *DRAFT,* MAYBE?
A DRAFT. I WISH.
CLIK CLIK
USUALLY I CAN SLIDE PAST MATTER LIKE IT WAS AIR.
THIS HOUSE HAS AN ANNOYING HABIT OF CHANGING THE RULES ON ME.
I JUST WANT TO BE ABLE TO MOVE THROUGH WALLS AGAIN. IS THAT TOO MUCH TO ASK?

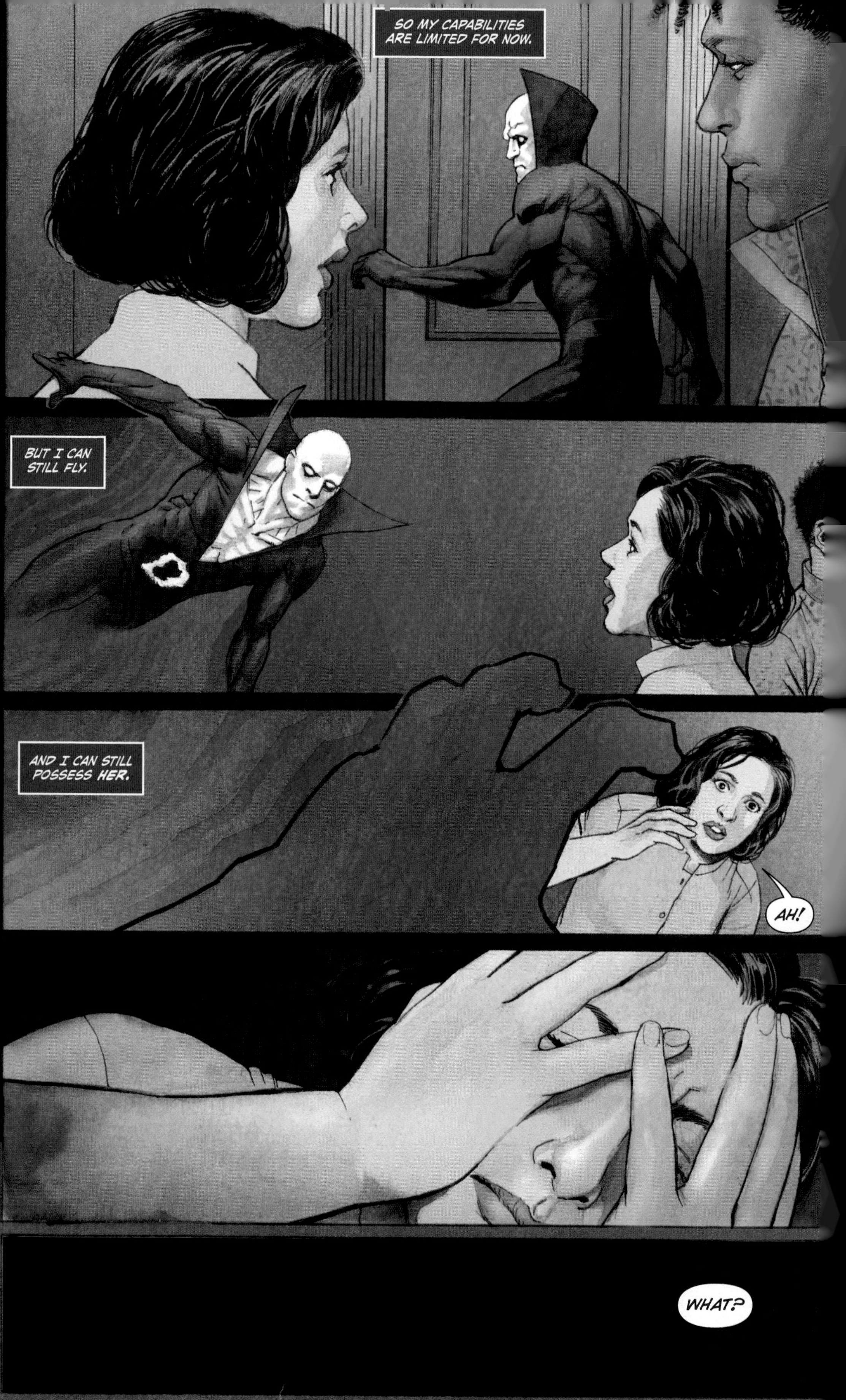
SO MY CAPABILITIES ARE LIMITED FOR NOW.
BUT I CAN STILL FLY.
AND I CAN STILL POSSESS HER.
AH!
WHAT?

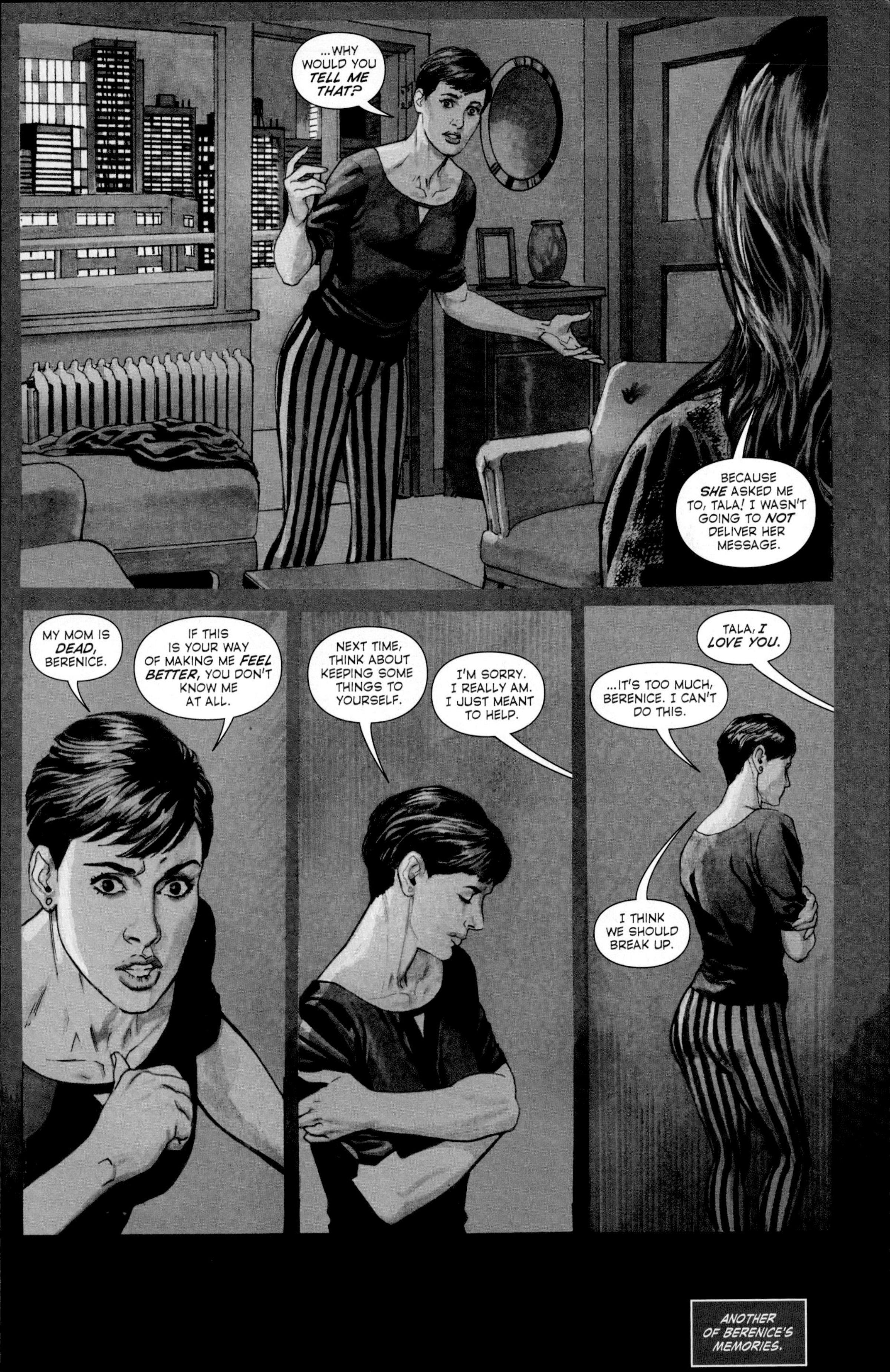
...WHY WOULD YOU TELL ME THAT?
BECAUSE SHE ASKED ME TO, TALA! I WASN'T GOING TO NOT DELIVER HER MESSAGE.
MY MOM IS DEAD, BERENICE.
IF THIS IS YOUR WAY OF MAKING ME FEEL BETTER, YOU DON'T KNOW ME AT ALL.
NEXT TIME, THINK ABOUT KEEPING SOME THINGS TO YOURSELF.
I'M SORRY. I REALLY AM. I JUST MEANT TO HELP.
TALA, I LOVE YOU.
...IT'S TOO MUCH, BERENICE. I CAN'T DO THIS.
I THINK WE SHOULD BREAK UP.
ANOTHER OF BERENICE'S MEMORIES.

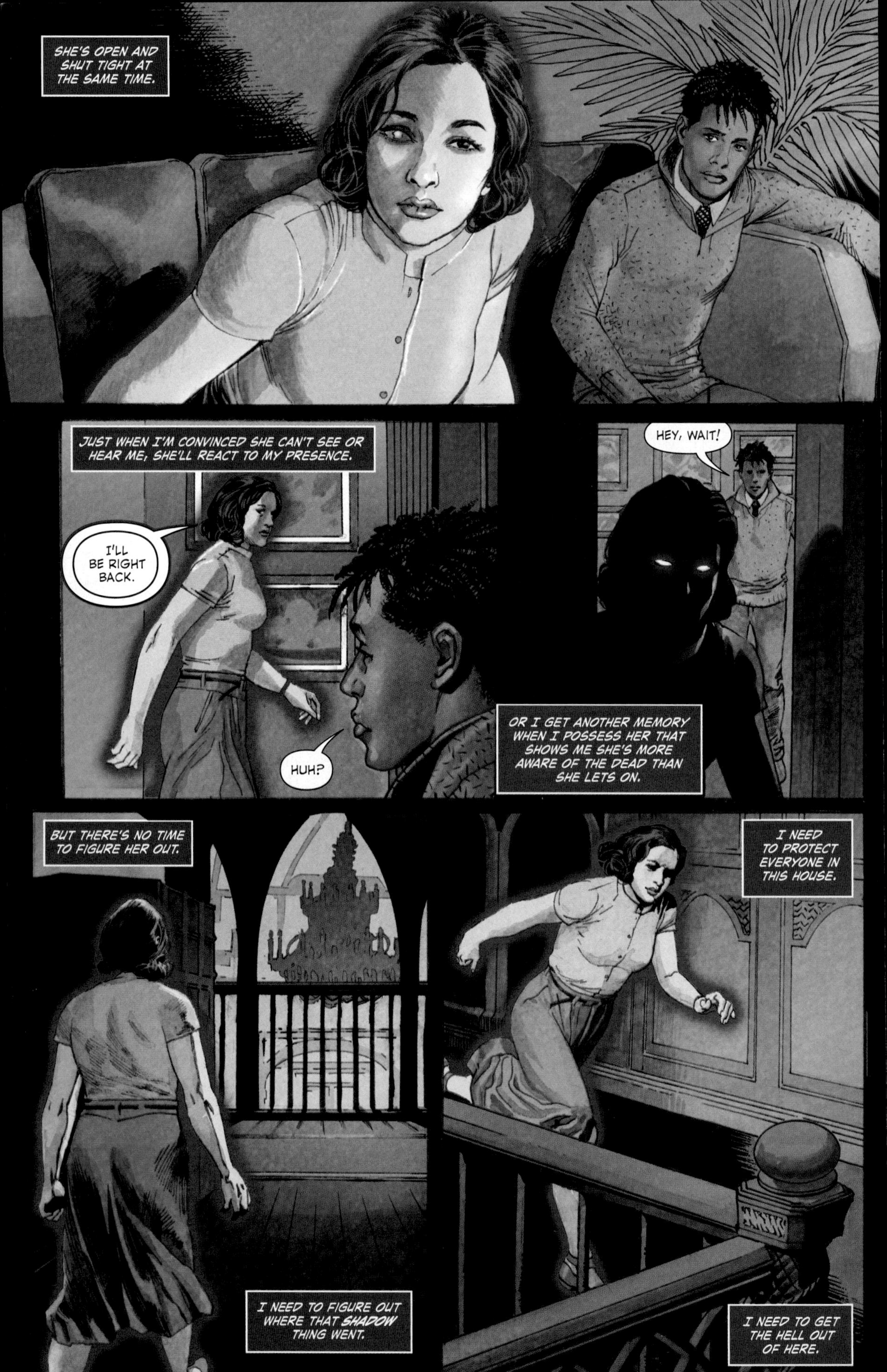
SHE'S OPEN AND SHUT TIGHT AT THE SAME TIME.
JUST WHEN I'M CONVINCED SHE CAN'T SEE OR HEAR ME, SHE'LL REACT TO MY PRESENCE.
I'LL BE RIGHT BACK.
HUH?
HEY, WAIT!
OR I GET ANOTHER MEMORY WHEN I POSSESS HER THAT SHOWS ME SHE'S MORE AWARE OF THE DEAD THAN SHE LETS ON.
BUT THERE'S NO TIME TO FIGURE HER OUT.
I NEED TO FIGURE OUT WHERE THAT SHADOW THING WENT.
I NEED TO PROTECT EVERYONE IN THIS HOUSE.
I NEED TO GET THE HELL OUT OF HERE.

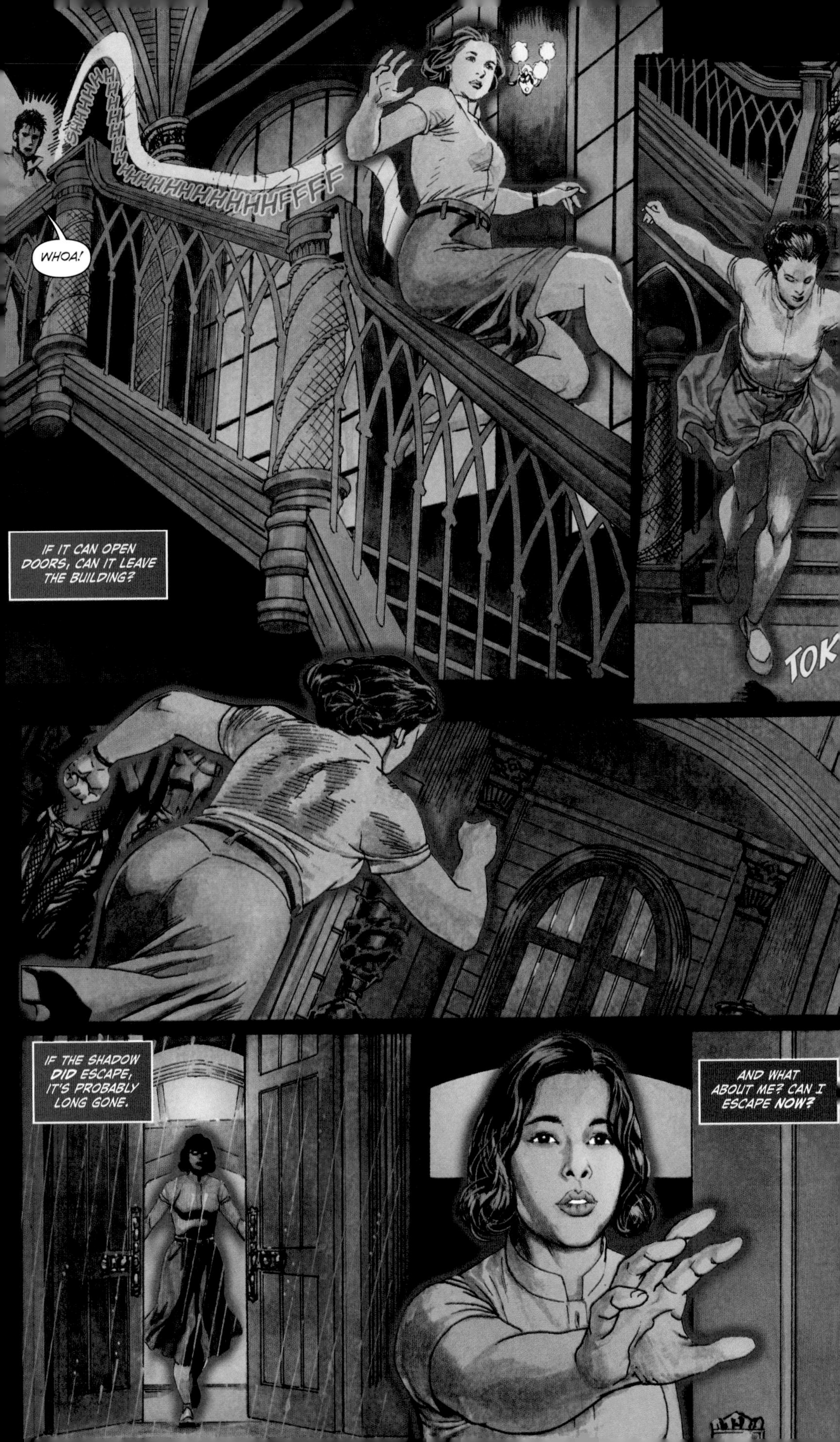
SHHHHHHHHHHHHHHHHHHHHHFFFFF
WHOA!
IF IT CAN OPEN DOORS, CAN IT LEAVE THE BUILDING?
TOK
IF THE SHADOW DID ESCAPE, IT'S PROBABLY LONG GONE.
AND WHAT ABOUT ME? CAN I ESCAPE NOW?

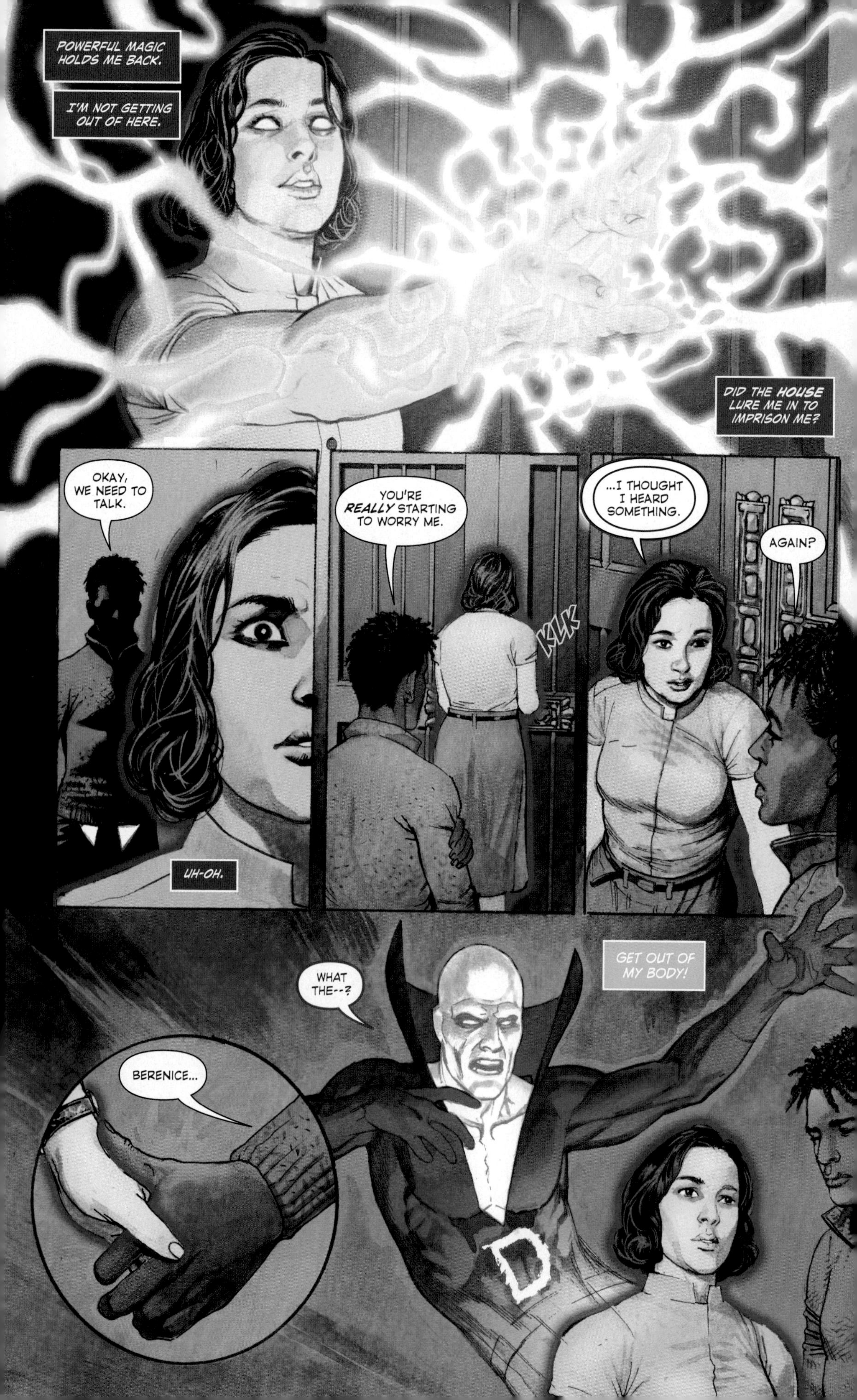
POWERFUL MAGIC HOLDS ME BACK.
I'M NOT GETTING OUT OF HERE.
DID THE HOUSE LURE ME IN TO IMPRISON ME?
OKAY, WE NEED TO TALK.
UH-OH.
YOU'RE REALLY STARTING TO WORRY ME.
KLK
...I THOUGHT I HEARD SOMETHING.
AGAIN?
WHAT THE--?
GET OUT OF MY BODY!
BERENICE...

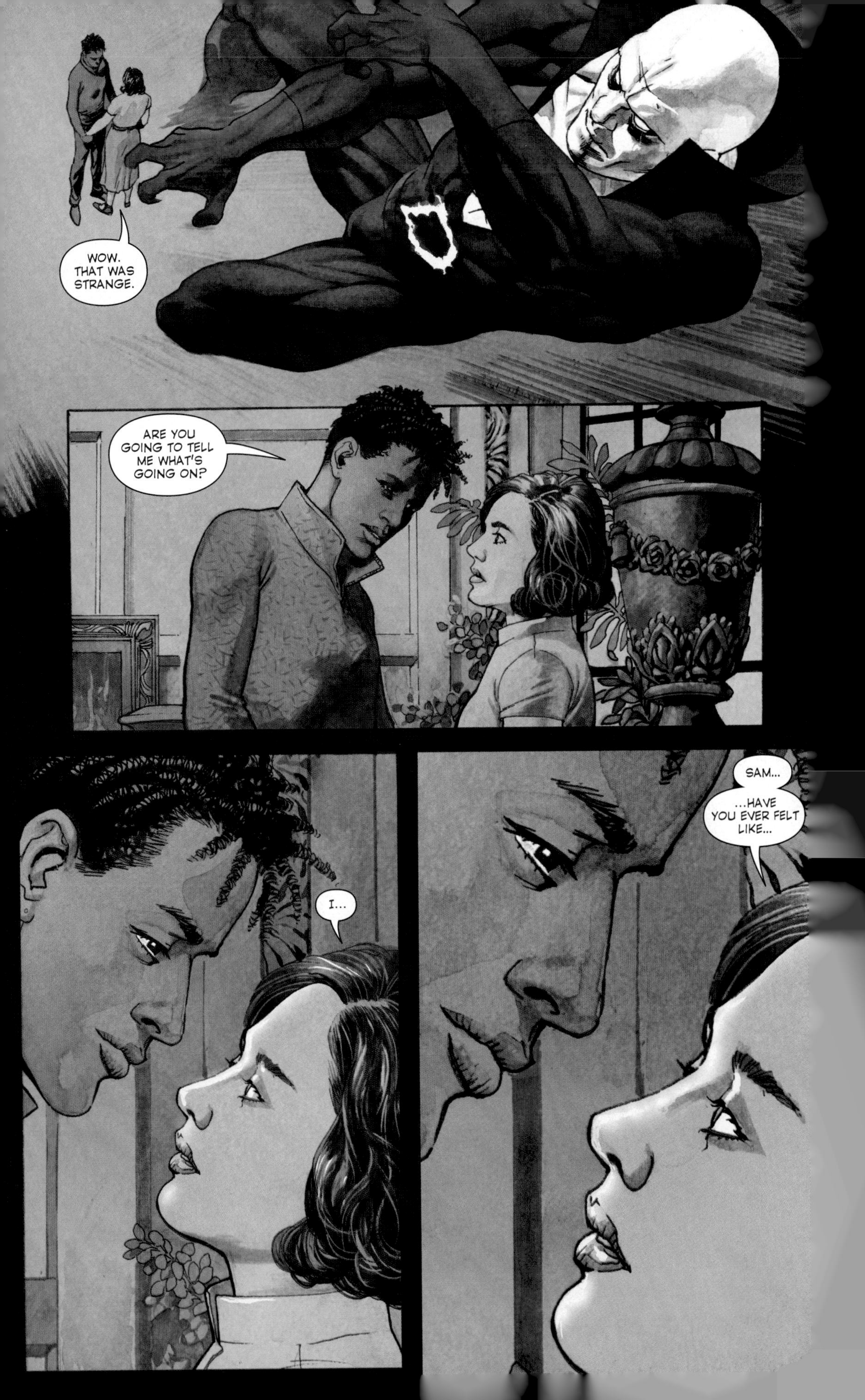
WOW. THAT WAS STRANGE.
ARE YOU GOING TO TELL ME WHAT'S GOING ON?
I...
SAM...
...HAVE YOU EVER FELT LIKE...

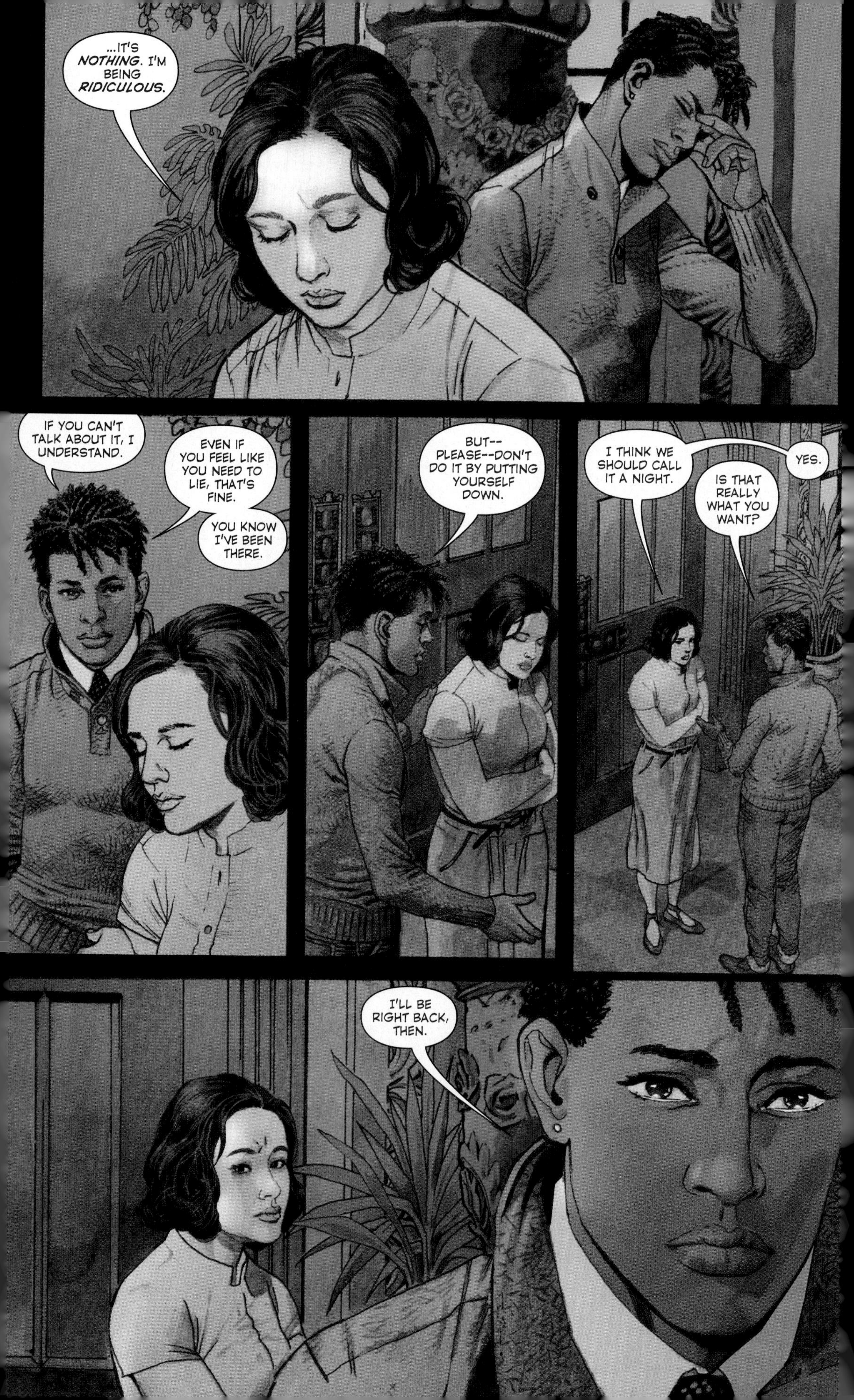
...IT'S NOTHING. I'M BEING RIDICULOUS.
IF YOU CAN'T TALK ABOUT IT, I UNDERSTAND.
EVEN IF YOU FEEL LIKE YOU NEED TO LIE, THAT'S FINE.
YOU KNOW I'VE BEEN THERE.
BUT-- PLEASE--DON'T DO IT BY PUTTING YOURSELF DOWN.
I THINK WE SHOULD CALL IT A NIGHT.
YES.
IS THAT REALLY WHAT YOU WANT?
I'LL BE RIGHT BACK, THEN.

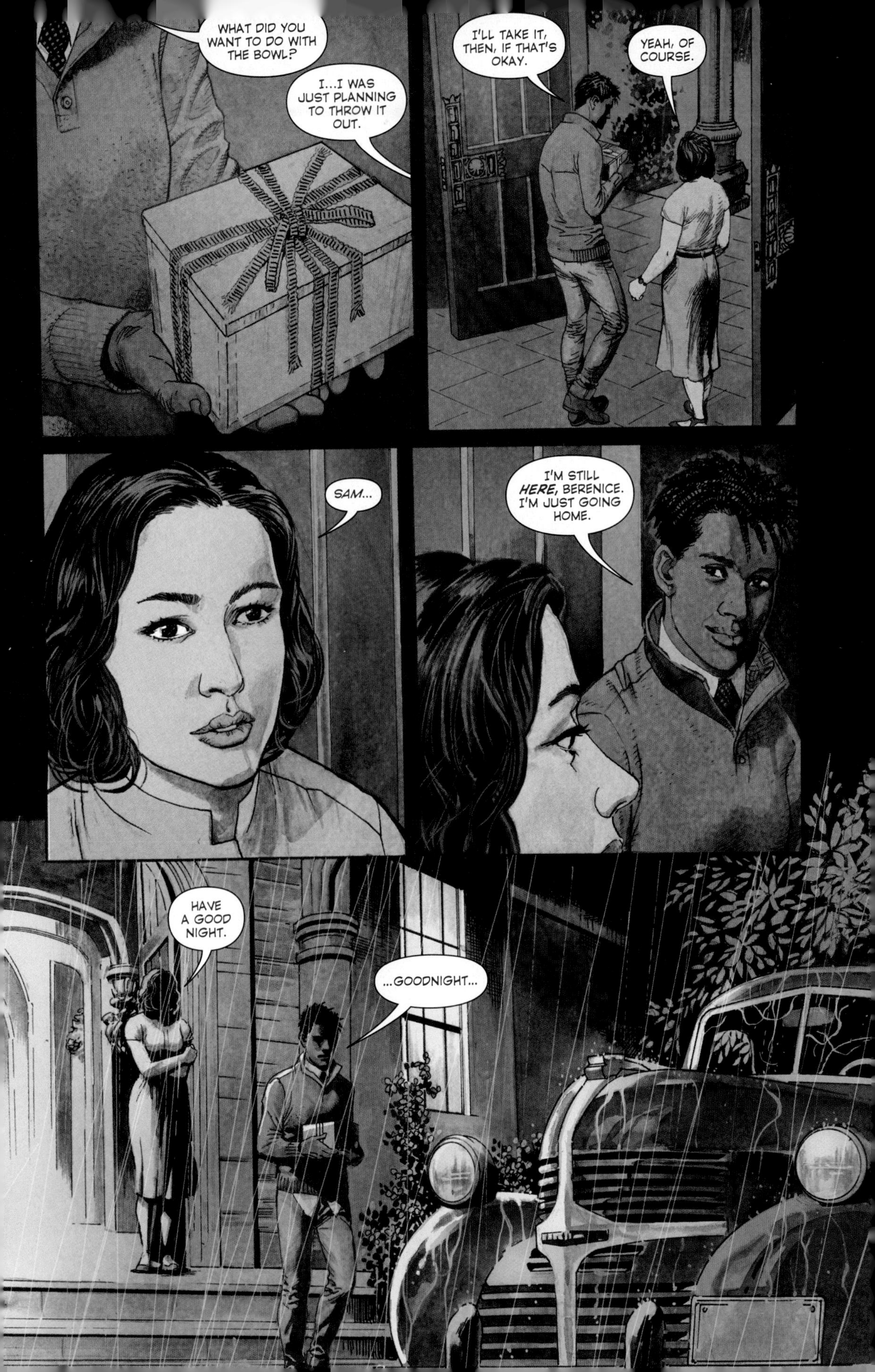
WHAT DID YOU WANT TO DO WITH THE BOWL?
I...I WAS JUST PLANNING TO THROW IT OUT.
I'LL TAKE IT, THEN, IF THAT'S OKAY.
YEAH, OF COURSE.
SAM...
I'M STILL *HERE,* BERENICE. I'M JUST GOING HOME.
HAVE A GOOD NIGHT.
...GOODNIGHT...

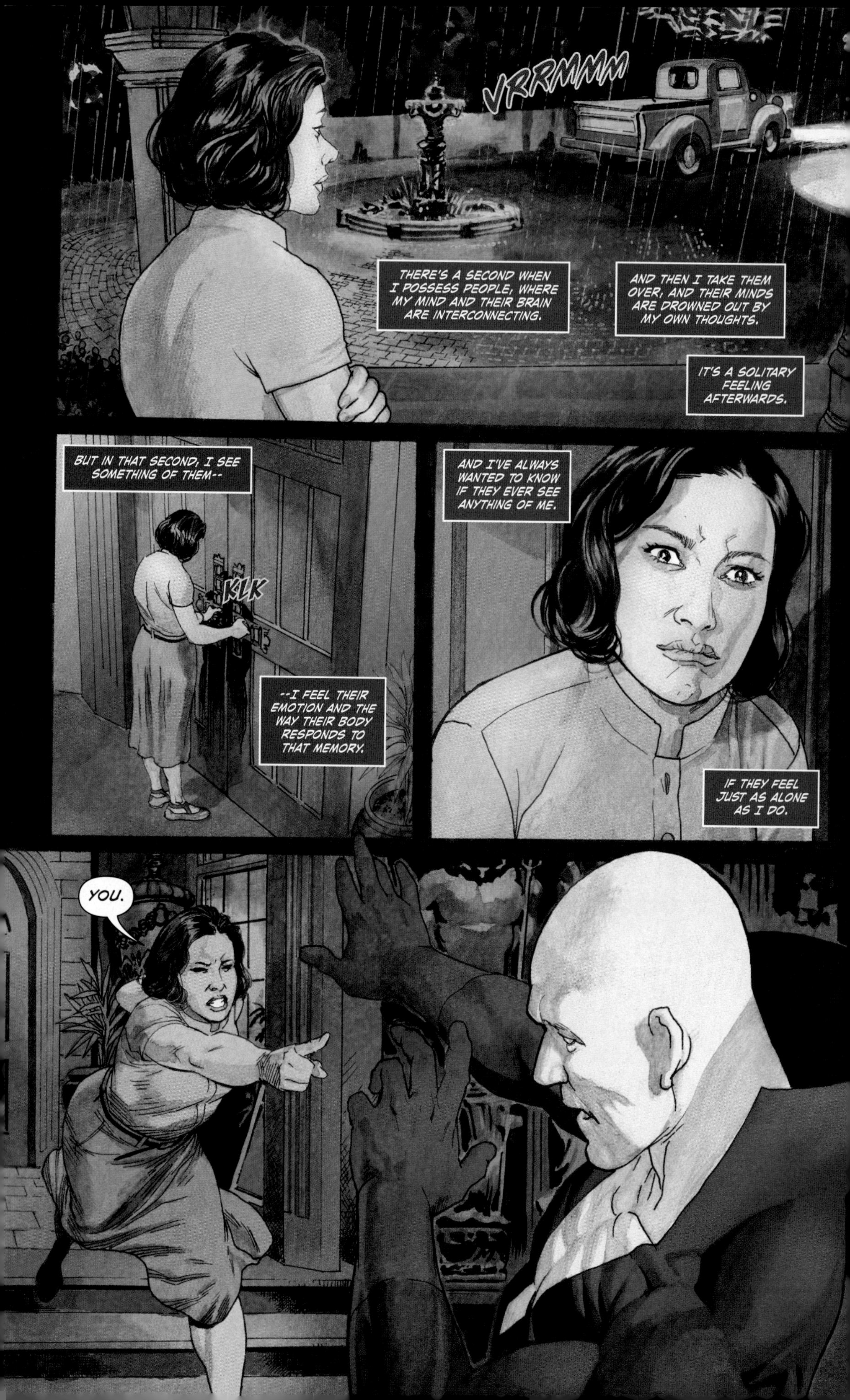
VRRMMM
THERE'S A SECOND WHEN I POSSESS PEOPLE, WHERE MY MIND AND THEIR BRAIN ARE INTERCONNECTING.
AND THEN I TAKE THEM OVER, AND THEIR MINDS ARE DROWNED OUT BY MY OWN THOUGHTS.
IT'S A SOLITARY FEELING AFTERWARDS.
BUT IN THAT SECOND, I SEE SOMETHING OF THEM--
KLK
--I FEEL THEIR EMOTION AND THE WAY THEIR BODY RESPONDS TO THAT MEMORY.
AND I'VE ALWAYS WANTED TO KNOW IF THEY EVER SEE ANYTHING OF ME.
IF THEY FEEL JUST AS ALONE AS I DO.
YOU.

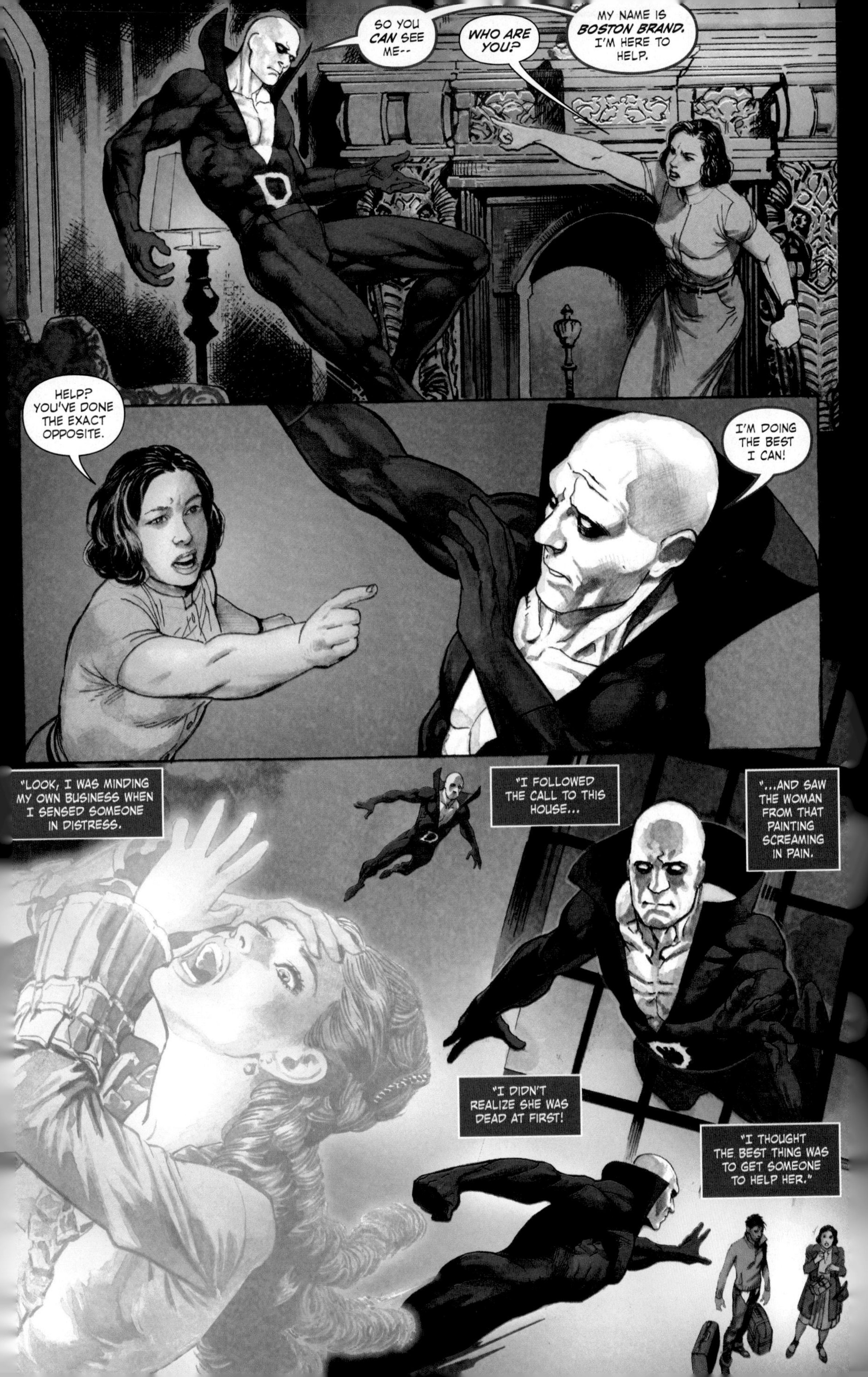
SO YOU CAN SEE ME--
WHO ARE YOU?
MY NAME IS BOSTON BRAND. I'M HERE TO HELP.
HELP? YOU'VE DONE THE EXACT OPPOSITE.
I'M DOING THE BEST I CAN!
"LOOK, I WAS MINDING MY OWN BUSINESS WHEN I SENSED SOMEONE IN DISTRESS.
"I FOLLOWED THE CALL TO THIS HOUSE...
"...AND SAW THE WOMAN FROM THAT PAINTING SCREAMING IN PAIN.
"I DIDN'T REALIZE SHE WAS DEAD AT FIRST!
"I THOUGHT THE BEST THING WAS TO GET SOMEONE TO HELP HER."

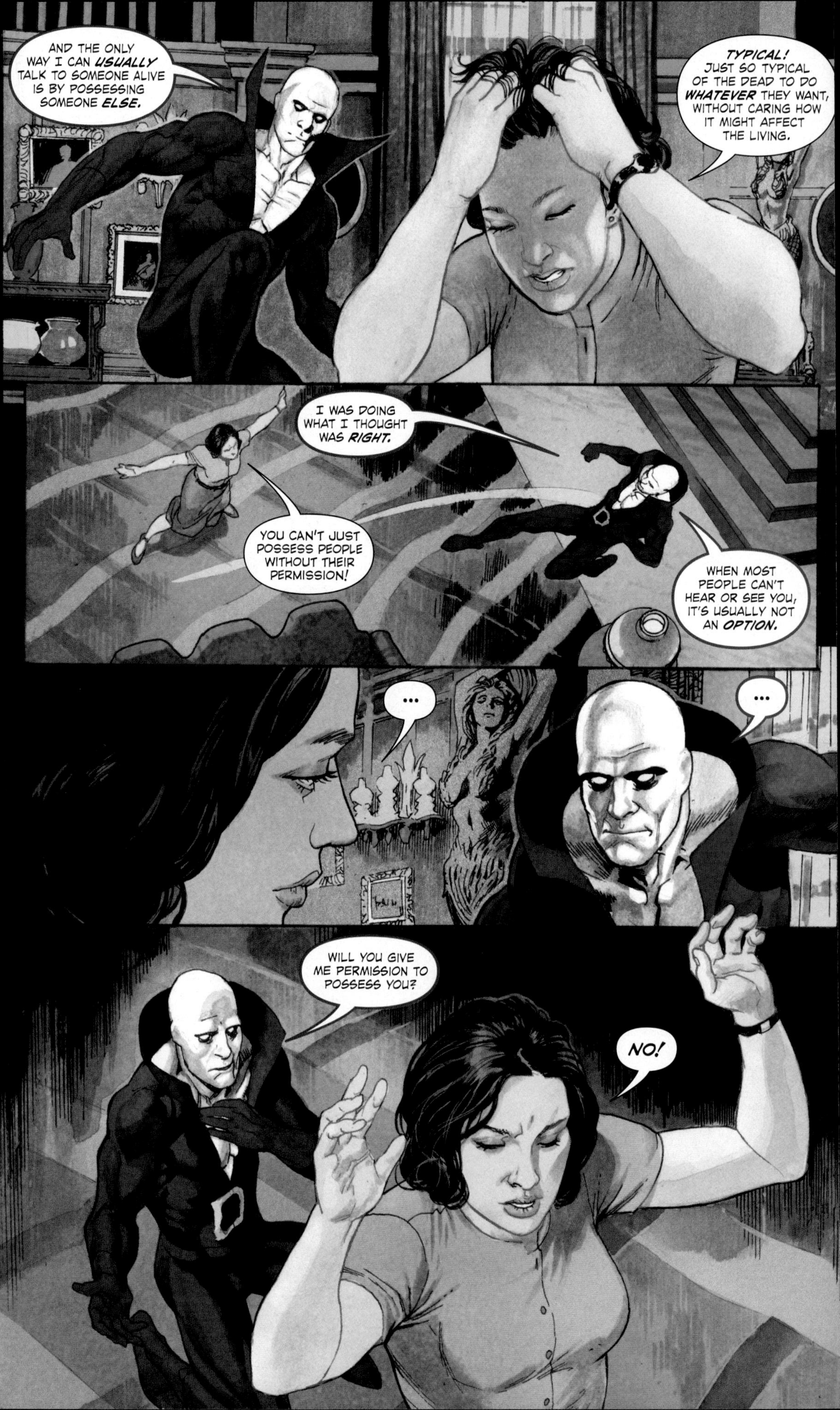
AND THE ONLY WAY I CAN USUALLY TALK TO SOMEONE ALIVE IS BY POSSESSING SOMEONE ELSE.
TYPICAL! JUST SO TYPICAL OF THE DEAD TO DO WHATEVER THEY WANT, WITHOUT CARING HOW IT MIGHT AFFECT THE LIVING.
I WAS DOING WHAT I THOUGHT WAS RIGHT.
YOU CAN'T JUST POSSESS PEOPLE WITHOUT THEIR PERMISSION!
WHEN MOST PEOPLE CAN'T HEAR OR SEE YOU, IT'S USUALLY NOT AN OPTION.
...
...
WILL YOU GIVE ME PERMISSION TO POSSESS YOU?
NO!

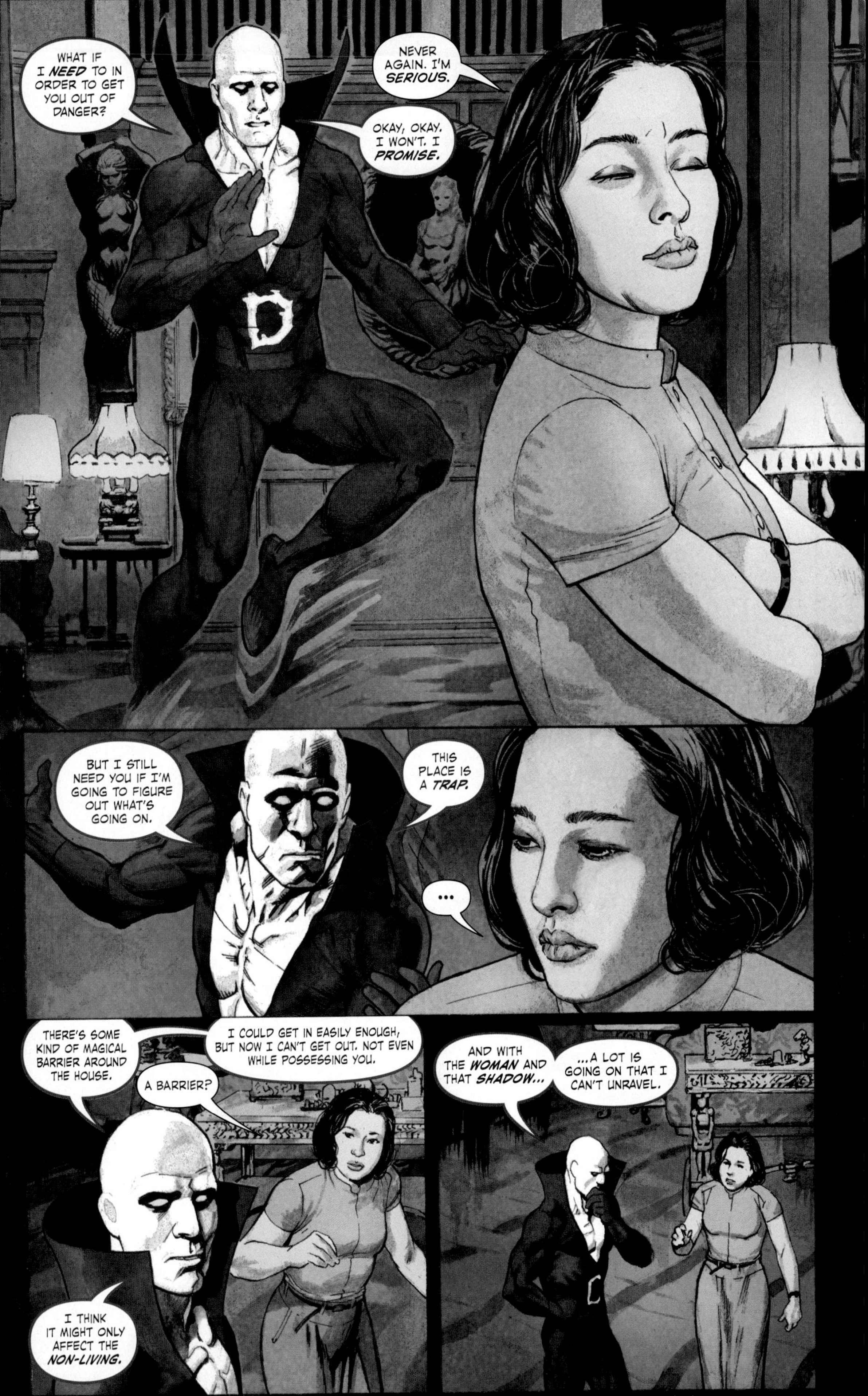
WHAT IF I NEED TO IN ORDER TO GET YOU OUT OF DANGER?
NEVER AGAIN. I'M SERIOUS.
OKAY, OKAY. I WON'T. I PROMISE.
BUT I STILL NEED YOU IF I'M GOING TO FIGURE OUT WHAT'S GOING ON.
THIS PLACE IS A TRAP.
...
THERE'S SOME KIND OF MAGICAL BARRIER AROUND THE HOUSE.
I COULD GET IN EASILY ENOUGH, BUT NOW I CAN'T GET OUT. NOT EVEN WHILE POSSESSING YOU.
A BARRIER?
I THINK IT MIGHT ONLY AFFECT THE NON-LIVING.
AND WITH THE WOMAN AND THAT SHADOW...
...A LOT IS GOING ON THAT I CAN'T UNRAVEL.

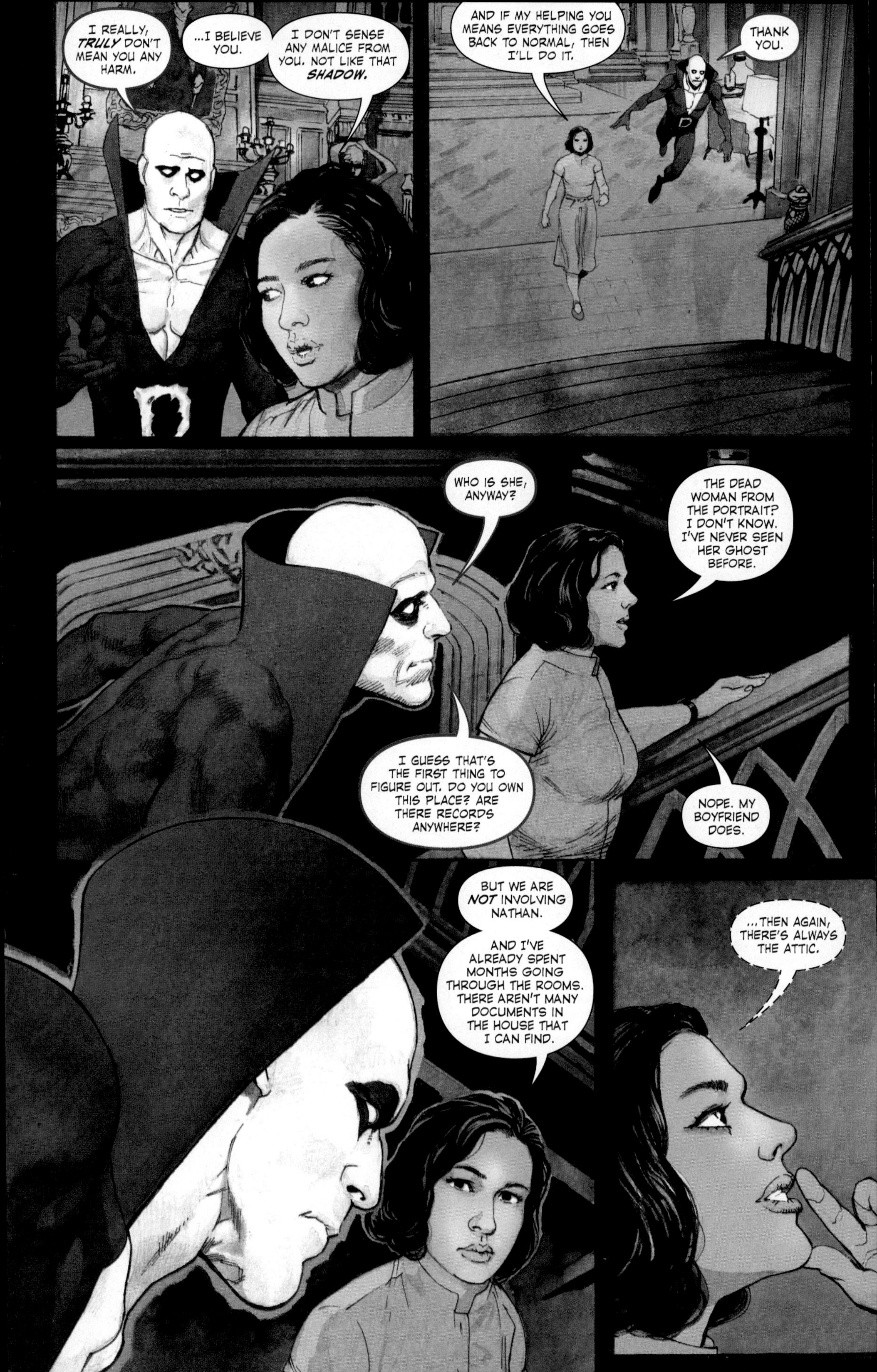
I REALLY, *TRULY* DON'T MEAN YOU ANY HARM.
...I BELIEVE YOU.
I DON'T SENSE ANY MALICE FROM YOU. NOT LIKE THAT *SHADOW.*
AND IF MY HELPING YOU MEANS EVERYTHING GOES BACK TO NORMAL, THEN I'LL DO IT.
THANK YOU.
WHO IS SHE, ANYWAY?
THE DEAD WOMAN FROM THE PORTRAIT? I DON'T KNOW. I'VE NEVER SEEN HER GHOST BEFORE.
I GUESS THAT'S THE FIRST THING TO FIGURE OUT. DO YOU OWN THIS PLACE? ARE THERE RECORDS ANYWHERE?
NOPE. MY BOYFRIEND DOES.
BUT WE ARE *NOT* INVOLVING NATHAN.
AND I'VE ALREADY SPENT MONTHS GOING THROUGH THE ROOMS. THERE AREN'T MANY DOCUMENTS IN THE HOUSE THAT I CAN FIND.
...THEN AGAIN, THERE'S ALWAYS THE ATTIC.

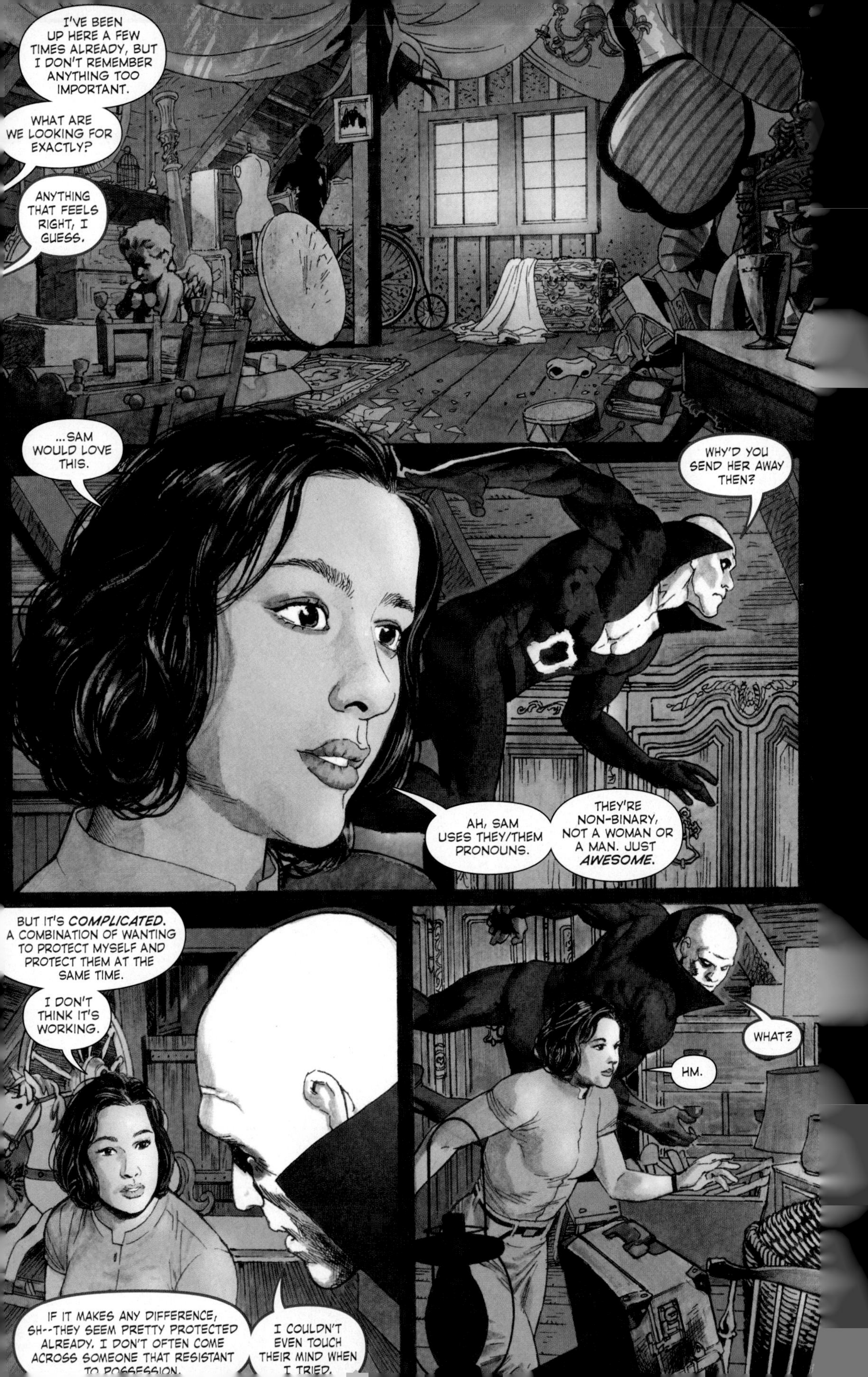
I'VE BEEN UP HERE A FEW TIMES ALREADY, BUT I DON'T REMEMBER ANYTHING TOO IMPORTANT.
WHAT ARE WE LOOKING FOR EXACTLY?
ANYTHING THAT FEELS RIGHT, I GUESS.
...SAM WOULD LOVE THIS.
WHY'D YOU SEND HER AWAY THEN?
AH, SAM USES THEY/THEM PRONOUNS.
THEY'RE NON-BINARY, NOT A WOMAN OR A MAN. JUST AWESOME.
BUT IT'S COMPLICATED. A COMBINATION OF WANTING TO PROTECT MYSELF AND PROTECT THEM AT THE SAME TIME.
I DON'T THINK IT'S WORKING.
IF IT MAKES ANY DIFFERENCE, SH--THEY SEEM PRETTY PROTECTED ALREADY. I DON'T OFTEN COME ACROSS SOMEONE THAT RESISTANT TO POSSESSION.
I COULDN'T EVEN TOUCH THEIR MIND WHEN I TRIED.
WHAT?
HM.

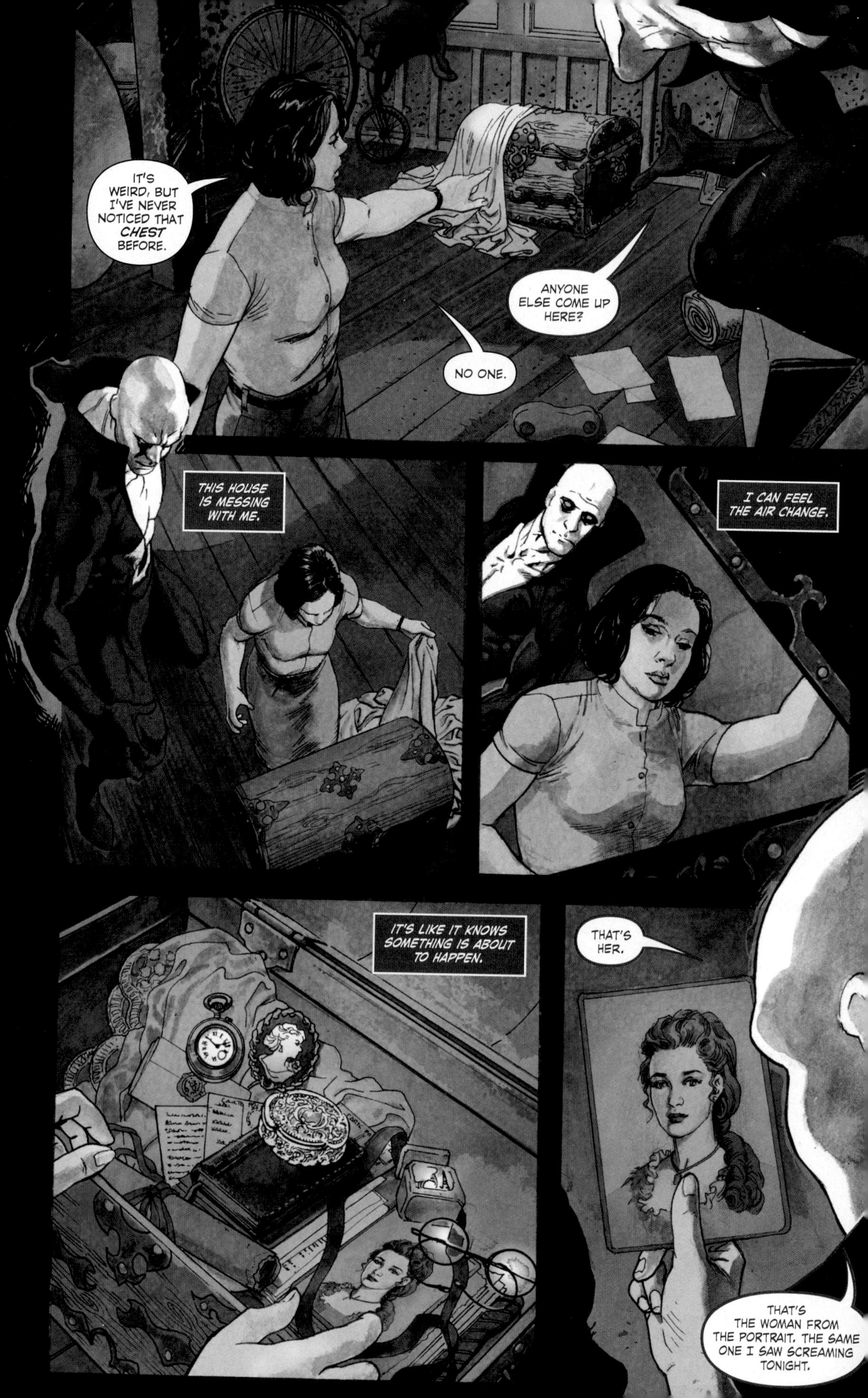
IT'S WEIRD, BUT I'VE NEVER NOTICED THAT CHEST BEFORE.
ANYONE ELSE COME UP HERE?
NO ONE.
THIS HOUSE IS MESSING WITH ME.
I CAN FEEL THE AIR CHANGE.
IT'S LIKE IT KNOWS SOMETHING IS ABOUT TO HAPPEN.
THAT'S HER.
THAT'S THE WOMAN FROM THE PORTRAIT. THE SAME ONE I SAW SCREAMING TONIGHT.

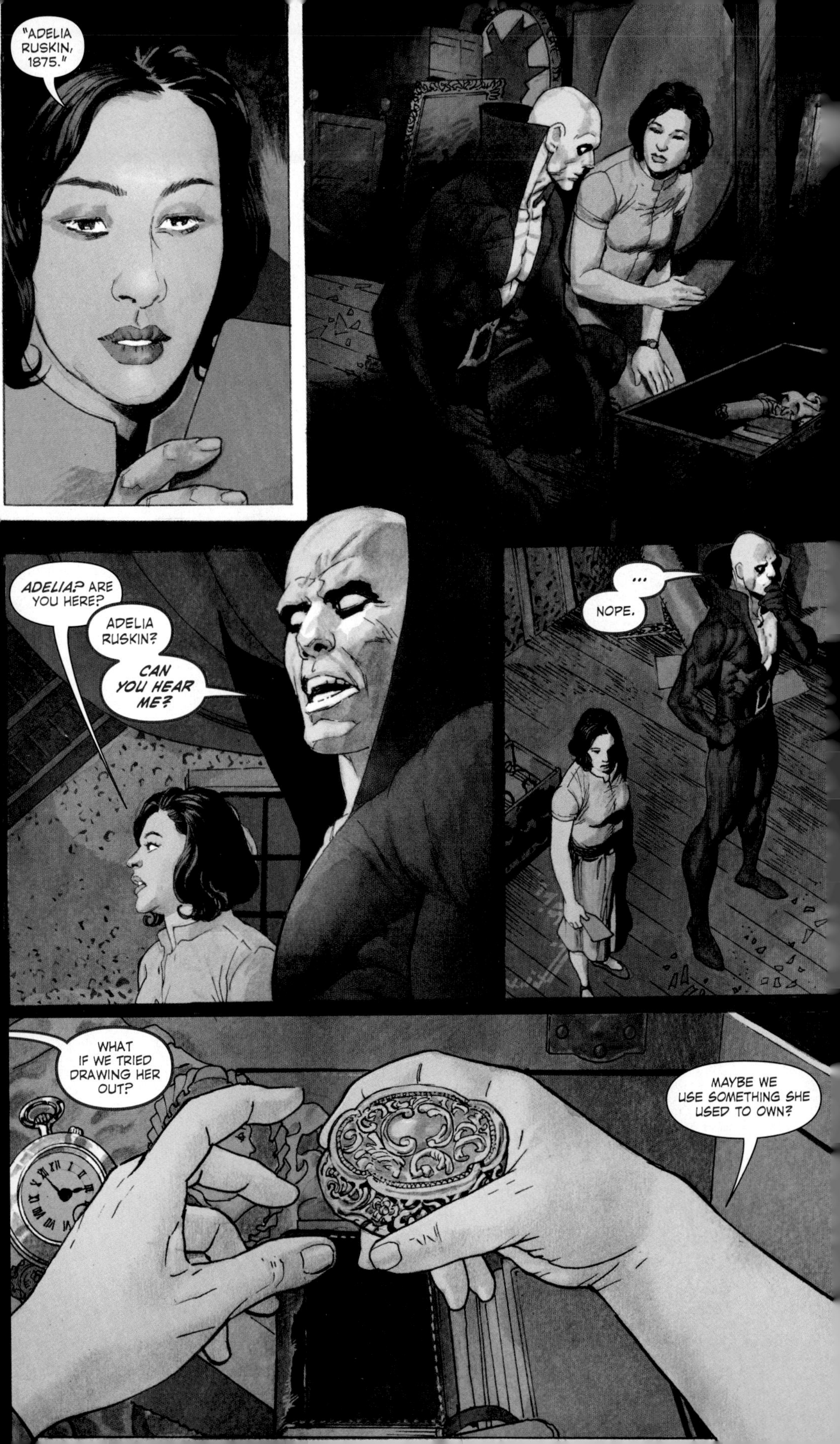
"ADELIA RUSKIN, 1875."
ADELIA? ARE YOU HERE?
ADELIA RUSKIN?
CAN YOU HEAR ME?
...
NOPE.
WHAT IF WE TRIED DRAWING HER OUT?
MAYBE WE USE SOMETHING SHE USED TO OWN?

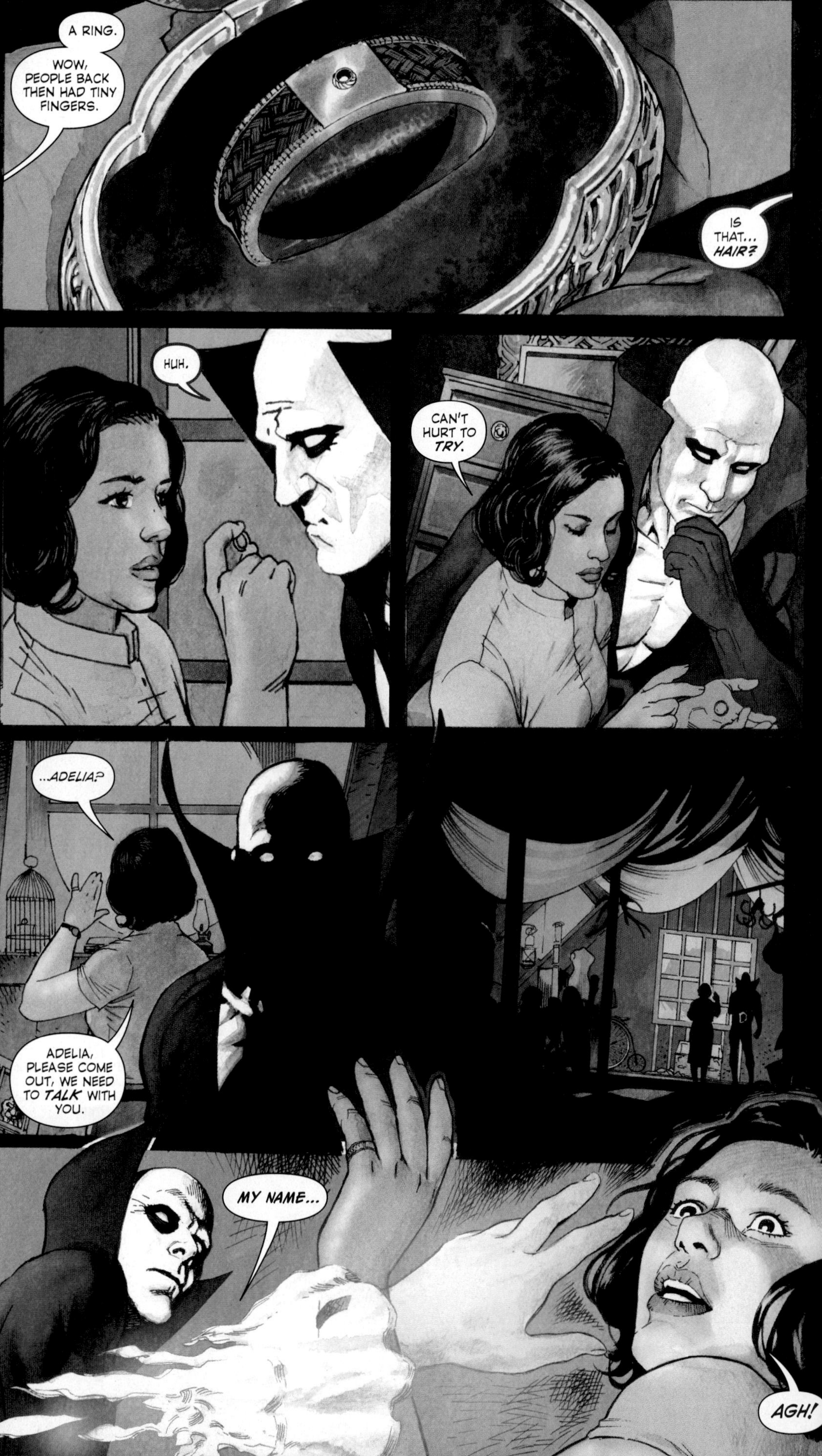
A RING.
WOW, PEOPLE BACK THEN HAD TINY FINGERS.
IS THAT... HAIR?
HUH.
CAN'T HURT TO TRY.
...ADELIA?
ADELIA, PLEASE COME OUT, WE NEED TO TALK WITH YOU.
MY NAME...
AGH!

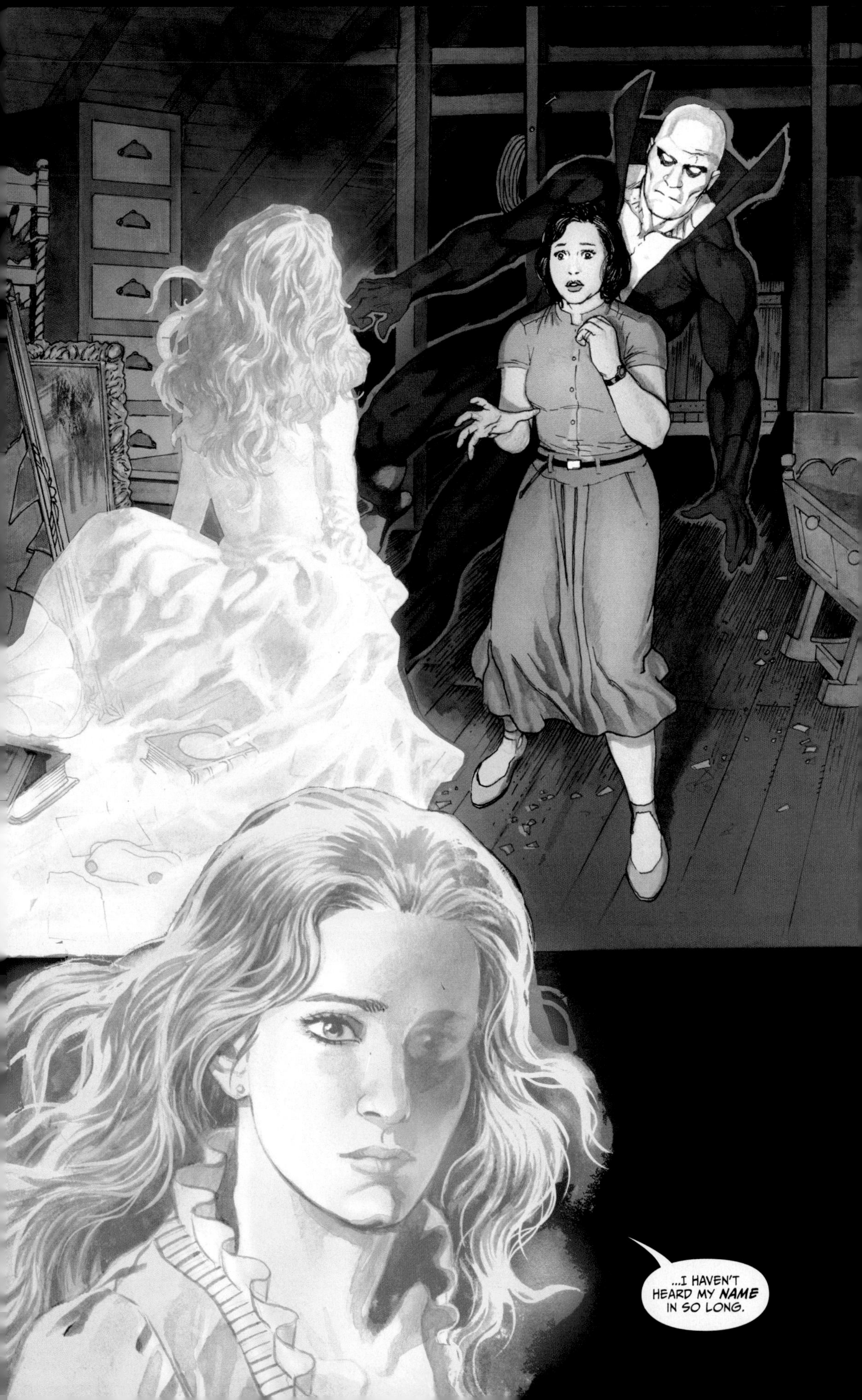
...I HAVEN'T HEARD MY **NAME** IN SO LONG.

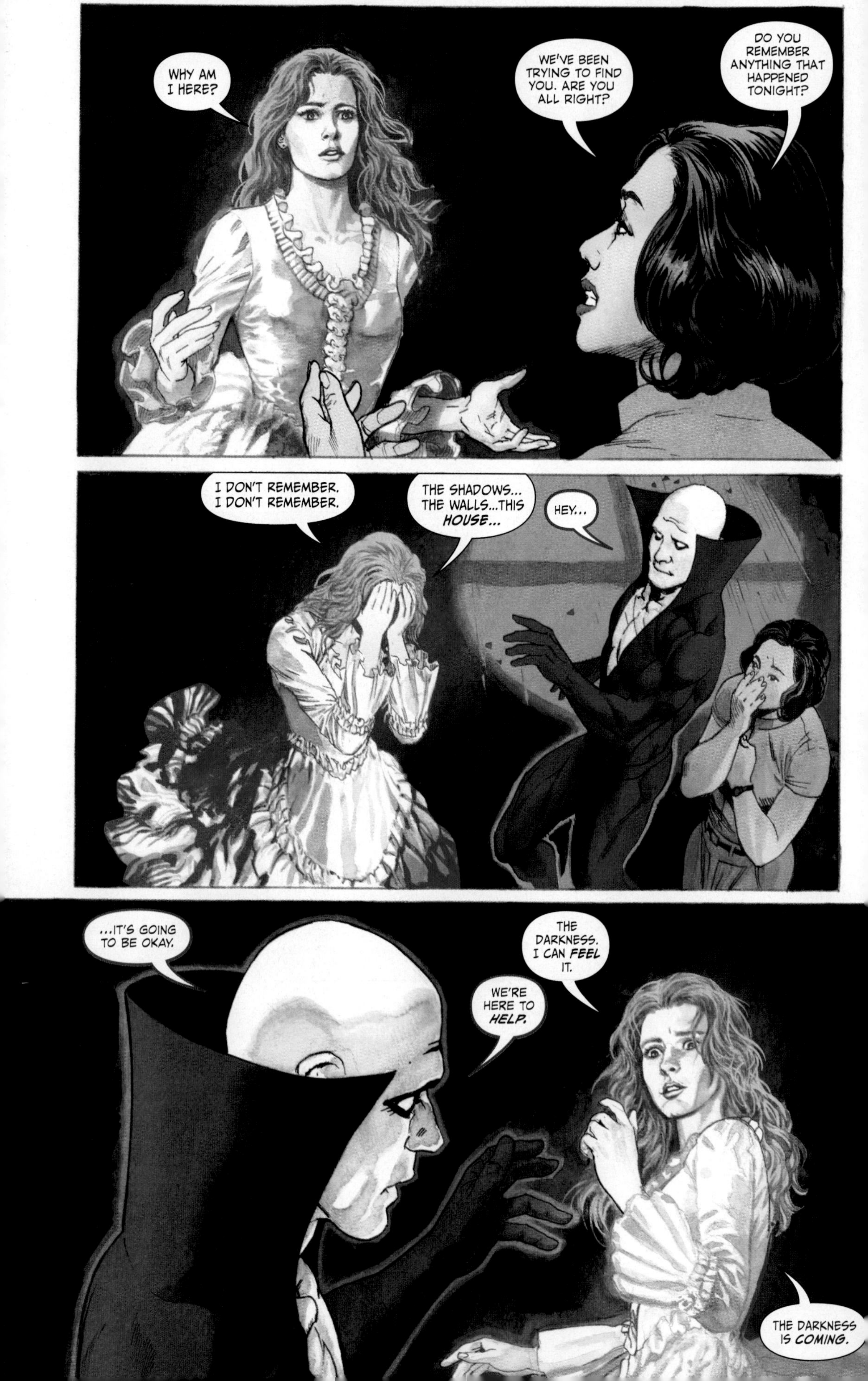
WHY AM I HERE?
WE'VE BEEN TRYING TO FIND YOU. ARE YOU ALL RIGHT?
DO YOU REMEMBER ANYTHING THAT HAPPENED TONIGHT?
I DON'T REMEMBER. I DON'T REMEMBER.
THE SHADOWS... THE WALLS...THIS *HOUSE*...
HEY...
...IT'S GOING TO BE OKAY.
WE'RE HERE TO *HELP*.
THE DARKNESS. I CAN *FEEL* IT.
THE DARKNESS IS *COMING*.

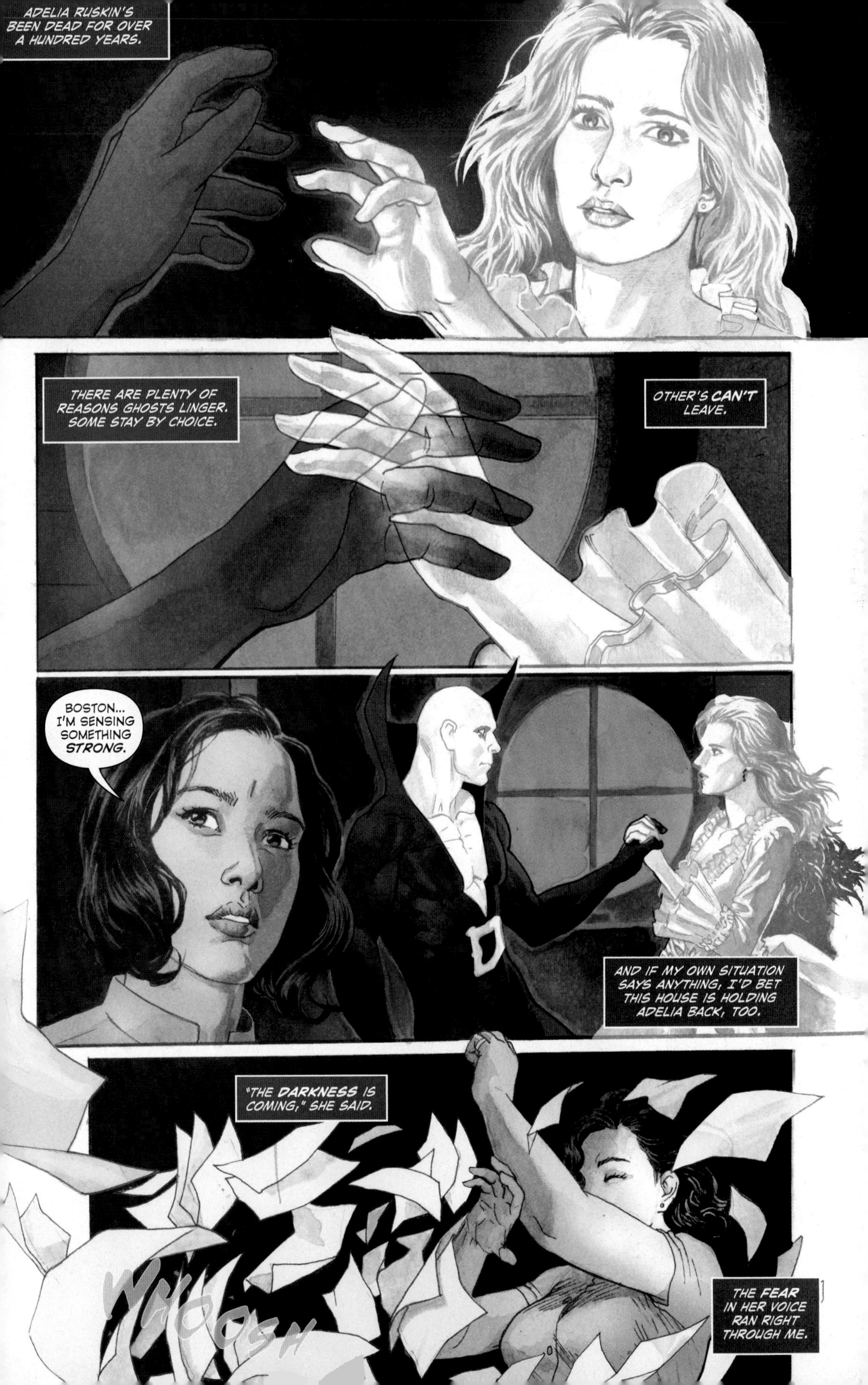
ADELIA RUSKIN'S BEEN DEAD FOR OVER A HUNDRED YEARS.
THERE ARE PLENTY OF REASONS GHOSTS LINGER. SOME STAY BY CHOICE.
OTHER'S **CAN'T** LEAVE.
BOSTON... I'M SENSING SOMETHING **STRONG**.
AND IF MY OWN SITUATION SAYS ANYTHING, I'D BET THIS HOUSE IS HOLDING ADELIA BACK, TOO.
"THE **DARKNESS** IS COMING," SHE SAID.
WHOOSH
THE **FEAR** IN HER VOICE RAN RIGHT THROUGH ME.

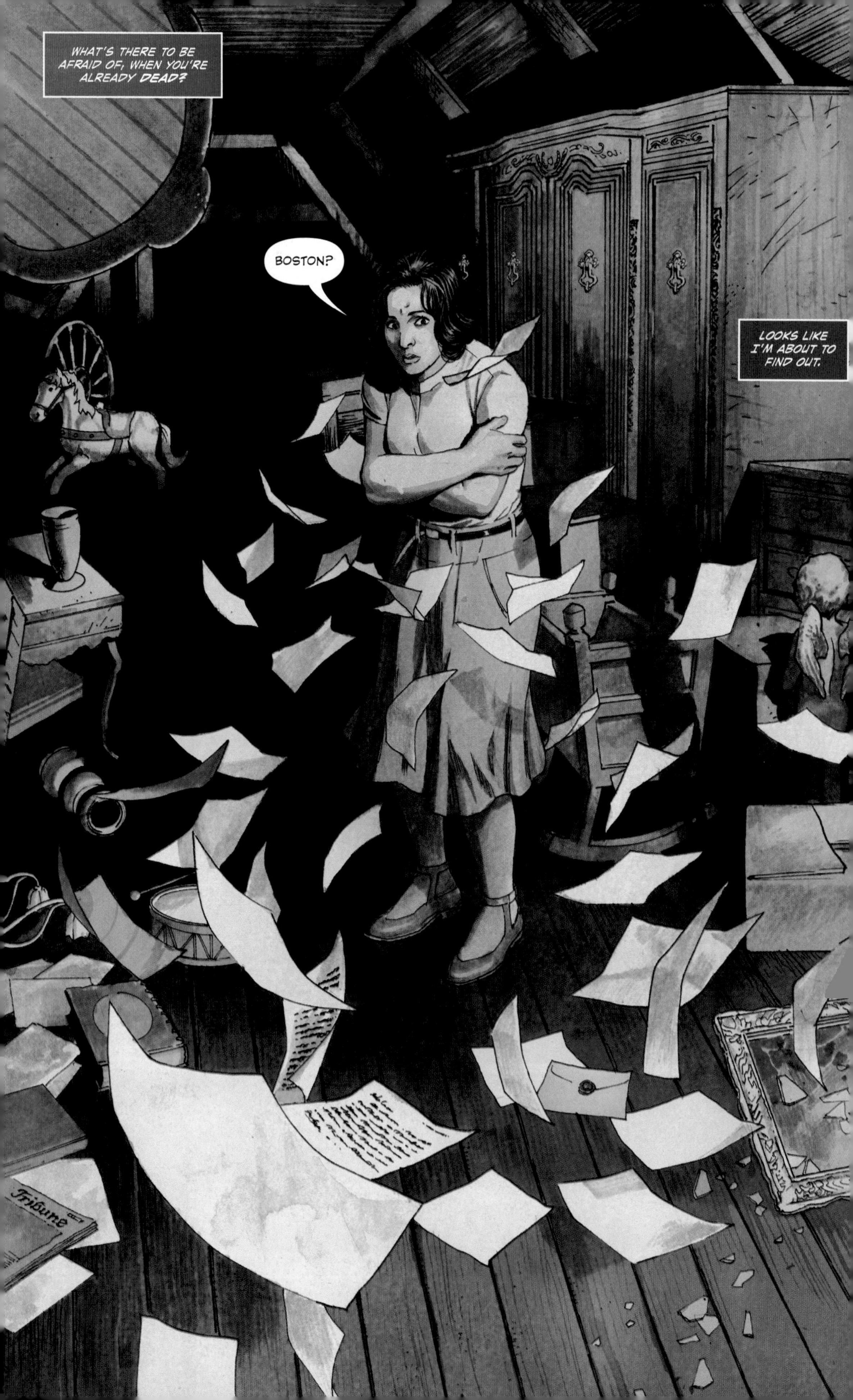
WHAT'S THERE TO BE AFRAID OF, WHEN YOU'RE ALREADY DEAD?
BOSTON?
LOOKS LIKE I'M ABOUT TO FIND OUT.

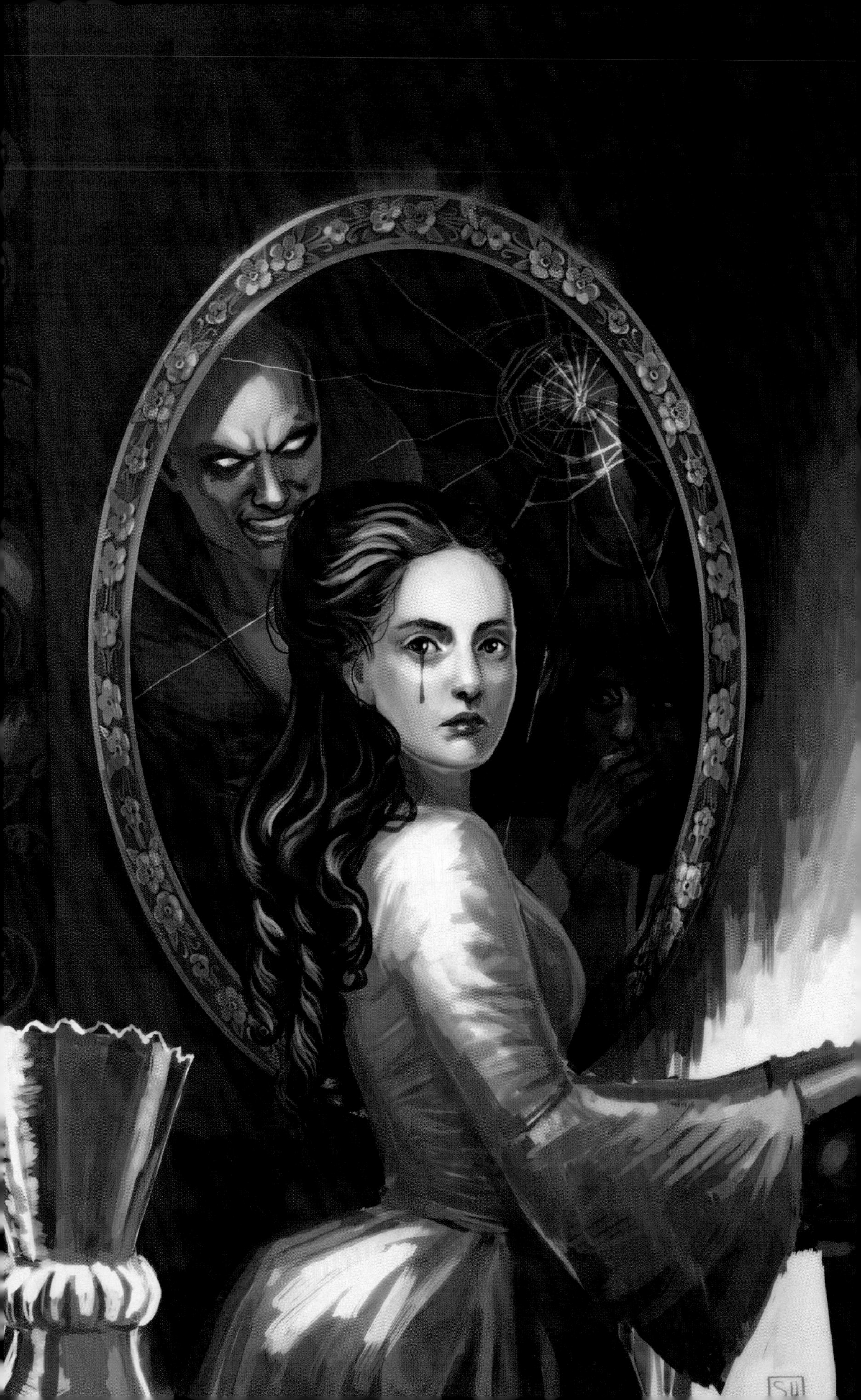

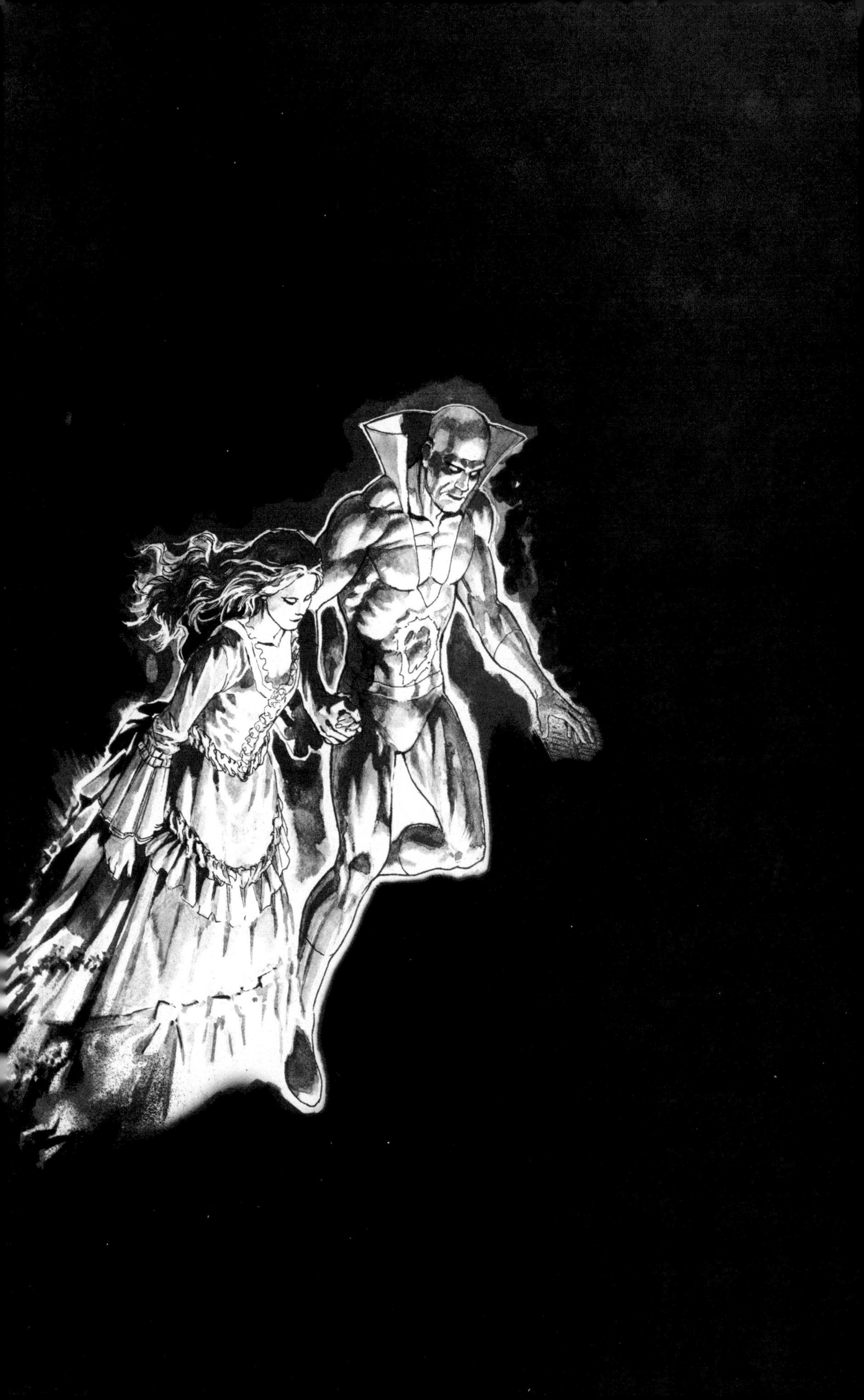

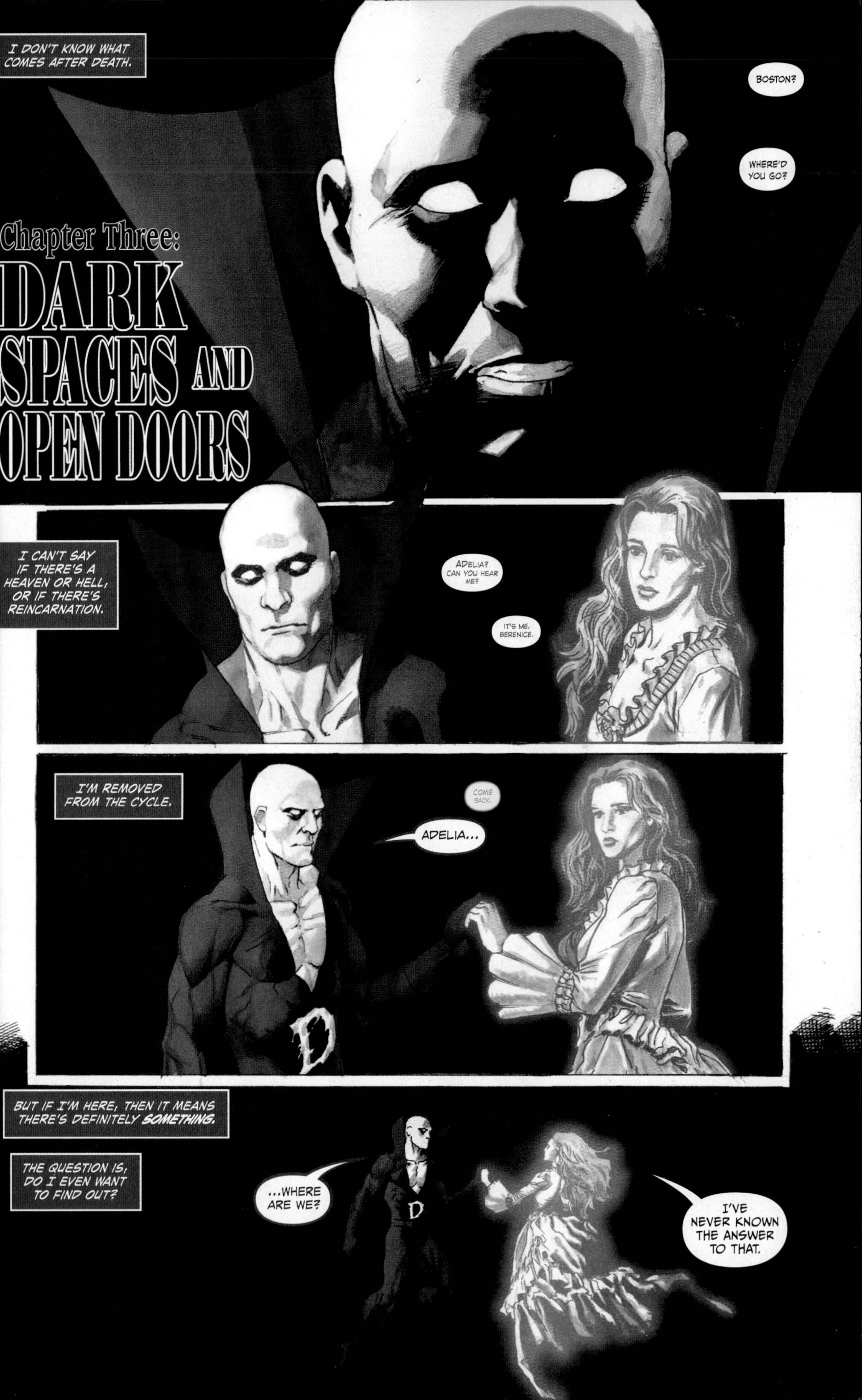
I DON'T KNOW WHAT COMES AFTER DEATH.
BOSTON?
WHERE'D YOU GO?
Chapter Three:
DARK SPACES AND OPEN DOORS
I CAN'T SAY IF THERE'S A HEAVEN OR HELL, OR IF THERE'S REINCARNATION.
ADELIA? CAN YOU HEAR ME?
IT'S ME, BERENICE.
I'M REMOVED FROM THE CYCLE.
COME BACK.
ADELIA...
BUT IF I'M HERE, THEN IT MEANS THERE'S DEFINITELY SOMETHING.
THE QUESTION IS, DO I EVEN WANT TO FIND OUT?
...WHERE ARE WE?
I'VE NEVER KNOWN THE ANSWER TO THAT.

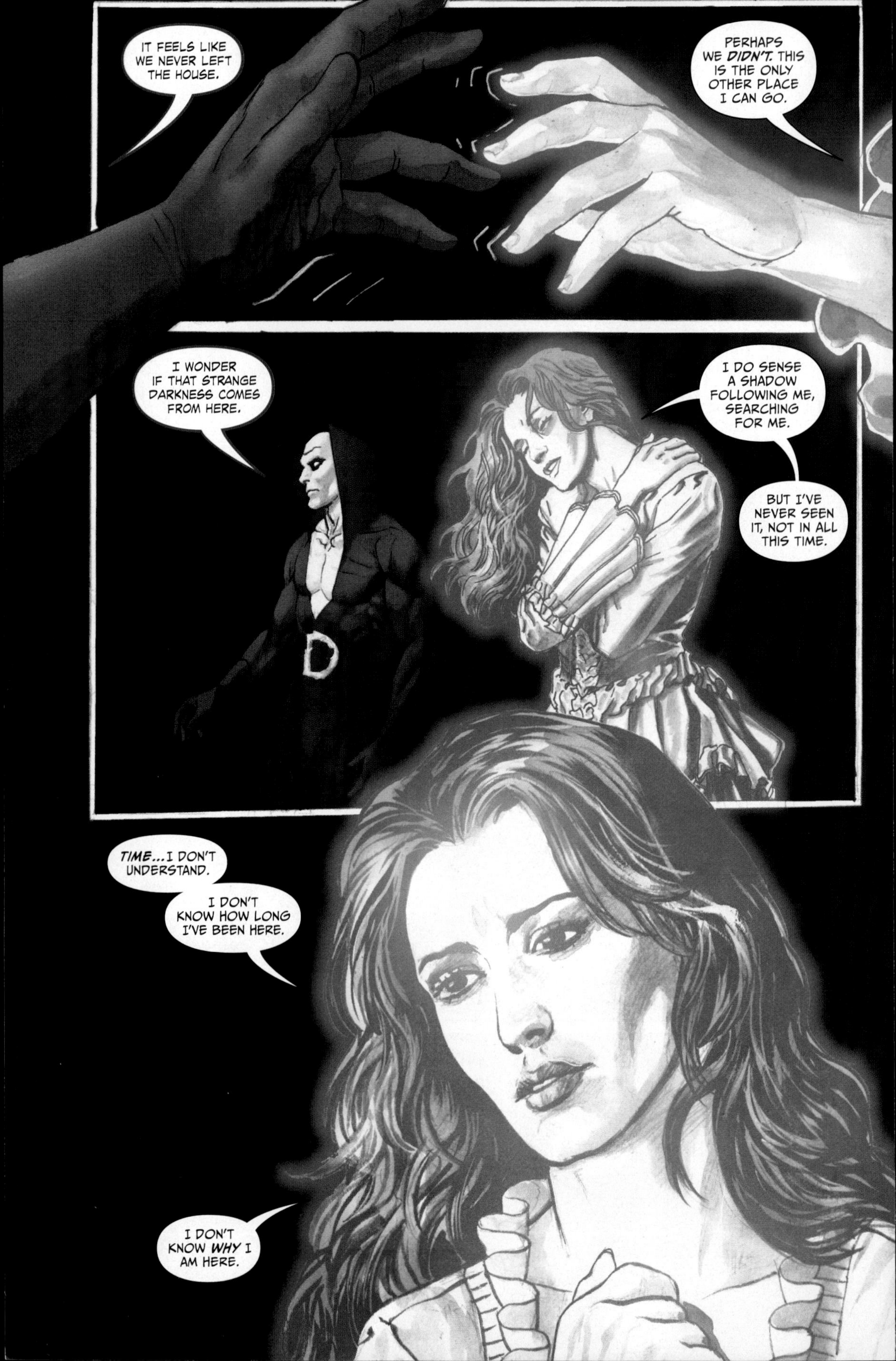
IT FEELS LIKE WE NEVER LEFT THE HOUSE.
PERHAPS WE *DIDN'T.* THIS IS THE ONLY OTHER PLACE I CAN GO.
I WONDER IF THAT STRANGE DARKNESS COMES FROM HERE.
I DO SENSE A SHADOW FOLLOWING ME, SEARCHING FOR ME.
BUT I'VE NEVER SEEN IT, NOT IN ALL THIS TIME.
*TIME...*I DON'T UNDERSTAND.
I DON'T KNOW HOW LONG I'VE BEEN HERE.
I DON'T KNOW *WHY* I AM HERE.

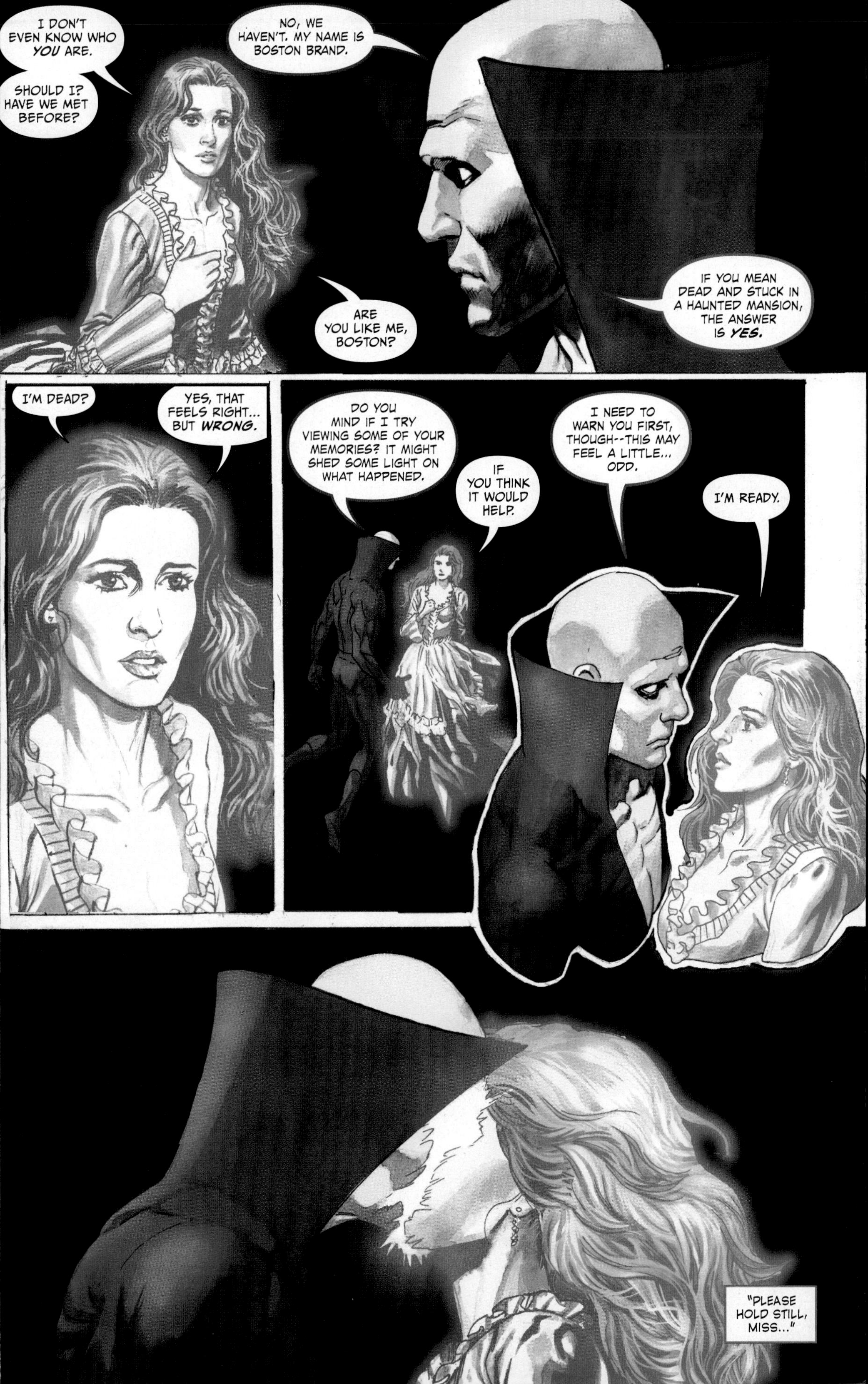
I DON'T EVEN KNOW WHO *YOU* ARE.
SHOULD I? HAVE WE MET BEFORE?
NO, WE HAVEN'T. MY NAME IS BOSTON BRAND.
ARE YOU LIKE ME, BOSTON?
IF YOU MEAN DEAD AND STUCK IN A HAUNTED MANSION, THE ANSWER IS ***YES.***
I'M DEAD?
YES, THAT FEELS RIGHT... BUT ***WRONG.***
DO YOU MIND IF I TRY VIEWING SOME OF YOUR MEMORIES? IT MIGHT SHED SOME LIGHT ON WHAT HAPPENED.
IF YOU THINK IT WOULD HELP.
I NEED TO WARN YOU FIRST, THOUGH--THIS MAY FEEL A LITTLE... ODD.
I'M READY.
"PLEASE HOLD STILL, MISS..."

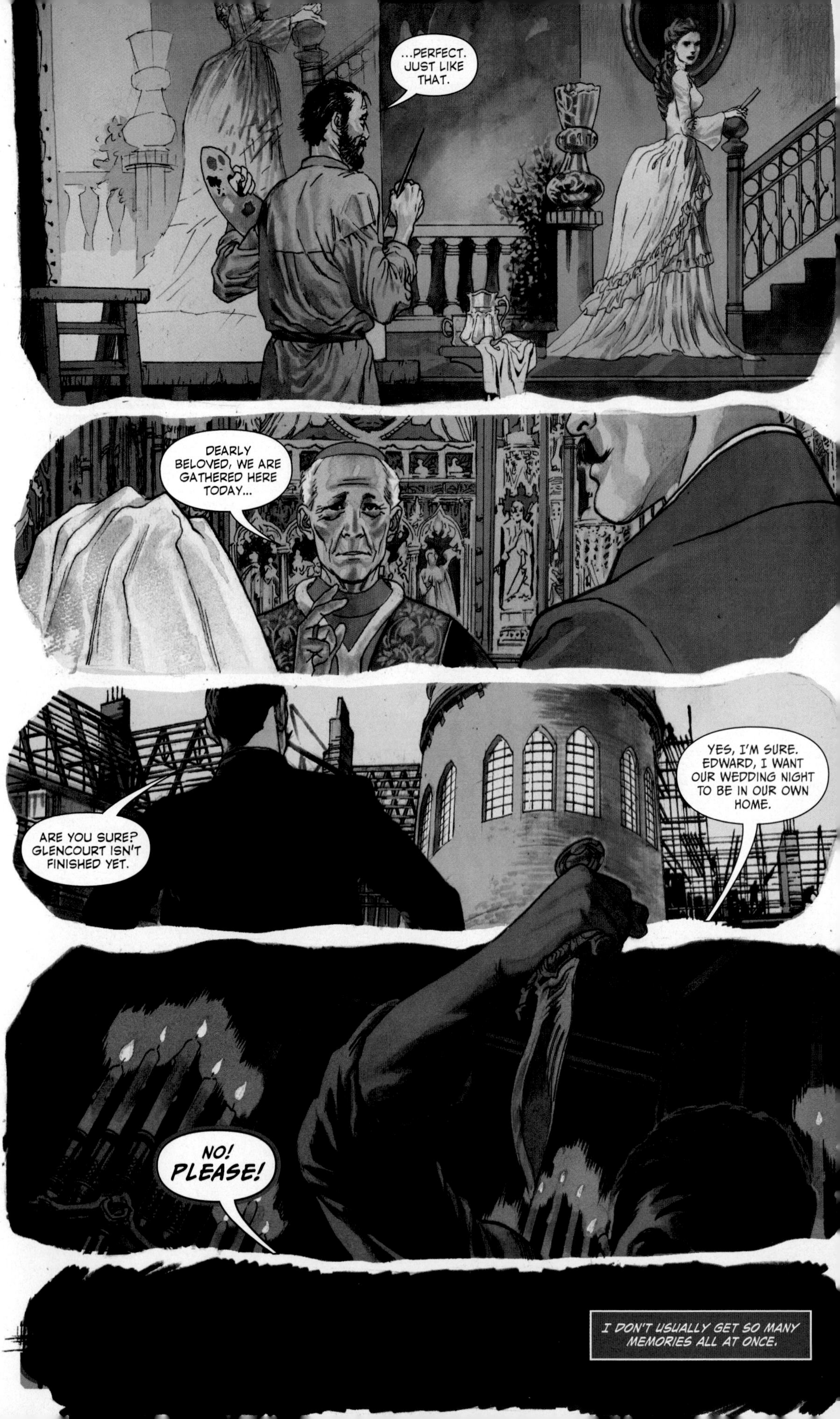
...PERFECT. JUST LIKE THAT.
DEARLY BELOVED, WE ARE GATHERED HERE TODAY...
ARE YOU SURE? GLENCOURT ISN'T FINISHED YET.
YES, I'M SURE. EDWARD, I WANT OUR WEDDING NIGHT TO BE IN OUR OWN HOME.
NO! PLEASE!
I DON'T USUALLY GET SO MANY MEMORIES ALL AT ONCE.

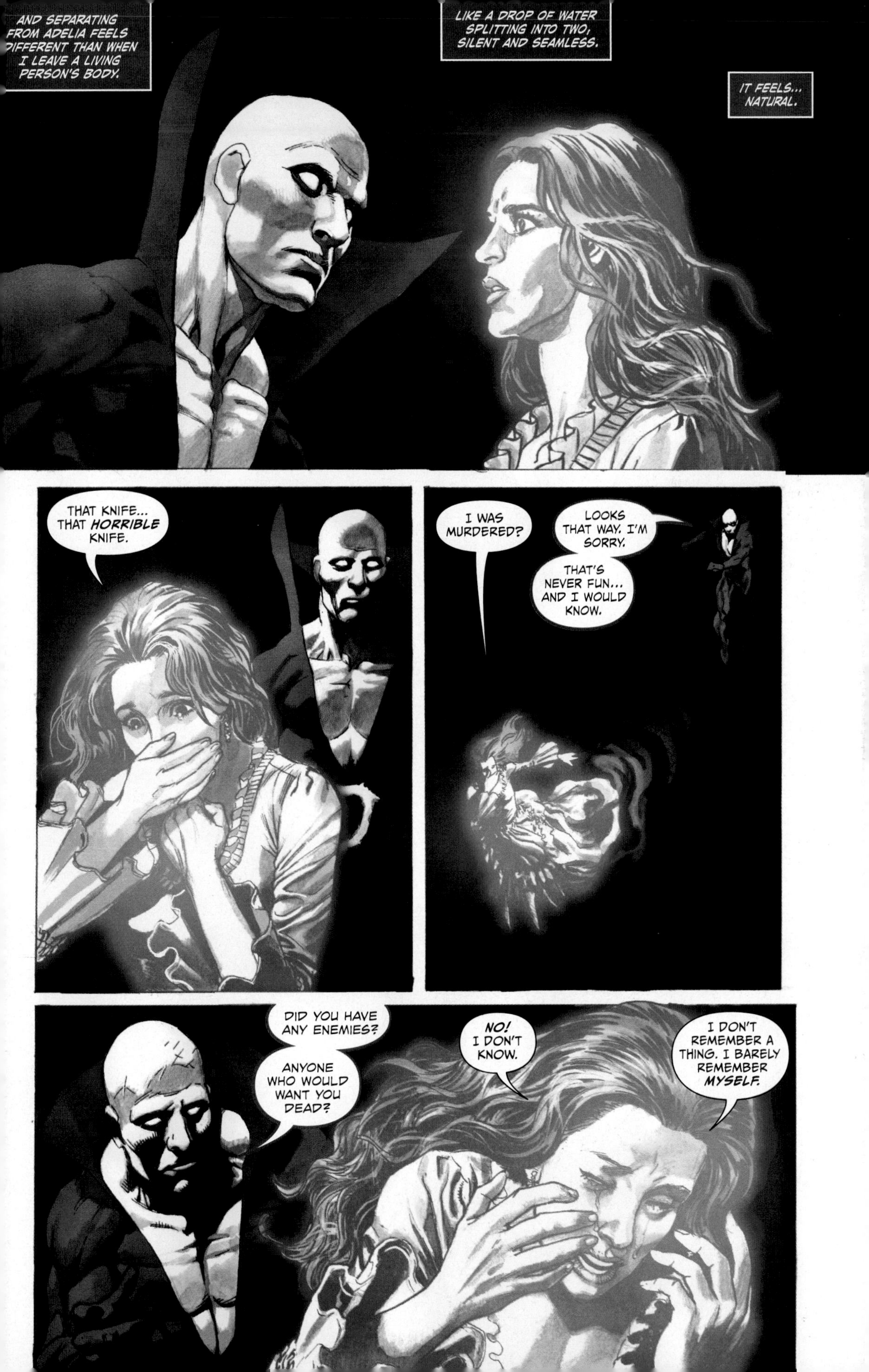
AND SEPARATING FROM ADELIA FEELS DIFFERENT THAN WHEN I LEAVE A LIVING PERSON'S BODY.
LIKE A DROP OF WATER SPLITTING INTO TWO, SILENT AND SEAMLESS.
IT FEELS... NATURAL.
THAT KNIFE... THAT HORRIBLE KNIFE.
I WAS MURDERED?
LOOKS THAT WAY. I'M SORRY.
THAT'S NEVER FUN... AND I WOULD KNOW.
DID YOU HAVE ANY ENEMIES?
ANYONE WHO WOULD WANT YOU DEAD?
NO! I DON'T KNOW.
I DON'T REMEMBER A THING. I BARELY REMEMBER MYSELF.

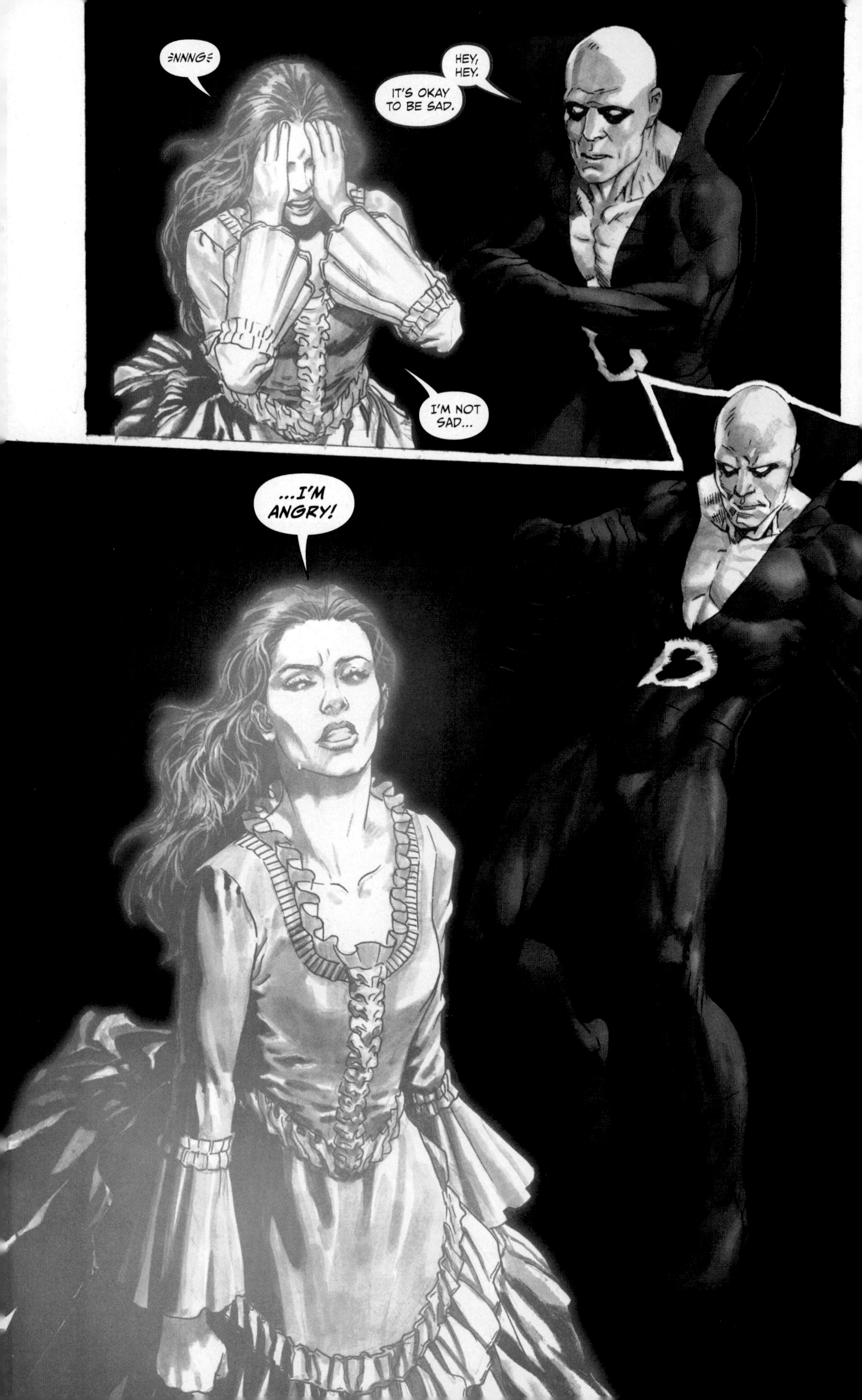

=NNNG=
HEY, HEY.
IT'S OKAY TO BE SAD.
I'M NOT SAD...
...I'M ANGRY!

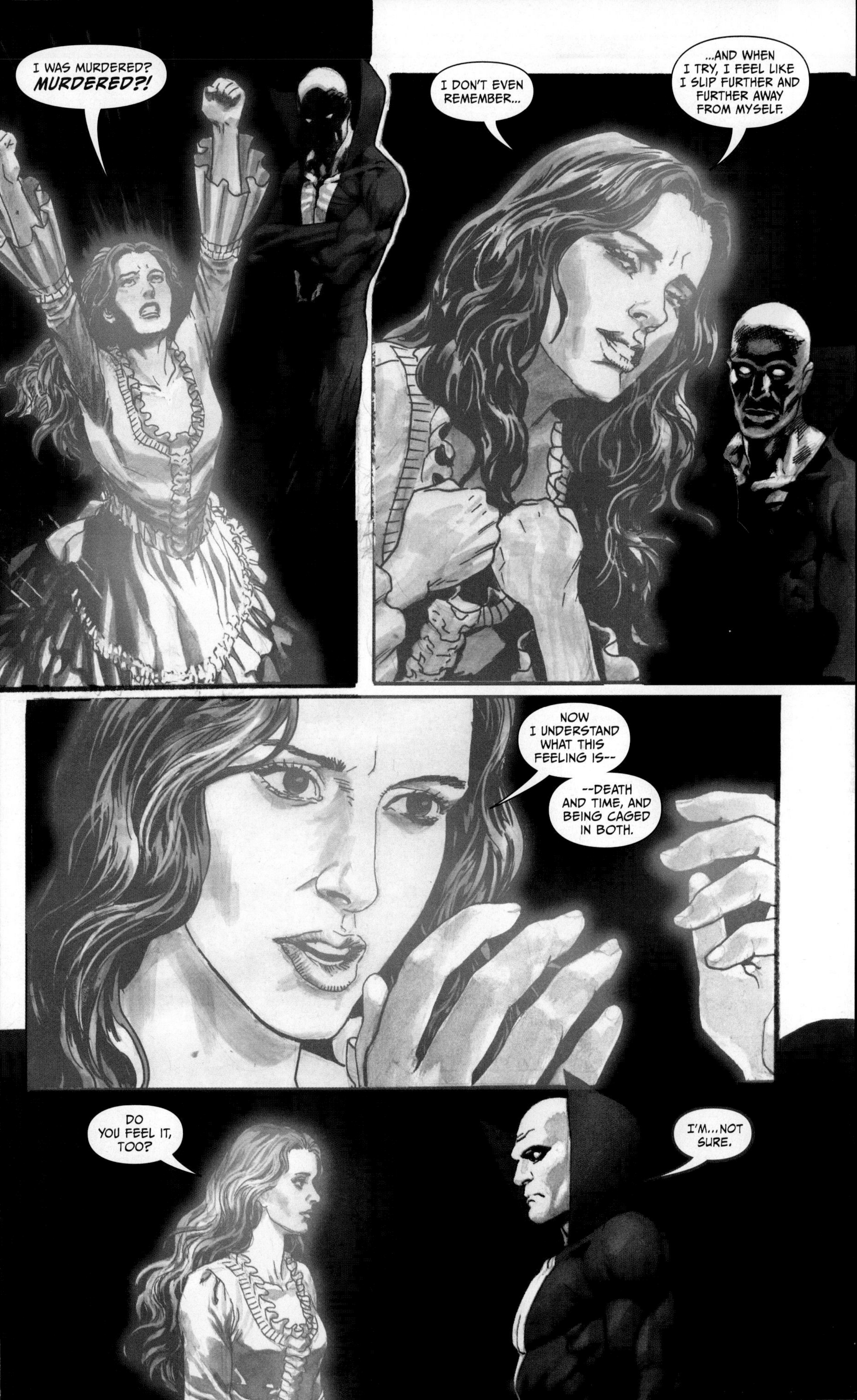
I WAS MURDERED? *MURDERED?!*
I DON'T EVEN REMEMBER...
...AND WHEN I TRY, I FEEL LIKE I SLIP FURTHER AND FURTHER AWAY FROM MYSELF.
NOW I UNDERSTAND WHAT THIS FEELING IS--
--DEATH AND TIME, AND BEING CAGED IN BOTH.
DO YOU FEEL IT, TOO?
I'M...NOT SURE.

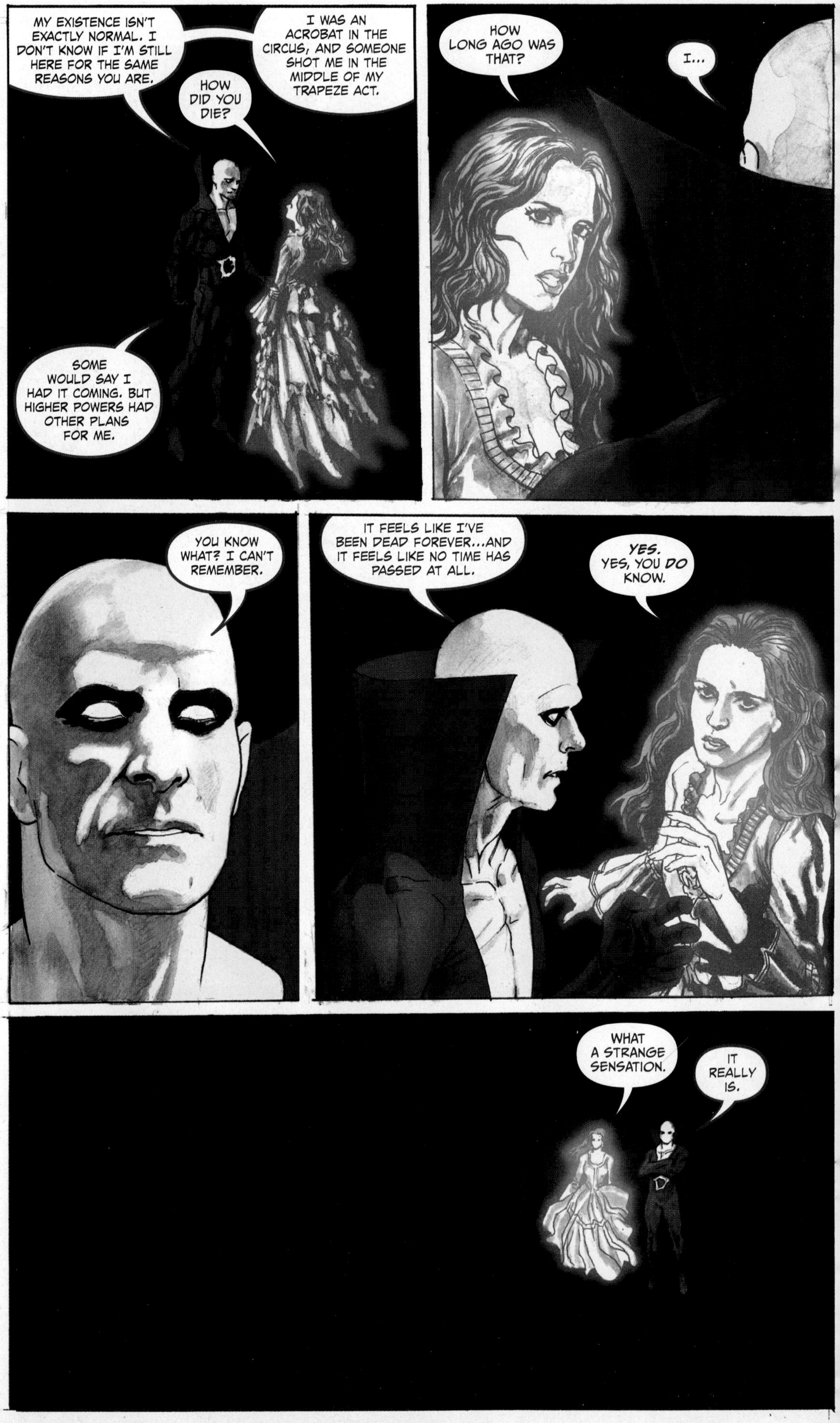
MY EXISTENCE ISN'T EXACTLY NORMAL. I DON'T KNOW IF I'M STILL HERE FOR THE SAME REASONS YOU ARE.
HOW DID YOU DIE?
I WAS AN ACROBAT IN THE CIRCUS, AND SOMEONE SHOT ME IN THE MIDDLE OF MY TRAPEZE ACT.
SOME WOULD SAY I HAD IT COMING. BUT HIGHER POWERS HAD OTHER PLANS FOR ME.
HOW LONG AGO WAS THAT?
I...
YOU KNOW WHAT? I CAN'T REMEMBER.
IT FEELS LIKE I'VE BEEN DEAD FOREVER...AND IT FEELS LIKE NO TIME HAS PASSED AT ALL.
YES. YES, YOU DO KNOW.
WHAT A STRANGE SENSATION.
IT REALLY IS.

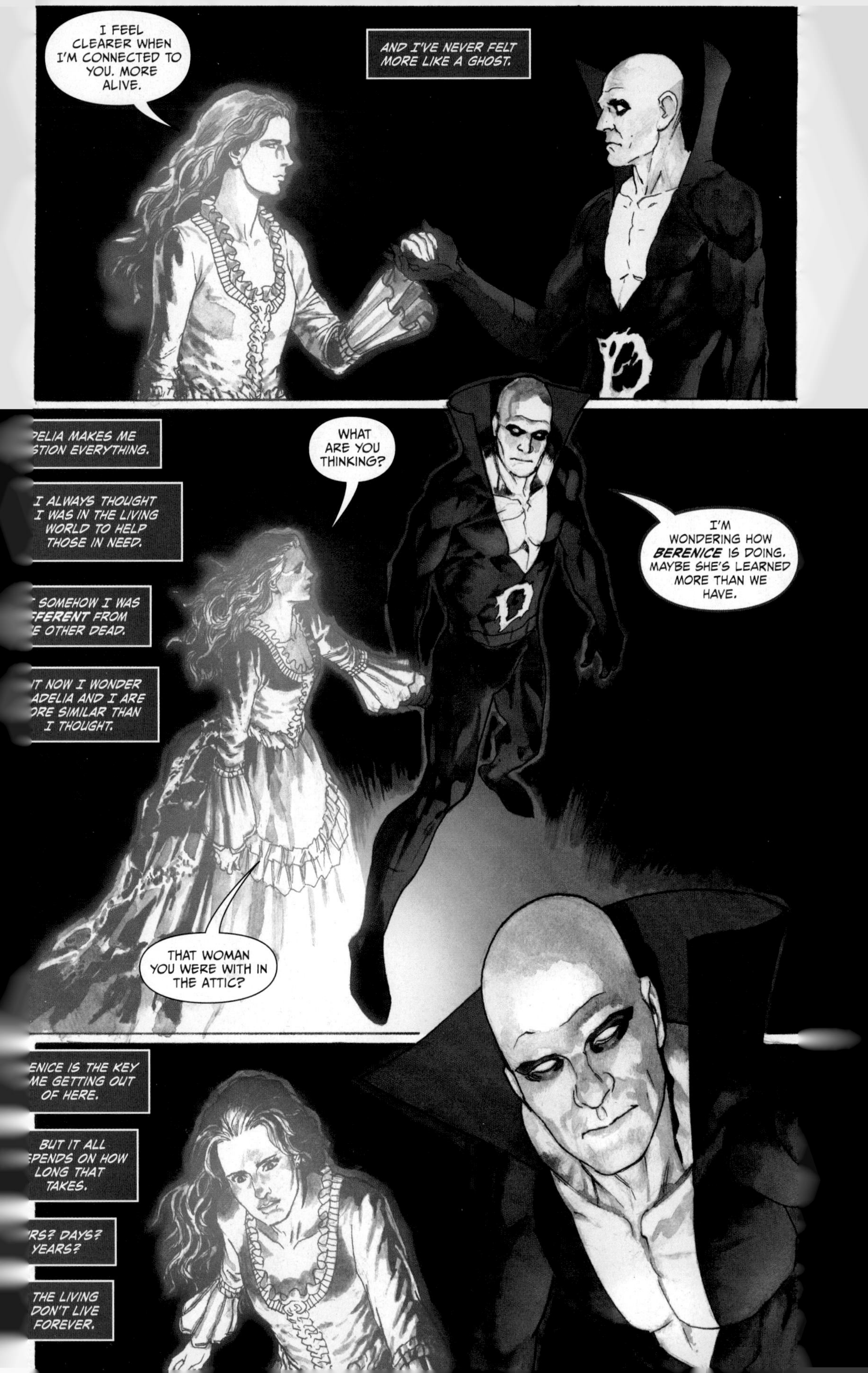

I FEEL CLEARER WHEN I'M CONNECTED TO YOU. MORE ALIVE.
AND I'VE NEVER FELT MORE LIKE A GHOST.
PELIA MAKES ME
STION EVERYTHING.
WHAT ARE YOU THINKING?
I'M WONDERING HOW BERENICE IS DOING. MAYBE SHE'S LEARNED MORE THAN WE HAVE.
I ALWAYS THOUGHT I WAS IN THE LIVING WORLD TO HELP THOSE IN NEED.
SOMEHOW I WAS
FFERENT FROM
E OTHER DEAD.
T NOW I WONDER
ADELIA AND I ARE
ORE SIMILAR THAN
I THOUGHT.
THAT WOMAN YOU WERE WITH IN THE ATTIC?
ENICE IS THE KEY
ME GETTING OUT
OF HERE.
BUT IT ALL
EPENDS ON HOW
LONG THAT TAKES.
RS? DAYS?
YEARS?
THE LIVING DON'T LIVE FOREVER.

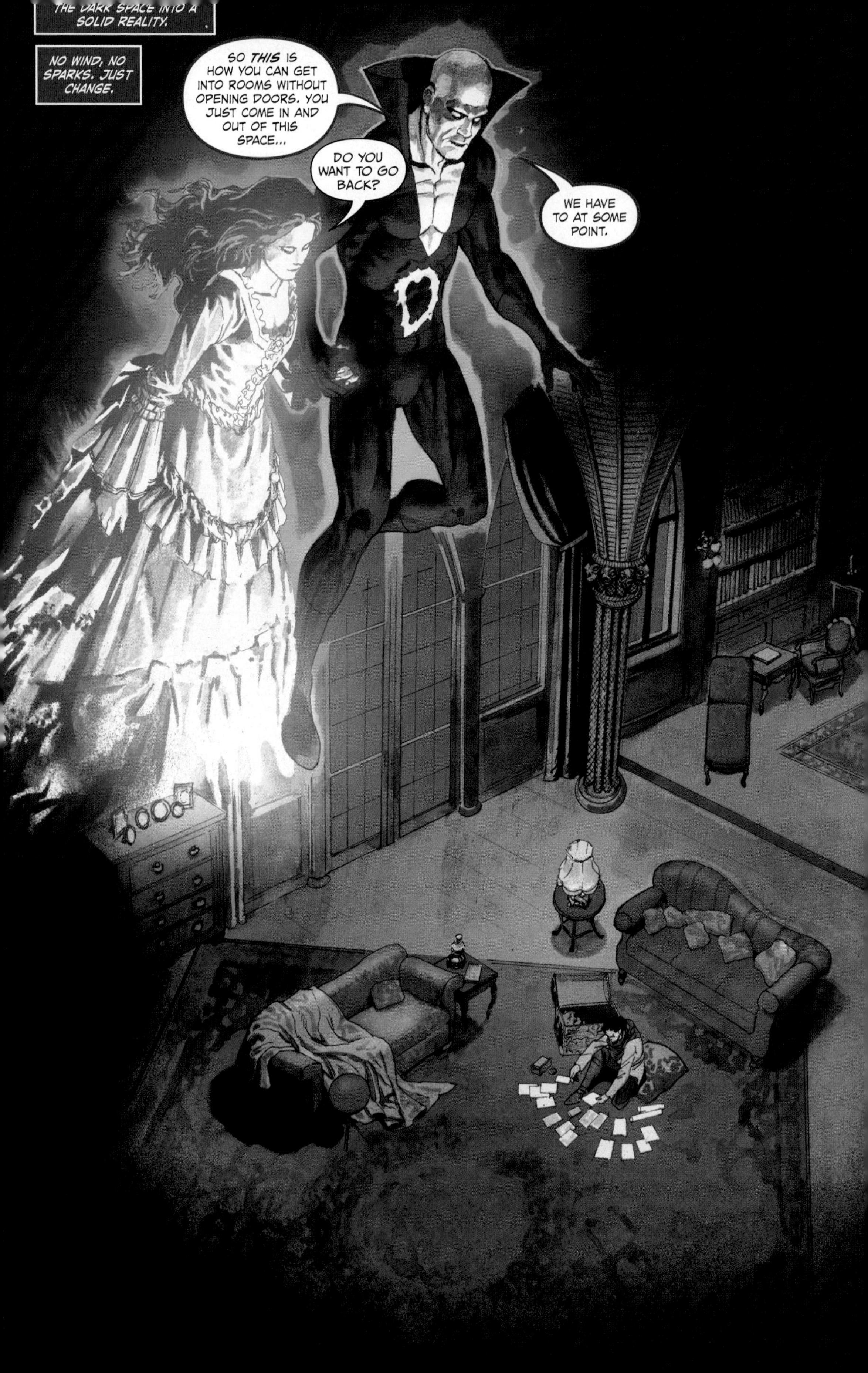
THE DARK SPACE INTO A SOLID REALITY.
NO WIND, NO SPARKS. JUST CHANGE.
SO THIS IS HOW YOU CAN GET INTO ROOMS WITHOUT OPENING DOORS. YOU JUST COME IN AND OUT OF THIS SPACE...
DO YOU WANT TO GO BACK?
WE HAVE TO AT SOME POINT.

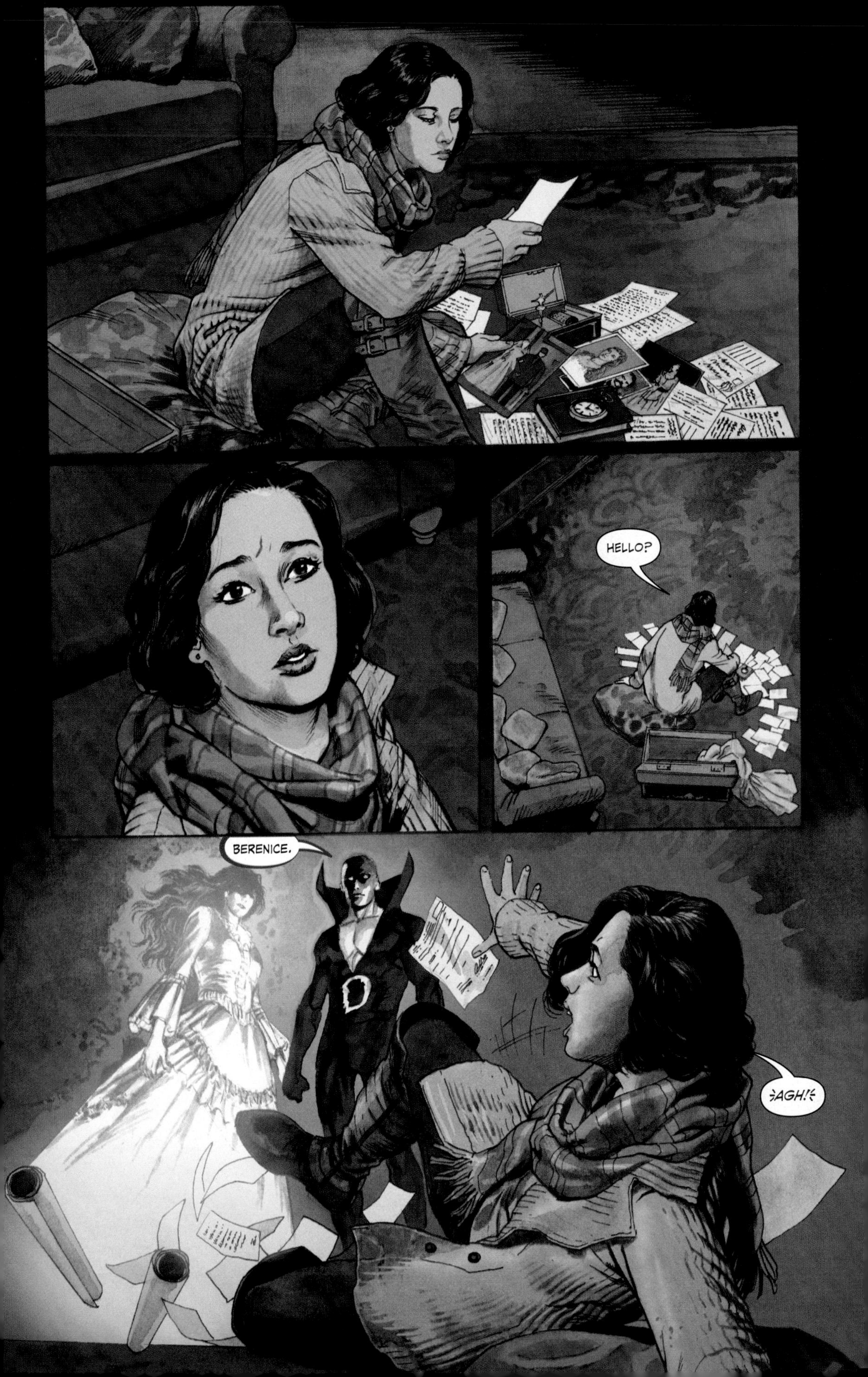
HELLO?
BERENICE.
AGH!

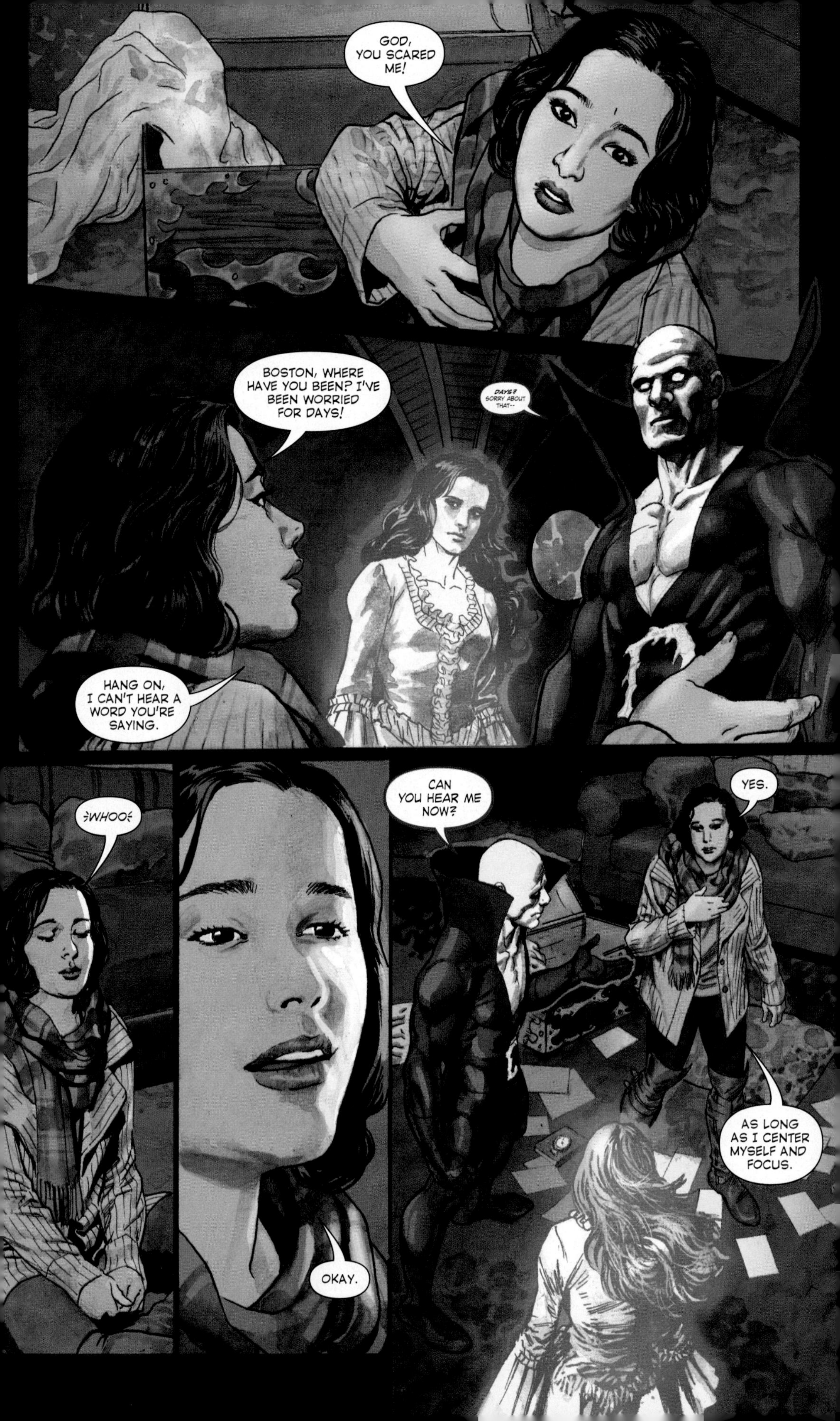
GOD, YOU SCARED ME!
BOSTON, WHERE HAVE YOU BEEN? I'VE BEEN WORRIED FOR DAYS!
DAYS? SORRY ABOUT THAT--
HANG ON, I CAN'T HEAR A WORD YOU'RE SAYING.
WHOO
OKAY.
CAN YOU HEAR ME NOW?
YES.
AS LONG AS I CENTER MYSELF AND FOCUS.

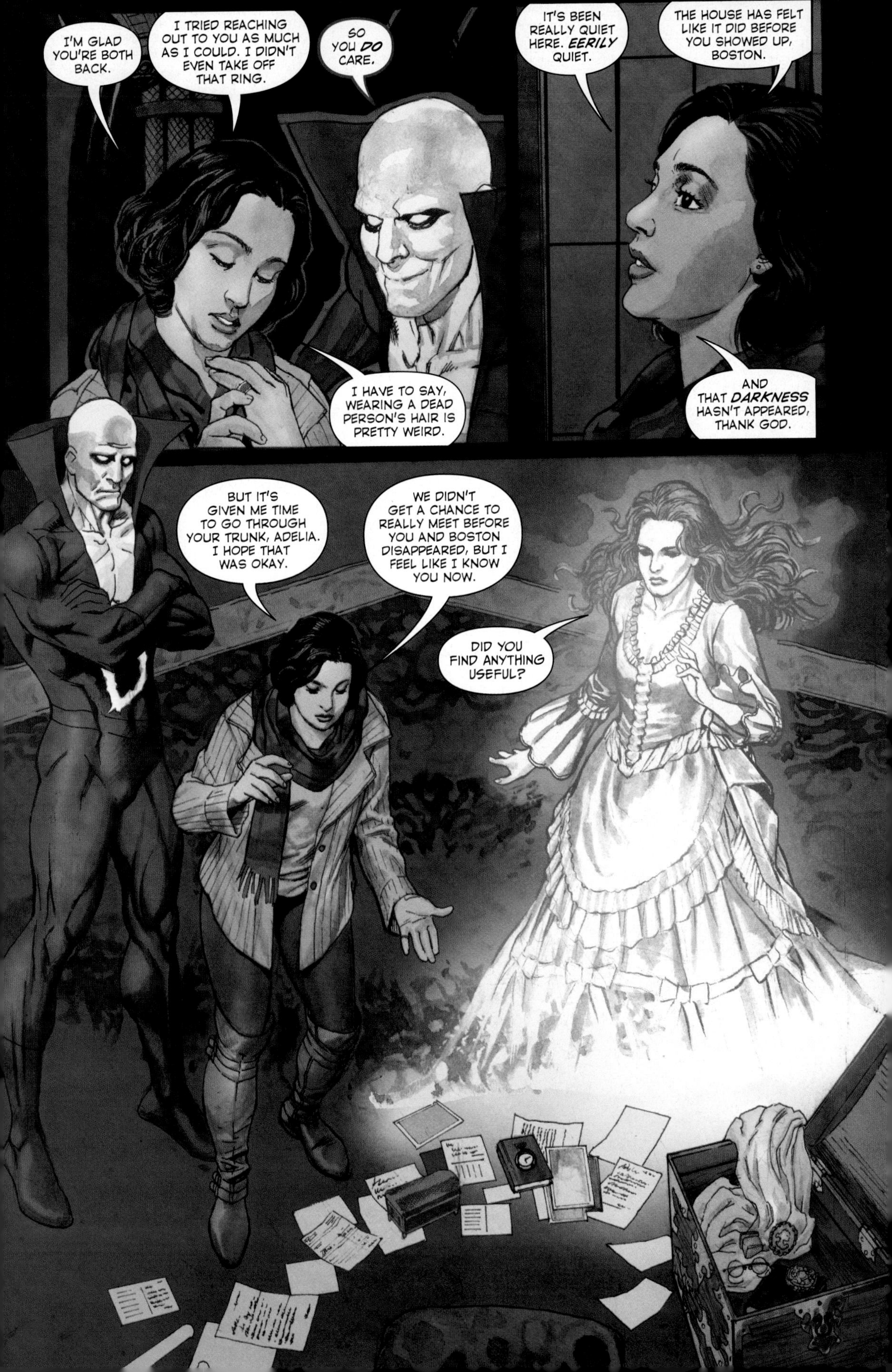

I'M GLAD YOU'RE BOTH BACK.
I TRIED REACHING OUT TO YOU AS MUCH AS I COULD. I DIDN'T EVEN TAKE OFF THAT RING.
SO YOU *DO* CARE.
I HAVE TO SAY, WEARING A DEAD PERSON'S HAIR IS PRETTY WEIRD.
IT'S BEEN REALLY QUIET HERE. *EERILY* QUIET.
THE HOUSE HAS FELT LIKE IT DID BEFORE YOU SHOWED UP, BOSTON.
AND THAT *DARKNESS* HASN'T APPEARED, THANK GOD.
BUT IT'S GIVEN ME TIME TO GO THROUGH YOUR TRUNK, ADELIA. I HOPE THAT WAS OKAY.
WE DIDN'T GET A CHANCE TO REALLY MEET BEFORE YOU AND BOSTON DISAPPEARED, BUT I FEEL LIKE I KNOW YOU NOW.
DID YOU FIND ANYTHING USEFUL?

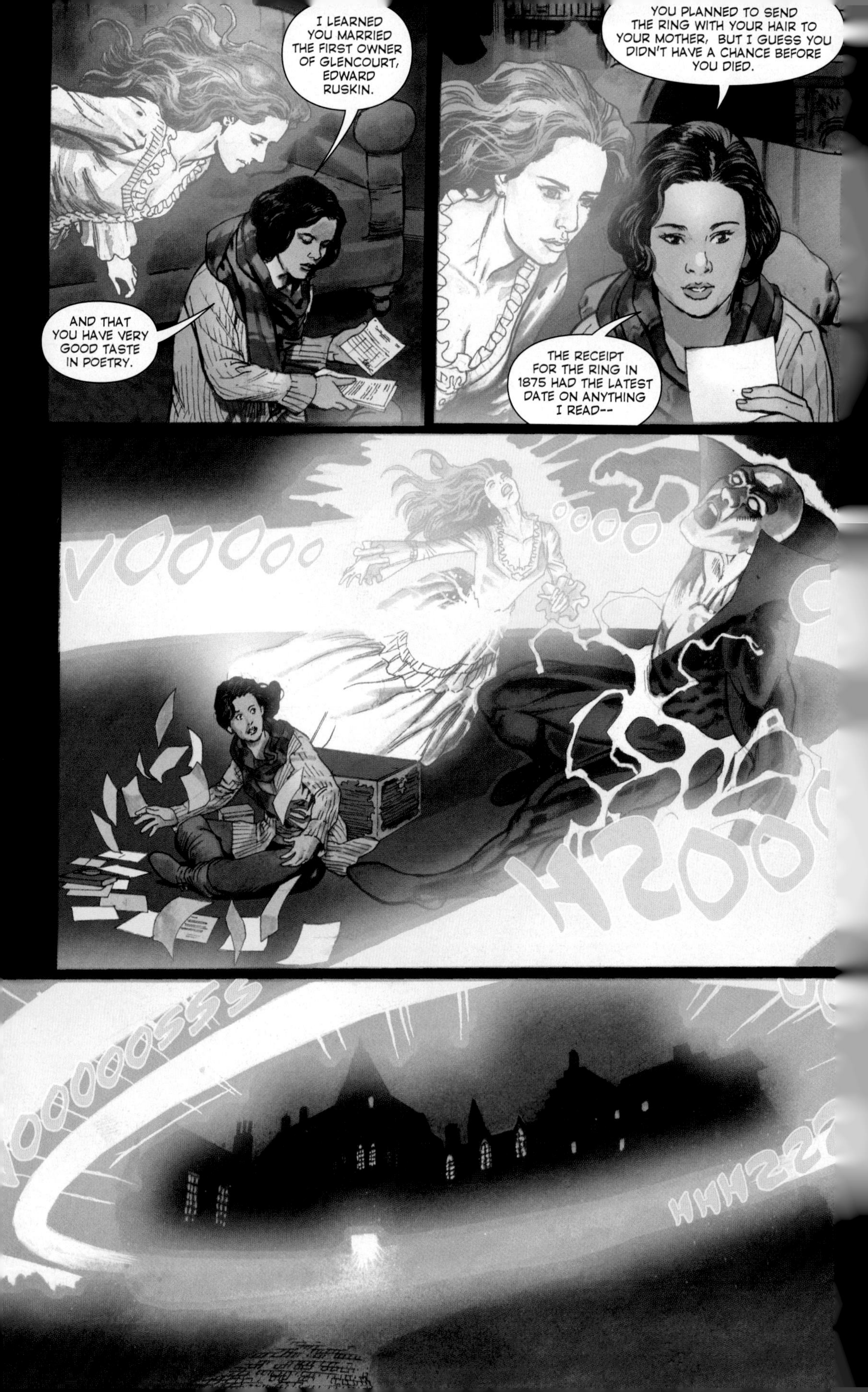
I LEARNED YOU MARRIED THE FIRST OWNER OF GLENCOURT, EDWARD RUSKIN.
AND THAT YOU HAVE VERY GOOD TASTE IN POETRY.
YOU PLANNED TO SEND THE RING WITH YOUR HAIR TO YOUR MOTHER, BUT I GUESS YOU DIDN'T HAVE A CHANCE BEFORE YOU DIED.
THE RECEIPT FOR THE RING IN 1875 HAD THE LATEST DATE ON ANYTHING I READ--
VOOOOoo

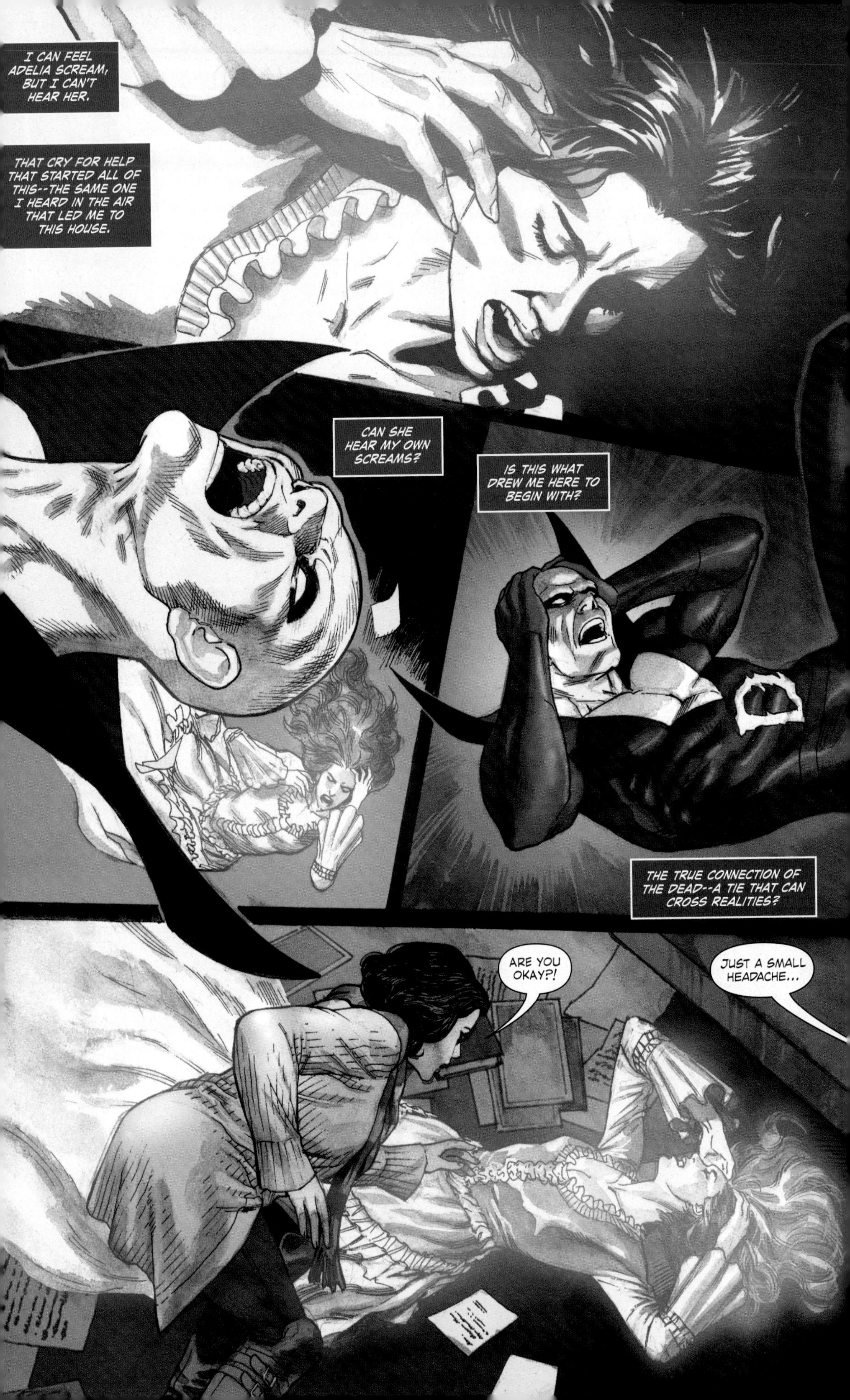
I CAN FEEL ADELIA SCREAM, BUT I CAN'T HEAR HER.
THAT CRY FOR HELP THAT STARTED ALL OF THIS--THE SAME ONE I HEARD IN THE AIR THAT LED ME TO THIS HOUSE.
CAN SHE HEAR MY OWN SCREAMS?
IS THIS WHAT DREW ME HERE TO BEGIN WITH?
THE TRUE CONNECTION OF THE DEAD--A TIE THAT CAN CROSS REALITIES?
ARE YOU OKAY?!
JUST A SMALL HEADACHE...

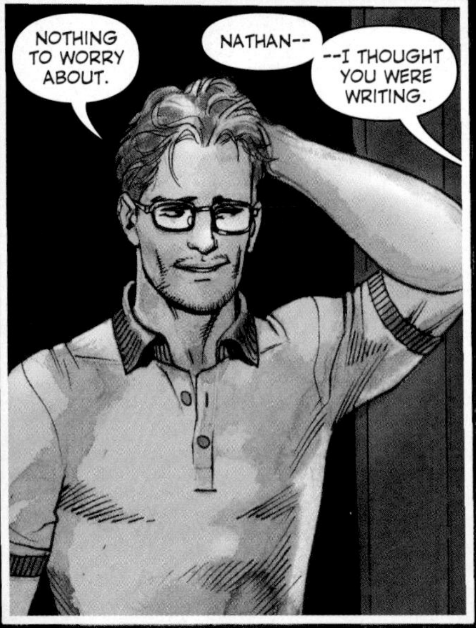
NOTHING TO WORRY ABOUT.
NATHAN--
--I THOUGHT YOU WERE WRITING.

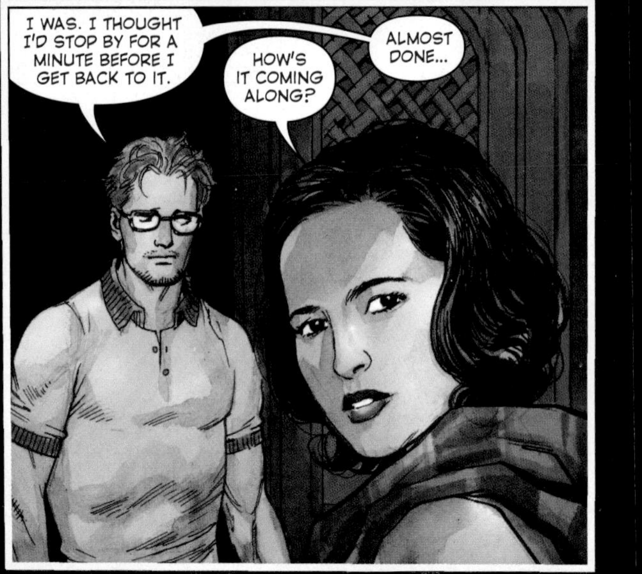
I WAS. I THOUGHT I'D STOP BY FOR A MINUTE BEFORE I GET BACK TO IT.
ALMOST DONE...
HOW'S IT COMING ALONG?

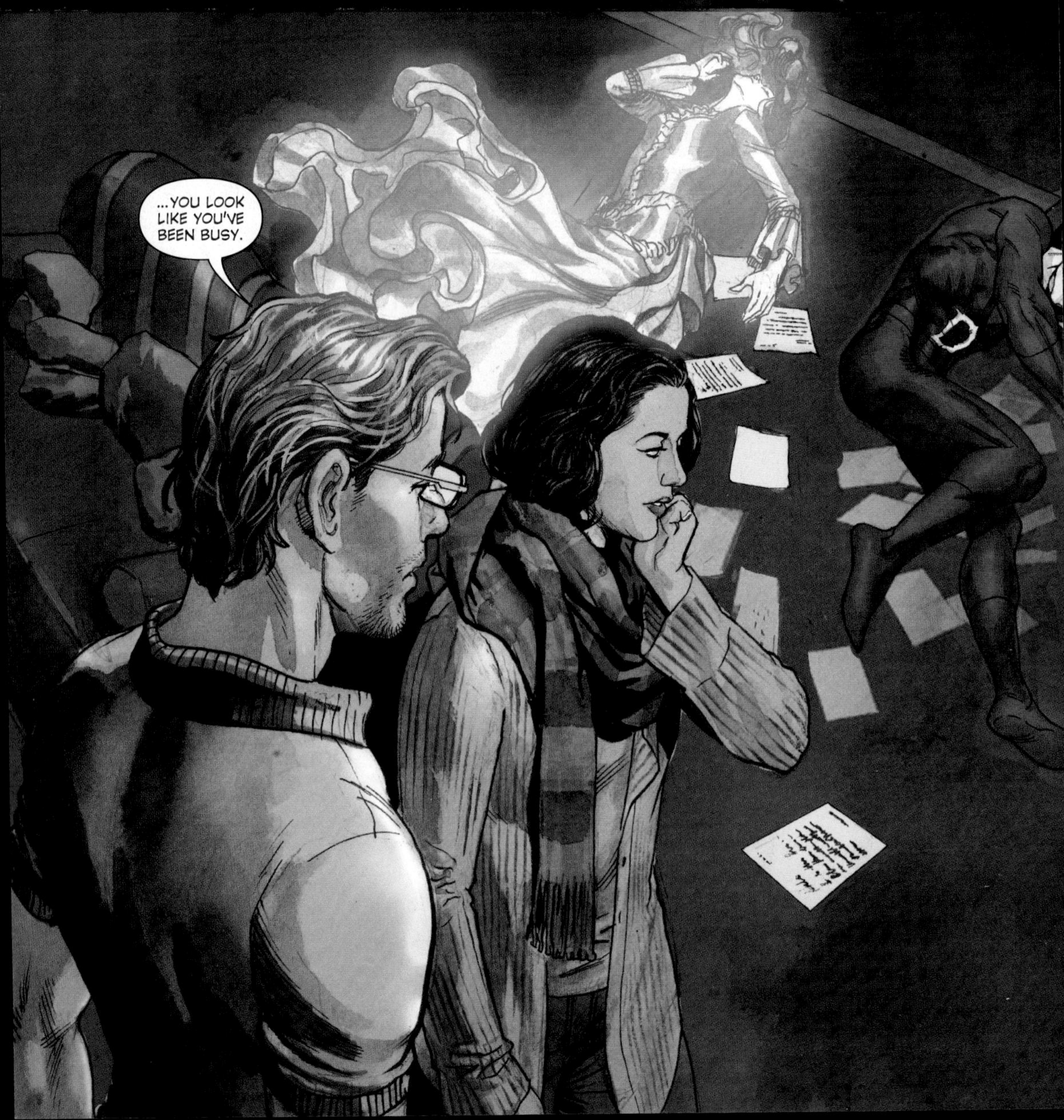
...YOU LOOK LIKE YOU'VE BEEN BUSY.

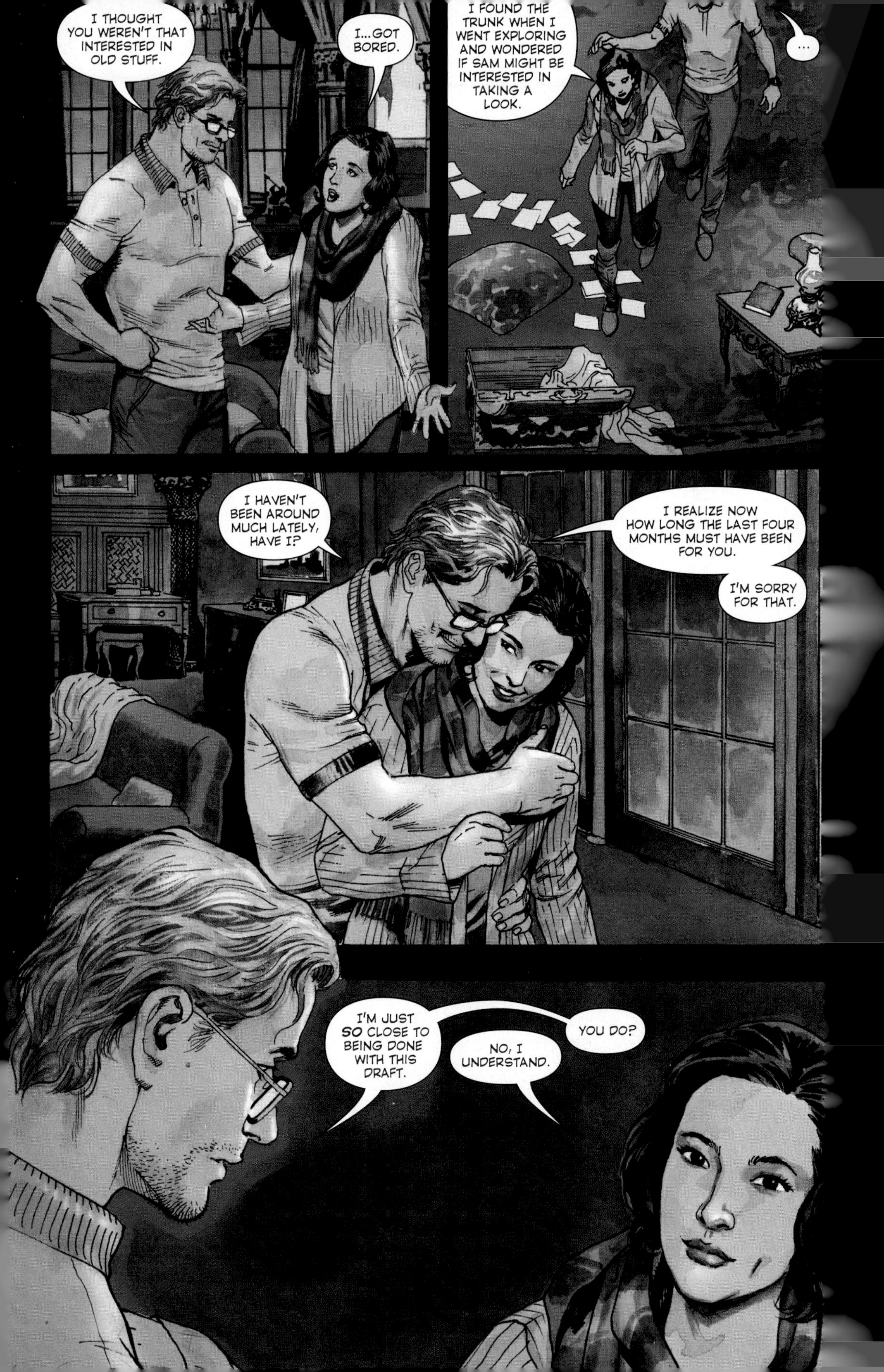
I THOUGHT YOU WEREN'T THAT INTERESTED IN OLD STUFF.
I...GOT BORED.
I FOUND THE TRUNK WHEN I WENT EXPLORING AND WONDERED IF SAM MIGHT BE INTERESTED IN TAKING A LOOK.
...
I HAVEN'T BEEN AROUND MUCH LATELY, HAVE I?
I REALIZE NOW HOW LONG THE LAST FOUR MONTHS MUST HAVE BEEN FOR YOU.
I'M SORRY FOR THAT.
NO, I UNDERSTAND.
YOU DO?
I'M JUST SO CLOSE TO BEING DONE WITH THIS DRAFT.

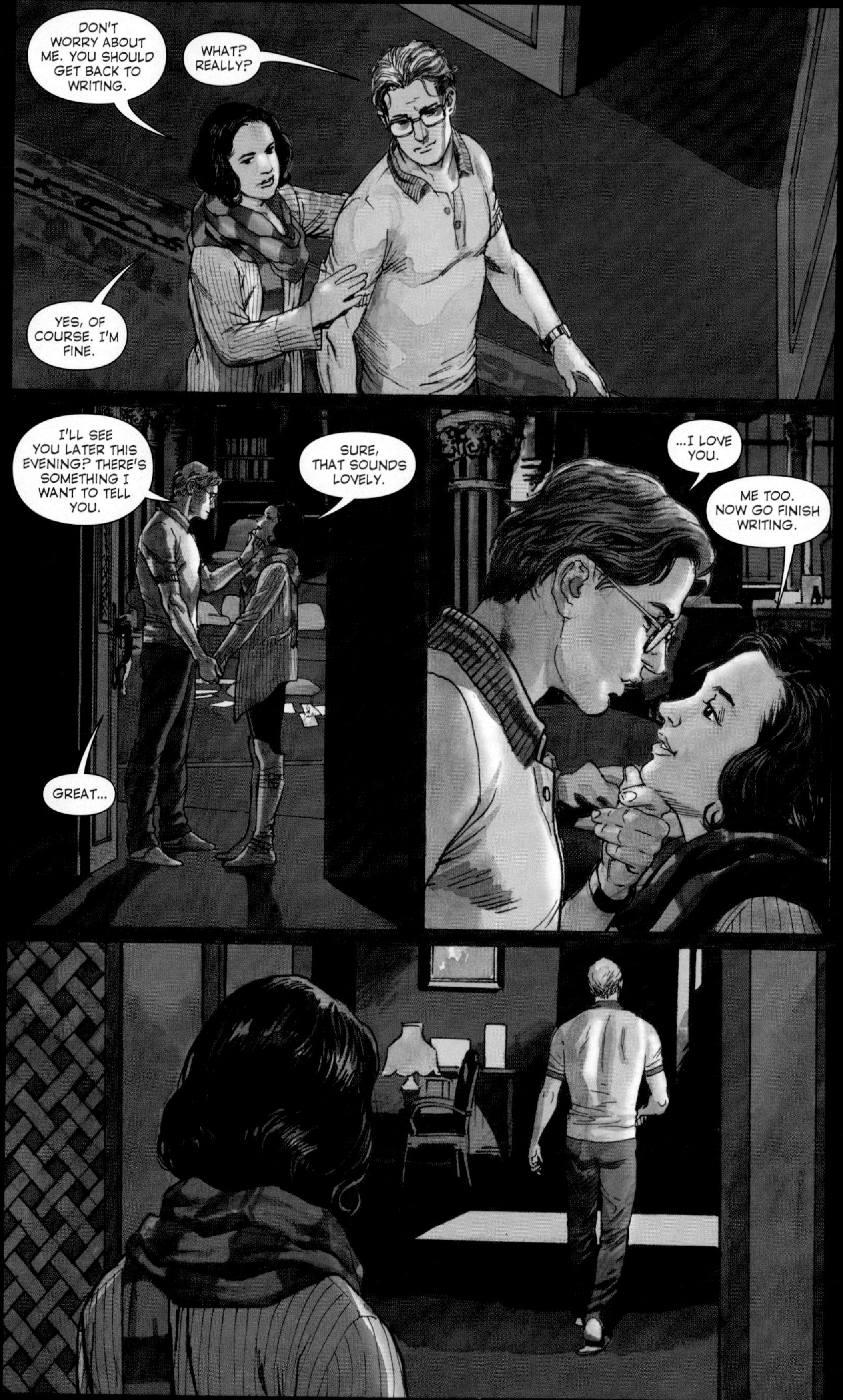
DON'T WORRY ABOUT ME. YOU SHOULD GET BACK TO WRITING.
WHAT? REALLY?
YES, OF COURSE. I'M FINE.
I'LL SEE YOU LATER THIS EVENING? THERE'S SOMETHING I WANT TO TELL YOU.
SURE, THAT SOUNDS LOVELY.
GREAT...
...I LOVE YOU.
ME TOO. NOW GO FINISH WRITING.

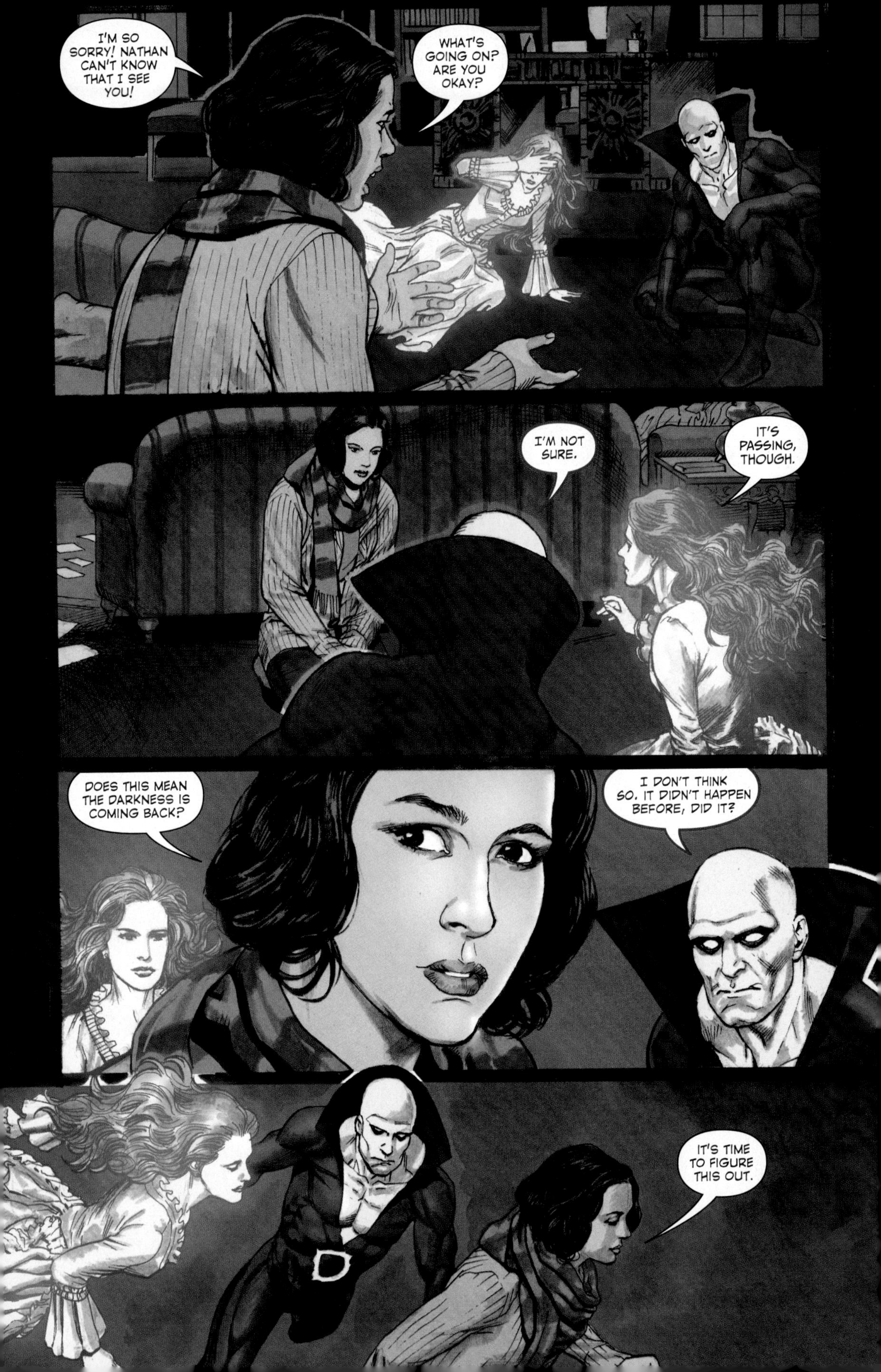

I'M SO SORRY! NATHAN CAN'T KNOW THAT I SEE YOU!
WHAT'S GOING ON? ARE YOU OKAY?
I'M NOT SURE.
IT'S PASSING, THOUGH.
DOES THIS MEAN THE DARKNESS IS COMING BACK?
I DON'T THINK SO. IT DIDN'T HAPPEN BEFORE, DID IT?
IT'S TIME TO FIGURE THIS OUT.

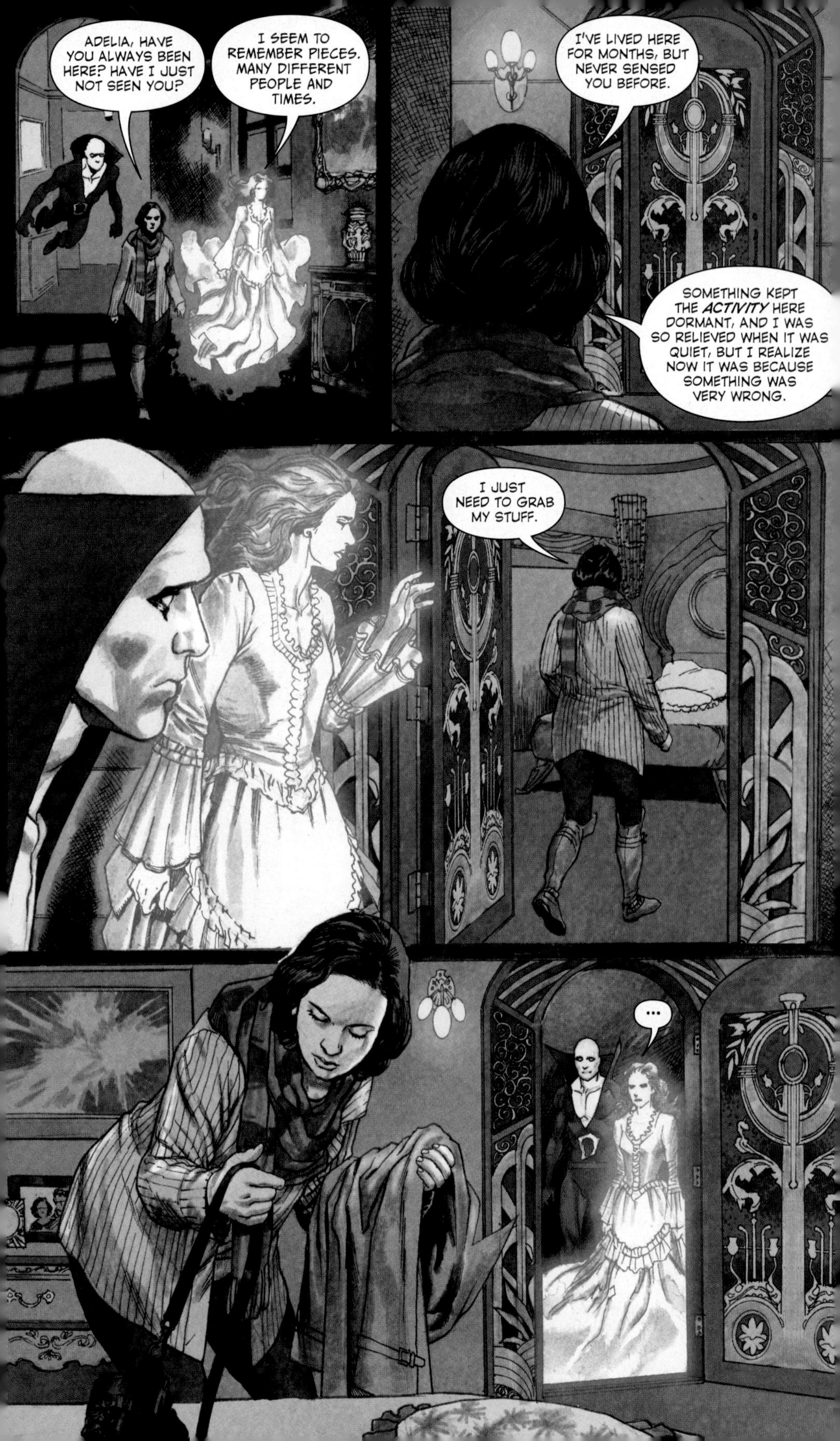
ADELIA, HAVE YOU ALWAYS BEEN HERE? HAVE I JUST NOT SEEN YOU?
I SEEM TO REMEMBER PIECES. MANY DIFFERENT PEOPLE AND TIMES.
I'VE LIVED HERE FOR MONTHS, BUT NEVER SENSED YOU BEFORE.
SOMETHING KEPT THE *ACTIVITY* HERE DORMANT, AND I WAS SO RELIEVED WHEN IT WAS QUIET, BUT I REALIZE NOW IT WAS BECAUSE SOMETHING WAS VERY WRONG.
I JUST NEED TO GRAB MY STUFF.
...

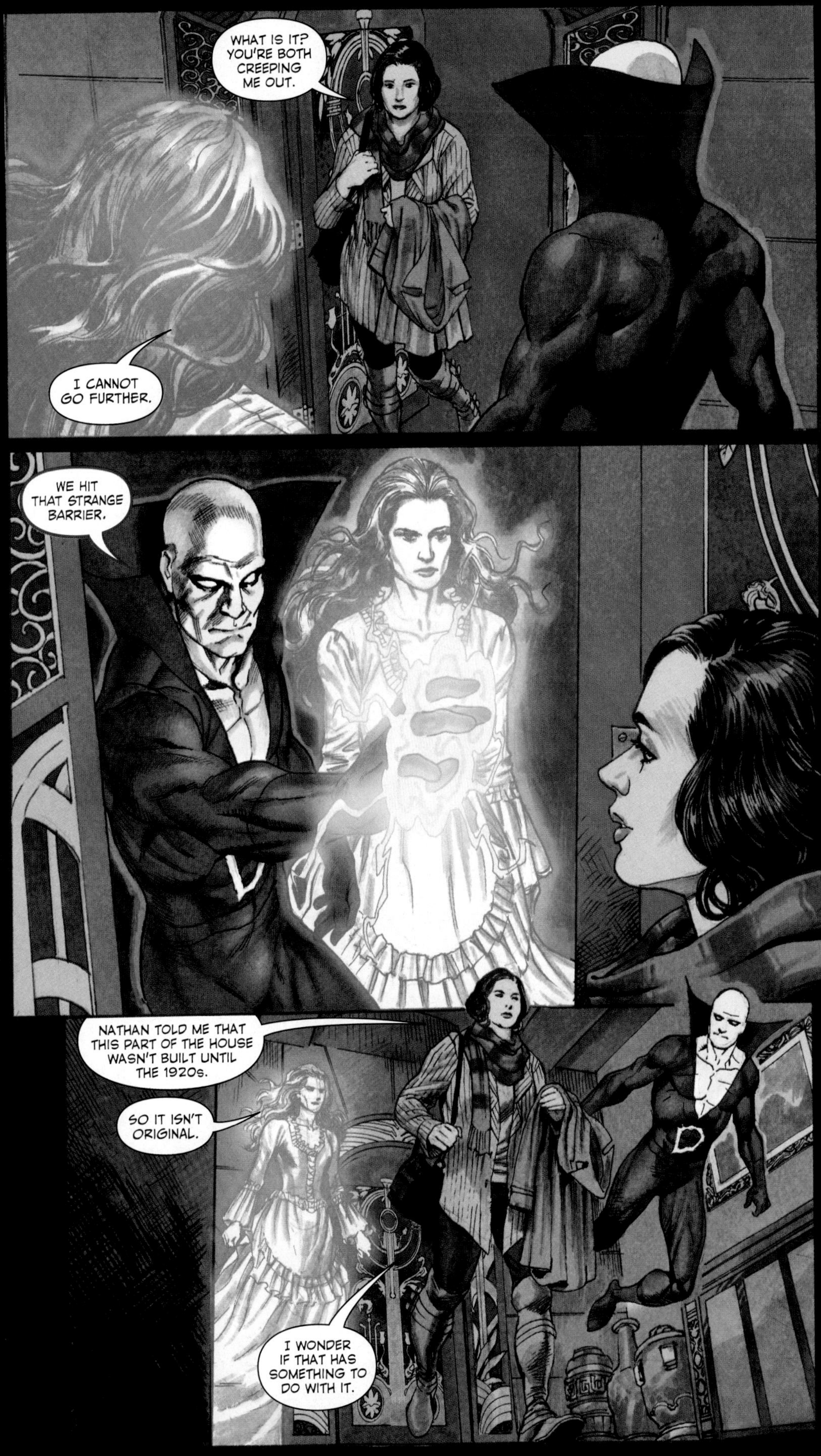
WHAT IS IT? YOU'RE BOTH CREEPING ME OUT.
I CANNOT GO FURTHER.
WE HIT THAT STRANGE BARRIER.
NATHAN TOLD ME THAT THIS PART OF THE HOUSE WASN'T BUILT UNTIL THE 1920s.
SO IT ISN'T ORIGINAL.
I WONDER IF THAT HAS SOMETHING TO DO WITH IT.

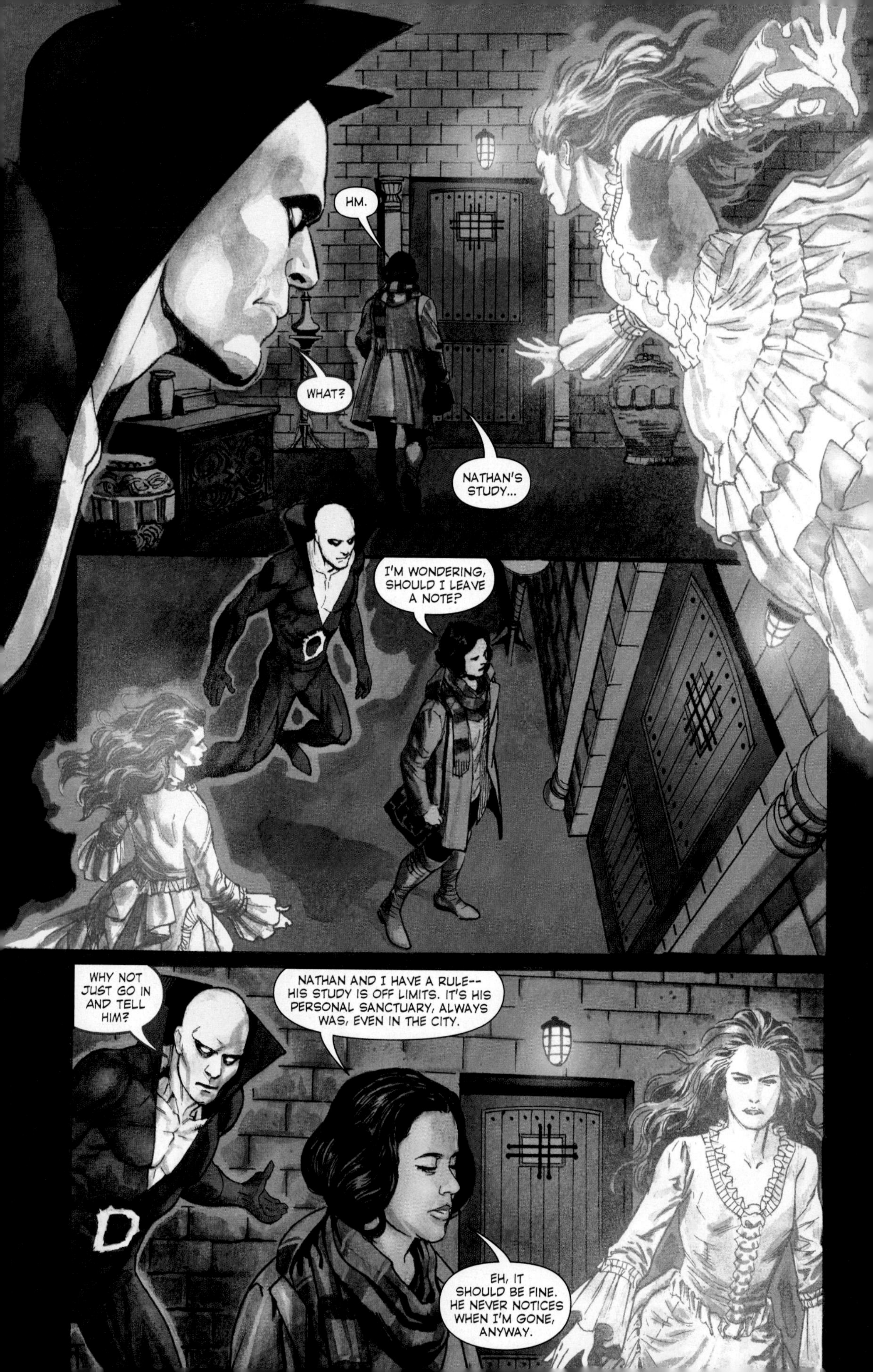
HM.
WHAT?
NATHAN'S STUDY...
I'M WONDERING, SHOULD I LEAVE A NOTE?
WHY NOT JUST GO IN AND TELL HIM?
NATHAN AND I HAVE A RULE-- HIS STUDY IS OFF LIMITS. IT'S HIS PERSONAL SANCTUARY, ALWAYS WAS, EVEN IN THE CITY.
EH, IT SHOULD BE FINE. HE NEVER NOTICES WHEN I'M GONE, ANYWAY.

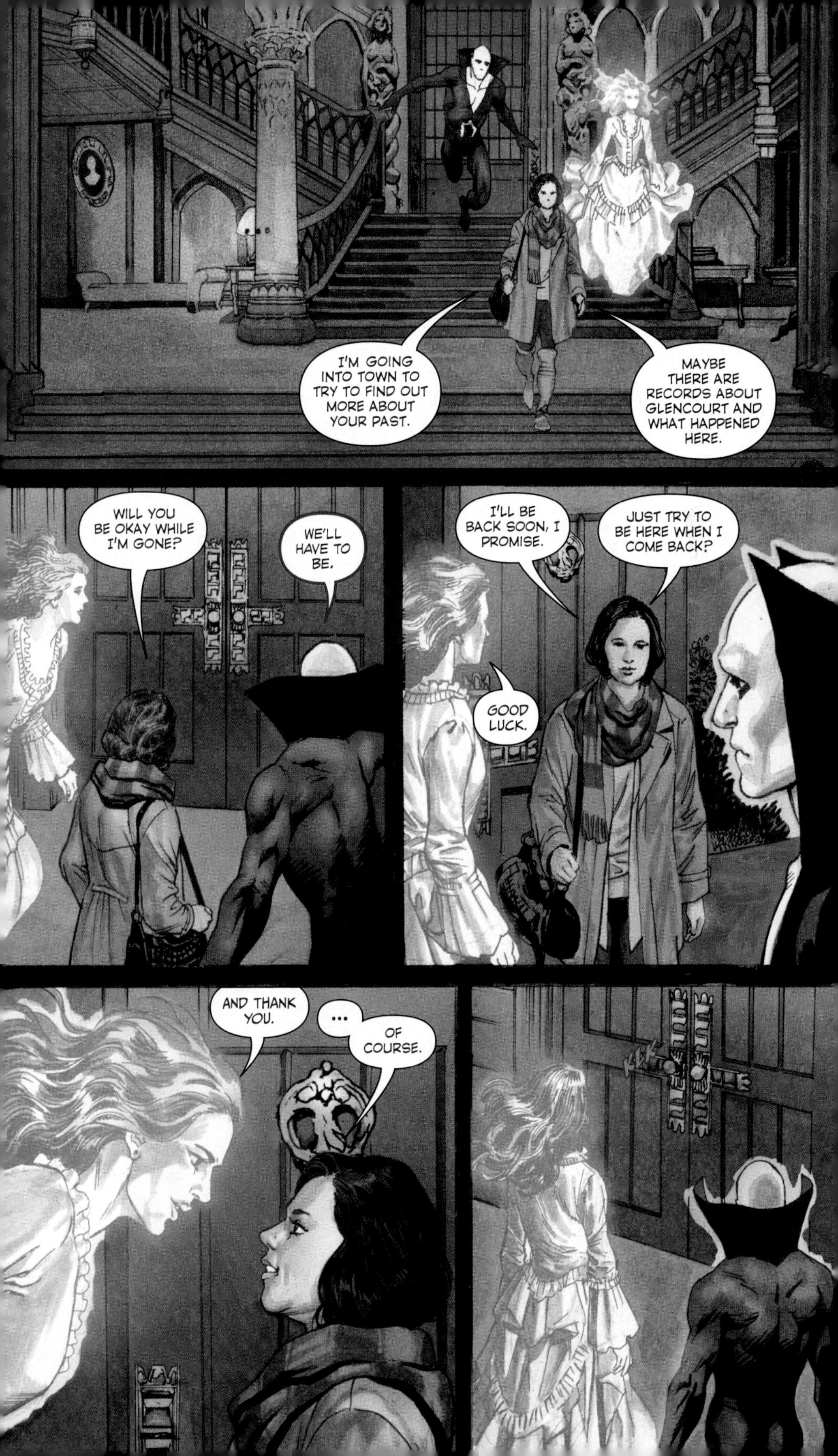
I'M GOING INTO TOWN TO TRY TO FIND OUT MORE ABOUT YOUR PAST.
MAYBE THERE ARE RECORDS ABOUT GLENCOURT AND WHAT HAPPENED HERE.
WILL YOU BE OKAY WHILE I'M GONE?
WE'LL HAVE TO BE.
I'LL BE BACK SOON, I PROMISE.
JUST TRY TO BE HERE WHEN I COME BACK?
GOOD LUCK.
AND THANK YOU.
...
OF COURSE.

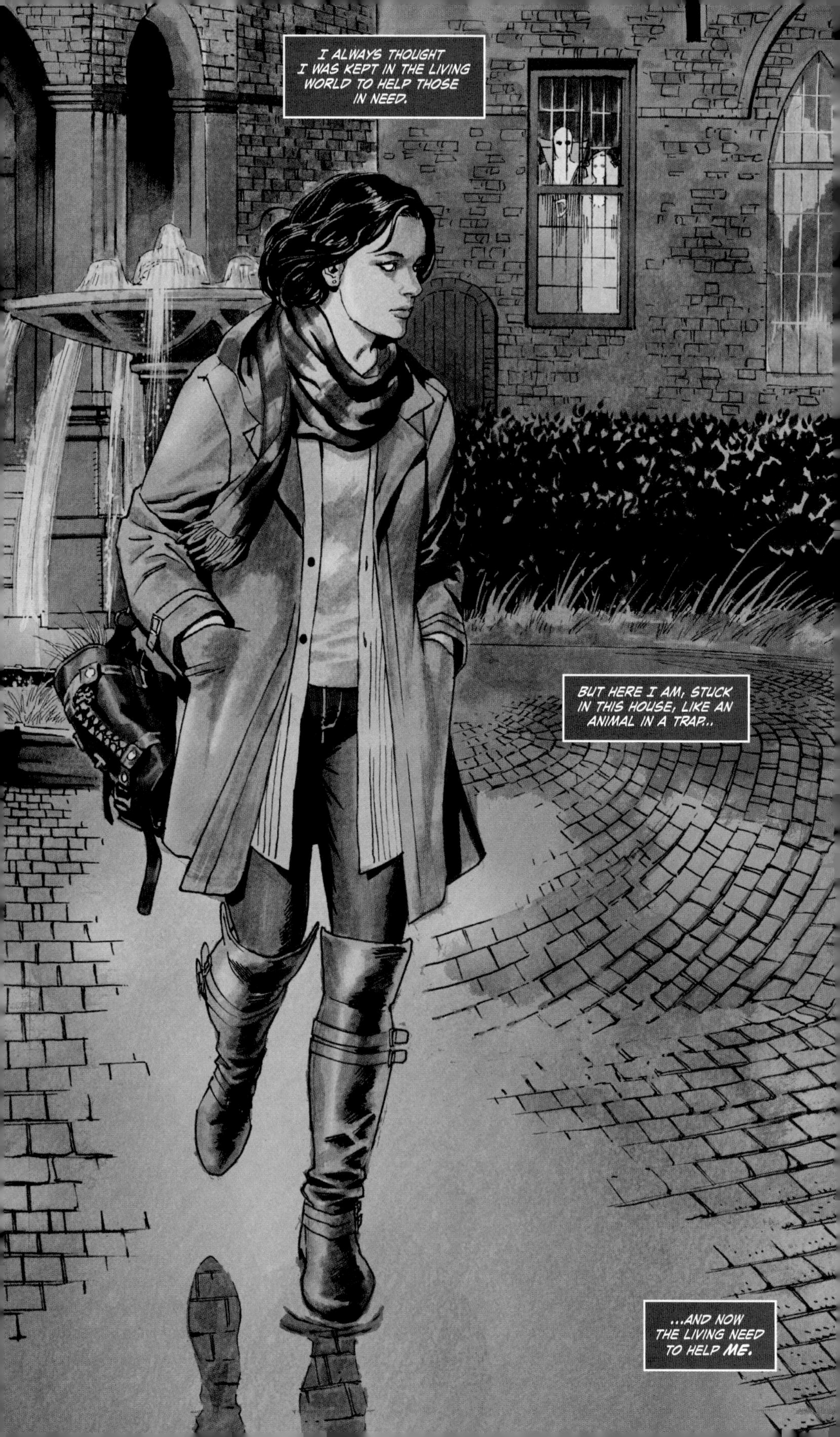
I ALWAYS THOUGHT I WAS KEPT IN THE LIVING WORLD TO HELP THOSE IN NEED.
BUT HERE I AM, STUCK IN THIS HOUSE, LIKE AN ANIMAL IN A TRAP...
...AND NOW THE LIVING NEED TO HELP **ME**.

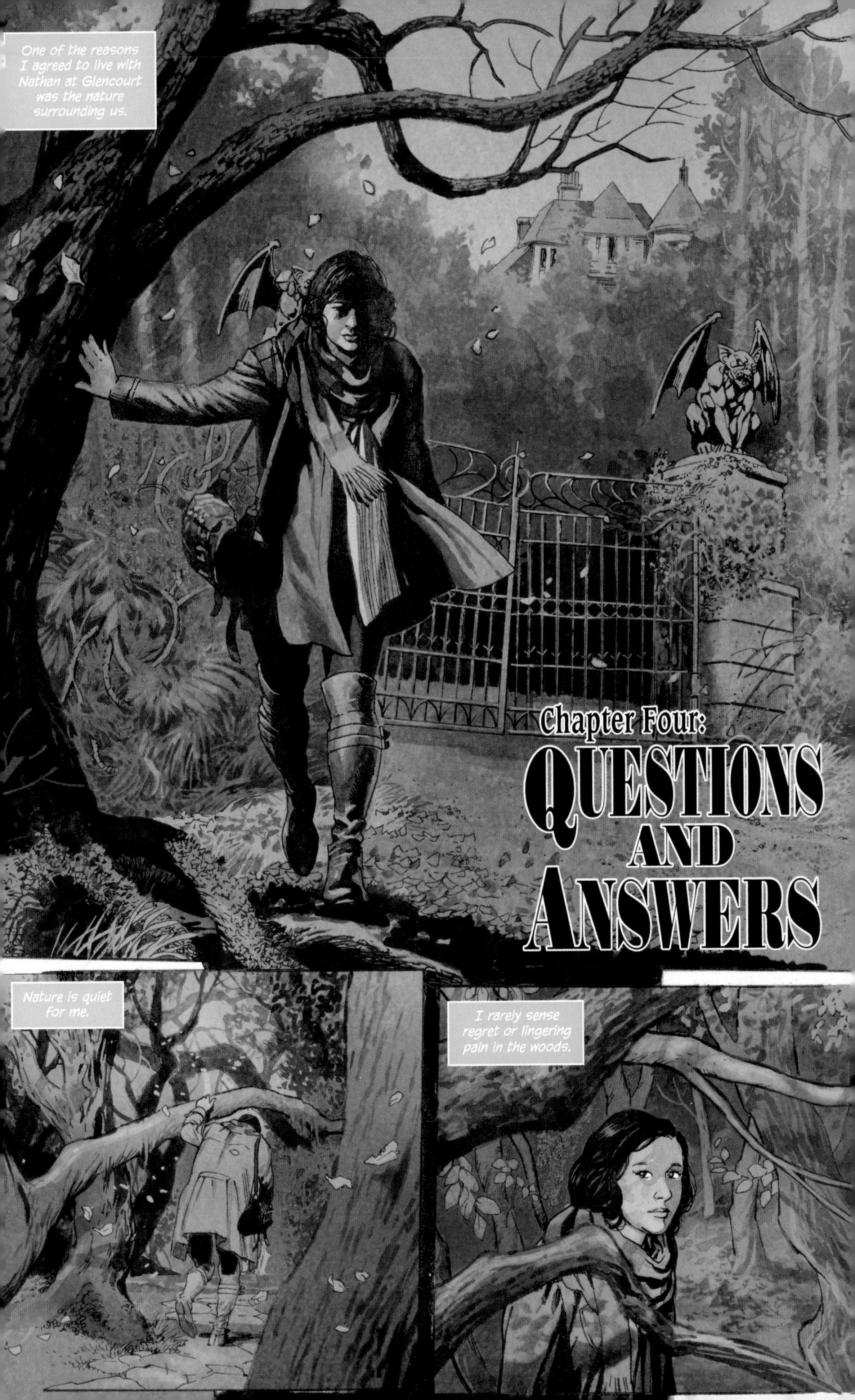
One of the reasons I agreed to live with Nathan at Glencourt was the nature surrounding us.
Chapter Four:
QUESTIONS AND ANSWERS
Nature is quiet for me.
I rarely sense regret or lingering pain in the woods.

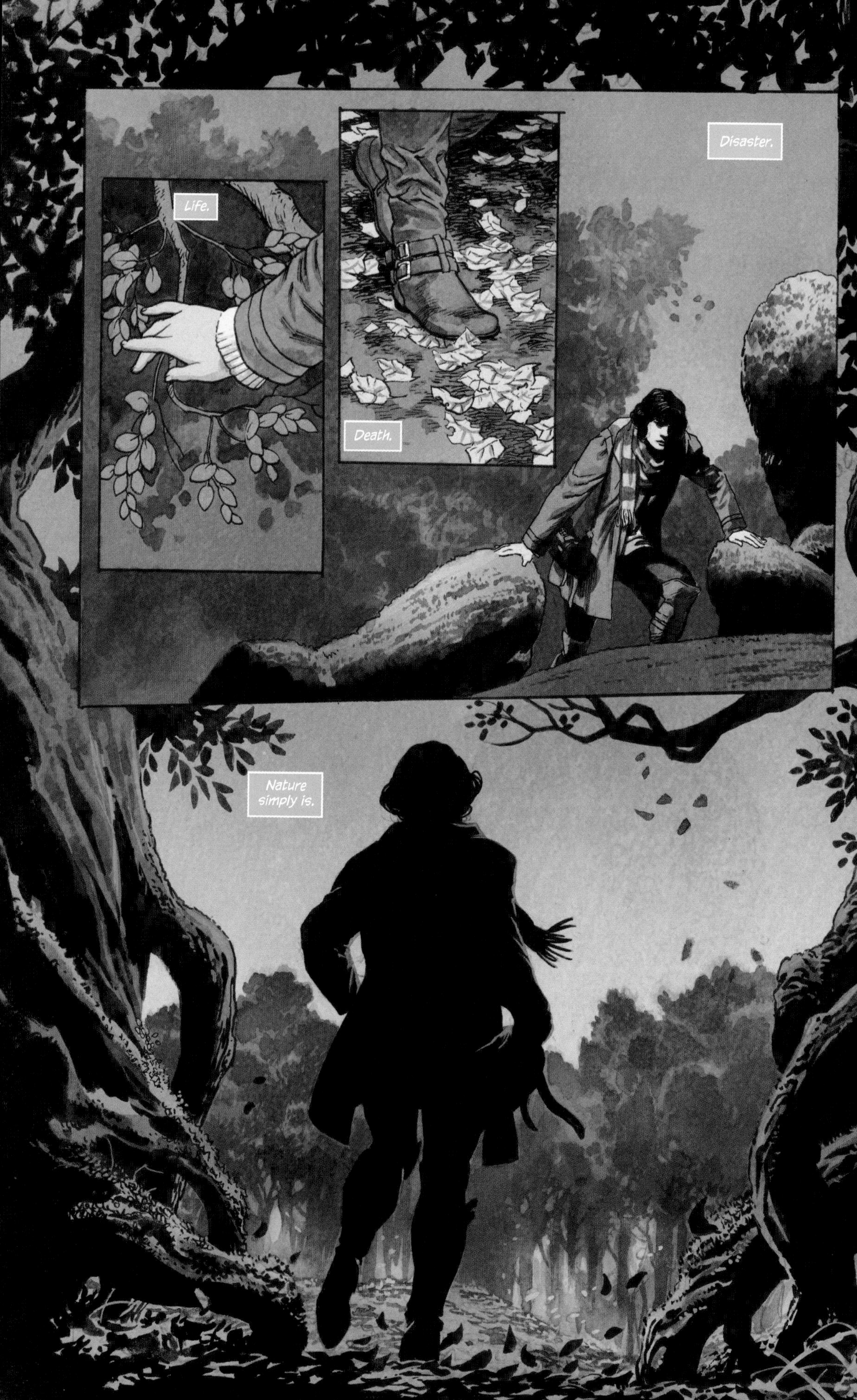
Life.
Death.
Disaster.
Nature simply is.

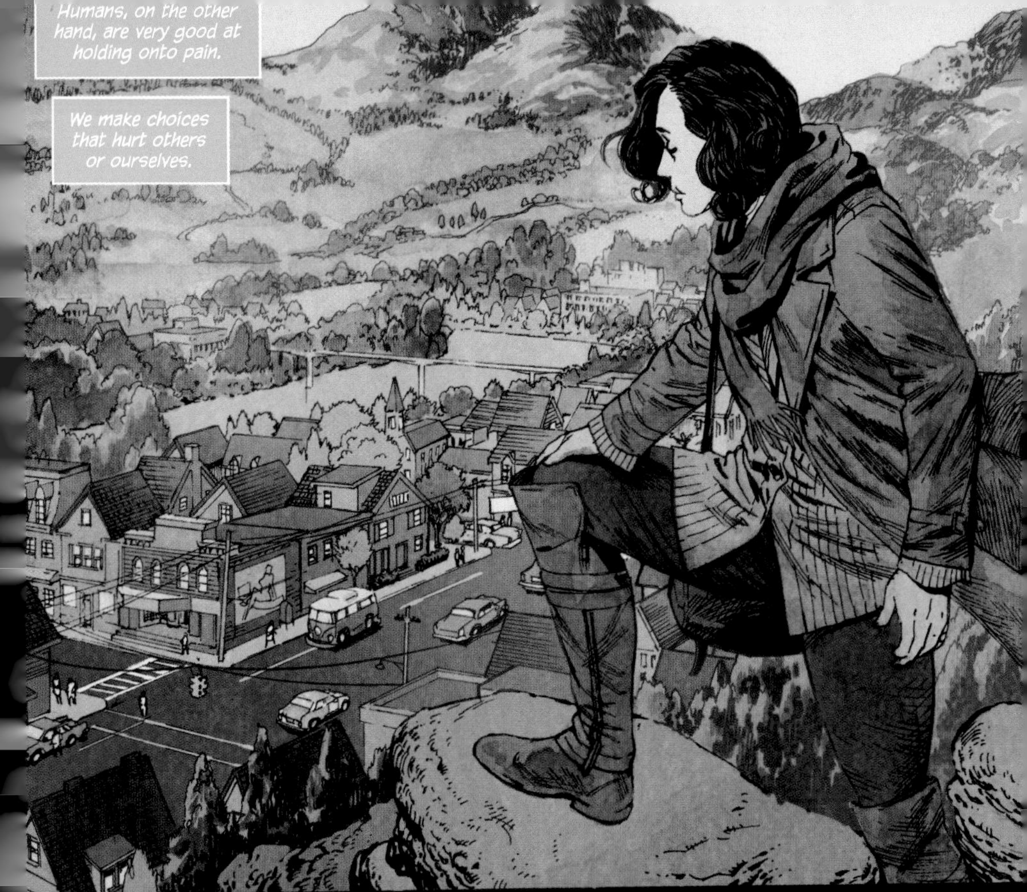
Humans, on the other hand, are very good at holding onto pain.
We make choices that hurt others or ourselves.

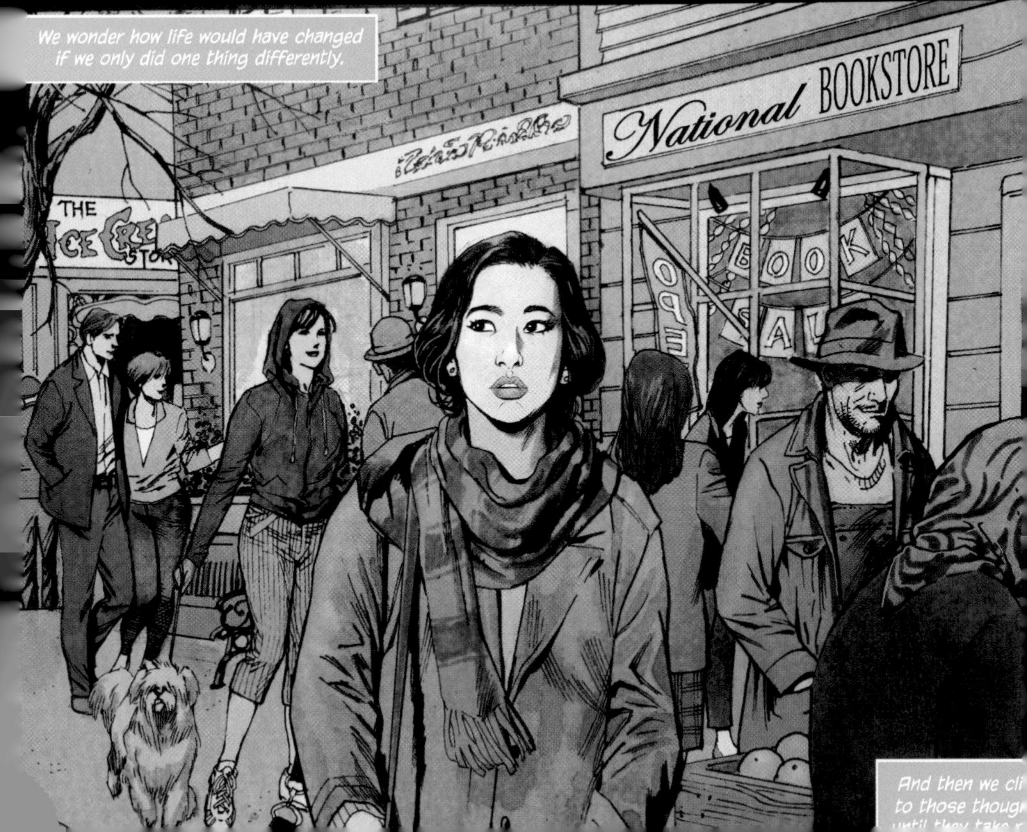
We wonder how life would have changed if we only did one thing differently.
National BOOKSTORE
THE
BOOK
And then we cli
to those thoug

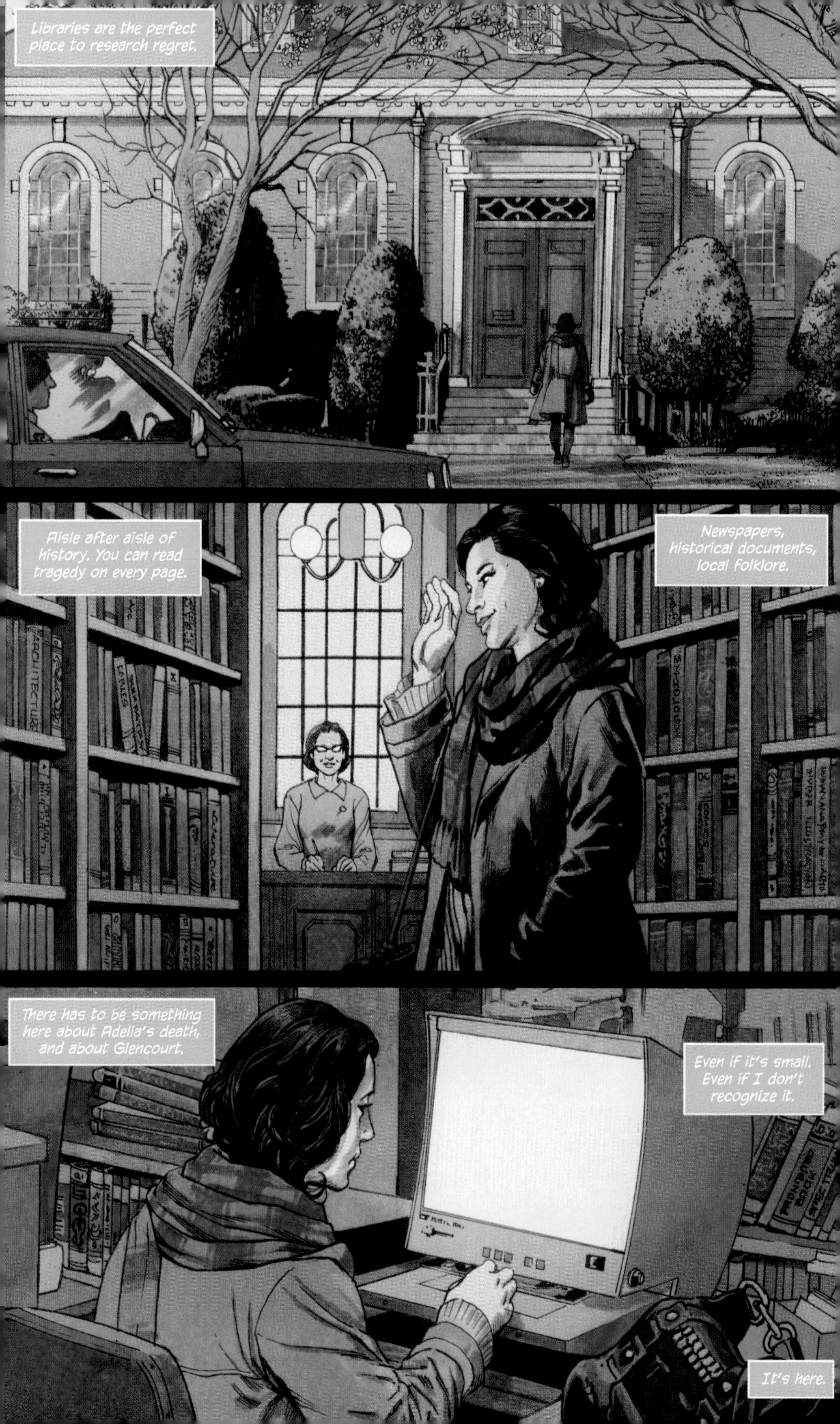
Libraries are the perfect place to research regret.
Aisle after aisle of history. You can read tragedy on every page.
Newspapers, historical documents, local folklore.
There has to be something here about Adelia's death, and about Glencourt.
Even if it's small. Even if I don't recognize it.
It's here.

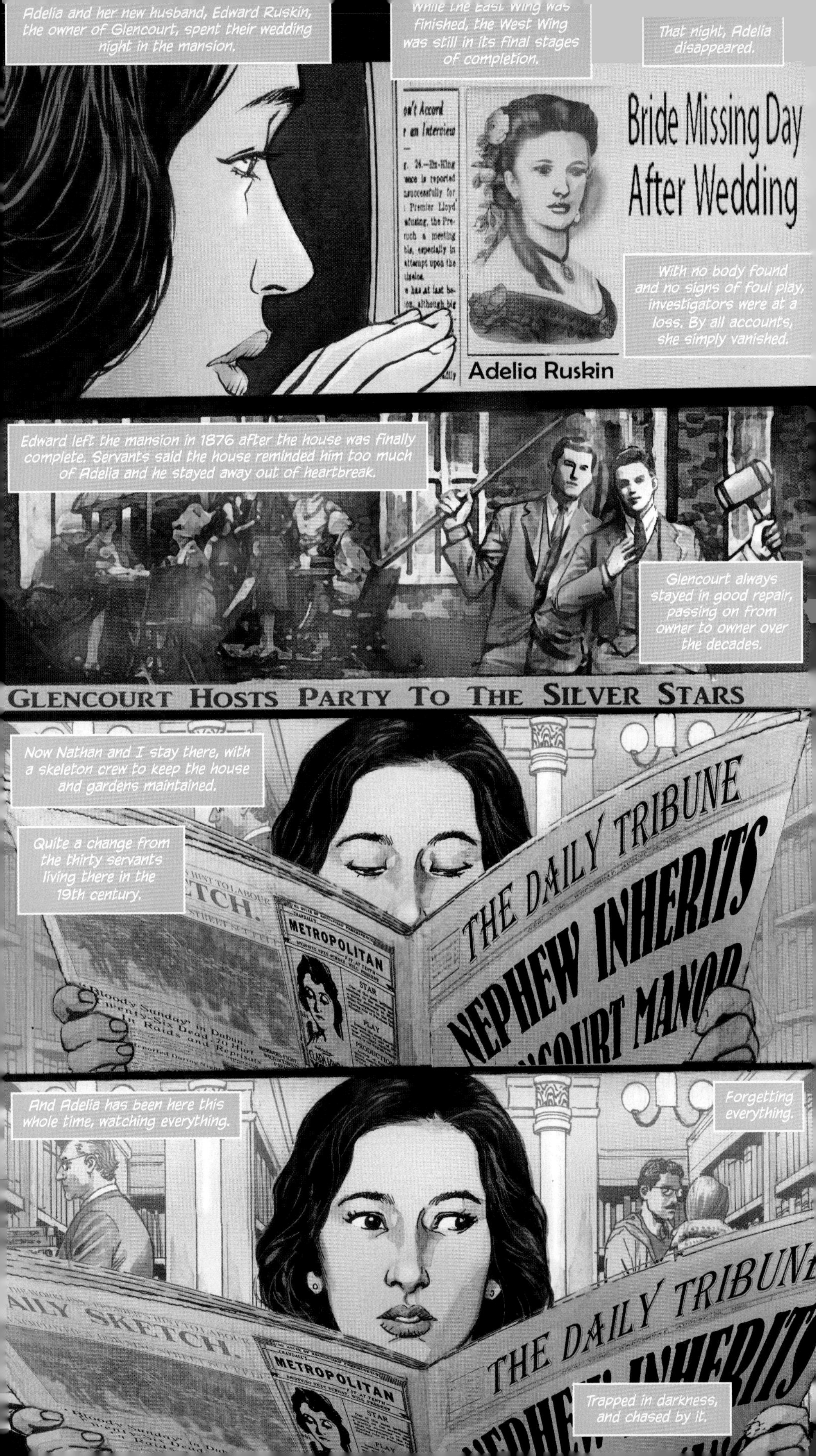

Adelia and her new husband, Edward Ruskin, the owner of Glencourt, spent their wedding night in the mansion.
While the East Wing was finished, the West Wing was still in its final stages of completion.
That night, Adelia disappeared.
Bride Missing Day After Wedding
Adelia Ruskin
With no body found and no signs of foul play, investigators were at a loss. By all accounts, she simply vanished.
Edward left the mansion in 1876 after the house was finally complete. Servants said the house reminded him too much of Adelia and he stayed away out of heartbreak.
Glencourt always stayed in good repair, passing on from owner to owner over the decades.
GLENCOURT HOSTS PARTY TO THE SILVER STARS
Now Nathan and I stay there, with a skeleton crew to keep the house and gardens maintained.
Quite a change from the thirty servants living there in the 19th century.
THE DAILY TRIBUNE
NEPHEW INHERITS
METROPOLITAN
And Adelia has been here this whole time, watching everything.
Forgetting everything.
Trapped in darkness, and chased by it.

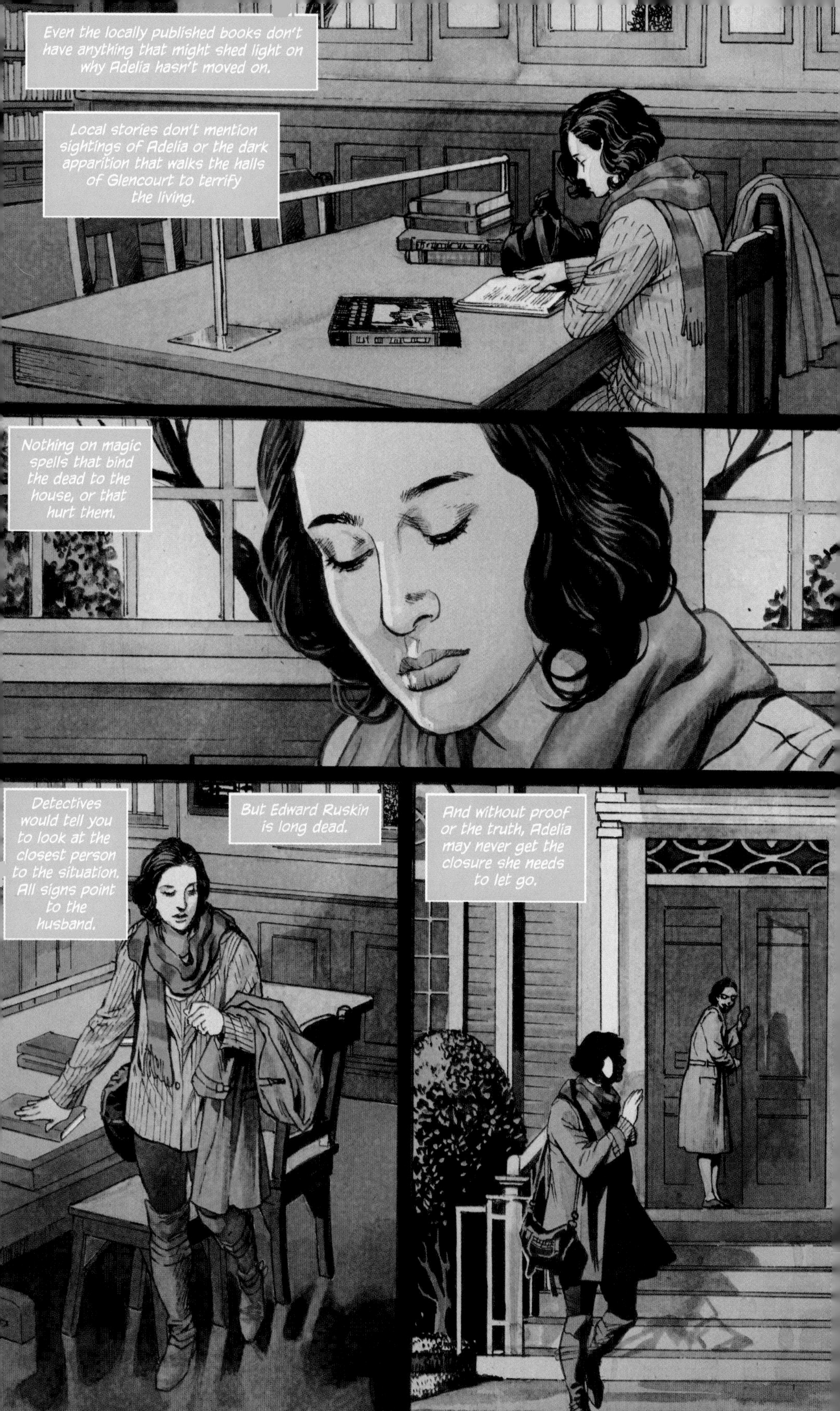
Even the locally published books don't have anything that might shed light on why Adelia hasn't moved on.
Local stories don't mention sightings of Adelia or the dark apparition that walks the halls of Glencourt to terrify the living.
Nothing on magic spells that bind the dead to the house, or that hurt them.
Detectives would tell you to look at the closest person to the situation. All signs point to the husband.
But Edward Ruskin is long dead.
And without proof or the truth, Adelia may never get the closure she needs to let go.

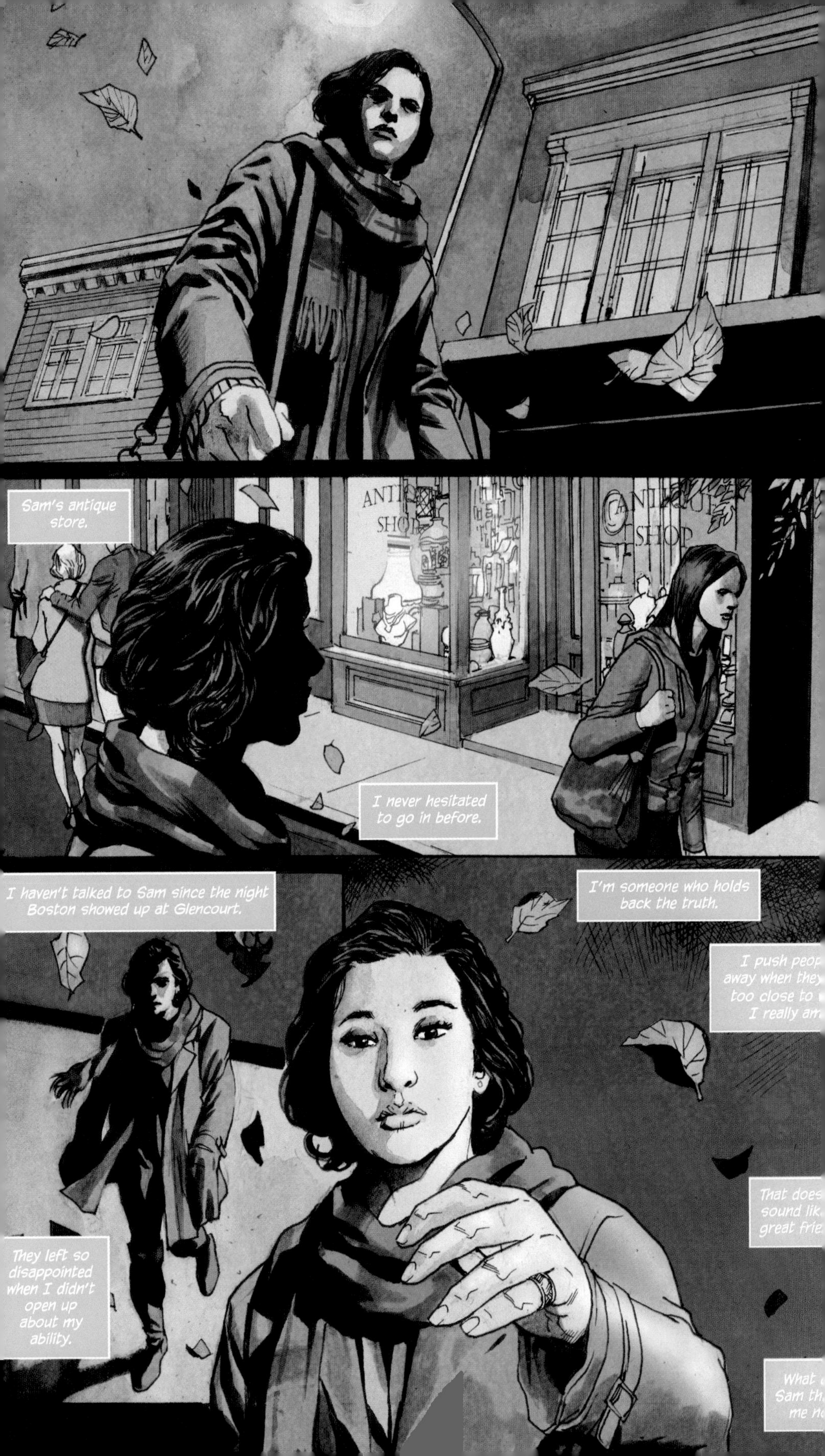

Sam's antique store.
ANTIQUE SHOP
ANTIQUE SHOP
I never hesitated to go in before.
I haven't talked to Sam since the night Boston showed up at Glencourt.
I'm someone who holds back the truth.
I push peop
away when they
too close to
I really am
They left so disappointed when I didn't open up about my ability.
That does
sound lik
great frie
What
Sam th
me no

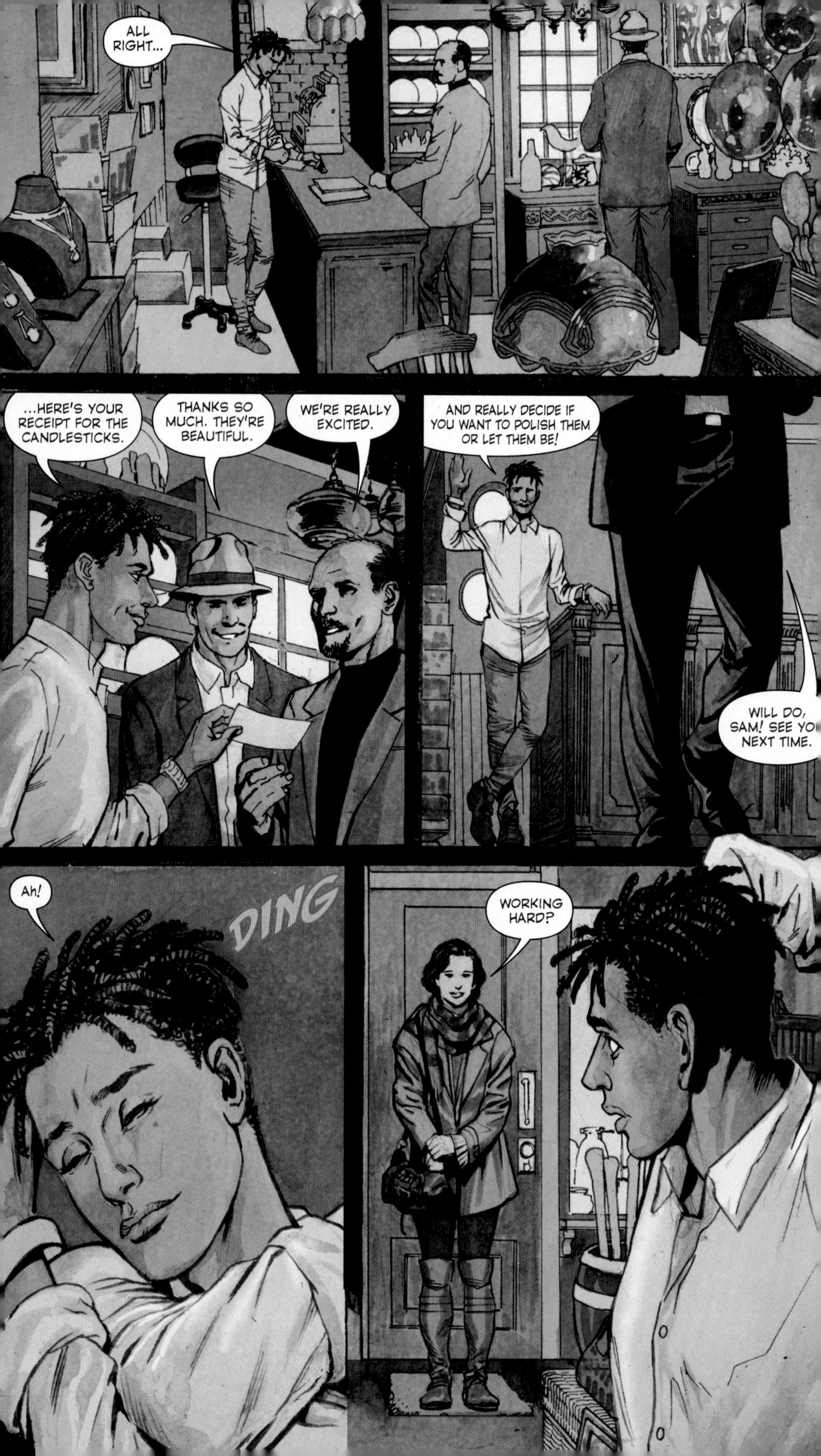
ALL RIGHT...
...HERE'S YOUR RECEIPT FOR THE CANDLESTICKS.
THANKS SO MUCH. THEY'RE BEAUTIFUL.
WE'RE REALLY EXCITED.
AND REALLY DECIDE IF YOU WANT TO POLISH THEM OR LET THEM BE!
WILL DO, SAM! SEE YO NEXT TIME.
Ah!
DING
WORKING HARD?

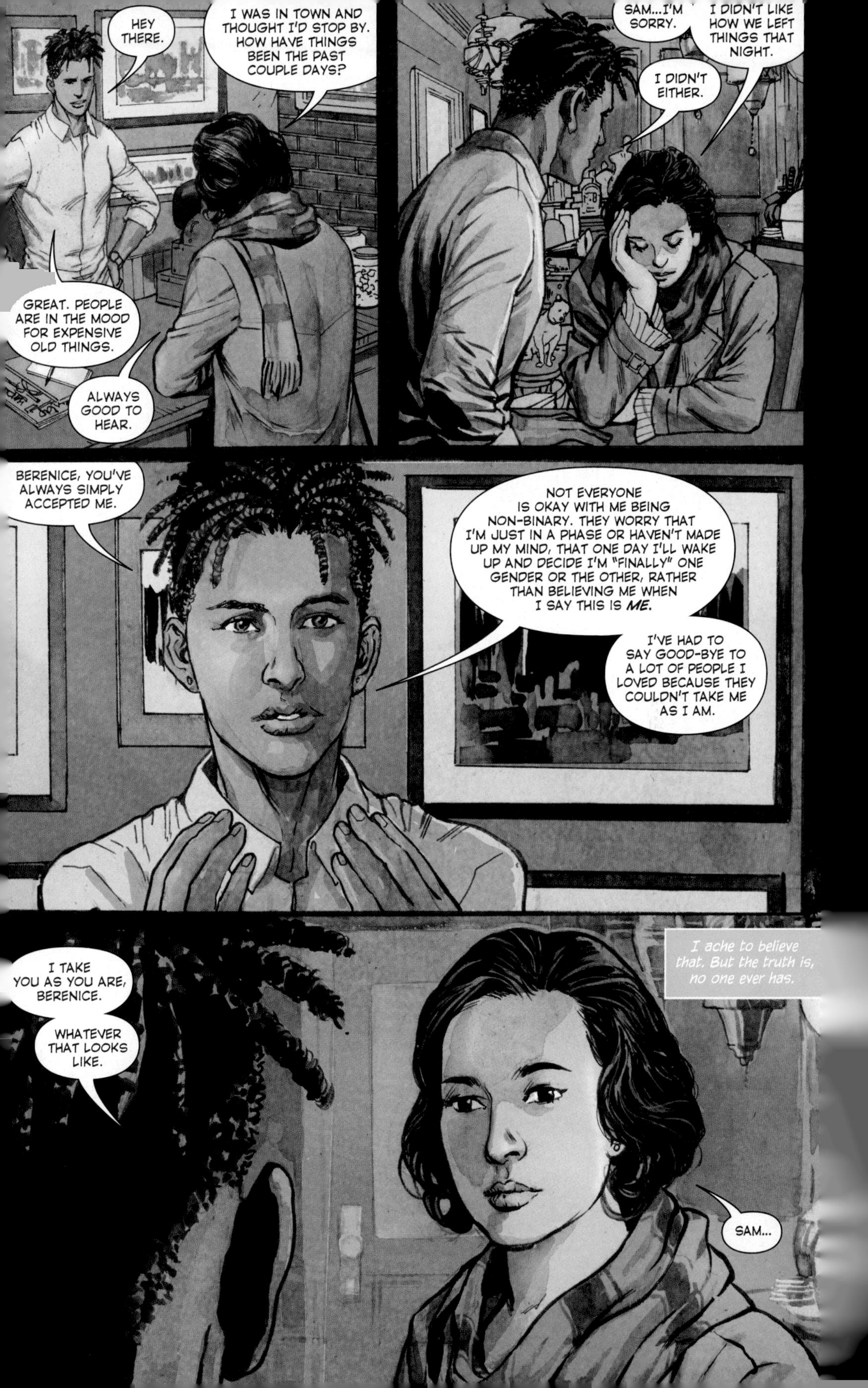
HEY THERE.
I WAS IN TOWN AND THOUGHT I'D STOP BY. HOW HAVE THINGS BEEN THE PAST COUPLE DAYS?
GREAT. PEOPLE ARE IN THE MOOD FOR EXPENSIVE OLD THINGS.
ALWAYS GOOD TO HEAR.
SAM...I'M SORRY.
I DIDN'T LIKE HOW WE LEFT THINGS THAT NIGHT.
I DIDN'T EITHER.
BERENICE, YOU'VE ALWAYS SIMPLY ACCEPTED ME.
NOT EVERYONE IS OKAY WITH ME BEING NON-BINARY. THEY WORRY THAT I'M JUST IN A PHASE OR HAVEN'T MADE UP MY MIND, THAT ONE DAY I'LL WAKE UP AND DECIDE I'M "FINALLY" ONE GENDER OR THE OTHER, RATHER THAN BELIEVING ME WHEN I SAY THIS IS ***ME.***
I'VE HAD TO SAY GOOD-BYE TO A LOT OF PEOPLE I LOVED BECAUSE THEY COULDN'T TAKE ME AS I AM.
I TAKE YOU AS YOU ARE, BERENICE.
WHATEVER THAT LOOKS LIKE.
I ache to believe that. But the truth is, no one ever has.
SAM...

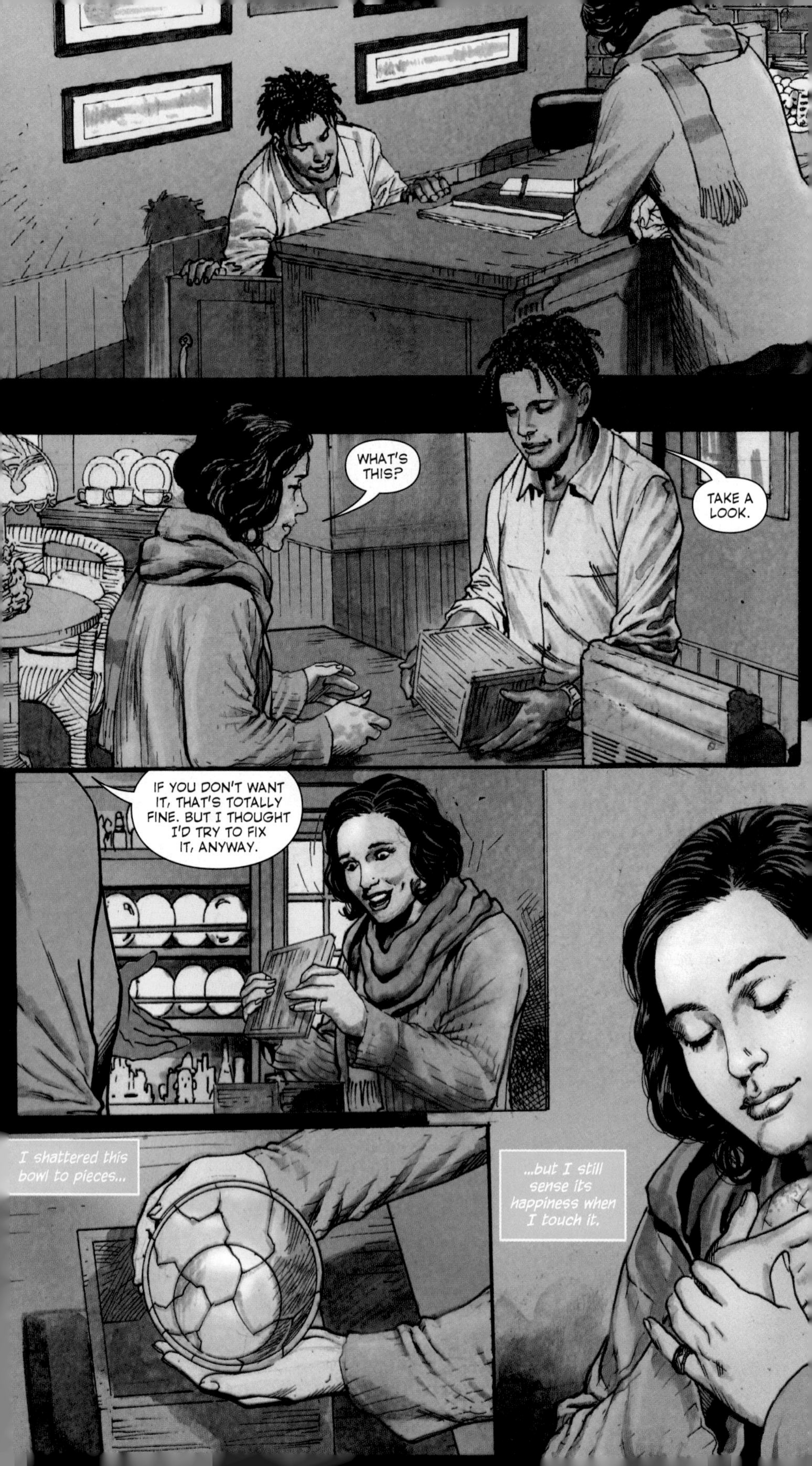
WHAT'S THIS?
TAKE A LOOK.
IF YOU DON'T WANT IT, THAT'S TOTALLY FINE. BUT I THOUGHT I'D TRY TO FIX IT, ANYWAY.
I shattered this bowl to pieces...
...but I still sense its happiness when I touch it.

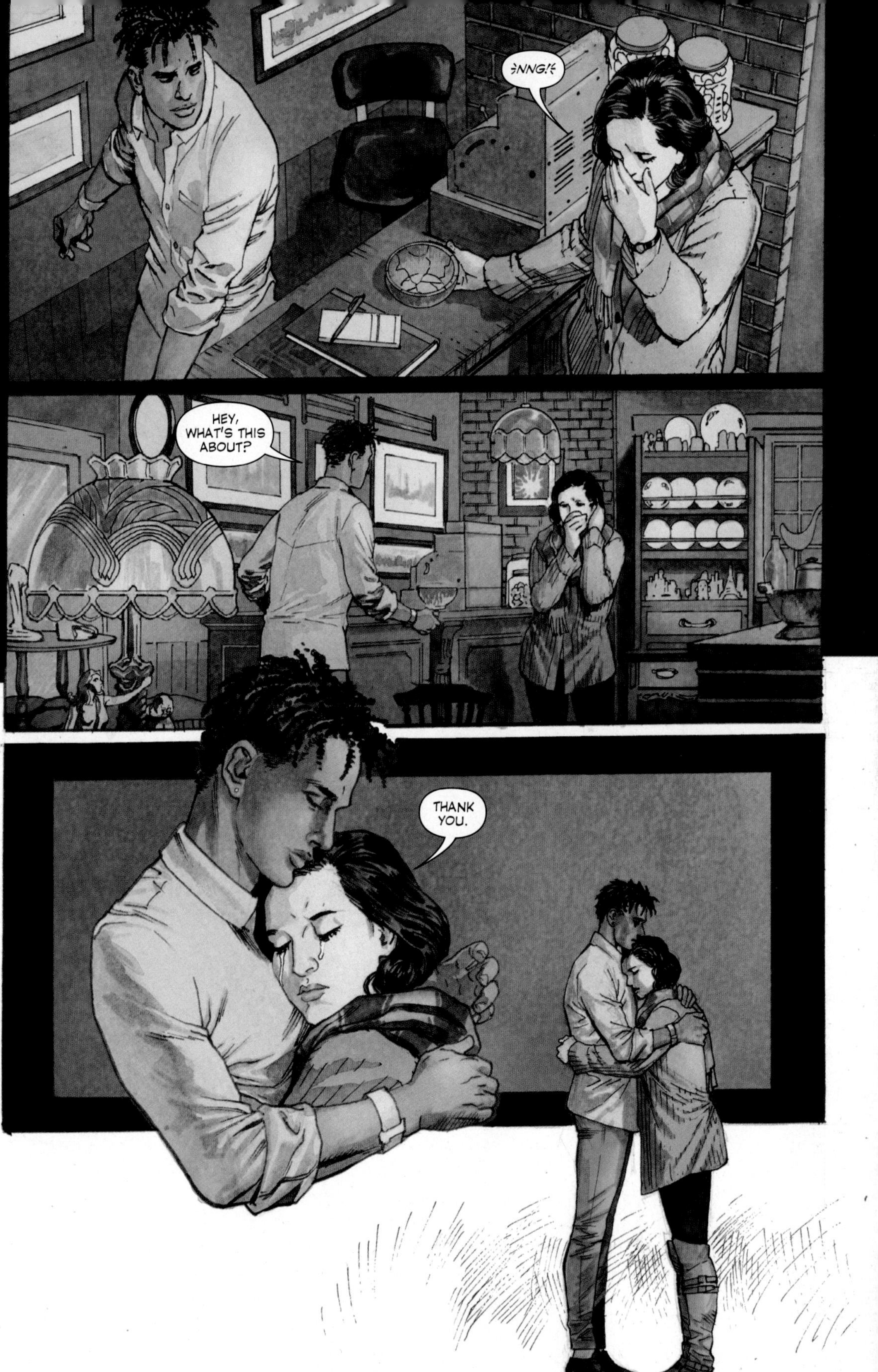
NNG!
HEY, WHAT'S THIS ABOUT?
THANK YOU.

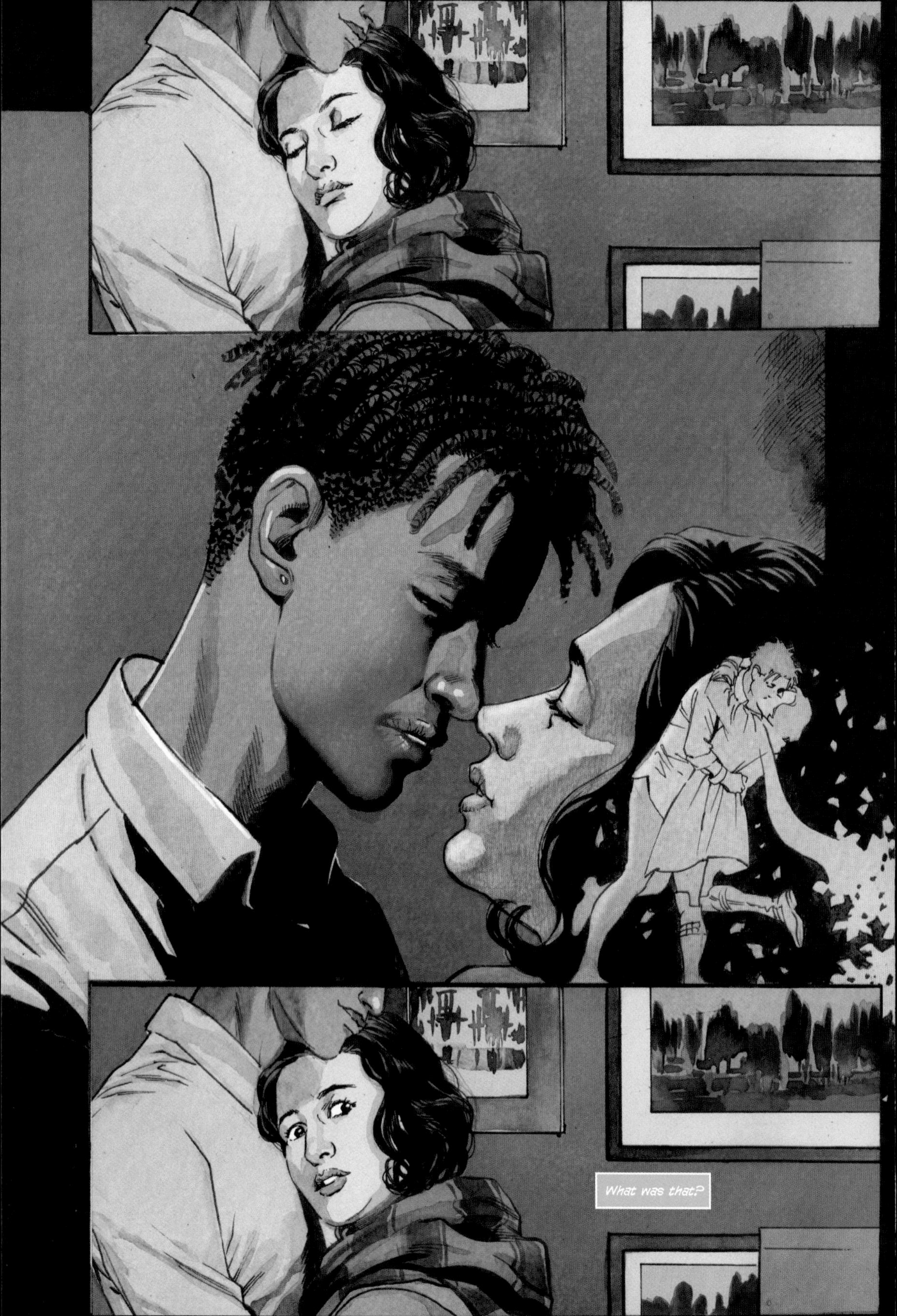
What was that?

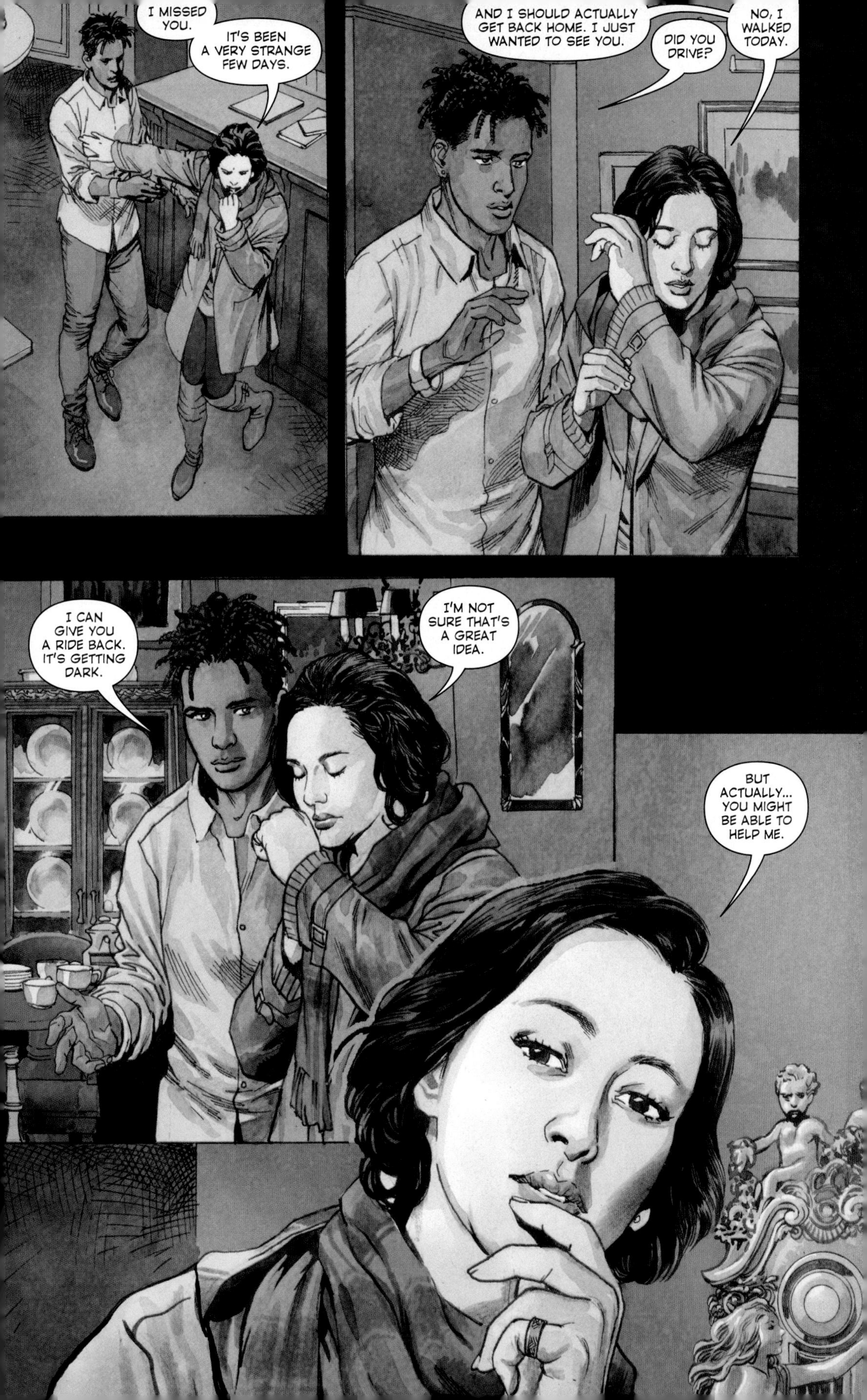
I MISSED YOU.
IT'S BEEN A VERY STRANGE FEW DAYS.
AND I SHOULD ACTUALLY GET BACK HOME. I JUST WANTED TO SEE YOU.
DID YOU DRIVE?
NO, I WALKED TODAY.
I CAN GIVE YOU A RIDE BACK. IT'S GETTING DARK.
I'M NOT SURE THAT'S A GREAT IDEA.
BUT ACTUALLY... YOU MIGHT BE ABLE TO HELP ME.

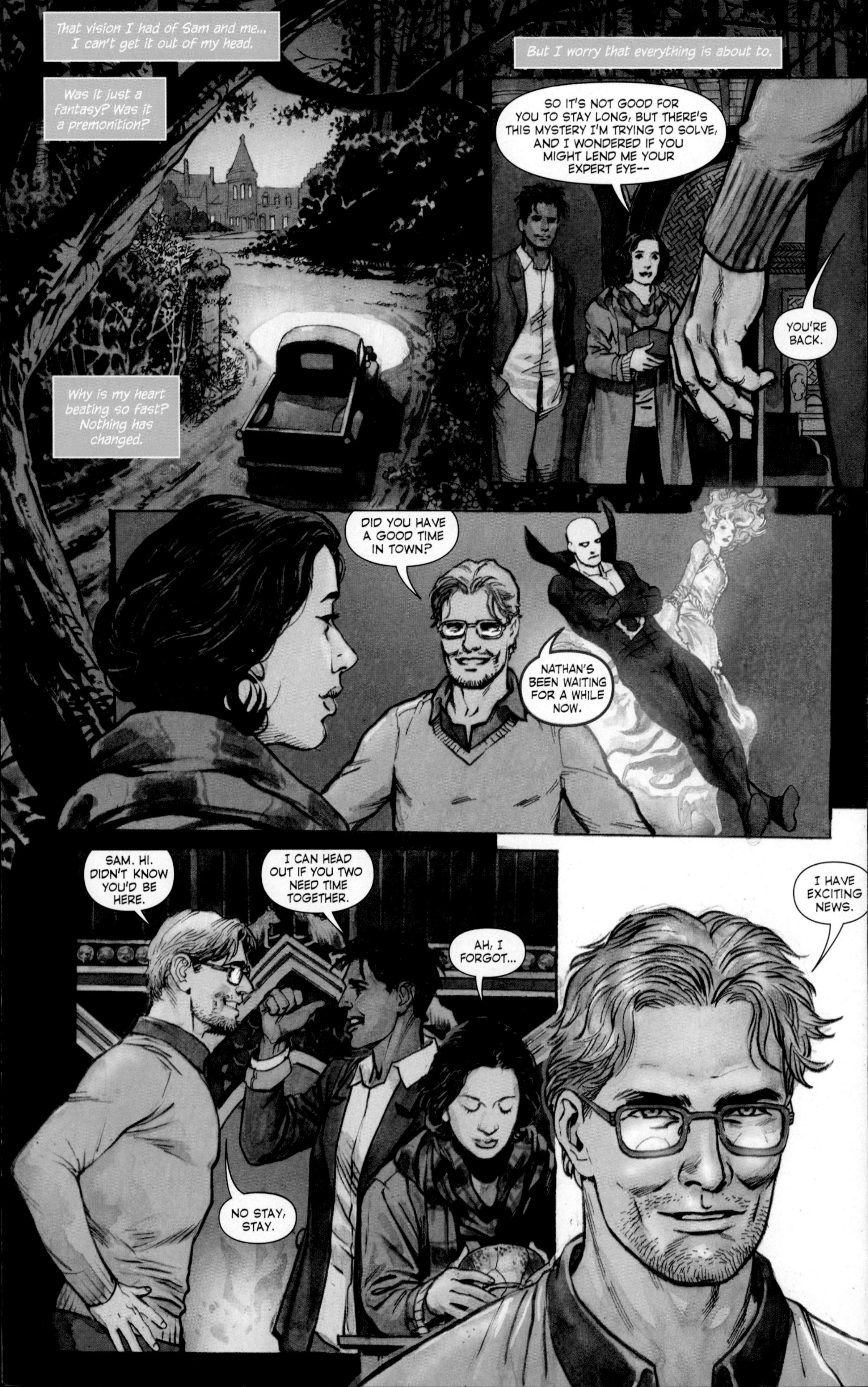
That vision I had of Sam and me... I can't get it out of my head.
Was it just a fantasy? Was it a premonition?
Why is my heart beating so fast? Nothing has changed.
But I worry that everything is about to.
SO IT'S NOT GOOD FOR YOU TO STAY LONG, BUT THERE'S THIS MYSTERY I'M TRYING TO SOLVE, AND I WONDERED IF YOU MIGHT LEND ME YOUR EXPERT EYE--
YOU'RE BACK.
DID YOU HAVE A GOOD TIME IN TOWN?
NATHAN'S BEEN WAITING FOR A WHILE NOW.
SAM. HI. DIDN'T KNOW YOU'D BE HERE.
I CAN HEAD OUT IF YOU TWO NEED TIME TOGETHER.
AH, I FORGOT...
NO STAY, STAY.
I HAVE EXCITING NEWS.

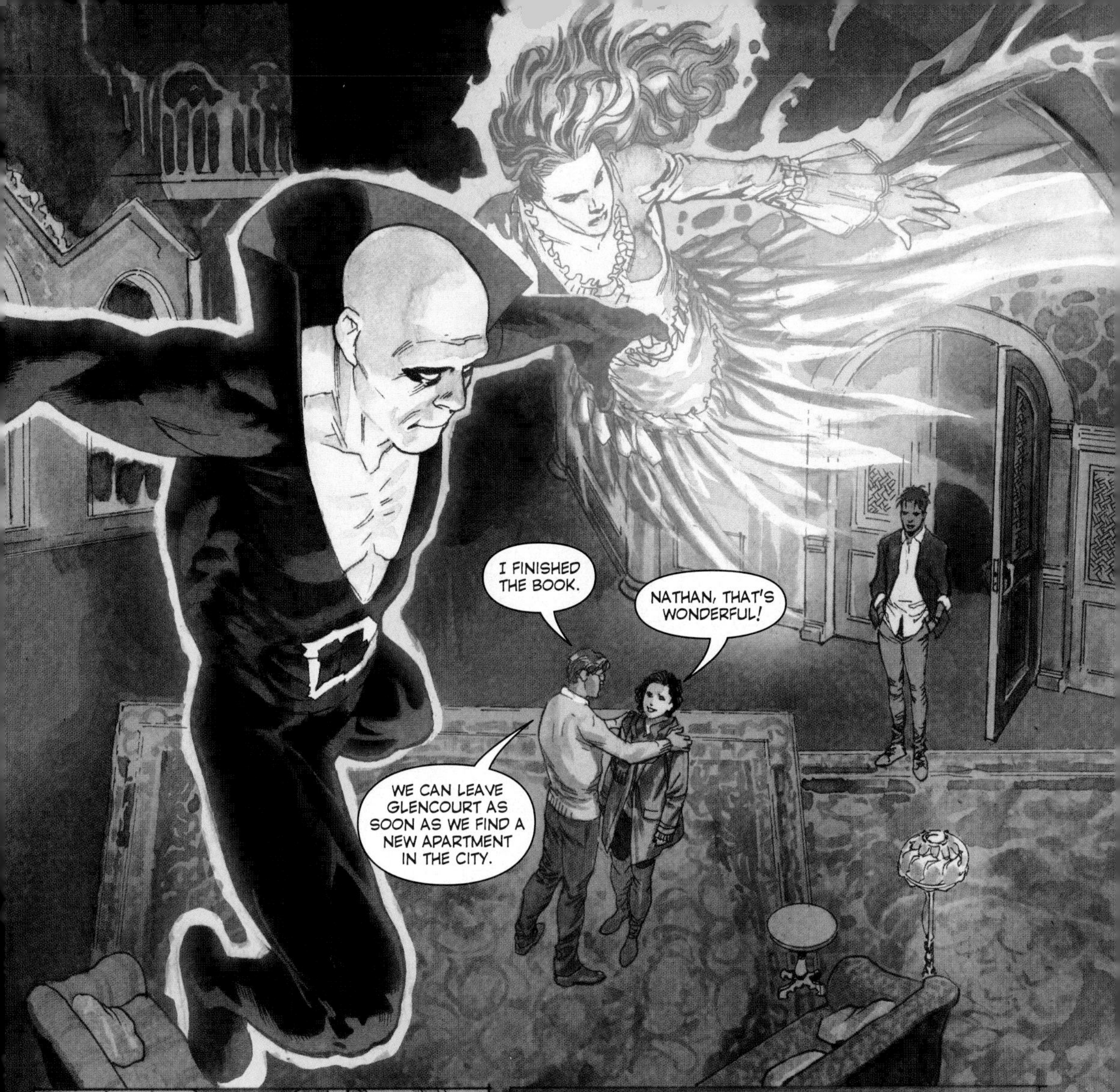
I FINISHED THE BOOK.
NATHAN, THAT'S WONDERFUL!
WE CAN LEAVE GLENCOURT AS SOON AS WE FIND A NEW APARTMENT IN THE CITY.

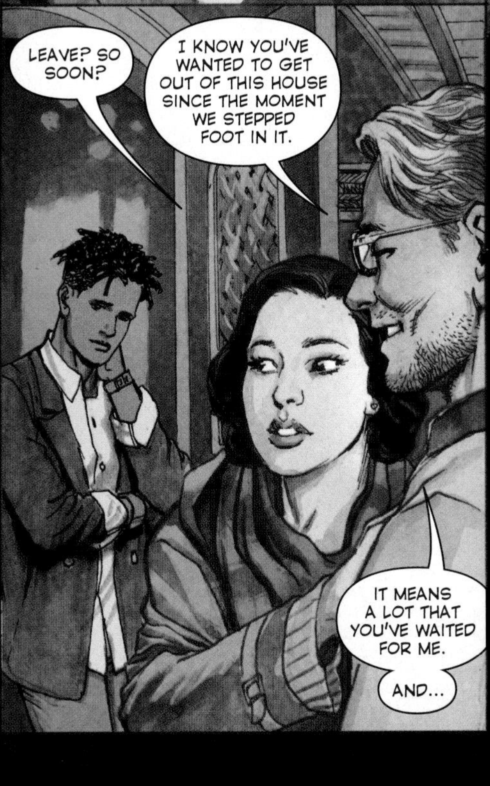
LEAVE? SO SOON?
I KNOW YOU'VE WANTED TO GET OUT OF THIS HOUSE SINCE THE MOMENT WE STEPPED FOOT IN IT.
IT MEANS A LOT THAT YOU'VE WAITED FOR ME.
AND...

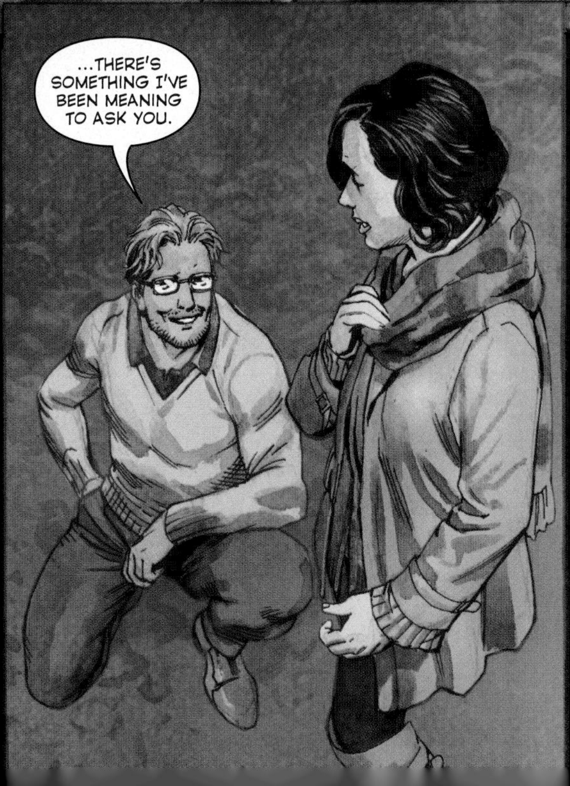
...THERE'S SOMETHING I'VE BEEN MEANING TO ASK YOU.

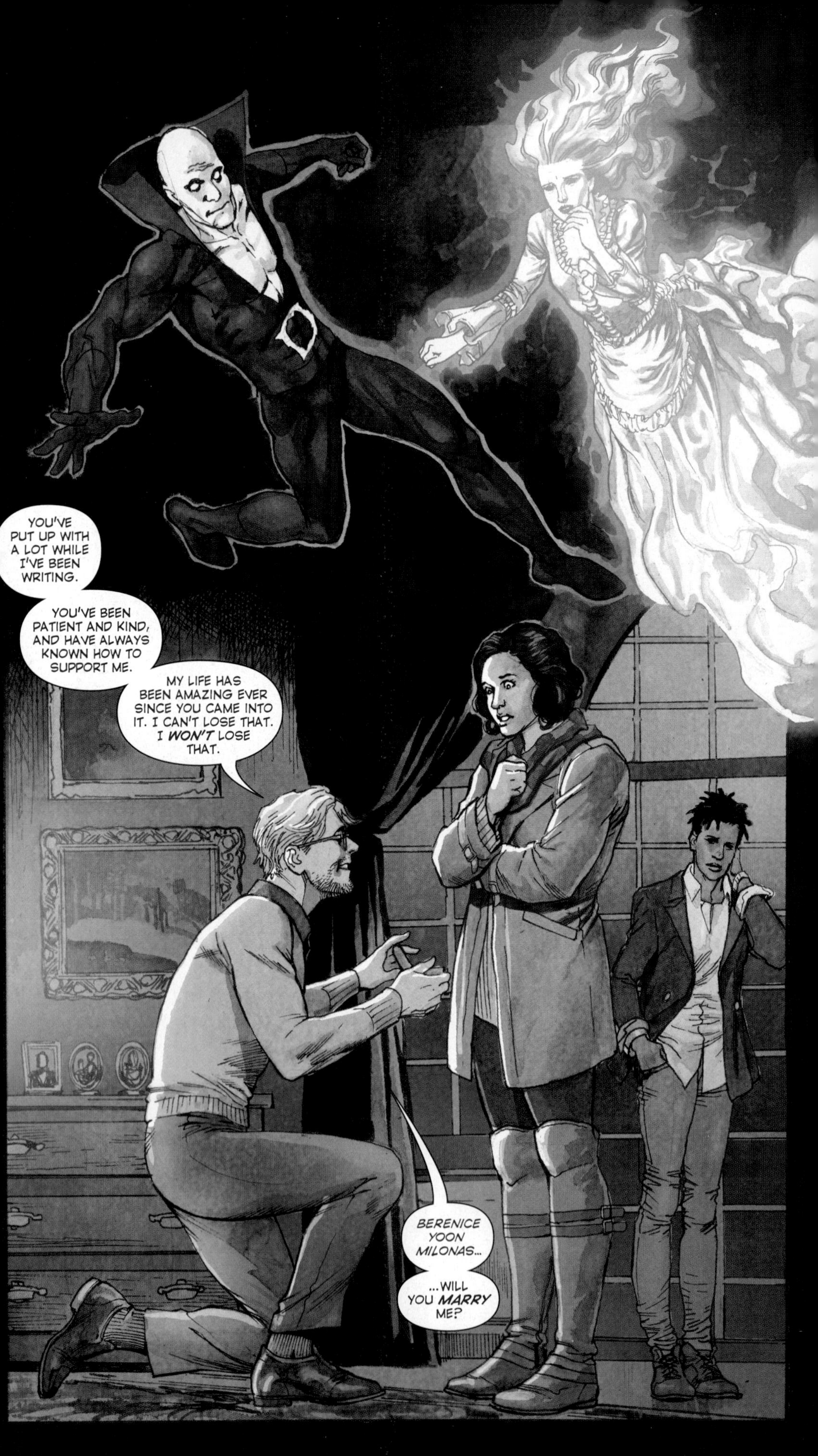
YOU'VE PUT UP WITH A LOT WHILE I'VE BEEN WRITING.
YOU'VE BEEN PATIENT AND KIND, AND HAVE ALWAYS KNOWN HOW TO SUPPORT ME.
MY LIFE HAS BEEN AMAZING EVER SINCE YOU CAME INTO IT. I CAN'T LOSE THAT. I *WON'T* LOSE THAT.
BERENICE YOON MILONAS...
...WILL YOU *MARRY* ME?

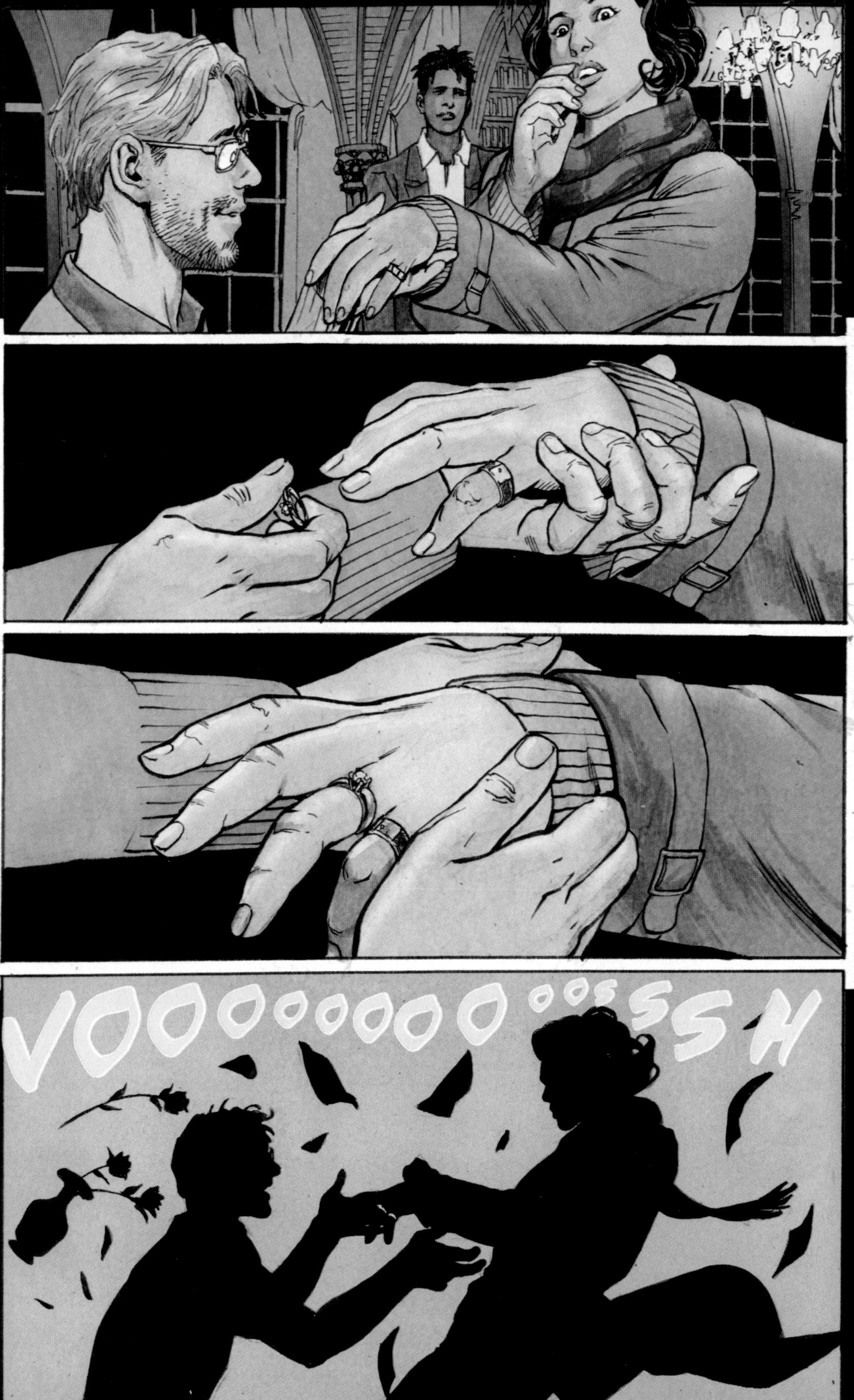
VOOOOOOOOOOSSH

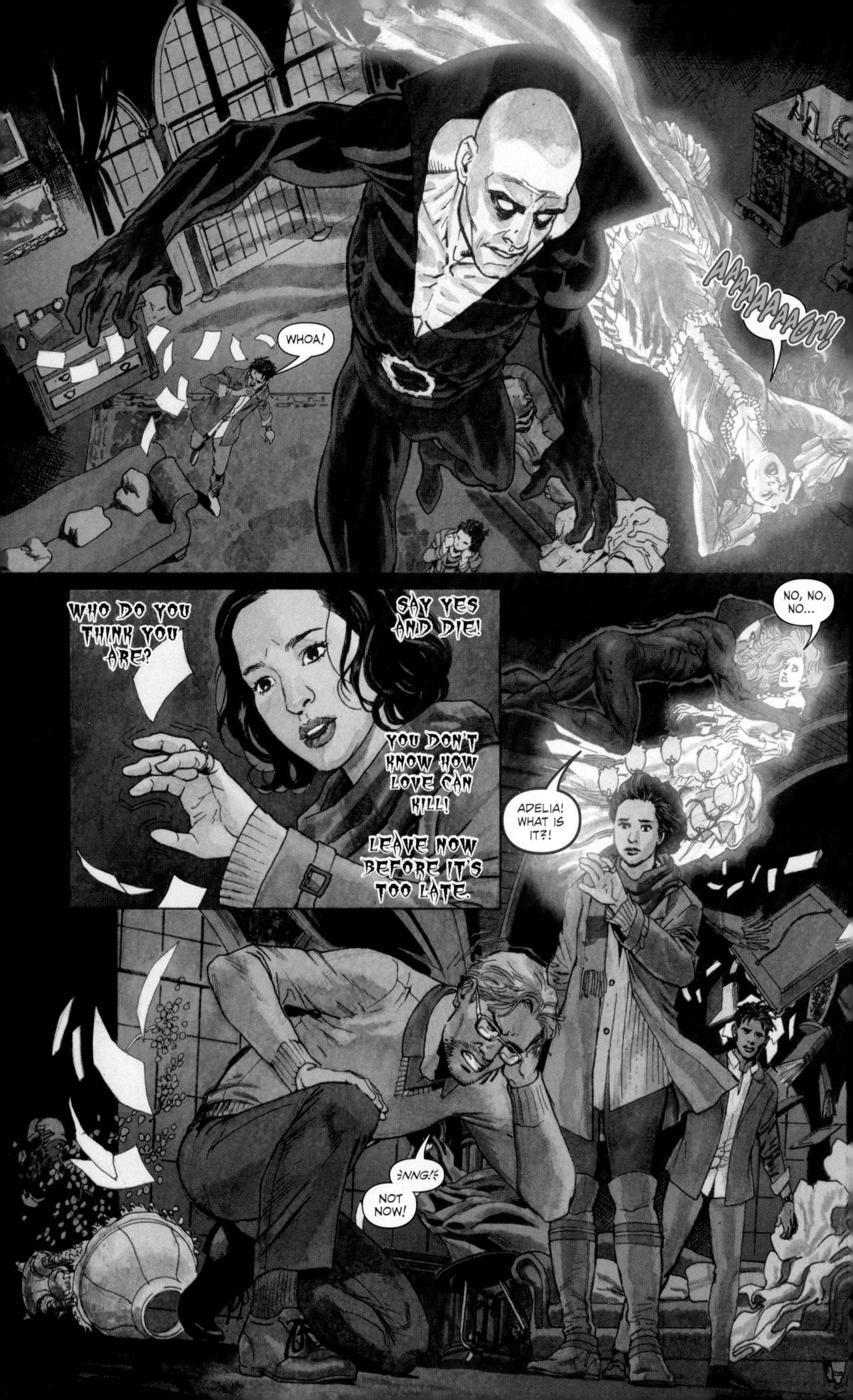
WHOA!
AAAAAAAAGH!
WHO DO YOU THINK YOU ARE?
SAY YES AND DIE!
YOU DON'T KNOW HOW LOVE CAN KILL!
LEAVE NOW BEFORE IT'S TOO LATE.
NO, NO, NO...
ADELIA! WHAT IS IT?!
NNG!
NOT NOW!

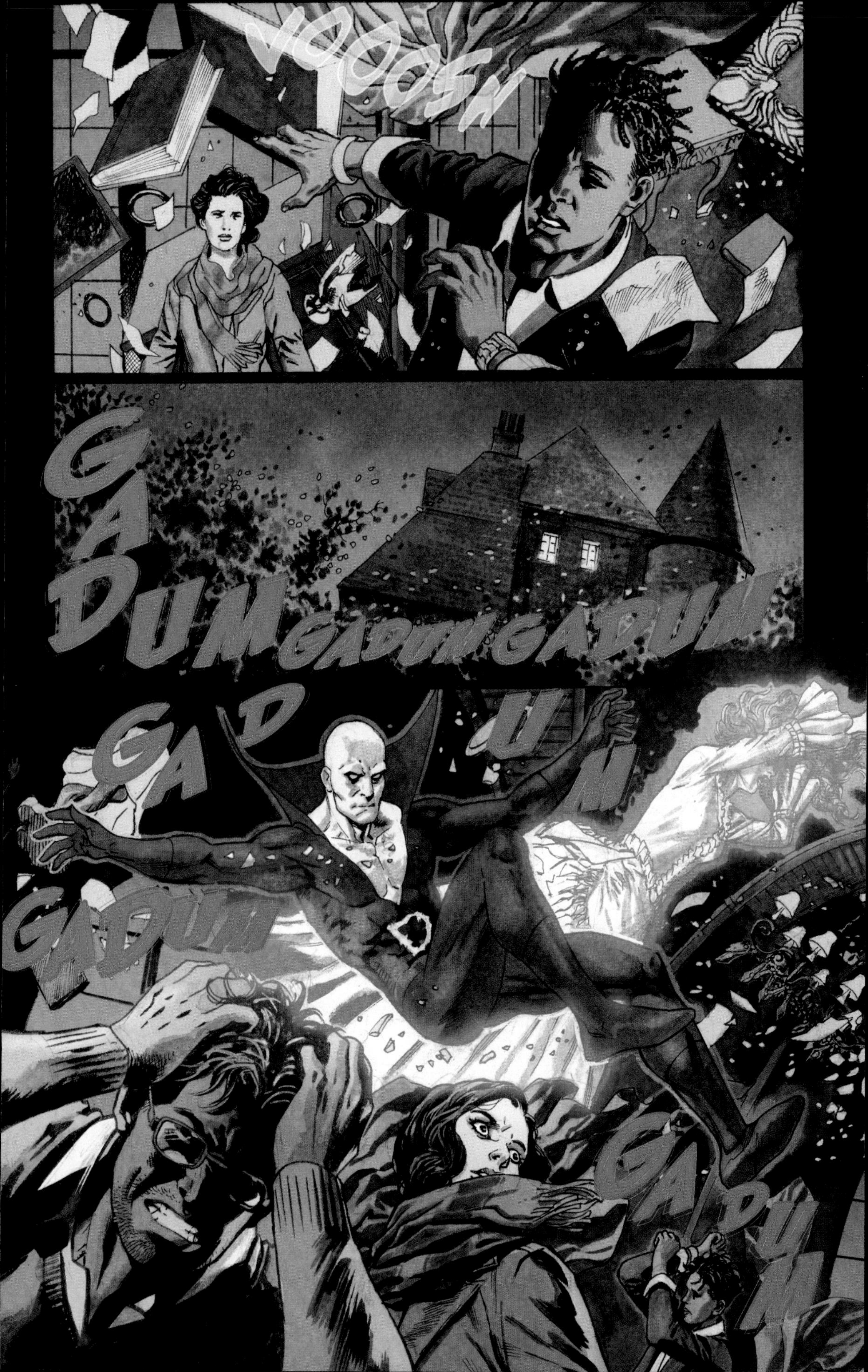
VOOOSH
GADUM
GADUM
GADUM
GADUM
GADUM
GADUM

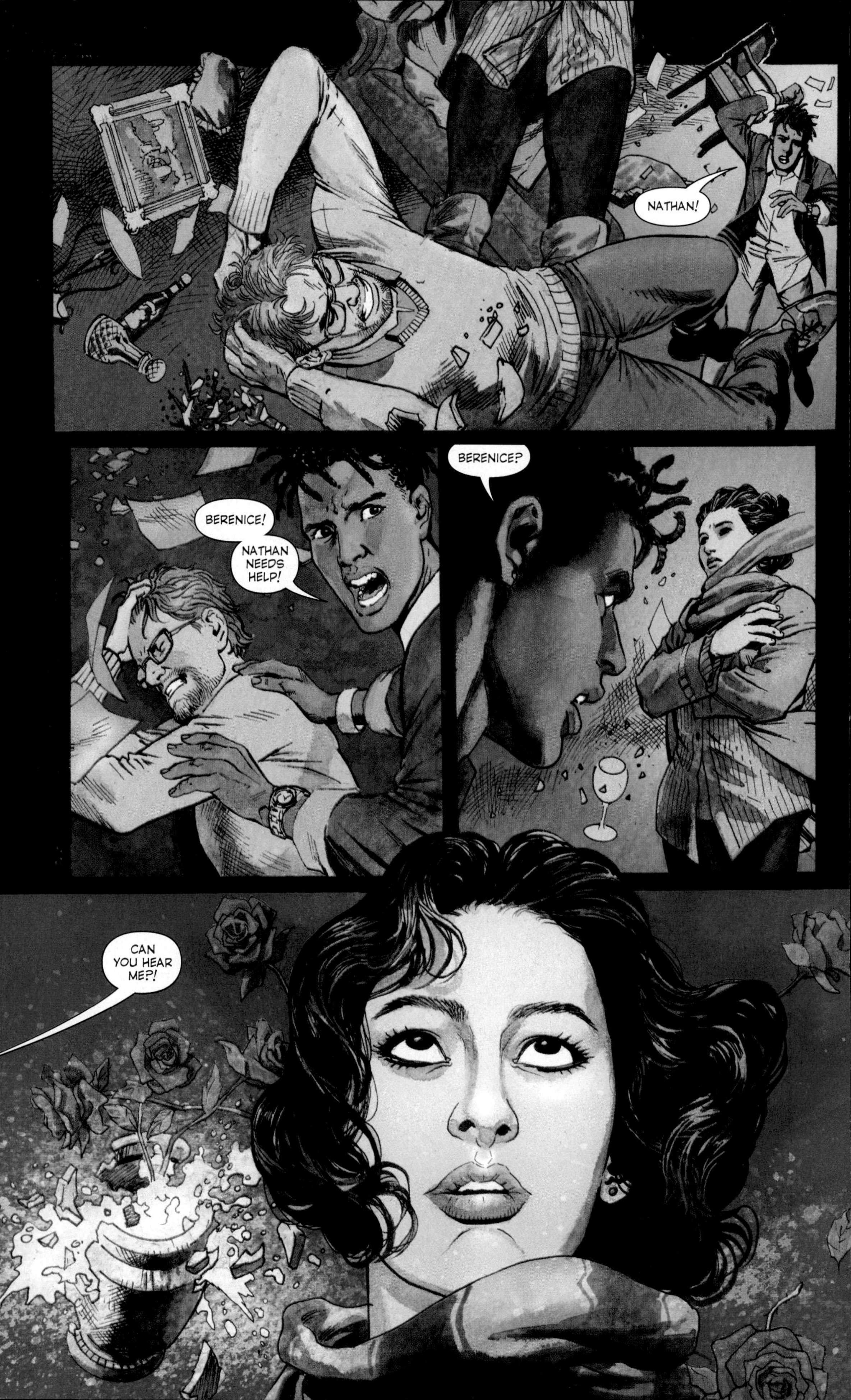
NATHAN!
BERENICE!
NATHAN NEEDS HELP!
BERENICE?
CAN YOU HEAR ME?!

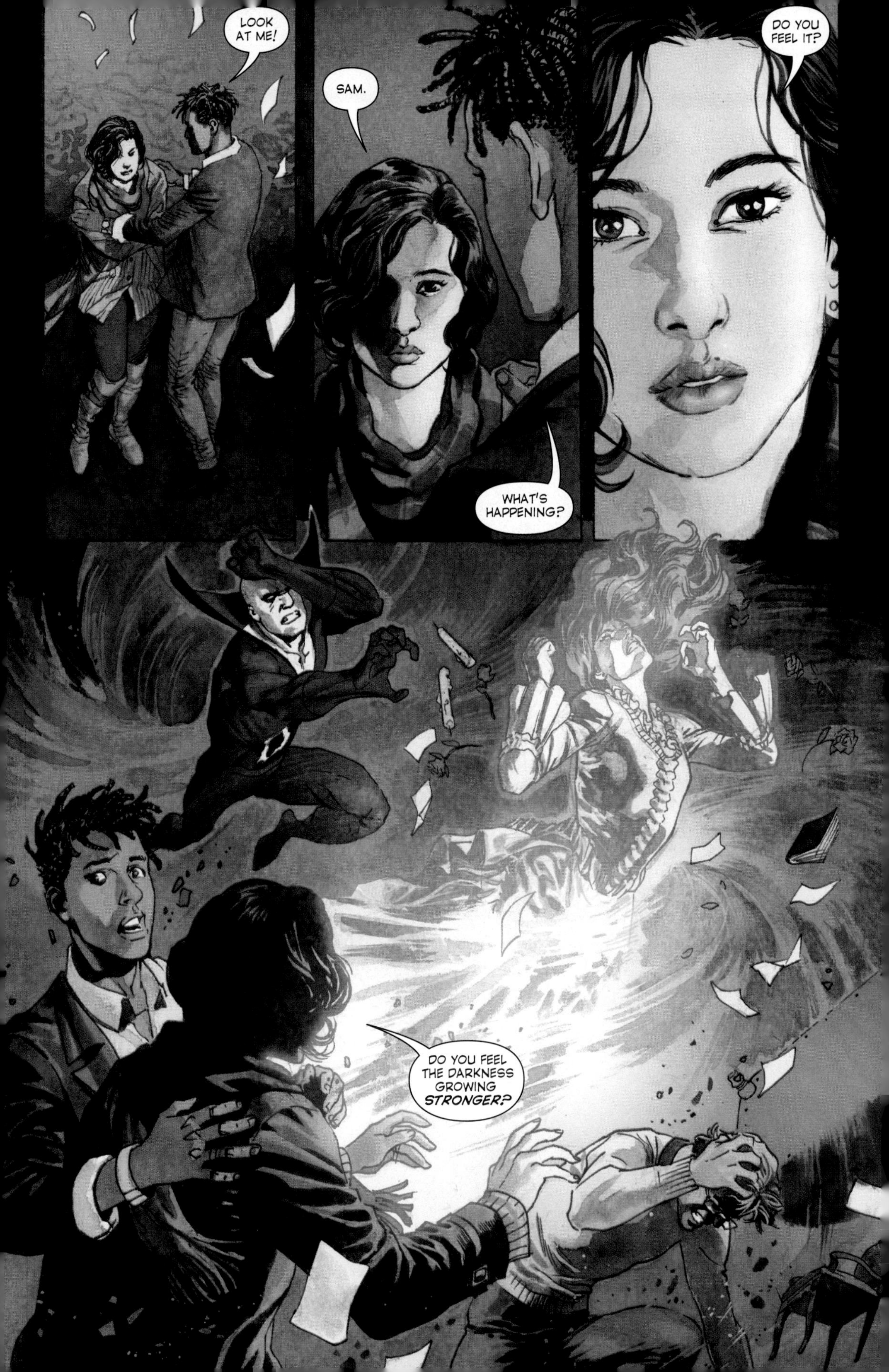
LOOK AT ME!
SAM.
WHAT'S HAPPENING?
DO YOU FEEL IT?
DO YOU FEEL THE DARKNESS GROWING *STRONGER?*

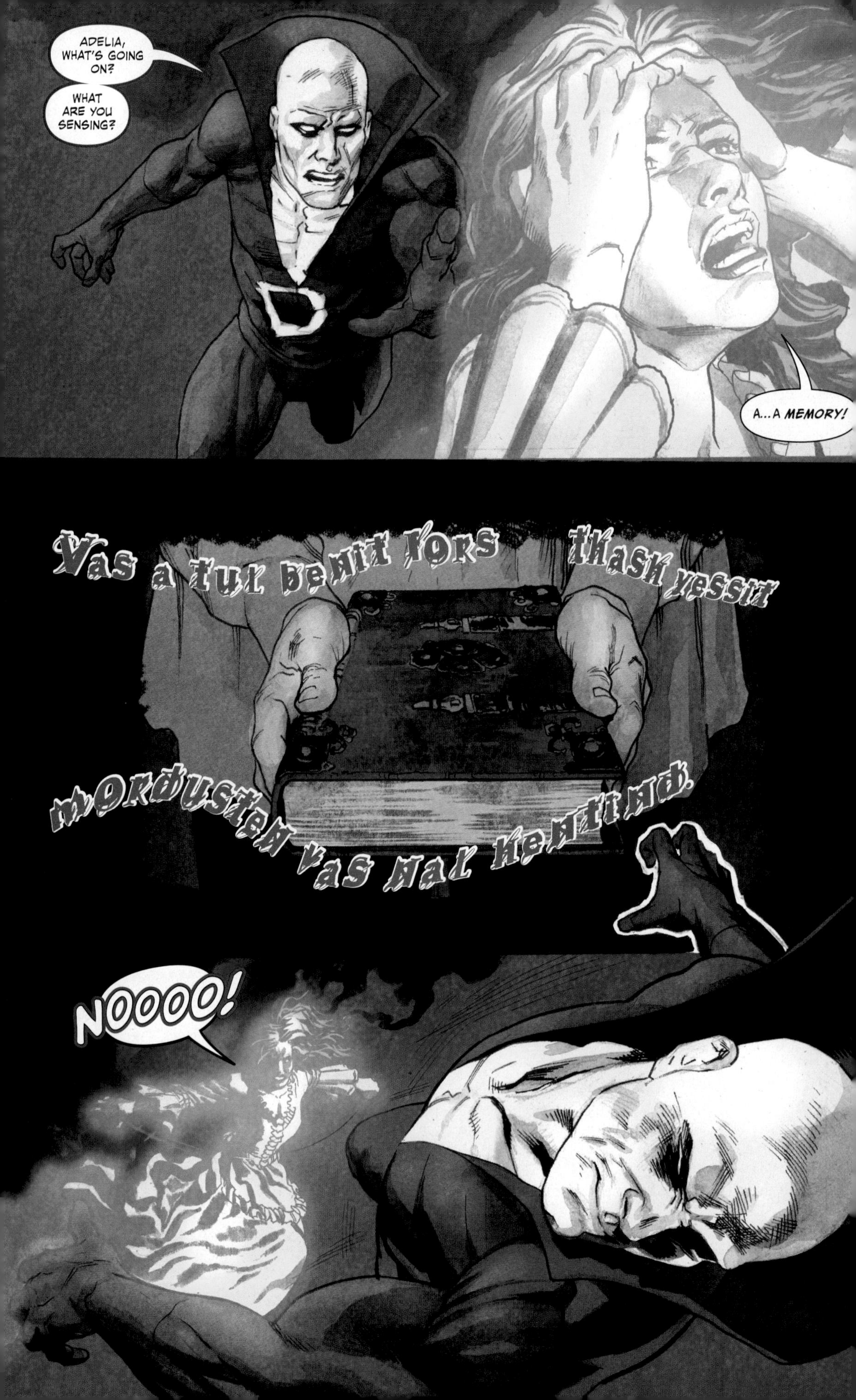
ADELIA, WHAT'S GOING ON?
WHAT ARE YOU SENSING?
A...A *MEMORY!*
Vas a tul benit fors thask yessit
morduster vas nal kentina.
NOOOO!

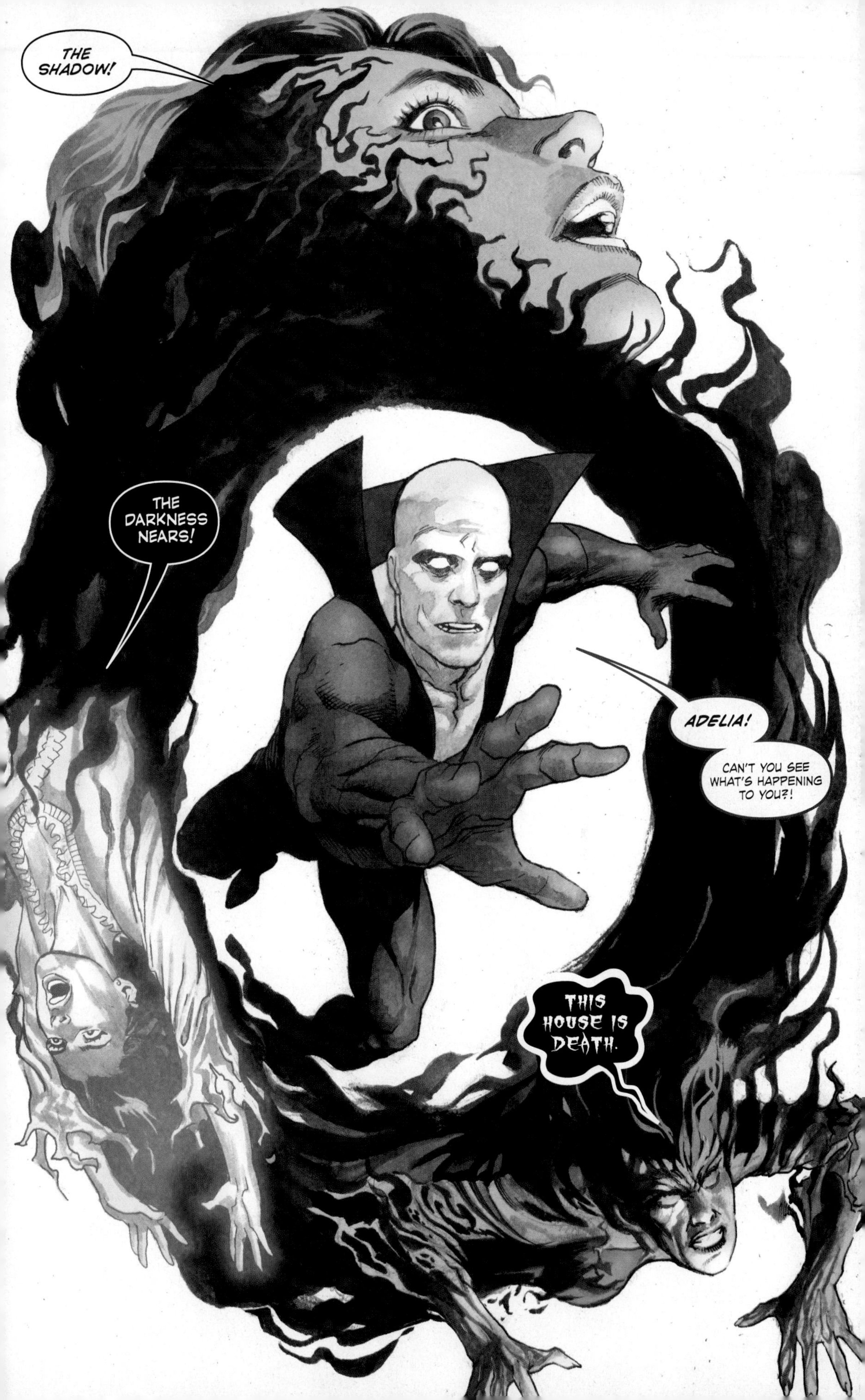
THE SHADOW!
THE DARKNESS NEARS!
ADELIA!
CAN'T YOU SEE WHAT'S HAPPENING TO YOU?!
THIS HOUSE IS DEATH.

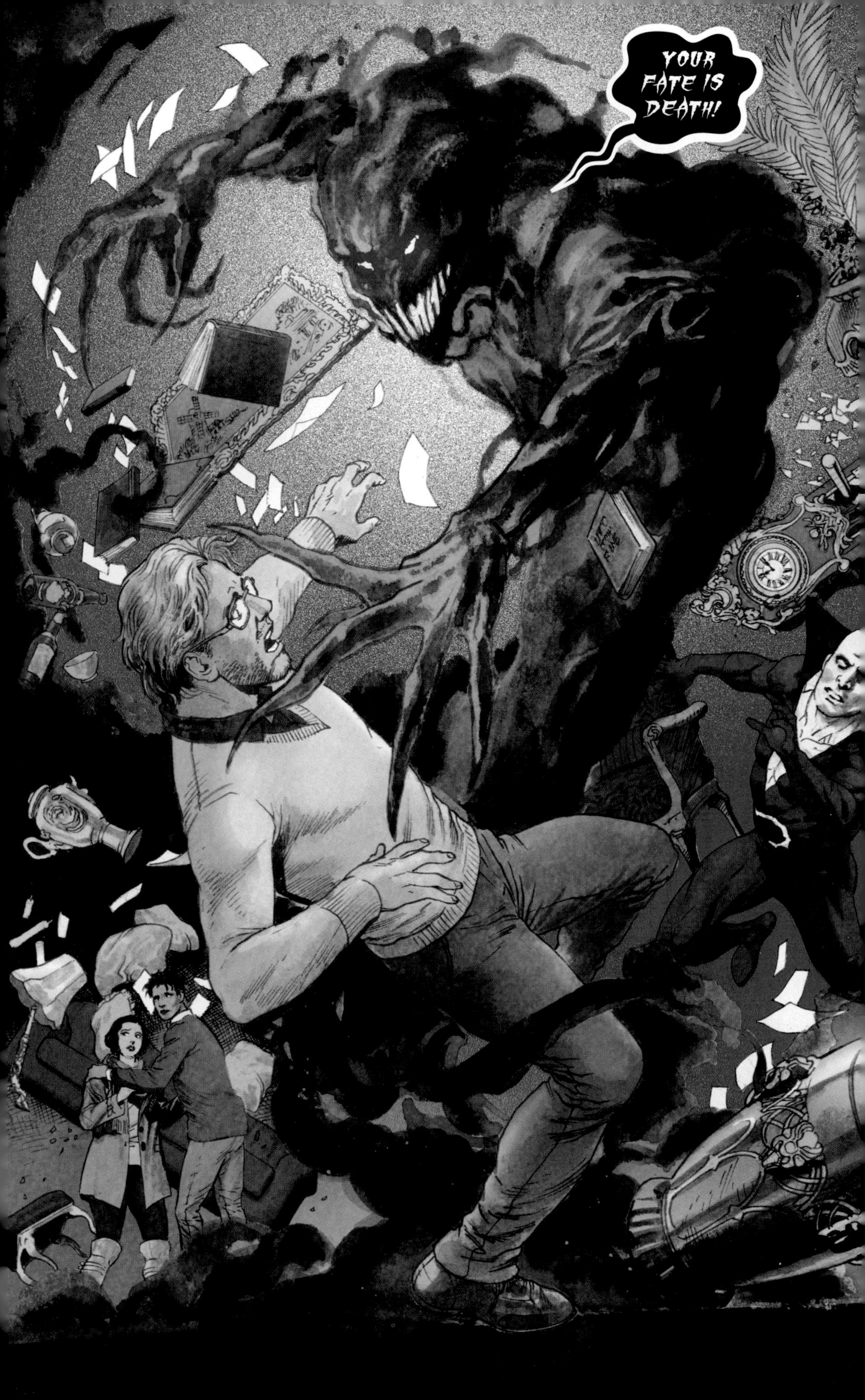
YOUR FATE IS DEATH!

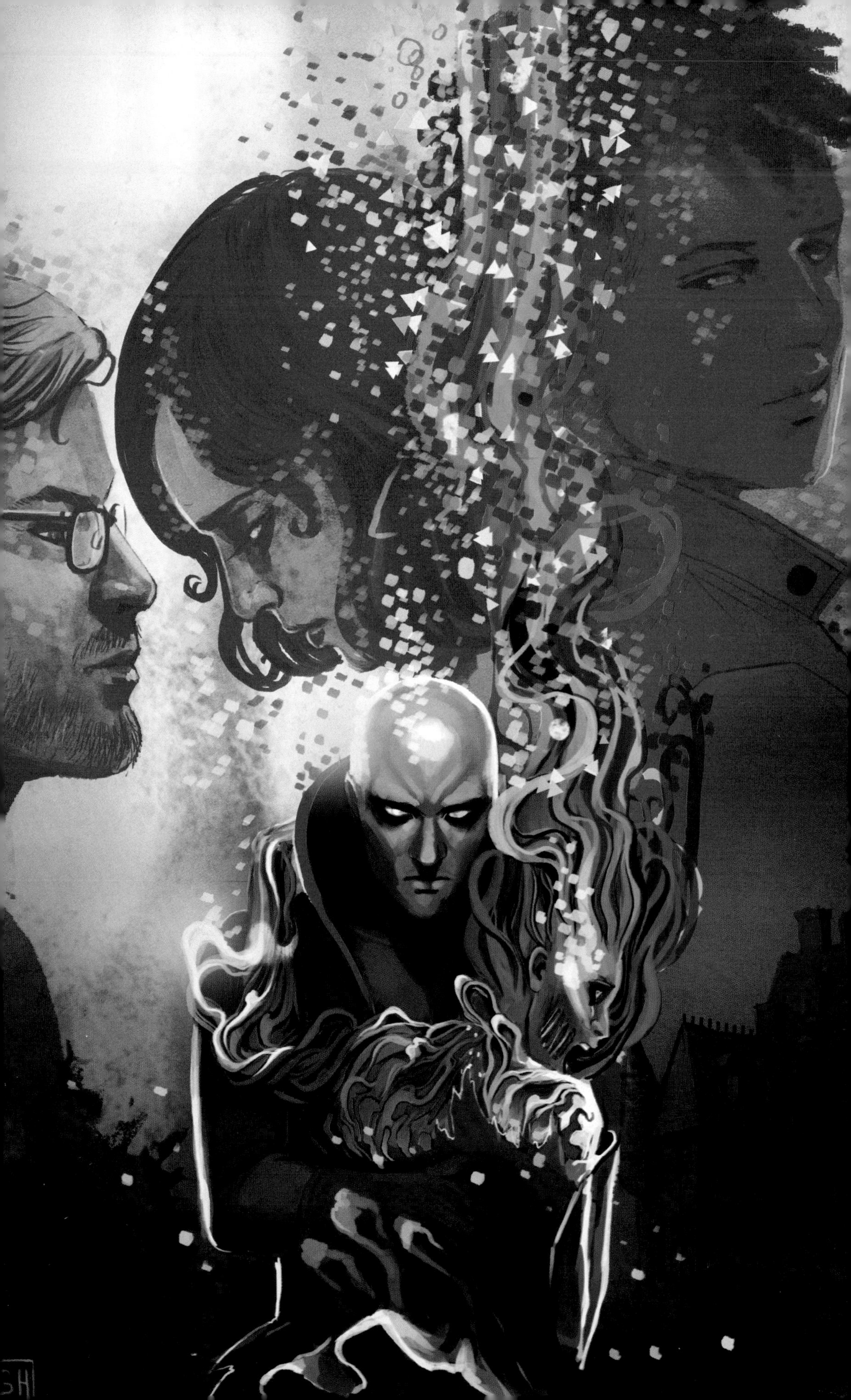
SH

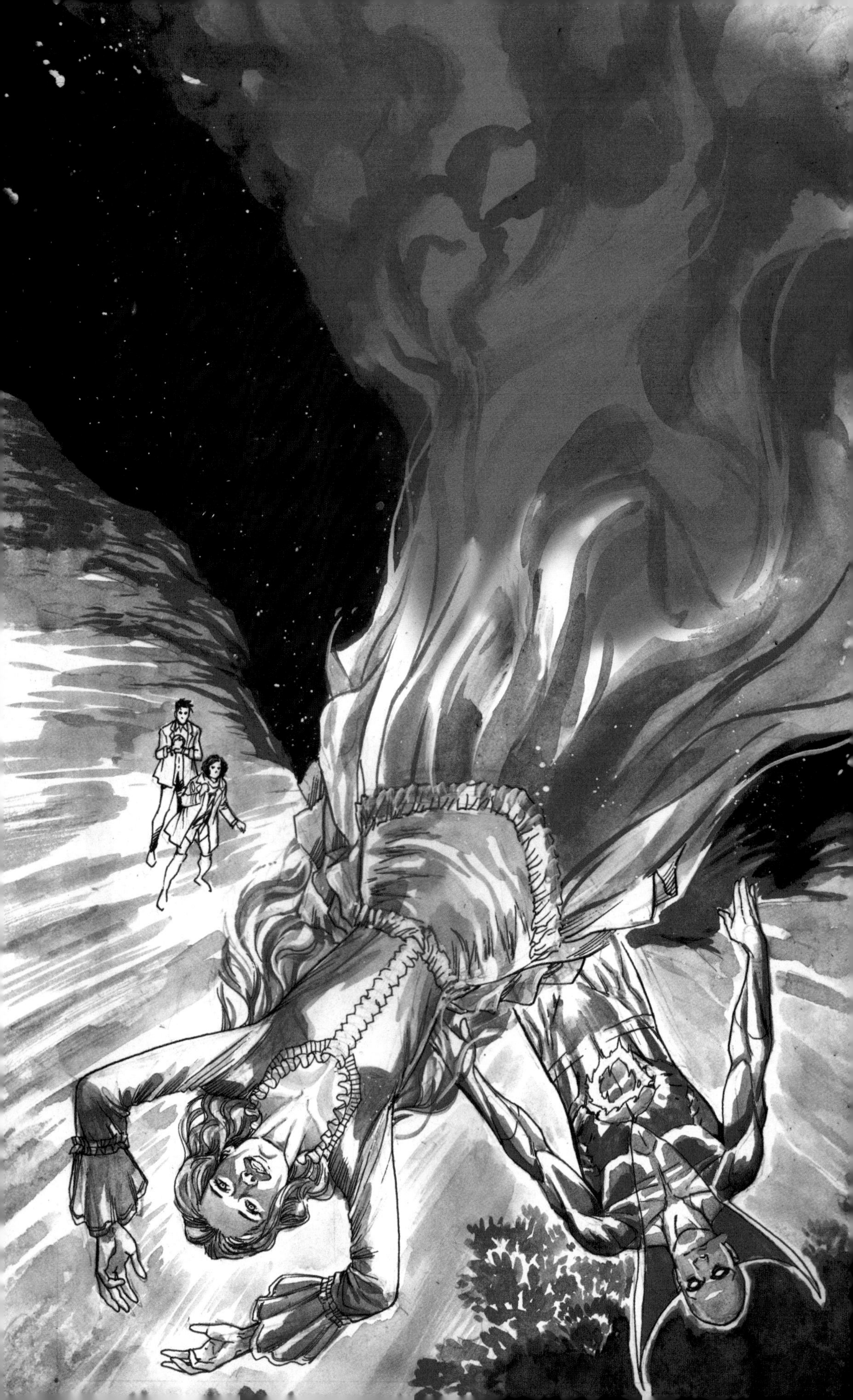

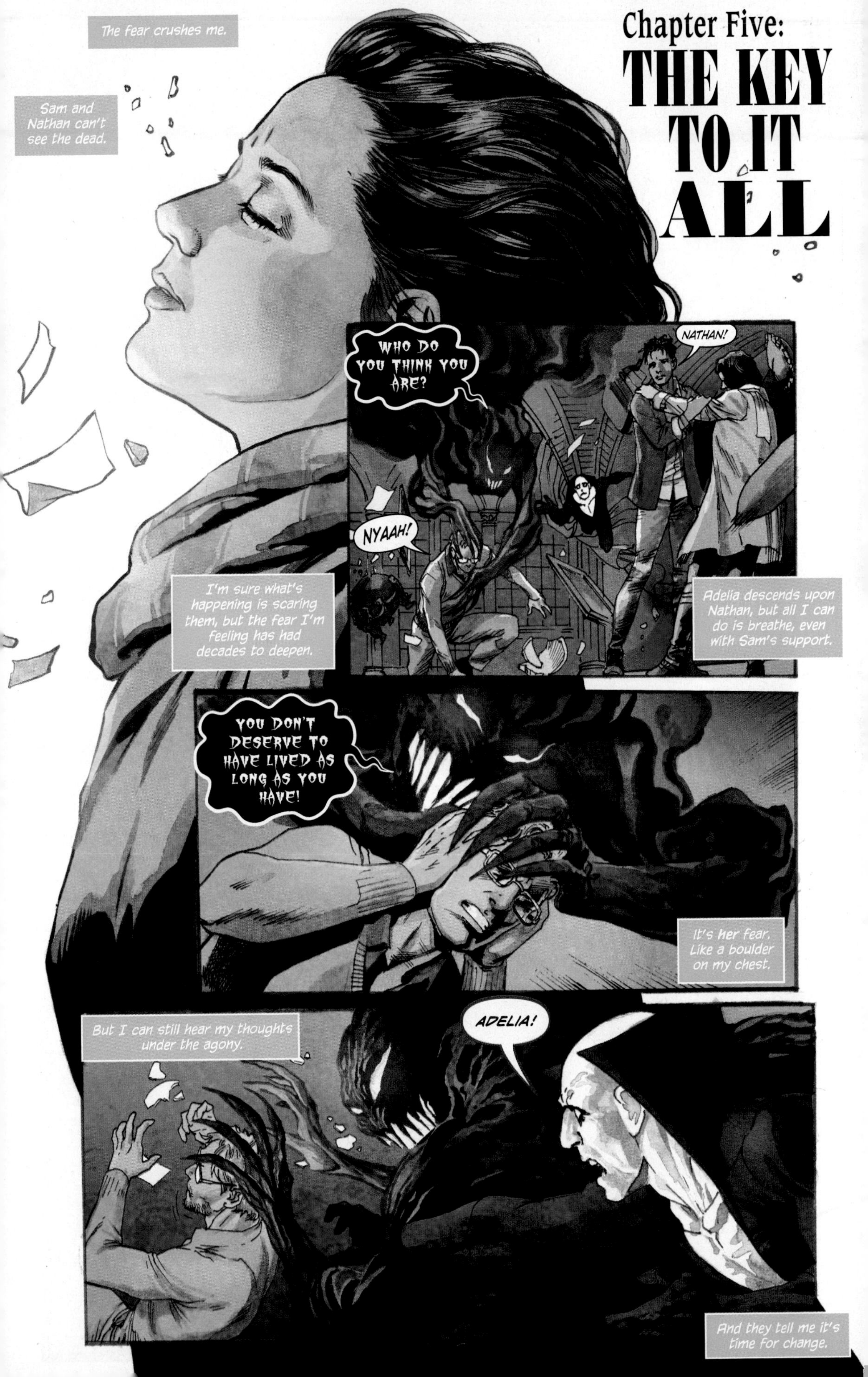
The fear crushes me.
Sam and Nathan can't see the dead.
Chapter Five:
THE KEY TO IT ALL
WHO DO YOU THINK YOU ARE?
NATHAN!
NYAAH!
I'm sure what's happening is scaring them, but the fear I'm feeling has had decades to deepen.
Adelia descends upon Nathan, but all I can do is breathe, even with Sam's support.
YOU DON'T DESERVE TO HAVE LIVED AS LONG AS YOU HAVE!
It's **her** fear. Like a boulder on my chest.
But I can still hear my thoughts under the agony.
ADELIA!
And they tell me it's time for change.

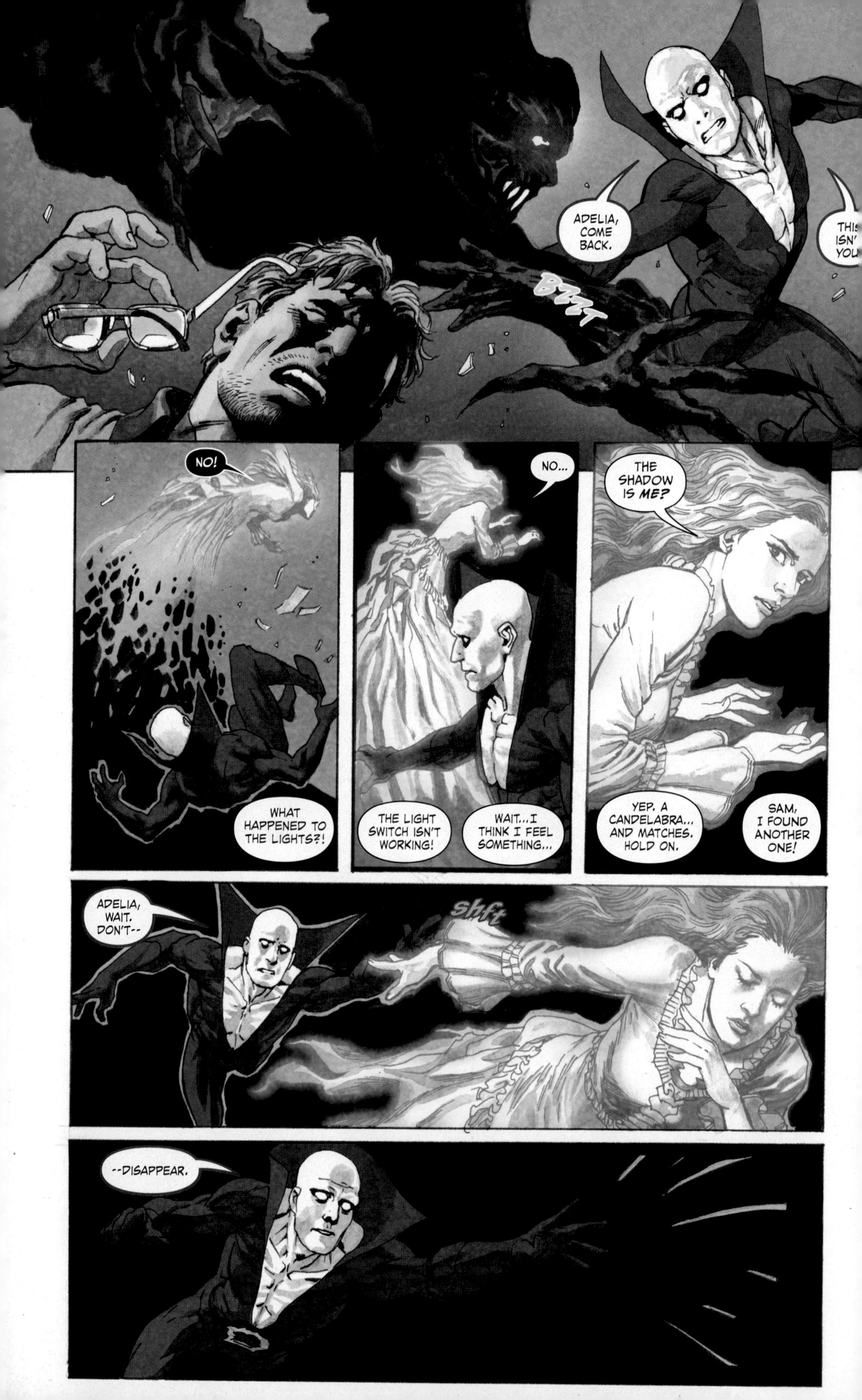
ADELIA, COME BACK.
THIS ISN'T YOU
BZZT
NO!
WHAT HAPPENED TO THE LIGHTS?!
NO...
THE LIGHT SWITCH ISN'T WORKING!
WAIT...I THINK I FEEL SOMETHING...
THE SHADOW IS *ME?*
YEP. A CANDELABRA... AND MATCHES. HOLD ON.
SAM, I FOUND ANOTHER ONE!
ADELIA, WAIT. DON'T--
shft
--DISAPPEAR.

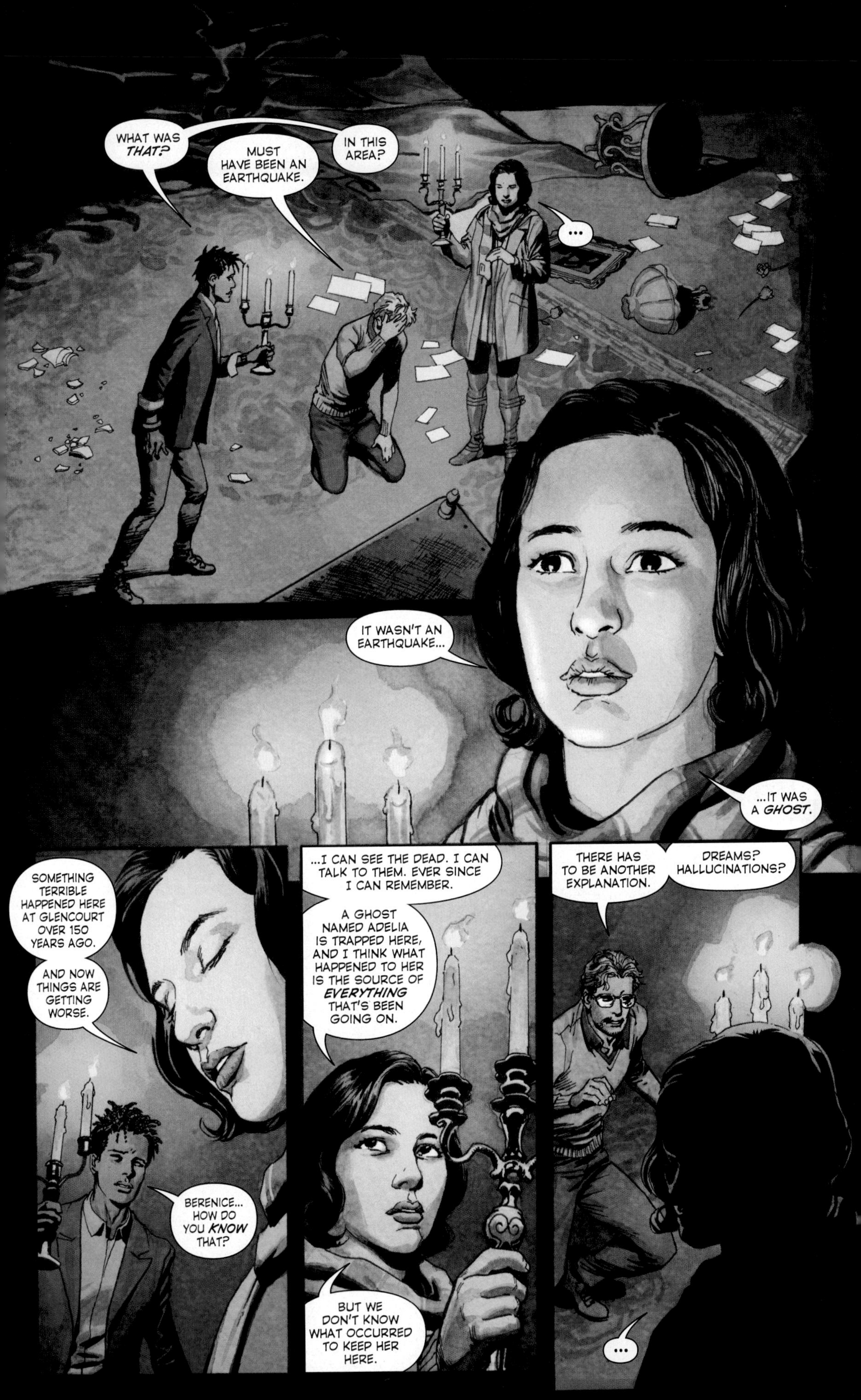
WHAT WAS *THAT?*
MUST HAVE BEEN AN EARTHQUAKE.
IN THIS AREA?
...
IT WASN'T AN EARTHQUAKE...
...IT WAS A *GHOST*.
SOMETHING TERRIBLE HAPPENED HERE AT GLENCOURT OVER 150 YEARS AGO.
AND NOW THINGS ARE GETTING WORSE.
BERENICE... HOW DO YOU *KNOW* THAT?
...I CAN SEE THE DEAD. I CAN TALK TO THEM. EVER SINCE I CAN REMEMBER.
A GHOST NAMED ADELIA IS TRAPPED HERE, AND I THINK WHAT HAPPENED TO HER IS THE SOURCE OF *EVERYTHING* THAT'S BEEN GOING ON.
BUT WE DON'T KNOW WHAT OCCURRED TO KEEP HER HERE.
THERE HAS TO BE ANOTHER EXPLANATION.
DREAMS? HALLUCINATIONS?
...

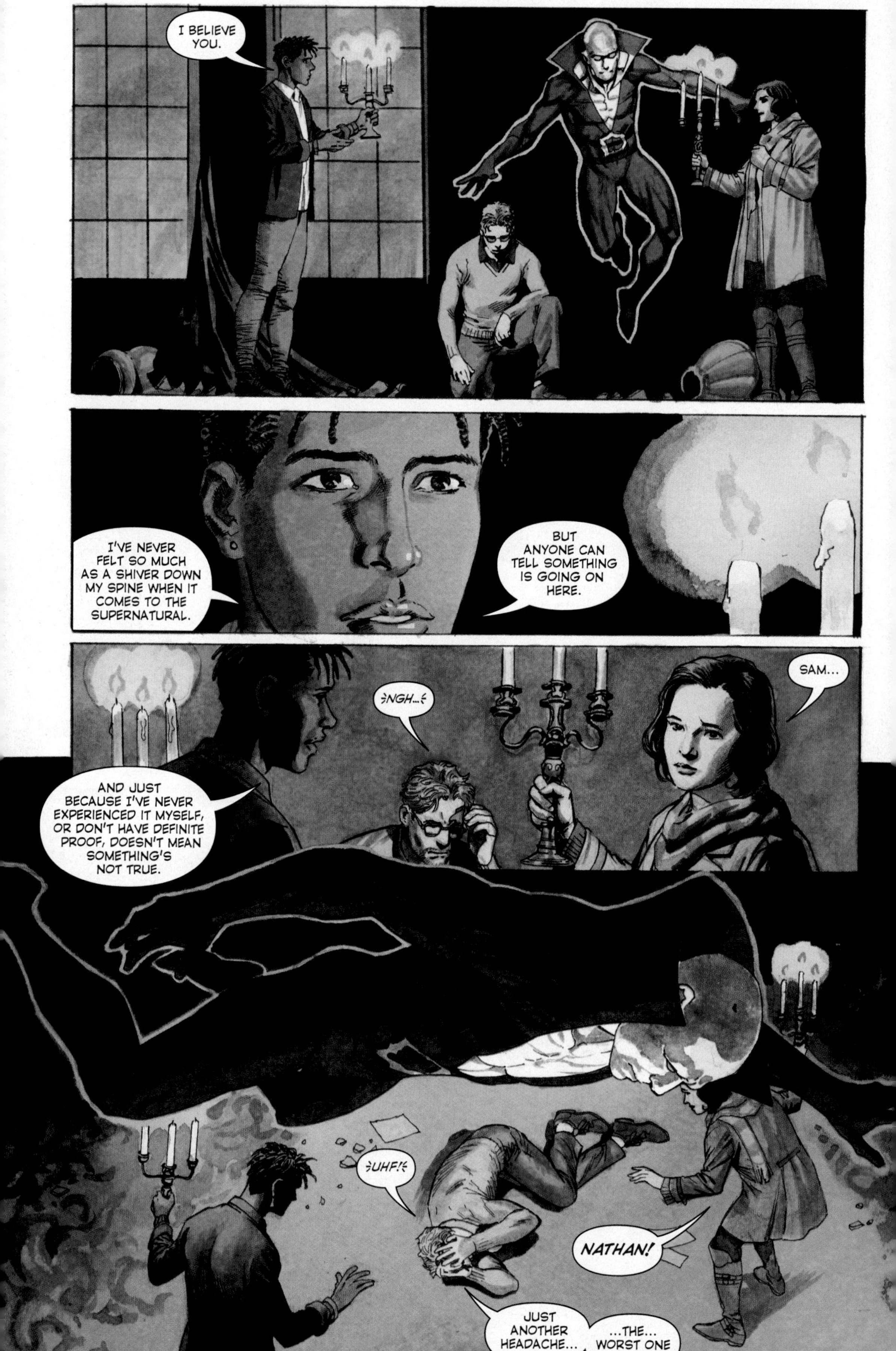
I BELIEVE YOU.
I'VE NEVER FELT SO MUCH AS A SHIVER DOWN MY SPINE WHEN IT COMES TO THE SUPERNATURAL.
BUT ANYONE CAN TELL SOMETHING IS GOING ON HERE.
AND JUST BECAUSE I'VE NEVER EXPERIENCED IT MYSELF, OR DON'T HAVE DEFINITE PROOF, DOESN'T MEAN SOMETHING'S NOT TRUE.
NGH...
SAM...
UHF!
NATHAN!
JUST ANOTHER HEADACHE...
...THE... WORST ONE YET.

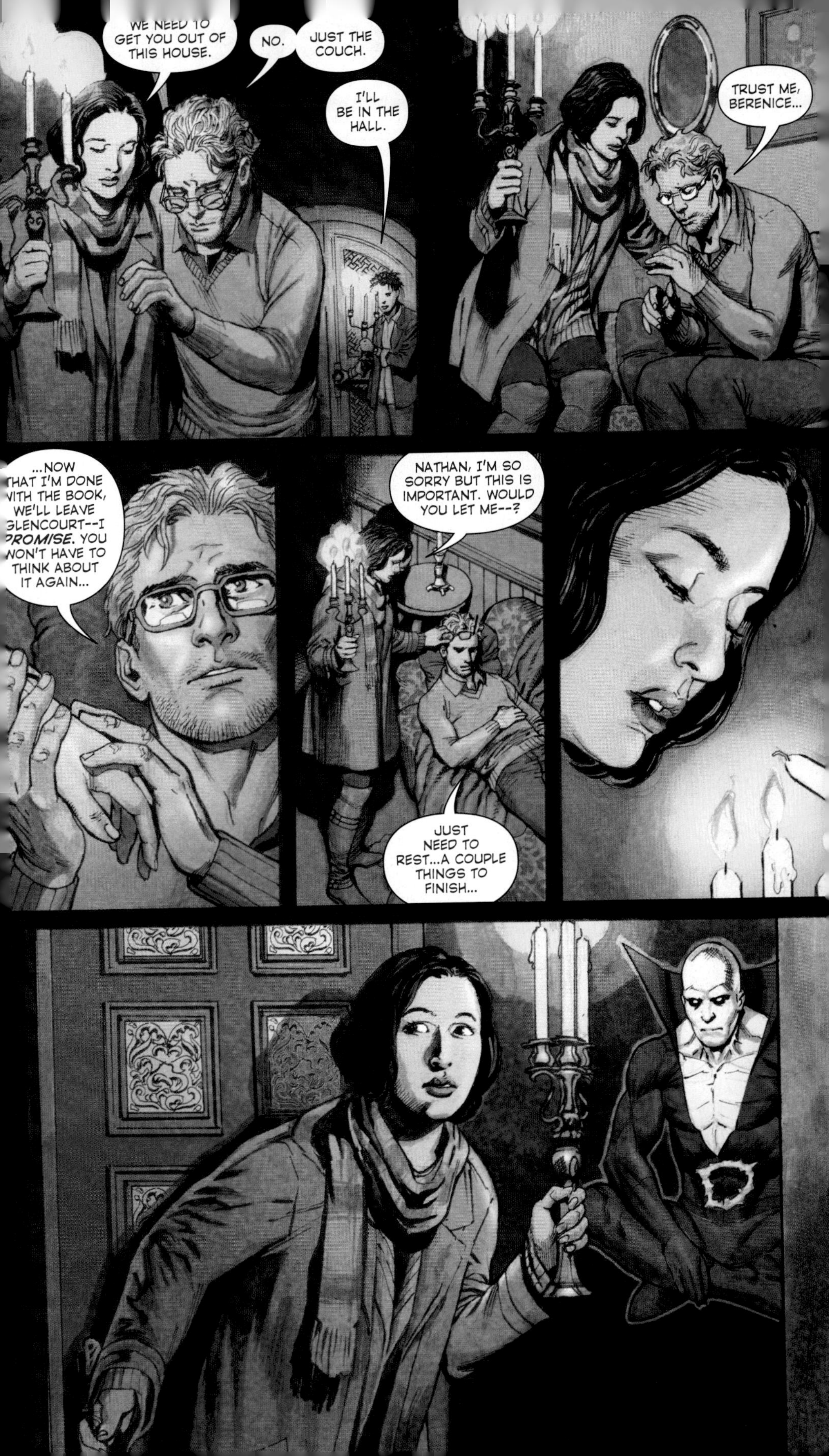
WE NEED TO GET YOU OUT OF THIS HOUSE.
NO.
JUST THE COUCH.
I'LL BE IN THE HALL.
TRUST ME, BERENICE...
...NOW THAT I'M DONE WITH THE BOOK, WE'LL LEAVE GLENCOURT--I PROMISE. YOU WON'T HAVE TO THINK ABOUT IT AGAIN...
NATHAN, I'M SO SORRY BUT THIS IS IMPORTANT. WOULD YOU LET ME--?
JUST NEED TO REST...A COUPLE THINGS TO FINISH...

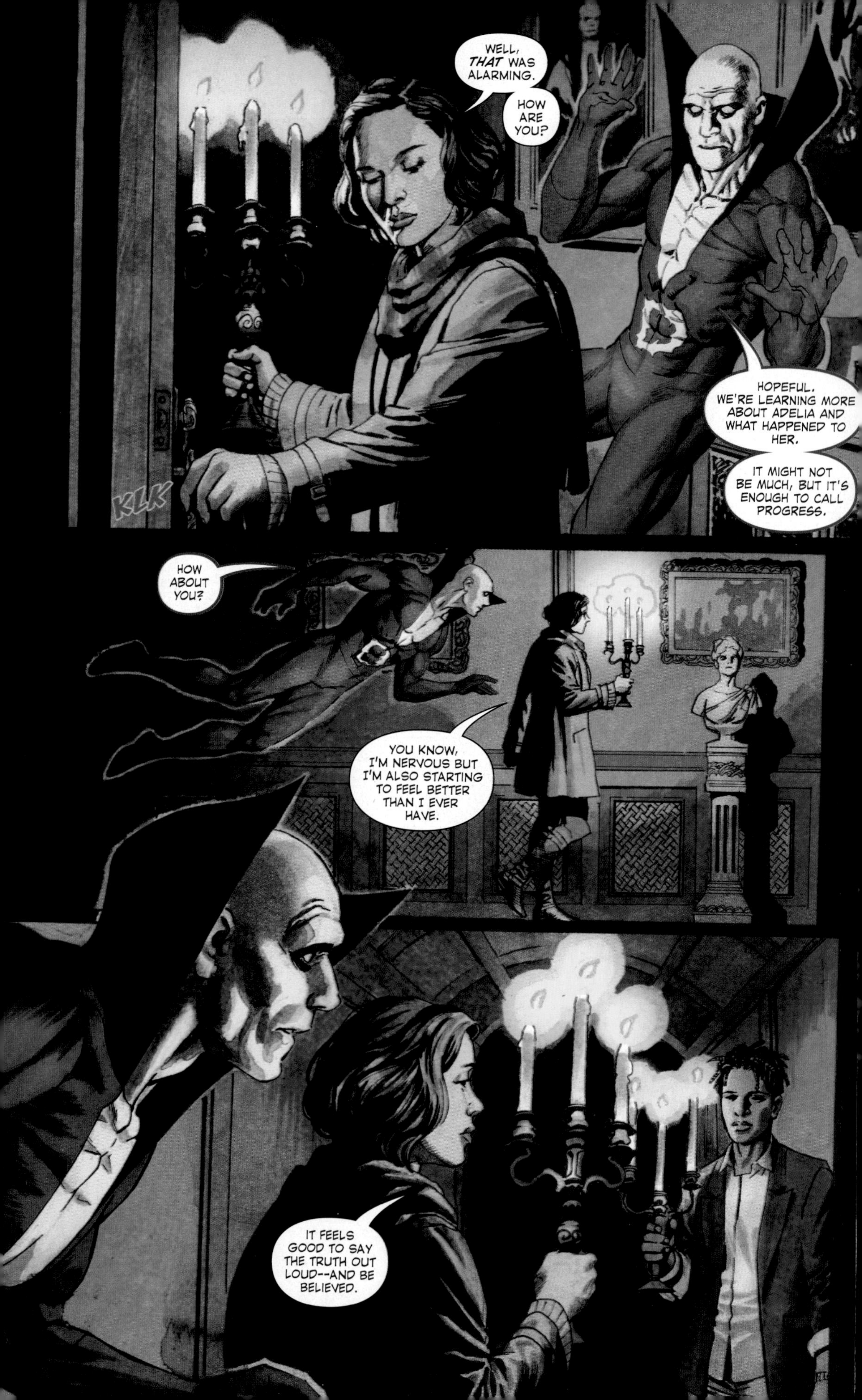
WELL, THAT WAS ALARMING.
HOW ARE YOU?
HOPEFUL. WE'RE LEARNING MORE ABOUT ADELIA AND WHAT HAPPENED TO HER.
IT MIGHT NOT BE MUCH, BUT IT'S ENOUGH TO CALL PROGRESS.
KLK
HOW ABOUT YOU?
YOU KNOW, I'M NERVOUS BUT I'M ALSO STARTING TO FEEL BETTER THAN I EVER HAVE.
IT FEELS GOOD TO SAY THE TRUTH OUT LOUD--AND BE BELIEVED.

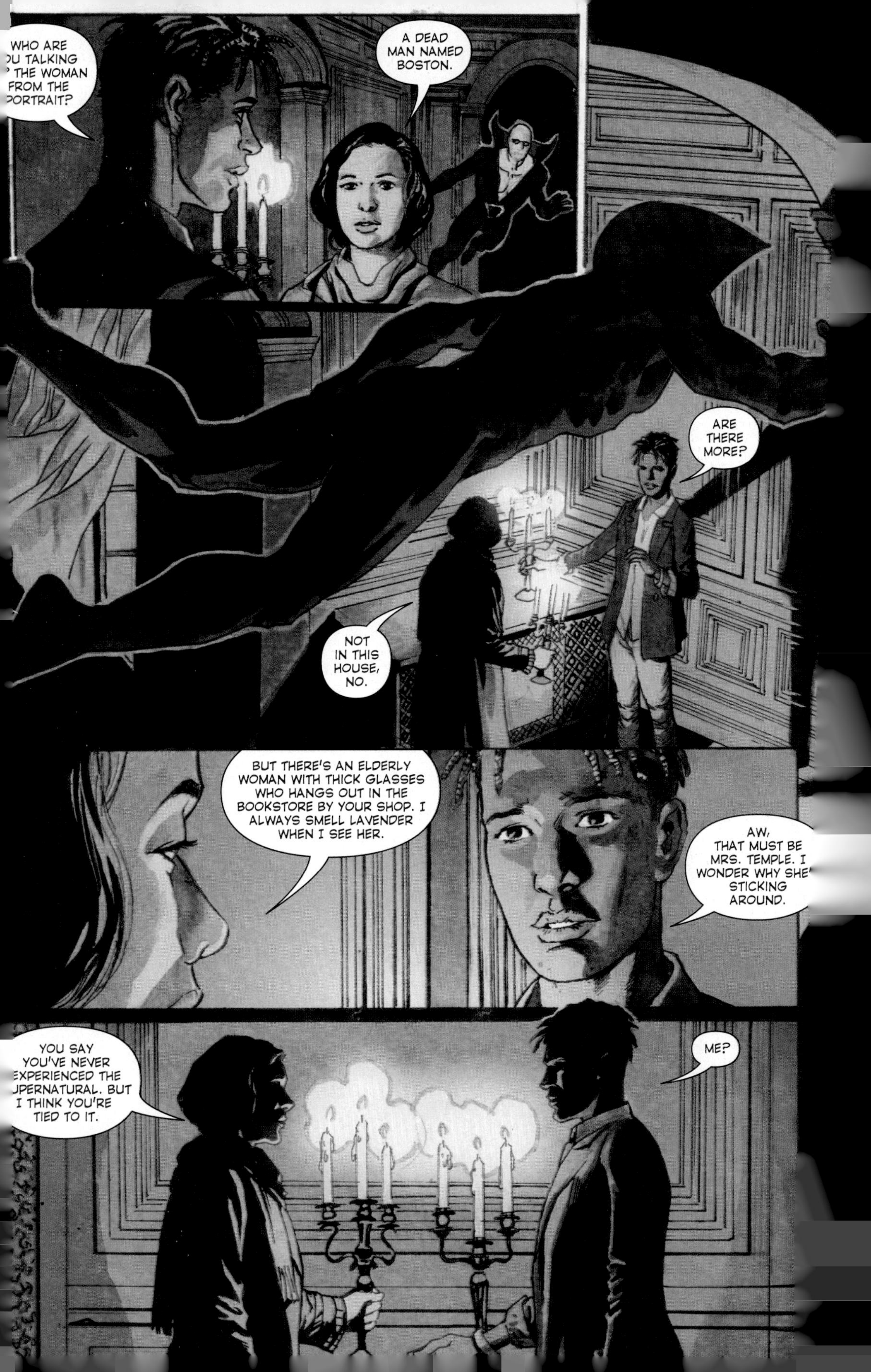
WHO ARE
OU TALKING
THE WOMAN
FROM THE
PORTRAIT?
A DEAD
MAN NAMED
BOSTON.
ARE
THERE
MORE?
NOT
IN THIS
HOUSE,
NO.
BUT THERE'S AN ELDERLY WOMAN WITH THICK GLASSES WHO HANGS OUT IN THE BOOKSTORE BY YOUR SHOP. I ALWAYS SMELL LAVENDER WHEN I SEE HER.
AW, THAT MUST BE MRS. TEMPLE. I WONDER WHY SHE' STICKING AROUND.
YOU SAY YOU'VE NEVER EXPERIENCED THE UPERNATURAL. BUT I THINK YOU'RE TIED TO IT.
ME?

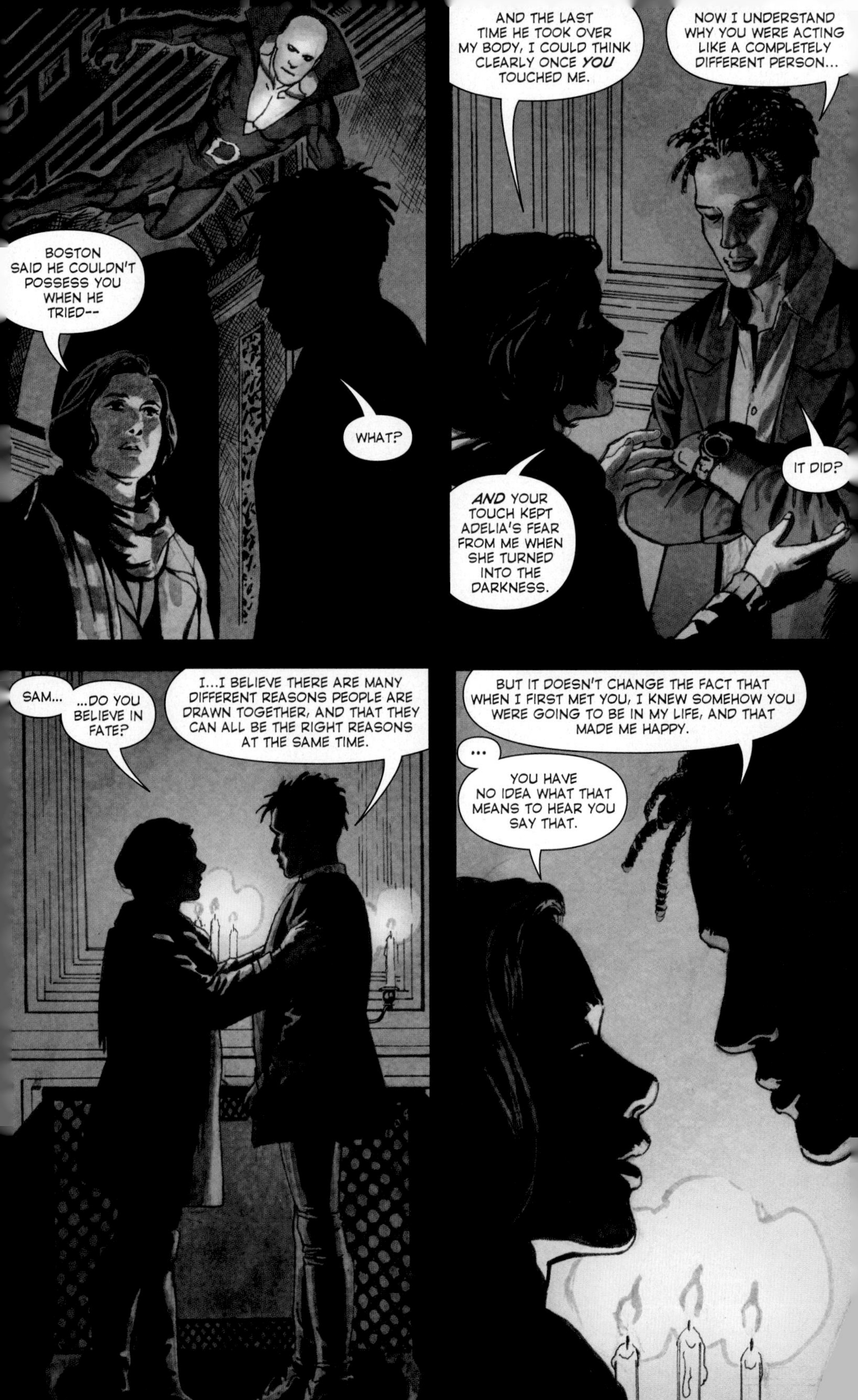
BOSTON SAID HE COULDN'T POSSESS YOU WHEN HE TRIED--
WHAT?
AND THE LAST TIME HE TOOK OVER MY BODY, I COULD THINK CLEARLY ONCE ***YOU*** TOUCHED ME.
NOW I UNDERSTAND WHY YOU WERE ACTING LIKE A COMPLETELY DIFFERENT PERSON...
AND YOUR TOUCH KEPT ADELIA'S FEAR FROM ME WHEN SHE TURNED INTO THE DARKNESS.
IT DID?
SAM...
...DO YOU BELIEVE IN FATE?
I...I BELIEVE THERE ARE MANY DIFFERENT REASONS PEOPLE ARE DRAWN TOGETHER, AND THAT THEY CAN ALL BE THE RIGHT REASONS AT THE SAME TIME.
BUT IT DOESN'T CHANGE THE FACT THAT WHEN I FIRST MET YOU, I KNEW SOMEHOW YOU WERE GOING TO BE IN MY LIFE, AND THAT MADE ME HAPPY.
...
YOU HAVE NO IDEA WHAT THAT MEANS TO HEAR YOU SAY THAT.

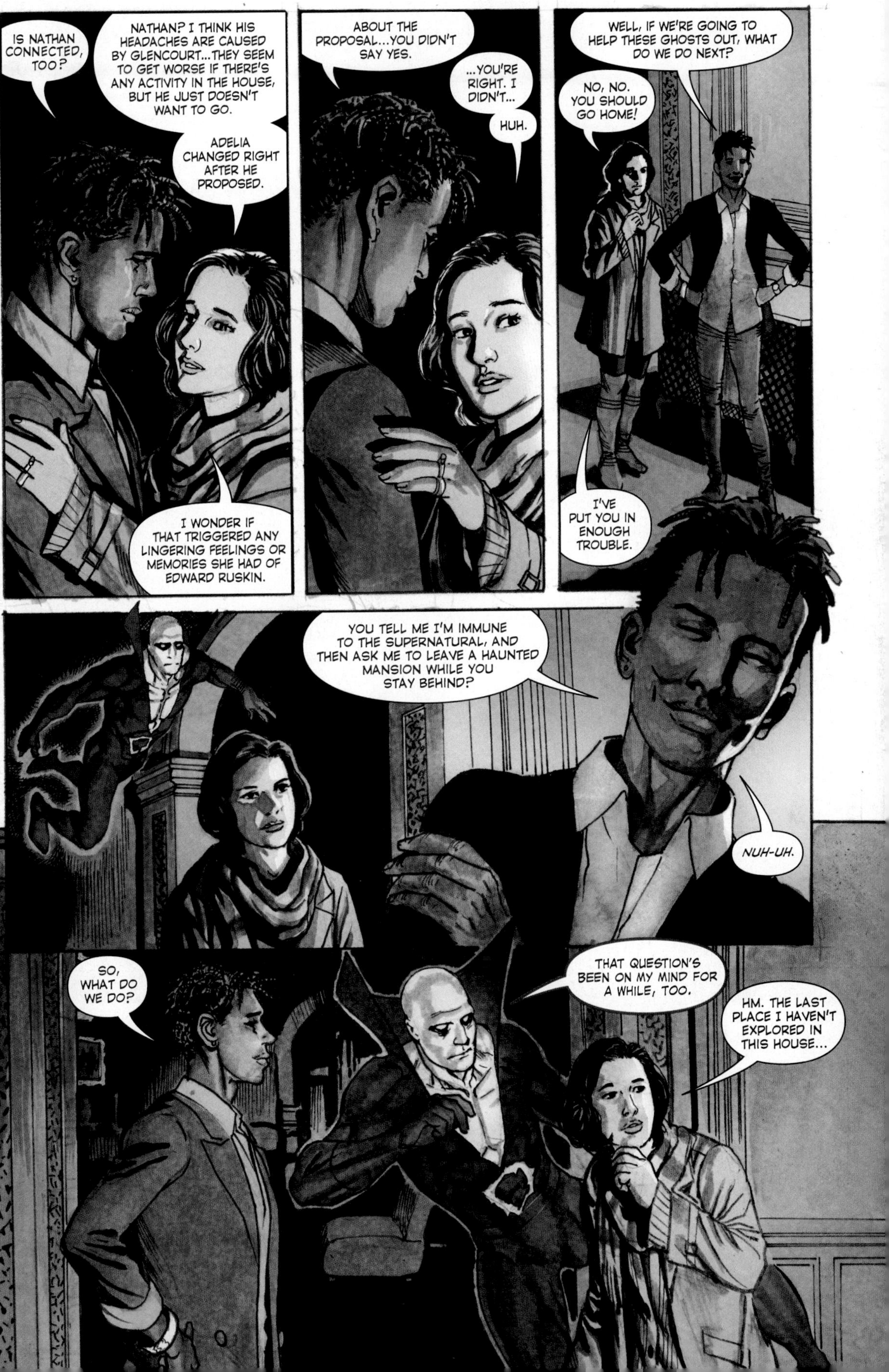
IS NATHAN CONNECTED, TOO?
NATHAN? I THINK HIS HEADACHES ARE CAUSED BY GLENCOURT...THEY SEEM TO GET WORSE IF THERE'S ANY ACTIVITY IN THE HOUSE, BUT HE JUST DOESN'T WANT TO GO.
ADELIA CHANGED RIGHT AFTER HE PROPOSED.
I WONDER IF THAT TRIGGERED ANY LINGERING FEELINGS OR MEMORIES SHE HAD OF EDWARD RUSKIN.
ABOUT THE PROPOSAL...YOU DIDN'T SAY YES.
...YOU'RE RIGHT. I DIDN'T...
HUH.
WELL, IF WE'RE GOING TO HELP THESE GHOSTS OUT, WHAT DO WE DO NEXT?
NO, NO. YOU SHOULD GO HOME!
I'VE PUT YOU IN ENOUGH TROUBLE.
YOU TELL ME I'M IMMUNE TO THE SUPERNATURAL, AND THEN ASK ME TO LEAVE A HAUNTED MANSION WHILE YOU STAY BEHIND?
NUH-UH.
SO, WHAT DO WE DO?
THAT QUESTION'S BEEN ON MY MIND FOR A WHILE, TOO.
HM. THE LAST PLACE I HAVEN'T EXPLORED IN THIS HOUSE...

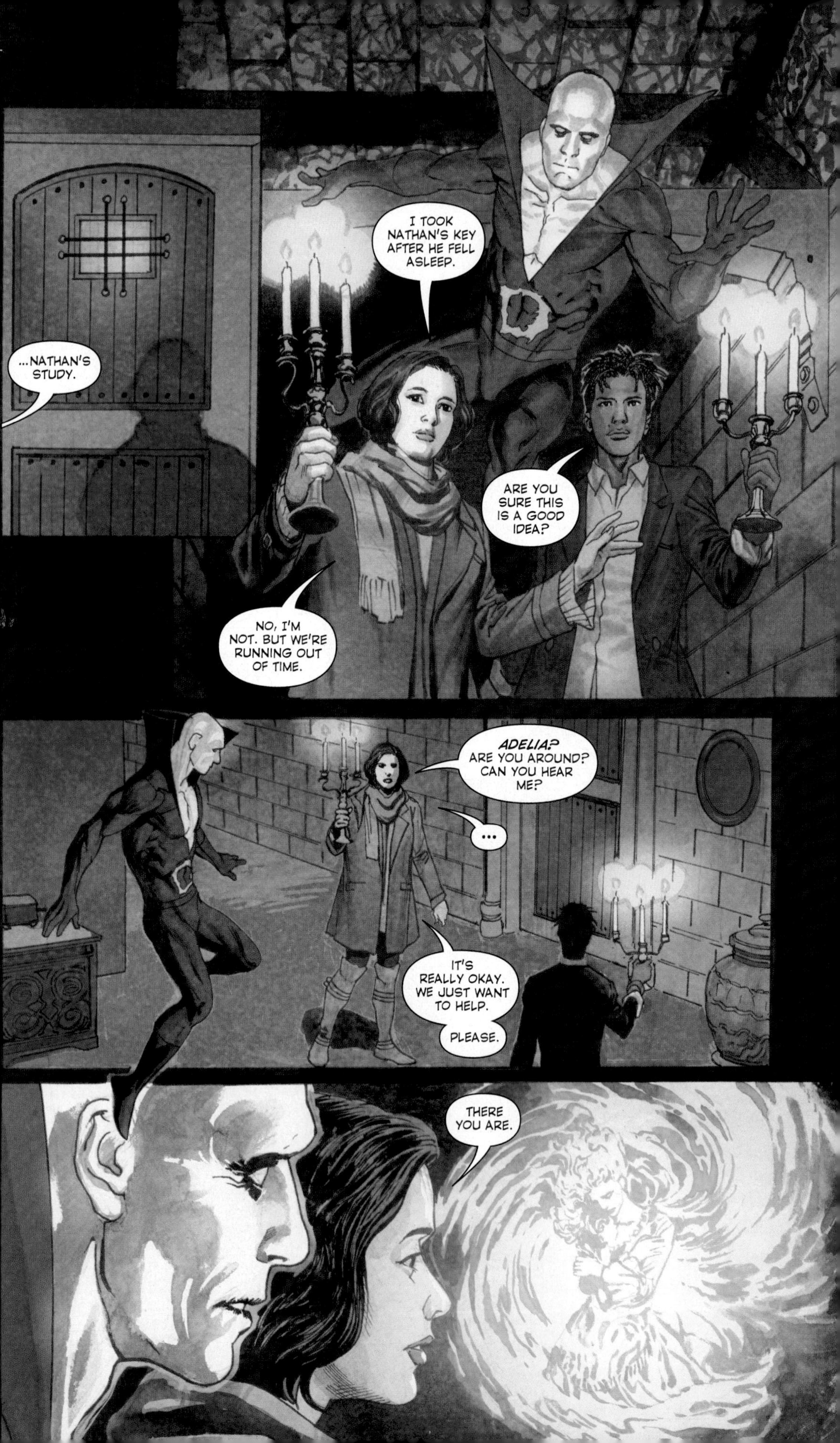
...NATHAN'S STUDY.
I TOOK NATHAN'S KEY AFTER HE FELL ASLEEP.
ARE YOU SURE THIS IS A GOOD IDEA?
NO, I'M NOT. BUT WE'RE RUNNING OUT OF TIME.
ADELIA? ARE YOU AROUND? CAN YOU HEAR ME?
...
IT'S REALLY OKAY. WE JUST WANT TO HELP.
PLEASE.
THERE YOU ARE.

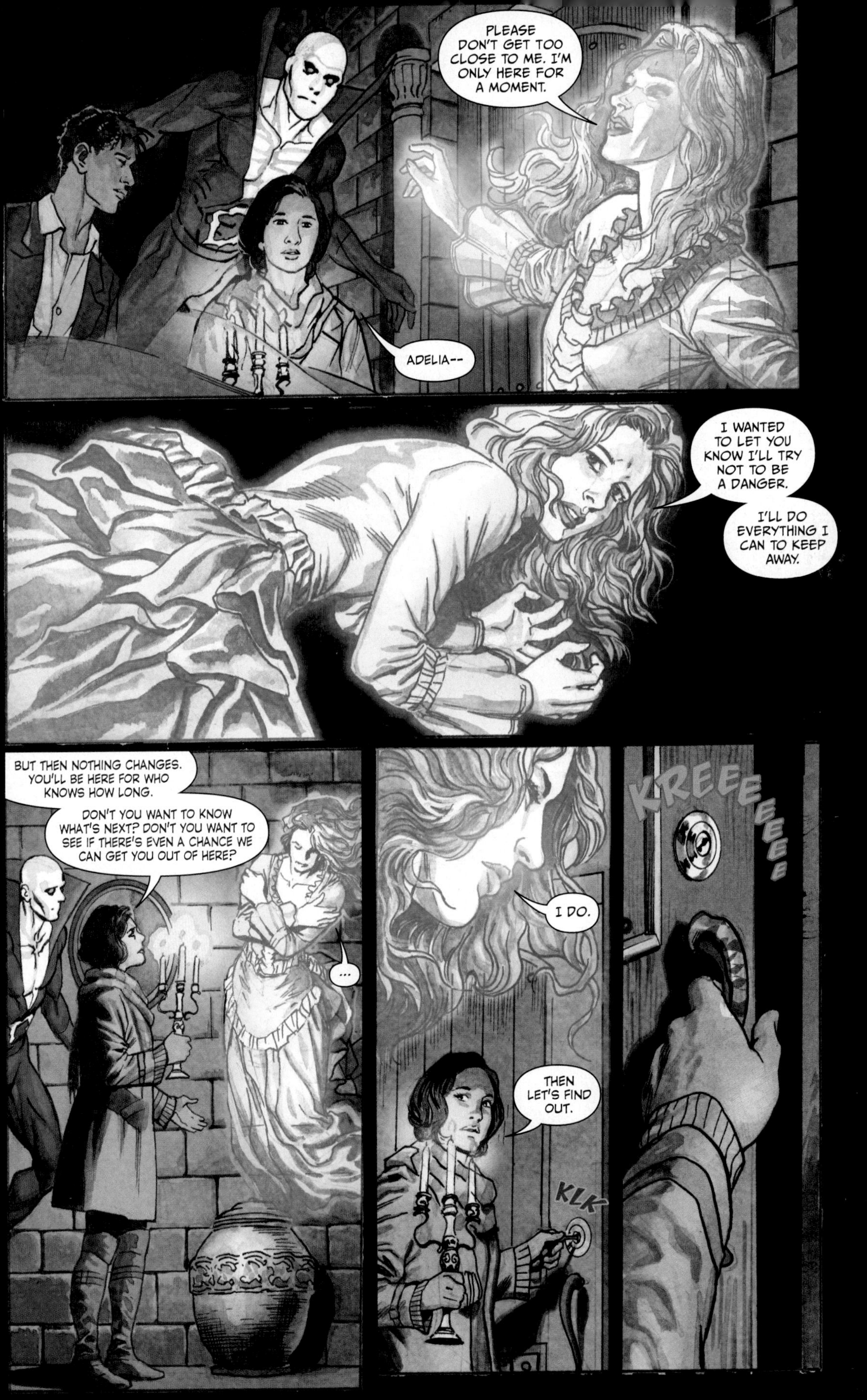

PLEASE DON'T GET TOO CLOSE TO ME. I'M ONLY HERE FOR A MOMENT.
ADELIA--
I WANTED TO LET YOU KNOW I'LL TRY NOT TO BE A DANGER.
I'LL DO EVERYTHING I CAN TO KEEP AWAY.
BUT THEN NOTHING CHANGES. YOU'LL BE HERE FOR WHO KNOWS HOW LONG.
DON'T YOU WANT TO KNOW WHAT'S NEXT? DON'T YOU WANT TO SEE IF THERE'S EVEN A CHANCE WE CAN GET YOU OUT OF HERE?
...
I DO.
THEN LET'S FIND OUT.
KLK
KREEEEEEEE

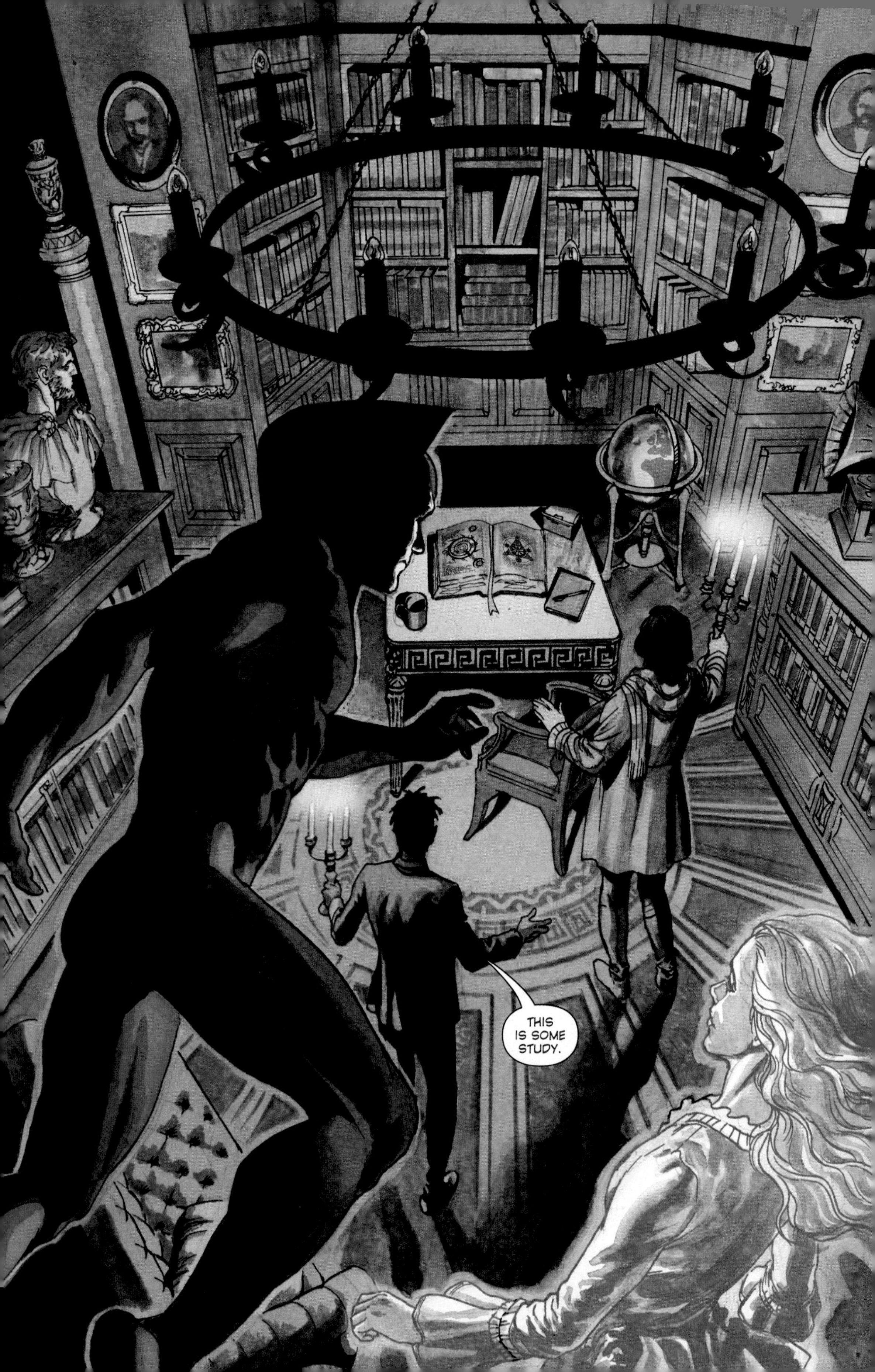
THIS IS SOME STUDY.

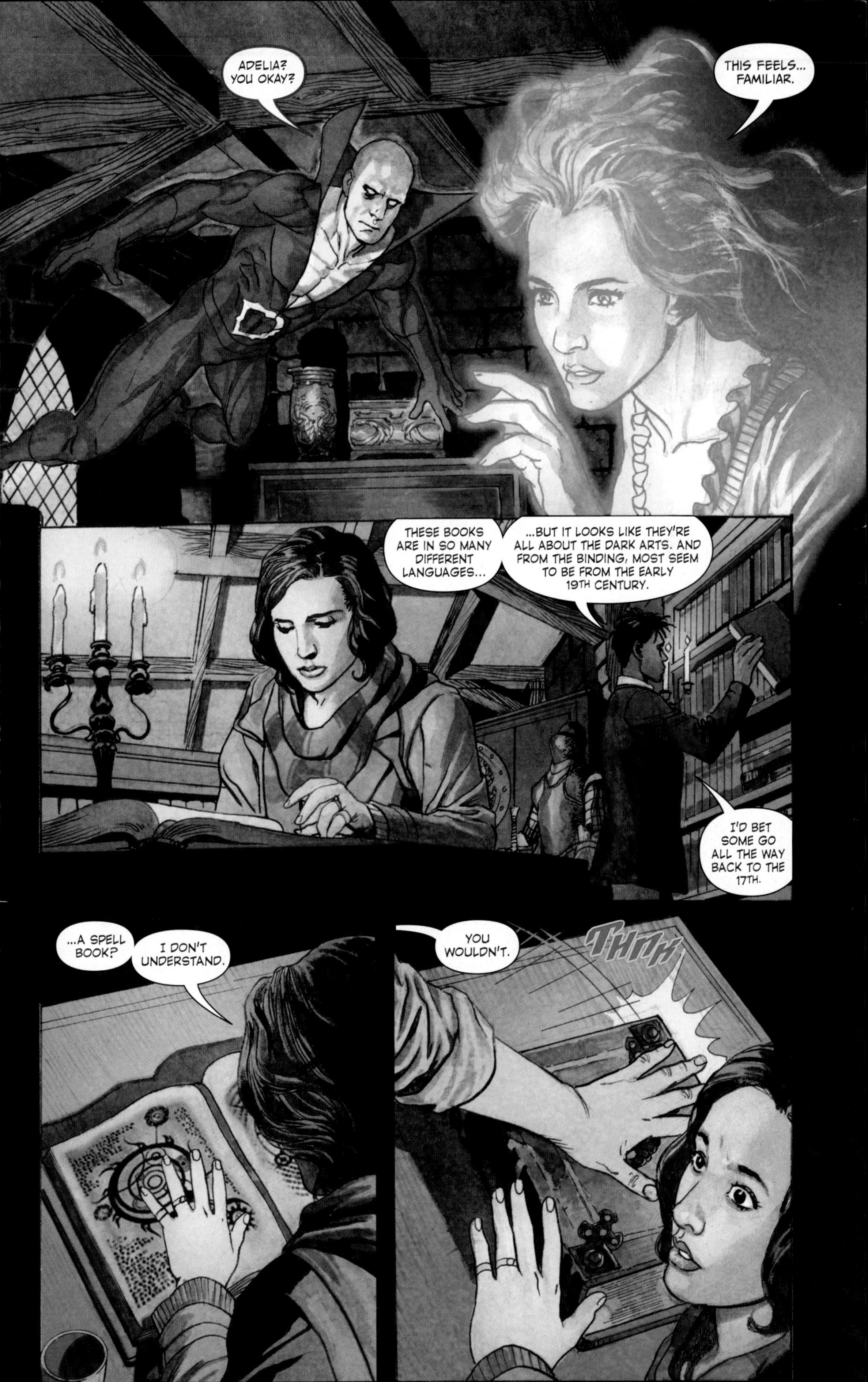
ADELIA? YOU OKAY?
THIS FEELS... FAMILIAR.
THESE BOOKS ARE IN SO MANY DIFFERENT LANGUAGES...
...BUT IT LOOKS LIKE THEY'RE ALL ABOUT THE DARK ARTS. AND FROM THE BINDING, MOST SEEM TO BE FROM THE EARLY 19TH CENTURY.
I'D BET SOME GO ALL THE WAY BACK TO THE 17TH.
...A SPELL BOOK?
I DON'T UNDERSTAND.
YOU WOULDN'T.
THNK

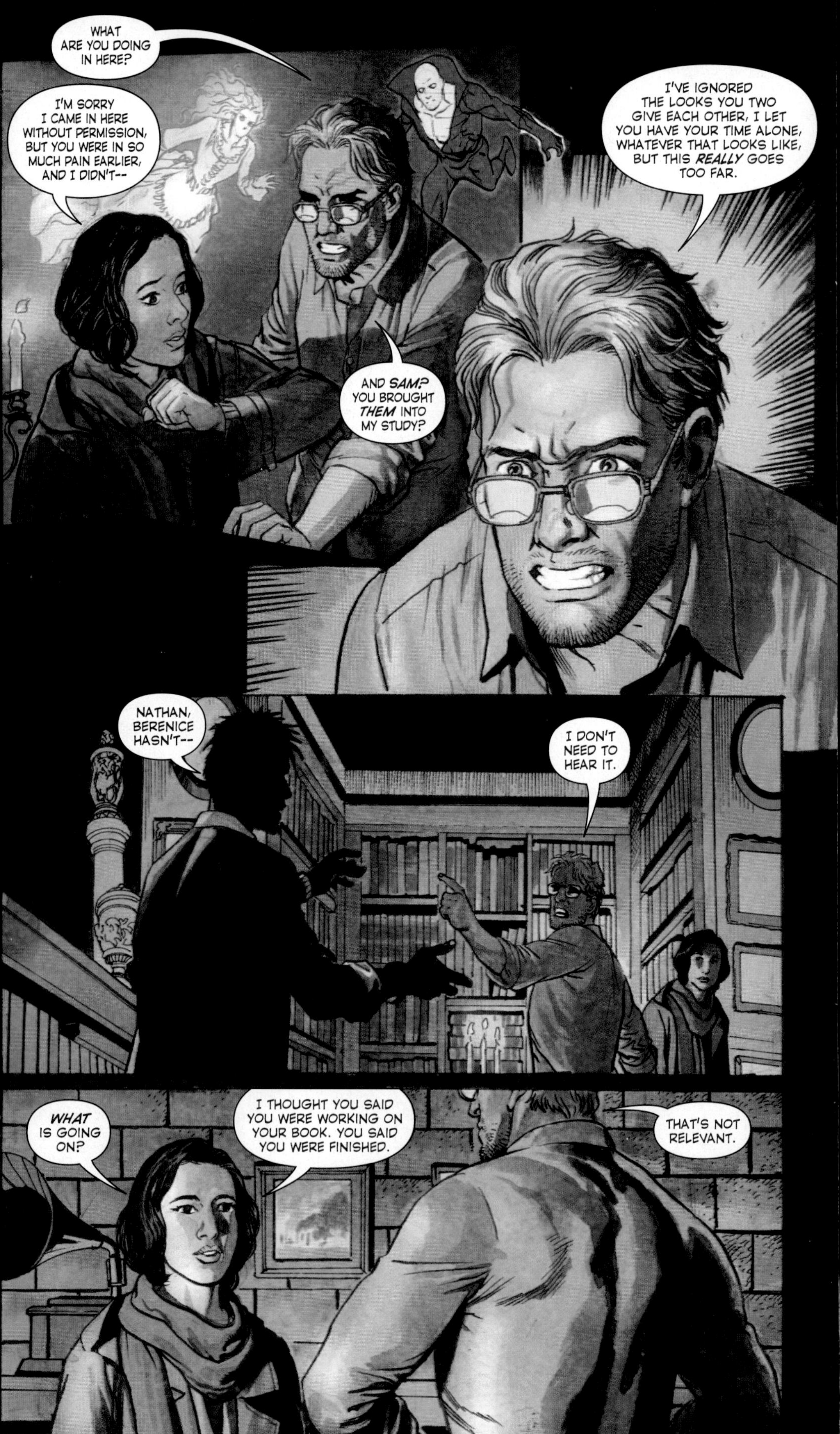
WHAT ARE YOU DOING IN HERE?
I'M SORRY I CAME IN HERE WITHOUT PERMISSION, BUT YOU WERE IN SO MUCH PAIN EARLIER, AND I DIDN'T--
AND SAM? YOU BROUGHT THEM INTO MY STUDY?
I'VE IGNORED THE LOOKS YOU TWO GIVE EACH OTHER, I LET YOU HAVE YOUR TIME ALONE, WHATEVER THAT LOOKS LIKE, BUT THIS REALLY GOES TOO FAR.
NATHAN, BERENICE HASN'T--
I DON'T NEED TO HEAR IT.
WHAT IS GOING ON?
I THOUGHT YOU SAID YOU WERE WORKING ON YOUR BOOK. YOU SAID YOU WERE FINISHED.
THAT'S NOT RELEVANT.

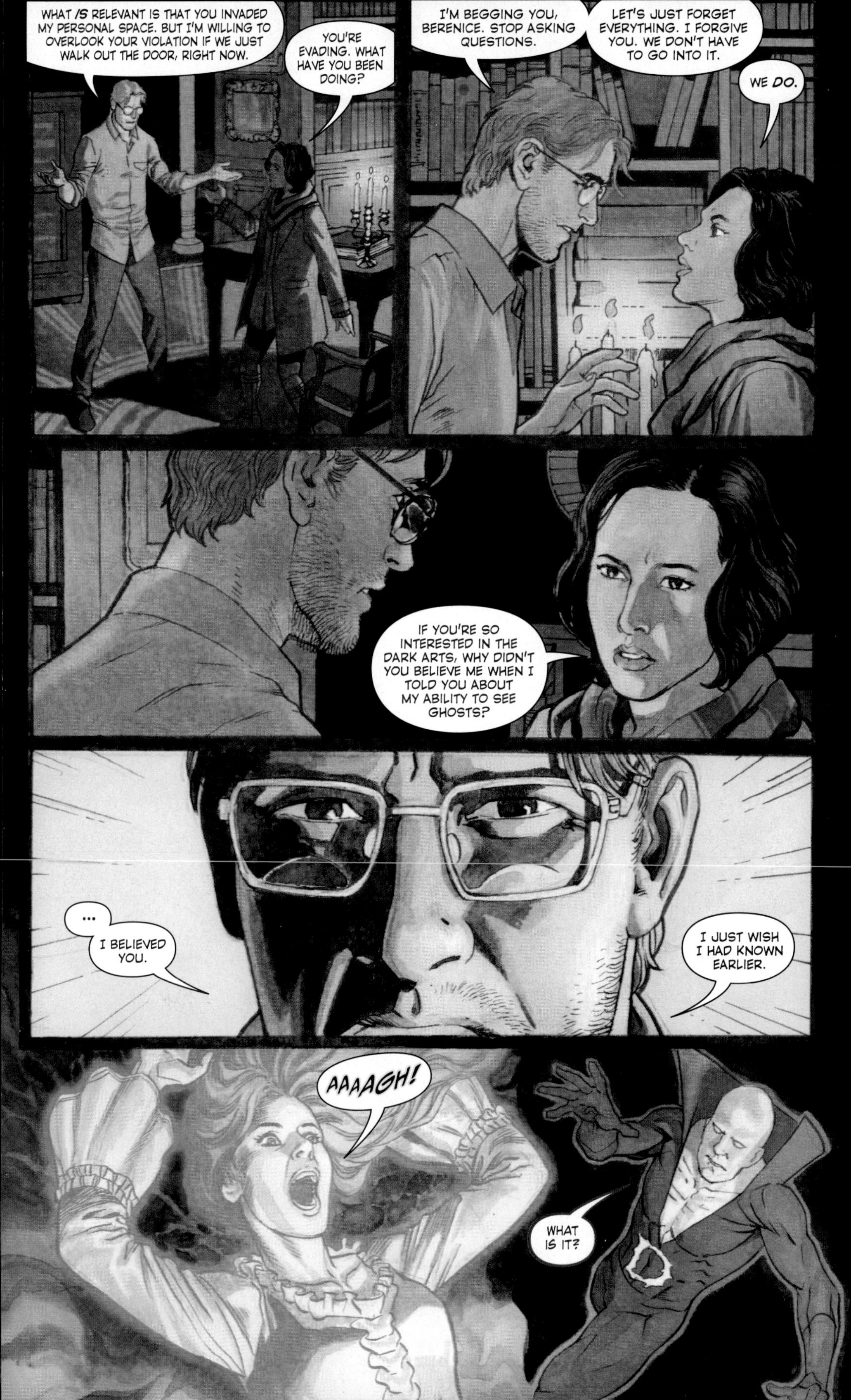
WHAT *IS* RELEVANT IS THAT YOU INVADED MY PERSONAL SPACE. BUT I'M WILLING TO OVERLOOK YOUR VIOLATION IF WE JUST WALK OUT THE DOOR, RIGHT NOW.
YOU'RE EVADING. WHAT HAVE YOU BEEN DOING?
I'M BEGGING YOU, BERENICE. STOP ASKING QUESTIONS.
LET'S JUST FORGET EVERYTHING. I FORGIVE YOU. WE DON'T HAVE TO GO INTO IT.
WE *DO*.
IF YOU'RE SO INTERESTED IN THE DARK ARTS, WHY DIDN'T YOU BELIEVE ME WHEN I TOLD YOU ABOUT MY ABILITY TO SEE GHOSTS?
... I BELIEVED YOU.
I JUST WISH I HAD KNOWN EARLIER.
AAAAGH!
WHAT IS IT?

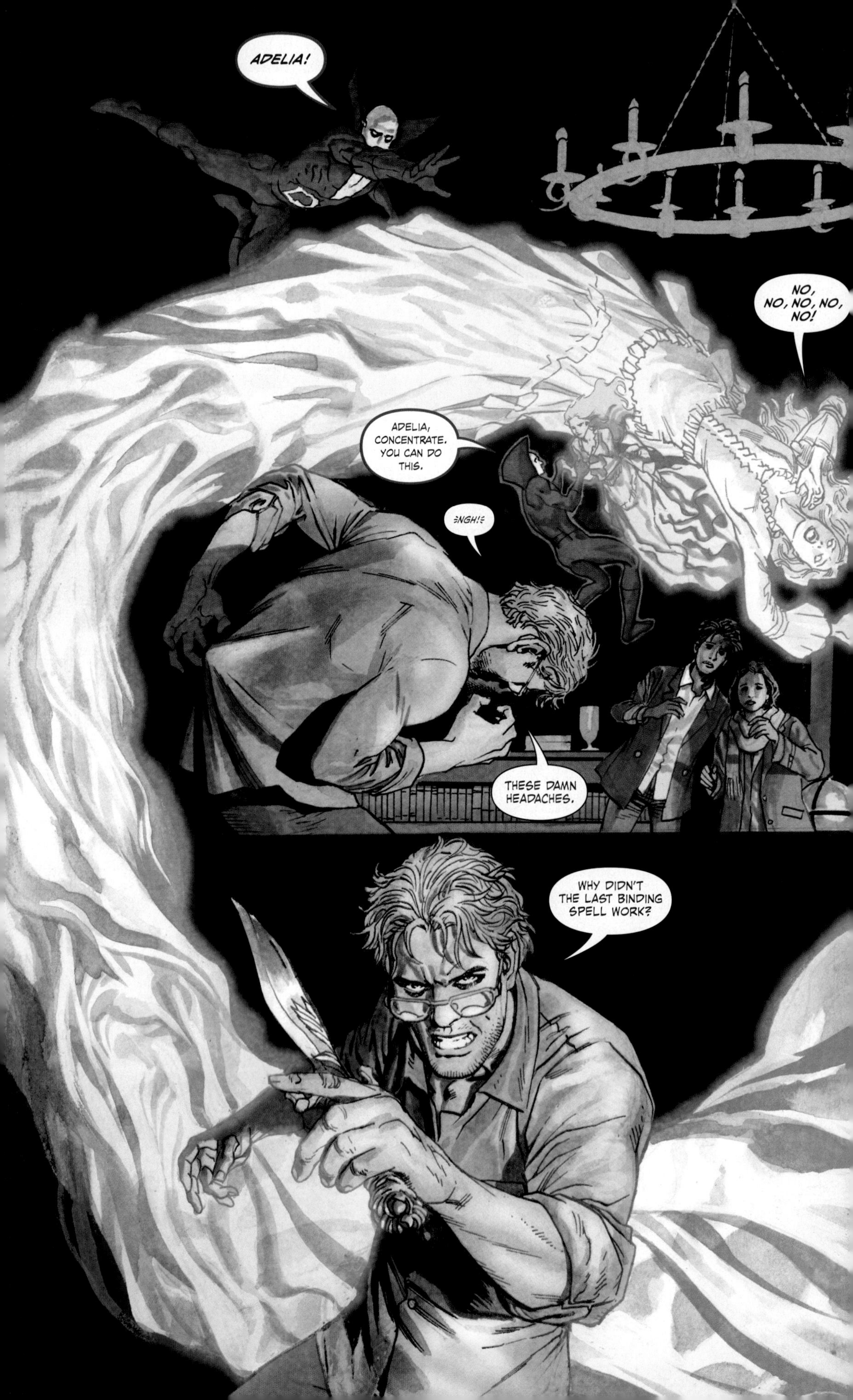
ADELIA!
NO, NO, NO, NO, NO!
ADELIA, CONCENTRATE. YOU CAN DO THIS.
ENGH!
THESE DAMN HEADACHES.
WHY DIDN'T THE LAST BINDING SPELL WORK?

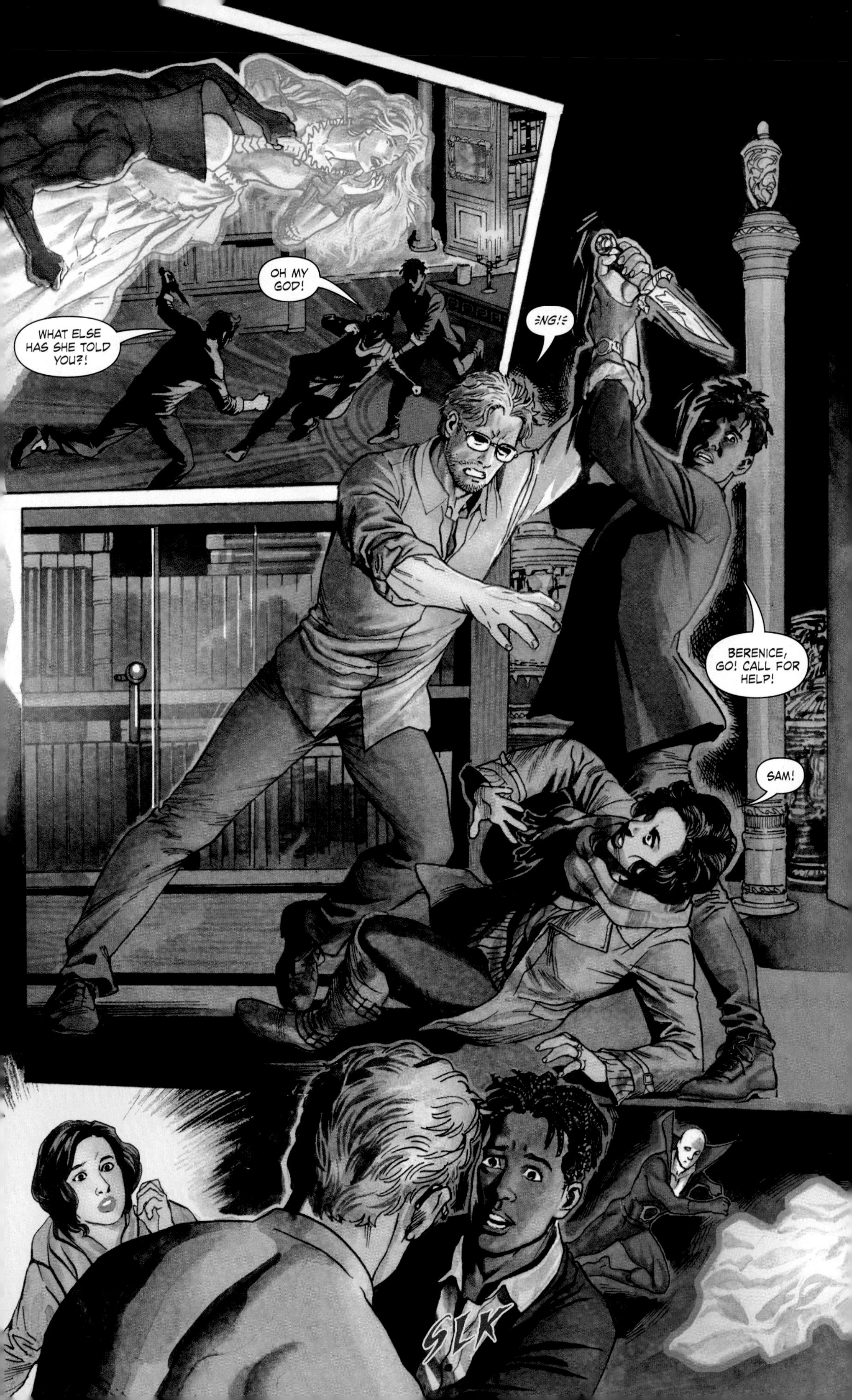
OH MY GOD!
WHAT ELSE HAS SHE TOLD YOU?!
NG!
BERENICE, GO! CALL FOR HELP!
SAM!
SLK

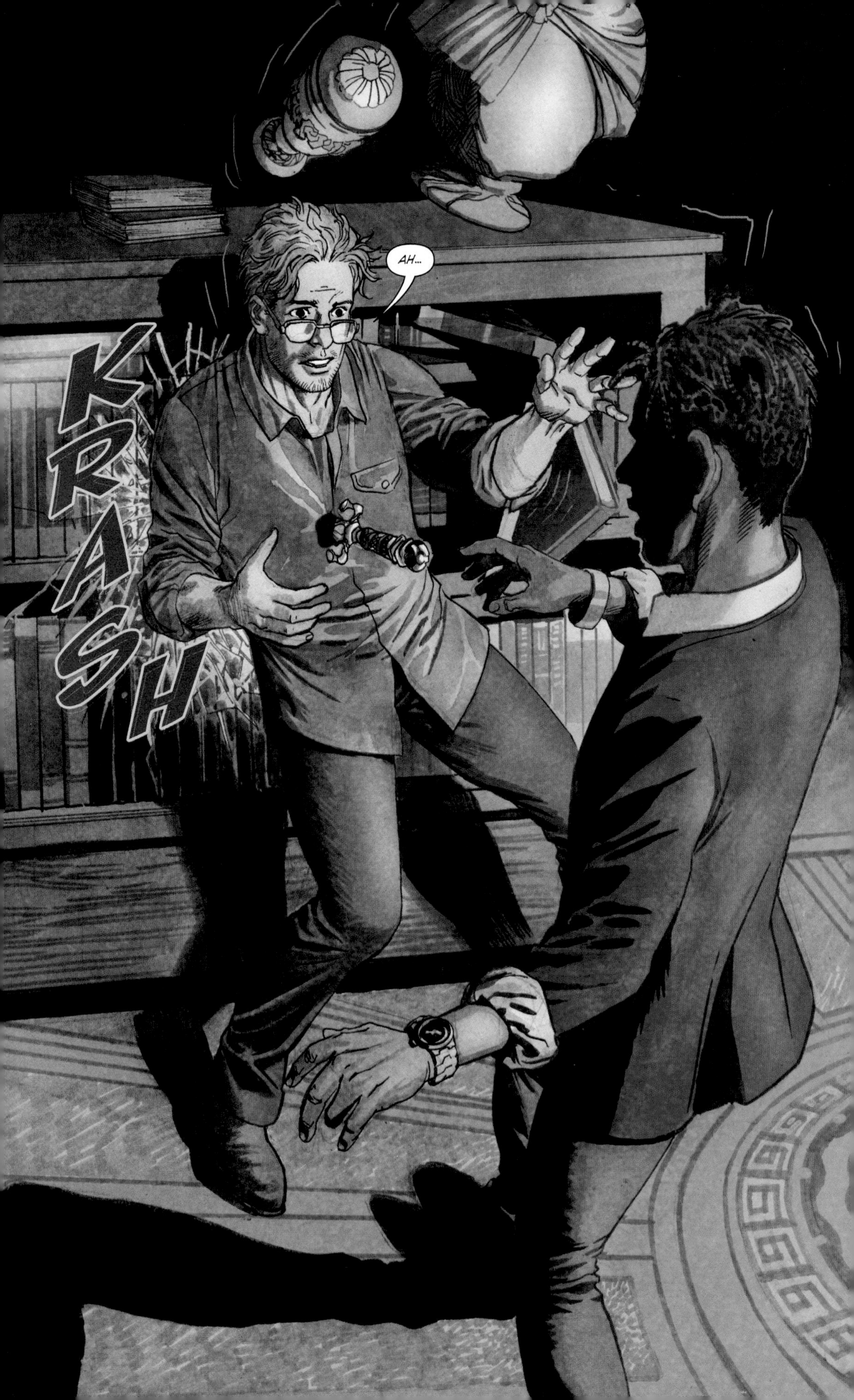
KRASH
AH...

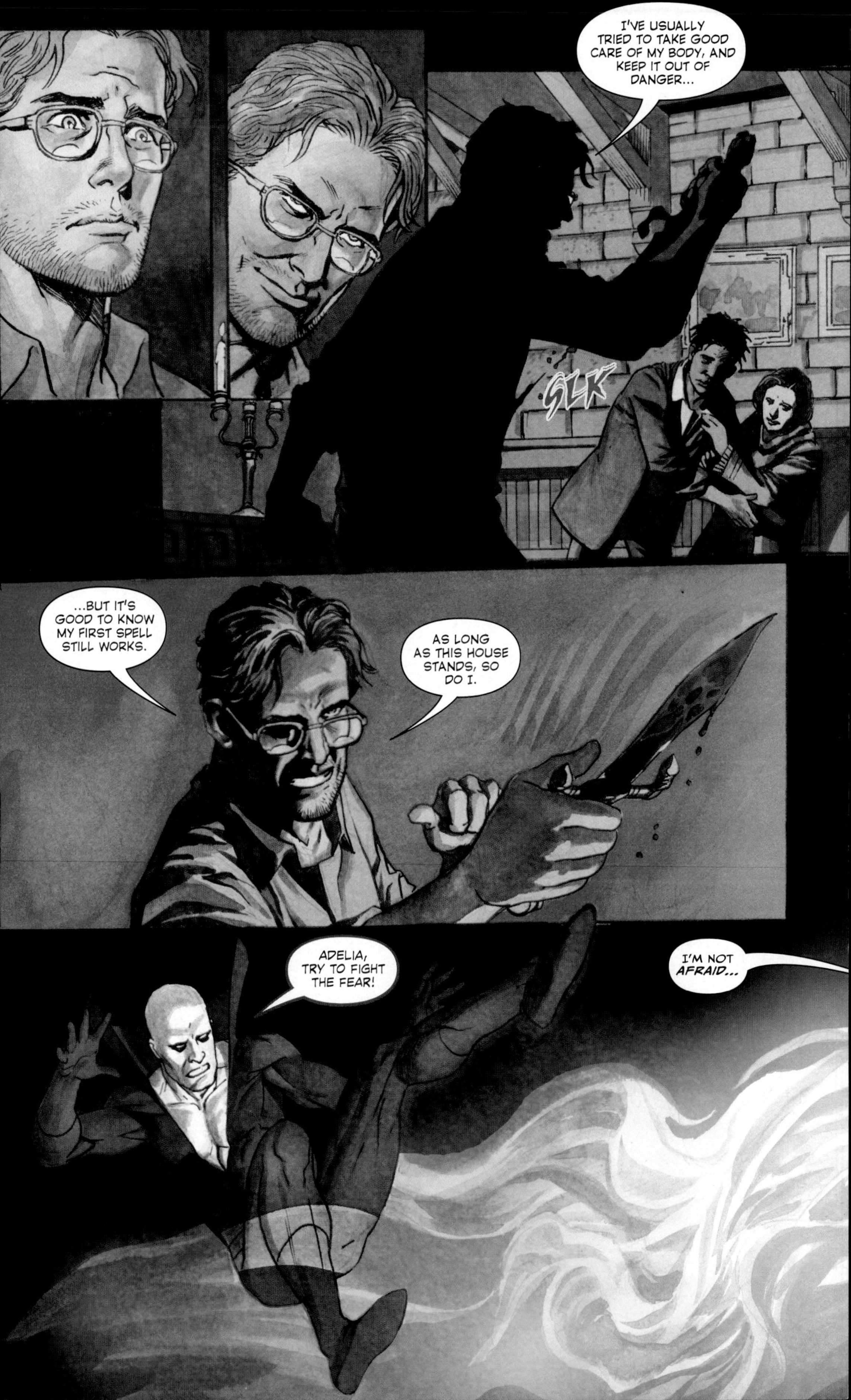
I'VE USUALLY TRIED TO TAKE GOOD CARE OF MY BODY, AND KEEP IT OUT OF DANGER...
SLK
...BUT IT'S GOOD TO KNOW MY FIRST SPELL STILL WORKS.
AS LONG AS THIS HOUSE STANDS, SO DO I.
ADELIA, TRY TO FIGHT THE FEAR!
I'M NOT AFRAID...

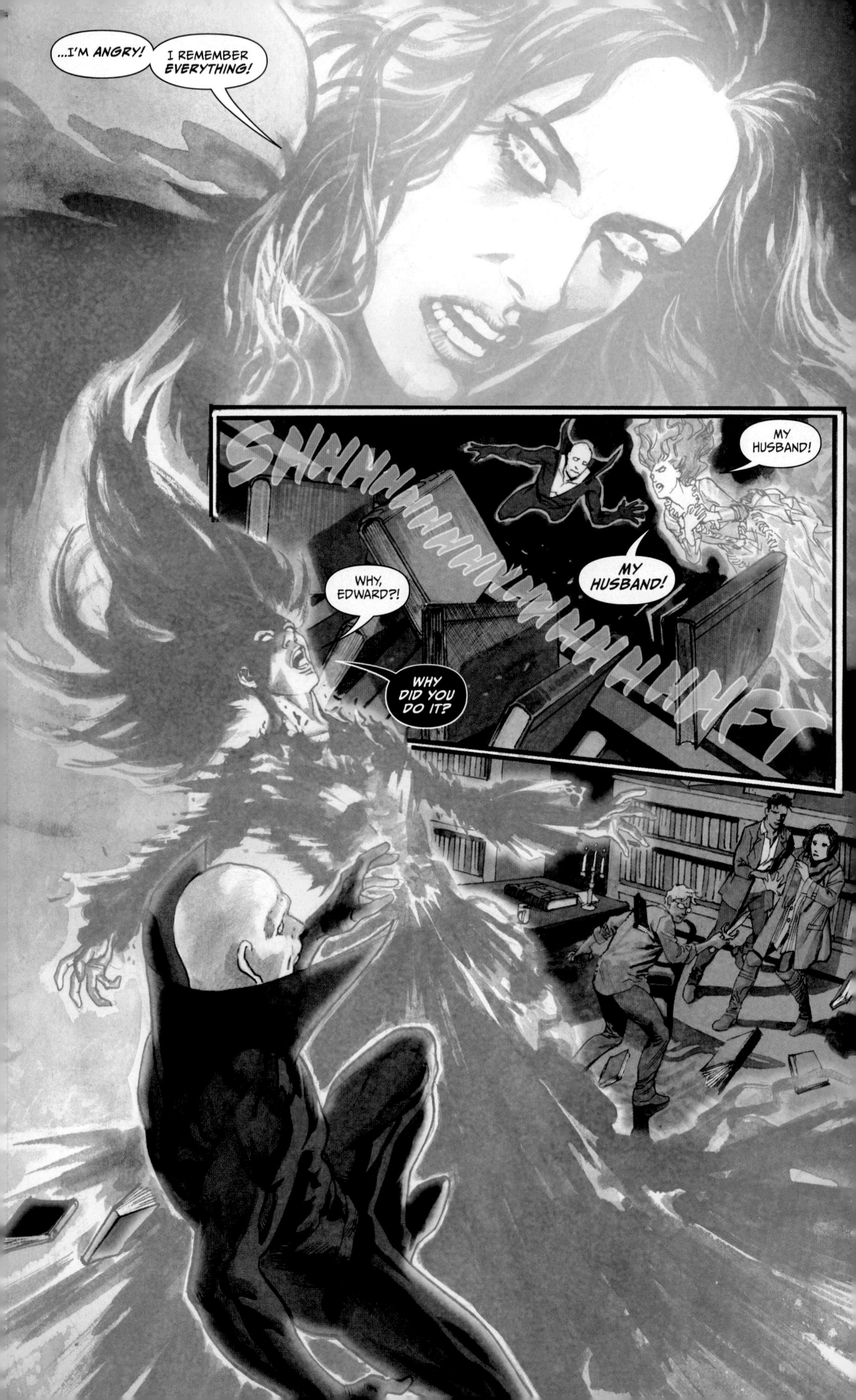
...I'M ANGRY!
I REMEMBER EVERYTHING!
SHHHHHHHHHHHHHHHHHHHHHHFT
MY HUSBAND!
MY HUSBAND!
WHY, EDWARD?!
WHY DID YOU DO IT?

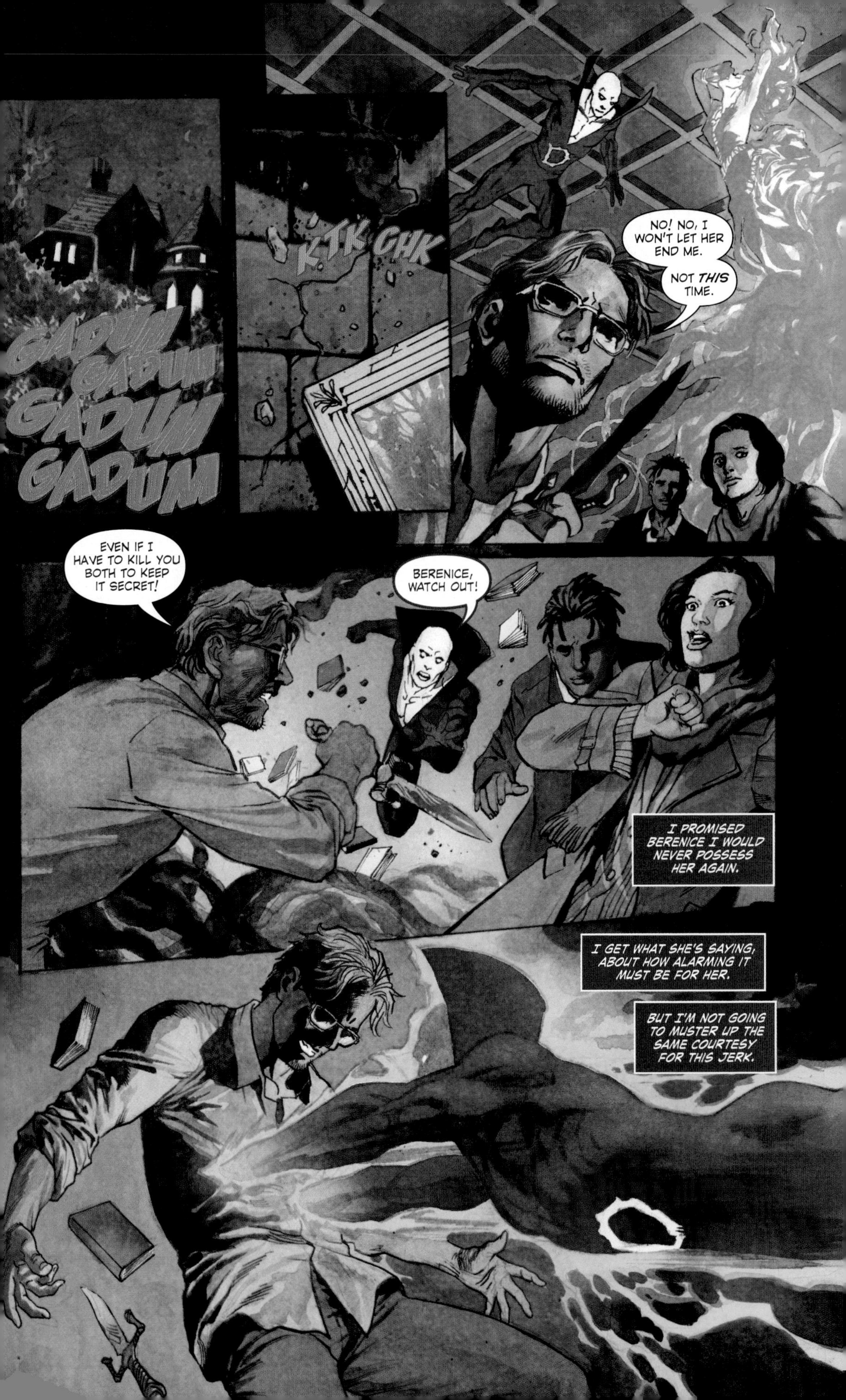

GADUM GADUM GADUM GADUM
KTK CHK
NO! NO, I WON'T LET HER END ME.
NOT THIS TIME.
EVEN IF I HAVE TO KILL YOU BOTH TO KEEP IT SECRET!
BERENICE, WATCH OUT!
I PROMISED BERENICE I WOULD NEVER POSSESS HER AGAIN.
I GET WHAT SHE'S SAYING, ABOUT HOW ALARMING IT MUST BE FOR HER.
BUT I'M NOT GOING TO MUSTER UP THE SAME COURTESY FOR THIS JERK.

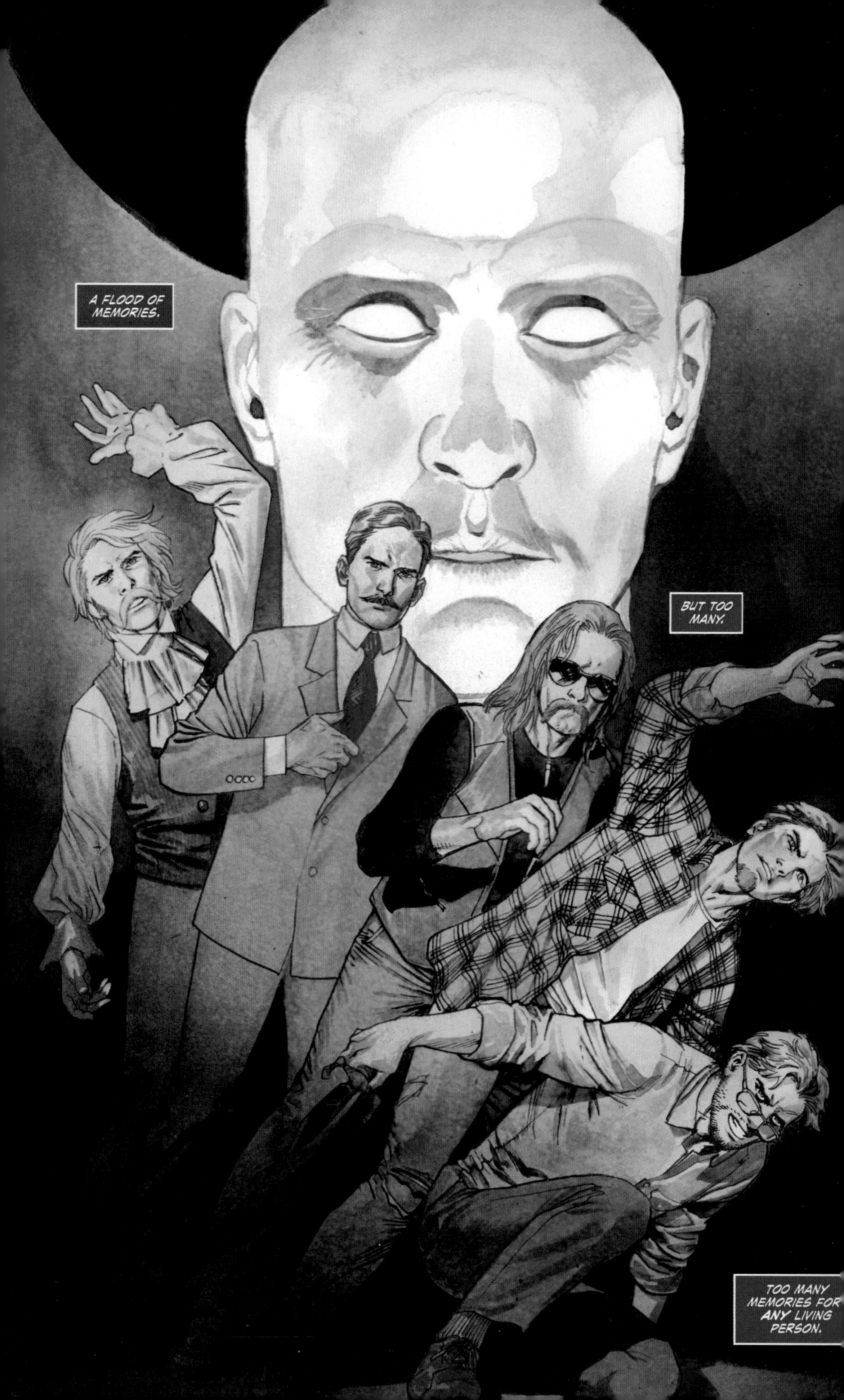
A FLOOD OF MEMORIES.
BUT TOO MANY.
TOO MANY MEMORIES FOR ANY LIVING PERSON.

EDWARD RUSKIN SPENT HIS WHOLE LIFE FEARING DEATH.

AND AFTER YEARS OF SEARCHING FOR THE ANSWER, HE FOUND IT.

HE NEEDED TO KILL TO STAY ALIVE INDEFINITELY.

SO HE CHOSE HIS OWN WIFE AS HIS VICTIM.

EDWARD!

NO! PLEASE!

VAS A TUL BEMIT IORS THASH YESSIT MORDUSTEN VAS HAL HEMTIMEG

HE MURDERED HER IN THE HOUSE HE HAD BUILT TO BEGIN HIS NEW AND ETERNAL LIFE.

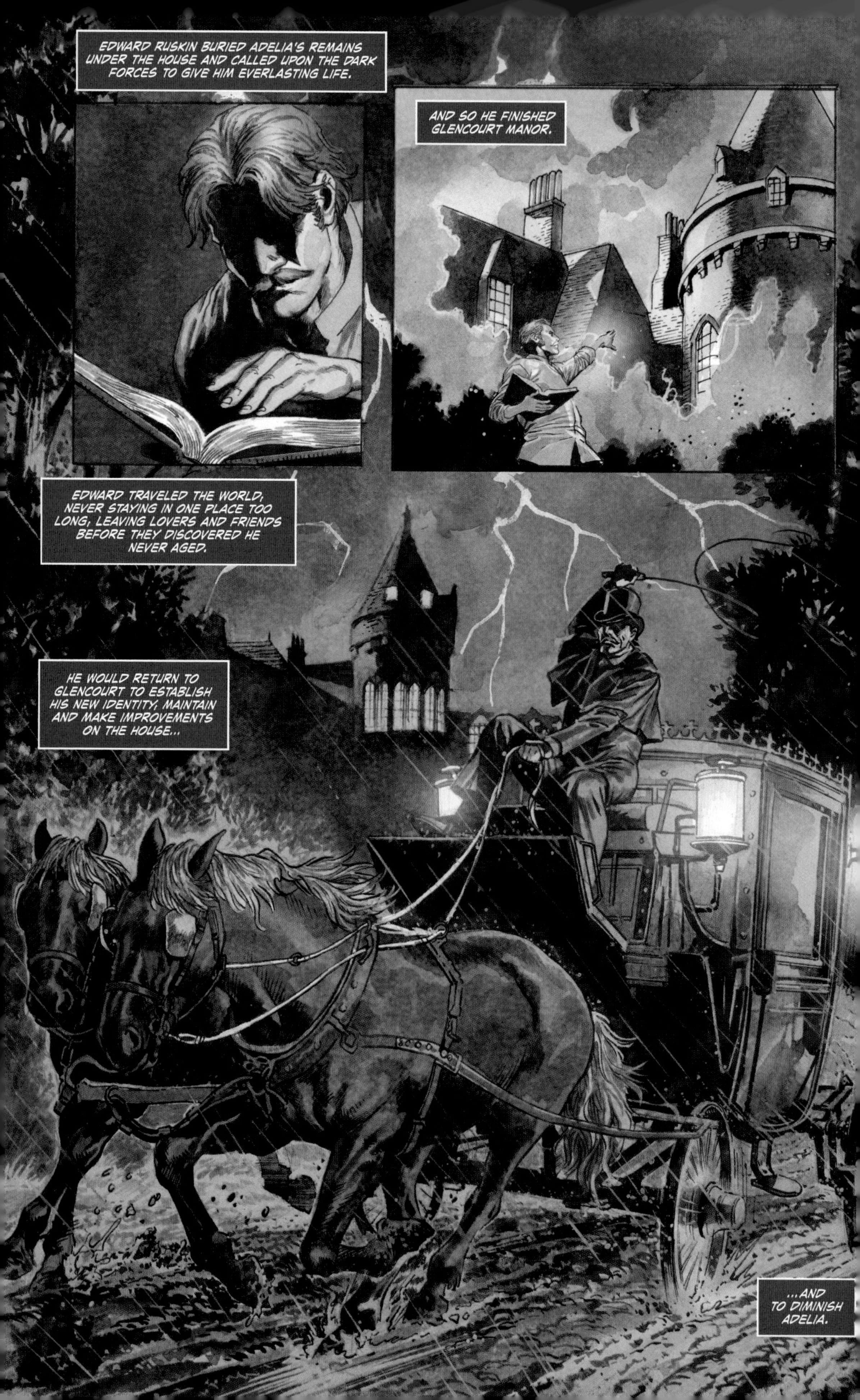
EDWARD RUSKIN BURIED ADELIA'S REMAINS UNDER THE HOUSE AND CALLED UPON THE DARK FORCES TO GIVE HIM EVERLASTING LIFE.
AND SO HE FINISHED GLENCOURT MANOR.
EDWARD TRAVELED THE WORLD, NEVER STAYING IN ONE PLACE TOO LONG, LEAVING LOVERS AND FRIENDS BEFORE THEY DISCOVERED HE NEVER AGED.
HE WOULD RETURN TO GLENCOURT TO ESTABLISH HIS NEW IDENTITY, MAINTAIN AND MAKE IMPROVEMENTS ON THE HOUSE...
...AND TO DIMINISH ADELIA.

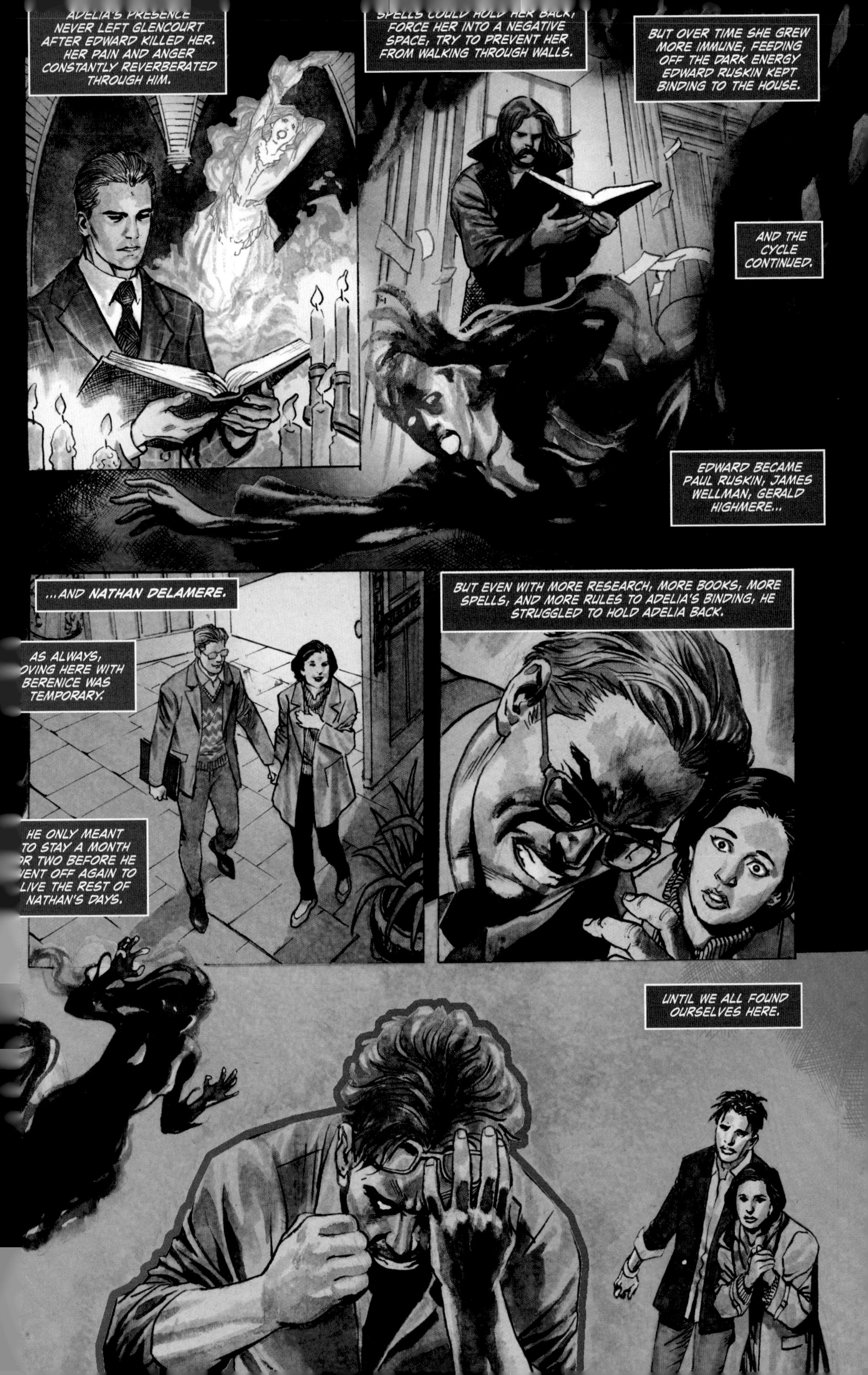
ADELIA'S PRESENCE NEVER LEFT GLENCOURT AFTER EDWARD KILLED HER. HER PAIN AND ANGER CONSTANTLY REVERBERATED THROUGH HIM.
SPELLS COULD HOLD HER BACK, FORCE HER INTO A NEGATIVE SPACE, TRY TO PREVENT HER FROM WALKING THROUGH WALLS.
BUT OVER TIME SHE GREW MORE IMMUNE, FEEDING OFF THE DARK ENERGY EDWARD RUSKIN KEPT BINDING TO THE HOUSE.
AND THE CYCLE CONTINUED.
EDWARD BECAME PAUL RUSKIN, JAMES WELLMAN, GERALD HIGHMERE...
...AND NATHAN DELAMERE.
AS ALWAYS, MOVING HERE WITH BERENICE WAS TEMPORARY.
HE ONLY MEANT TO STAY A MONTH OR TWO BEFORE HE WENT OFF AGAIN TO LIVE THE REST OF NATHAN'S DAYS.
BUT EVEN WITH MORE RESEARCH, MORE BOOKS, MORE SPELLS, AND MORE RULES TO ADELIA'S BINDING, HE STRUGGLED TO HOLD ADELIA BACK.
UNTIL WE ALL FOUND OURSELVES HERE.

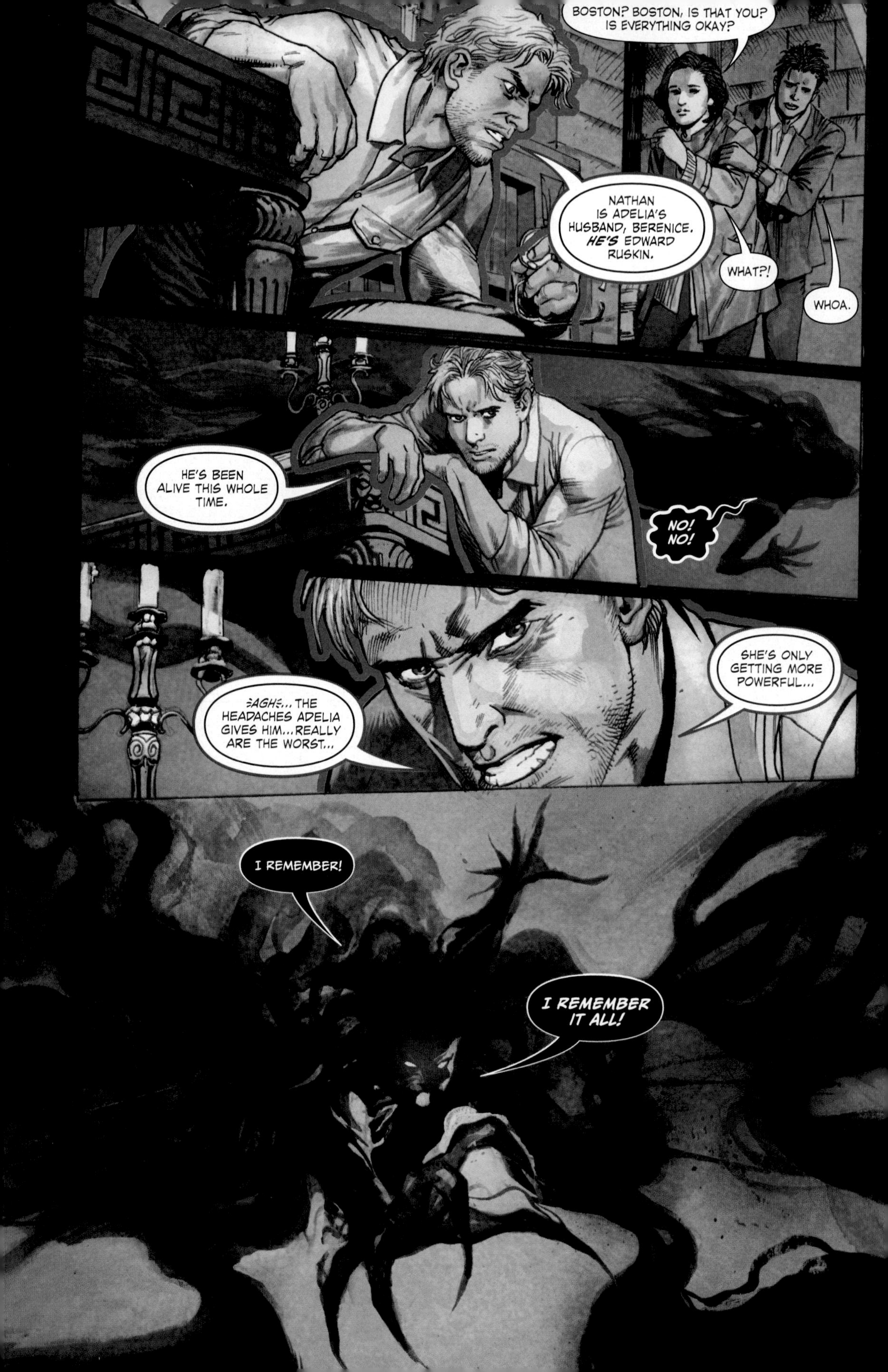

BOSTON? BOSTON, IS THAT YOU? IS EVERYTHING OKAY?
NATHAN IS ADELIA'S HUSBAND, BERENICE. **HE'S** EDWARD RUSKIN.
WHAT?!
WHOA.
HE'S BEEN ALIVE THIS WHOLE TIME.
NO! NO!
AGH... THE HEADACHES ADELIA GIVES HIM... REALLY ARE THE WORST...
SHE'S ONLY GETTING MORE POWERFUL...
I REMEMBER!
I REMEMBER IT ALL!

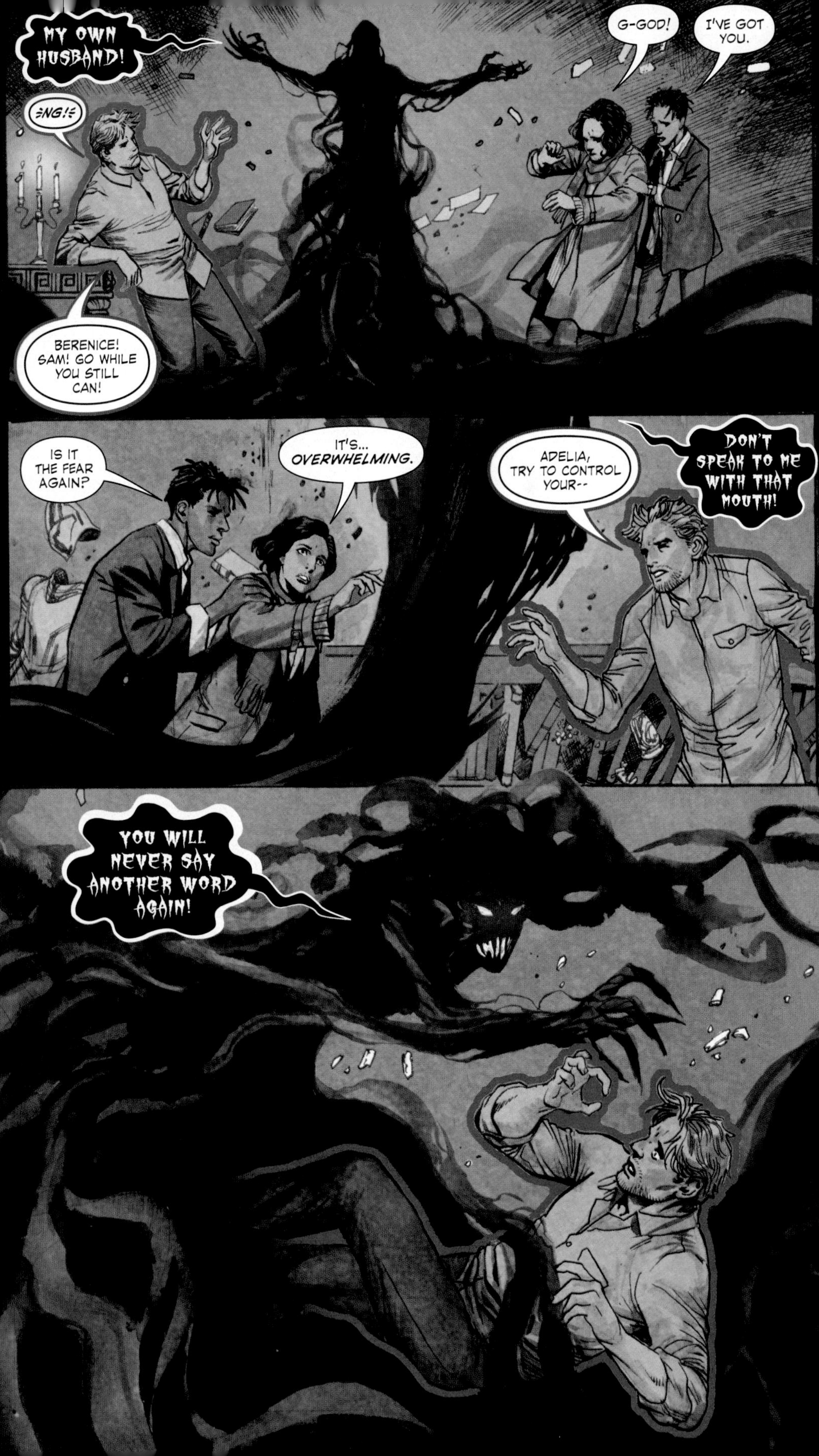
MY OWN HUSBAND!
NG!
G-GOD!
I'VE GOT YOU.
BERENICE! SAM! GO WHILE YOU STILL CAN!
IS IT THE FEAR AGAIN?
IT'S... OVERWHELMING.
ADELIA, TRY TO CONTROL YOUR--
DON'T SPEAK TO ME WITH THAT MOUTH!
YOU WILL NEVER SAY ANOTHER WORD AGAIN!

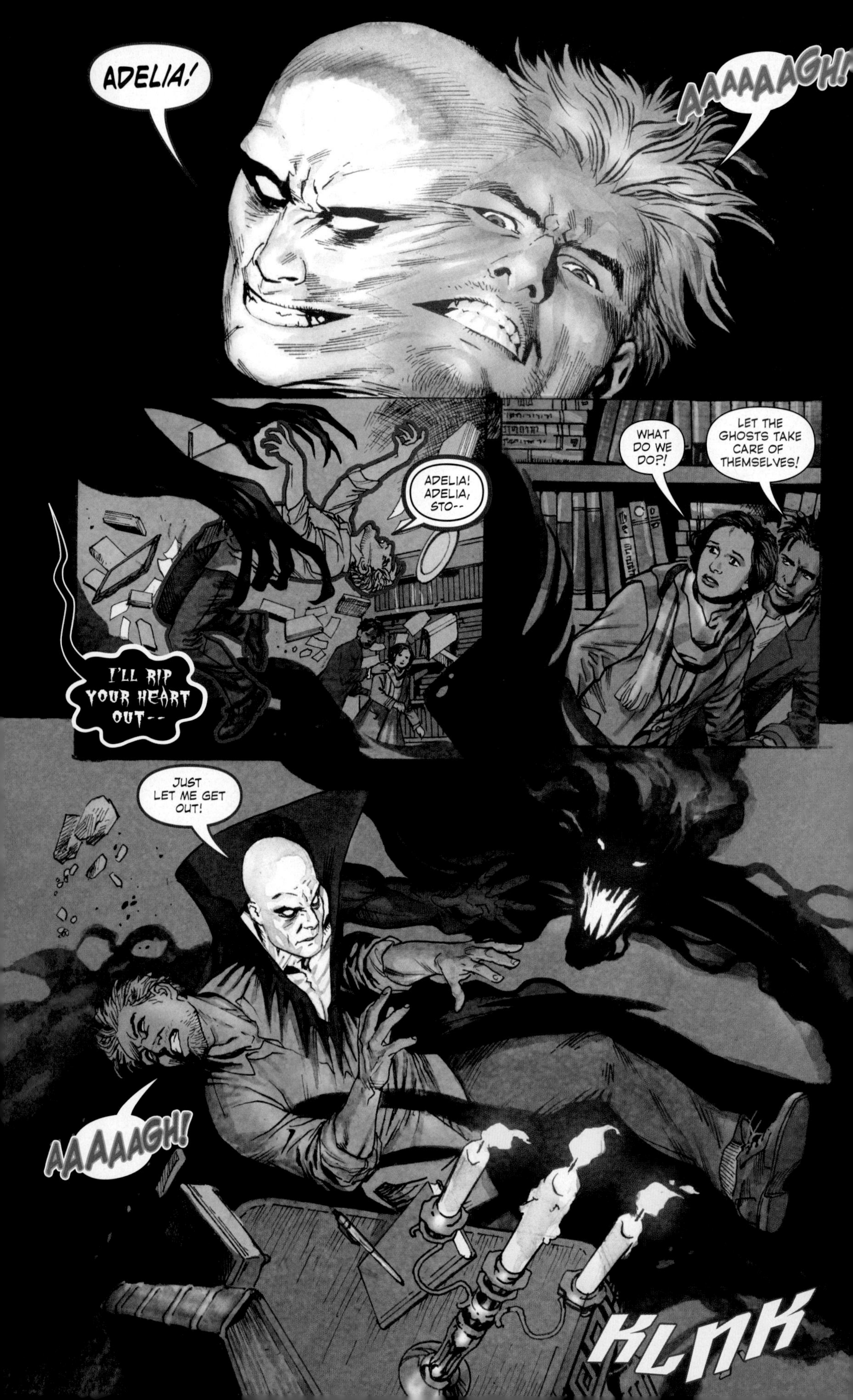
ADELIA!
AAAAAAGH!
ADELIA! ADELIA, STO--
I'LL RIP YOUR HEART OUT--
WHAT DO WE DO?!
LET THE GHOSTS TAKE CARE OF THEMSELVES!
JUST LET ME GET OUT!
AAAAAGH!
KLNK

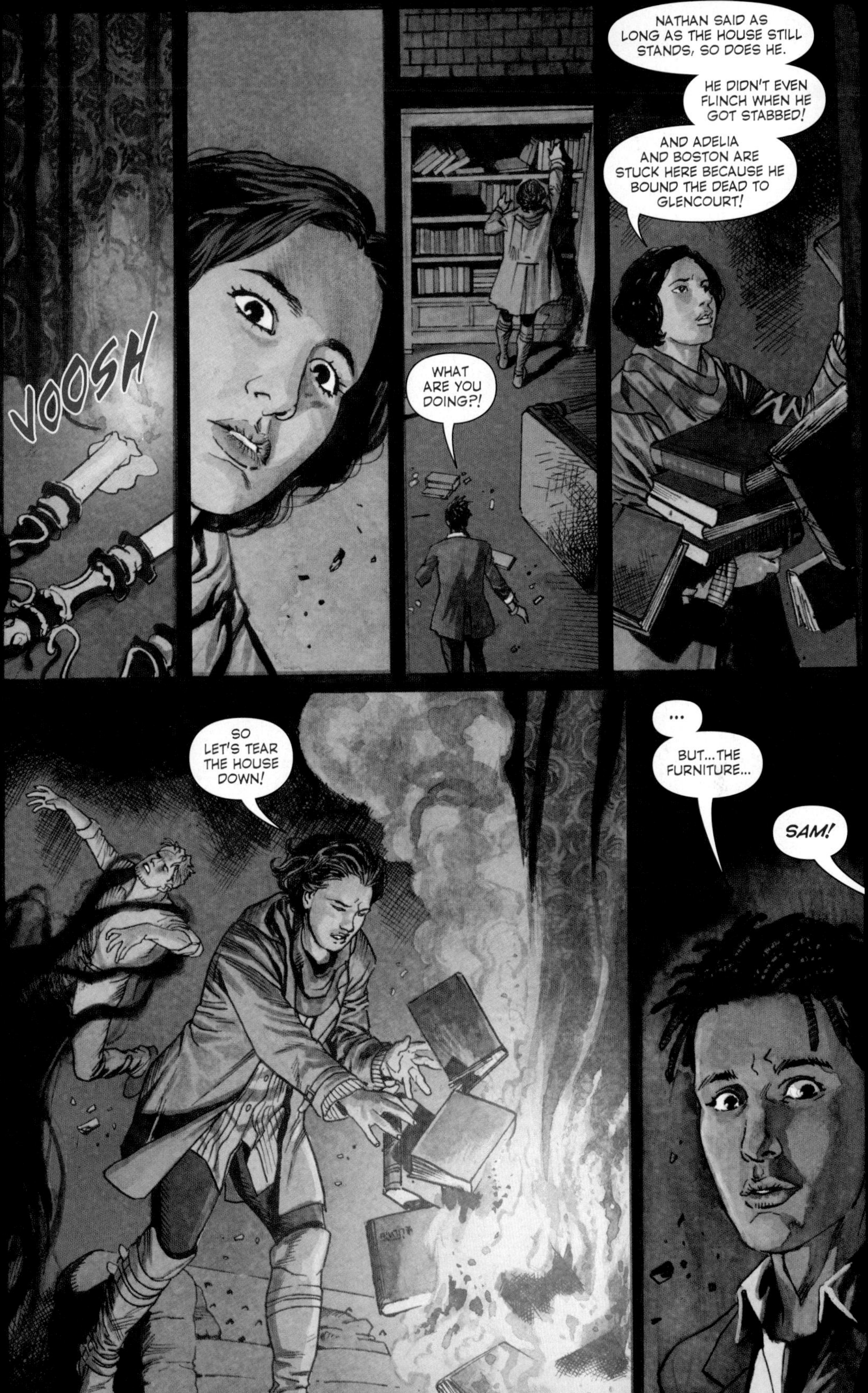
VOOSH
NATHAN SAID AS LONG AS THE HOUSE STILL STANDS, SO DOES HE.
HE DIDN'T EVEN FLINCH WHEN HE GOT STABBED!
AND ADELIA AND BOSTON ARE STUCK HERE BECAUSE HE BOUND THE DEAD TO GLENCOURT!
WHAT ARE YOU DOING?!
SO LET'S TEAR THE HOUSE DOWN!
...
BUT...THE FURNITURE...
SAM!

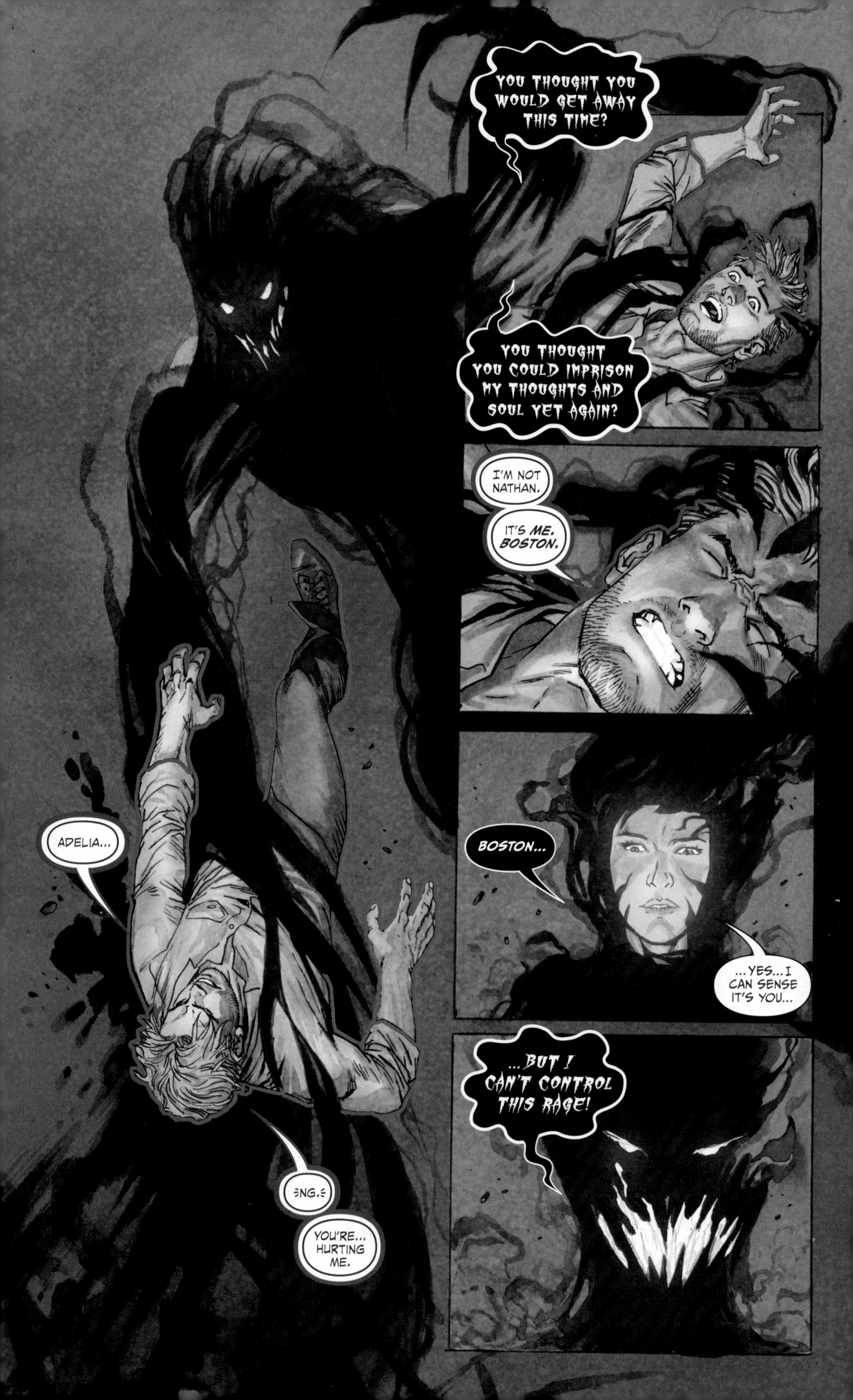
YOU THOUGHT YOU WOULD GET AWAY THIS TIME?
YOU THOUGHT YOU COULD IMPRISON MY THOUGHTS AND SOUL YET AGAIN?
I'M NOT NATHAN.
IT'S ME. BOSTON.
BOSTON...
...YES...I CAN SENSE IT'S YOU...
...BUT I CAN'T CONTROL THIS RAGE!
ADELIA...
NG.
YOU'RE... HURTING ME.

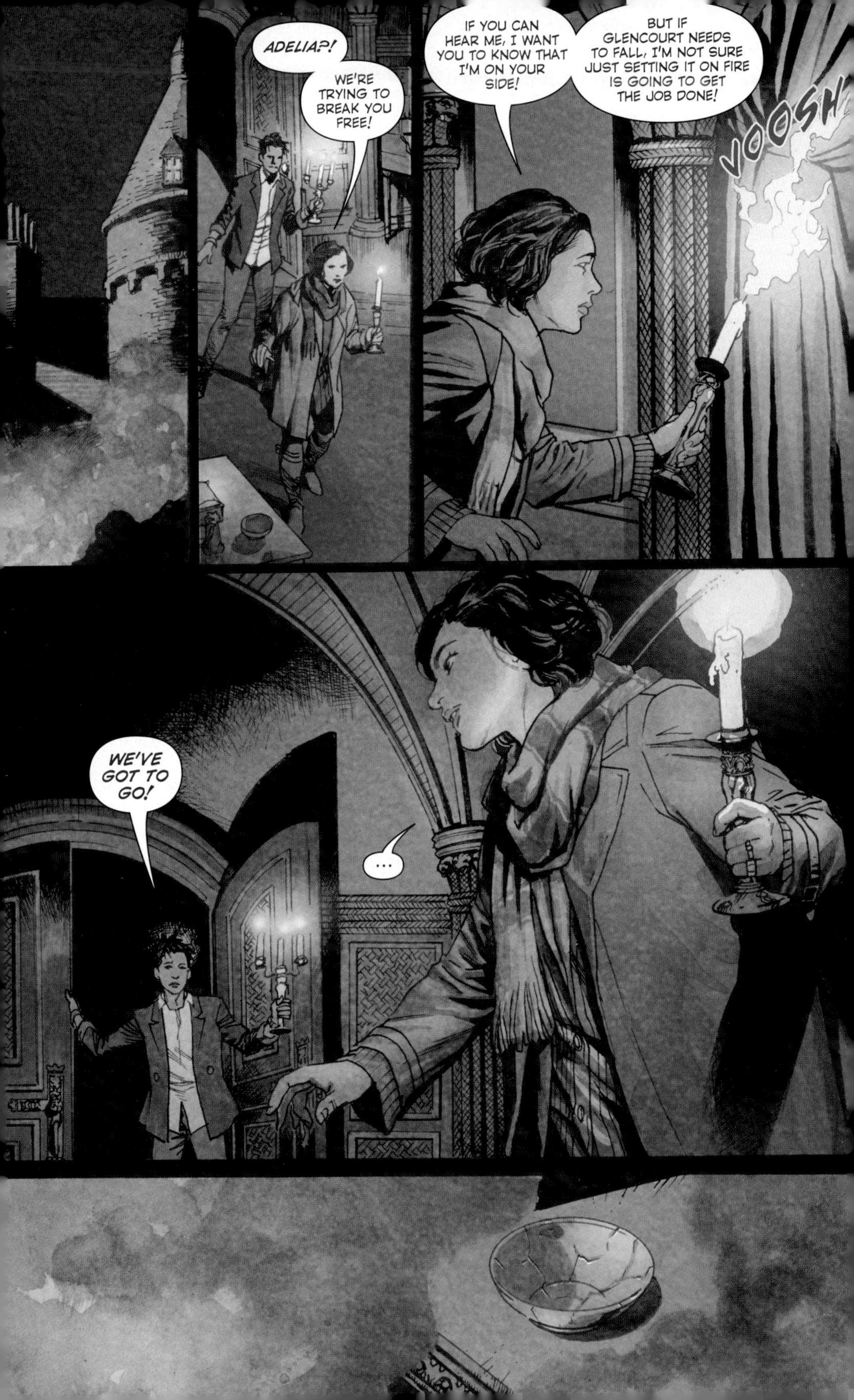
ADELIA?!
WE'RE TRYING TO BREAK YOU FREE!
IF YOU CAN HEAR ME, I WANT YOU TO KNOW THAT I'M ON YOUR SIDE!
BUT IF GLENCOURT NEEDS TO FALL, I'M NOT SURE JUST SETTING IT ON FIRE IS GOING TO GET THE JOB DONE!
VOOSH
WE'VE GOT TO GO!
...

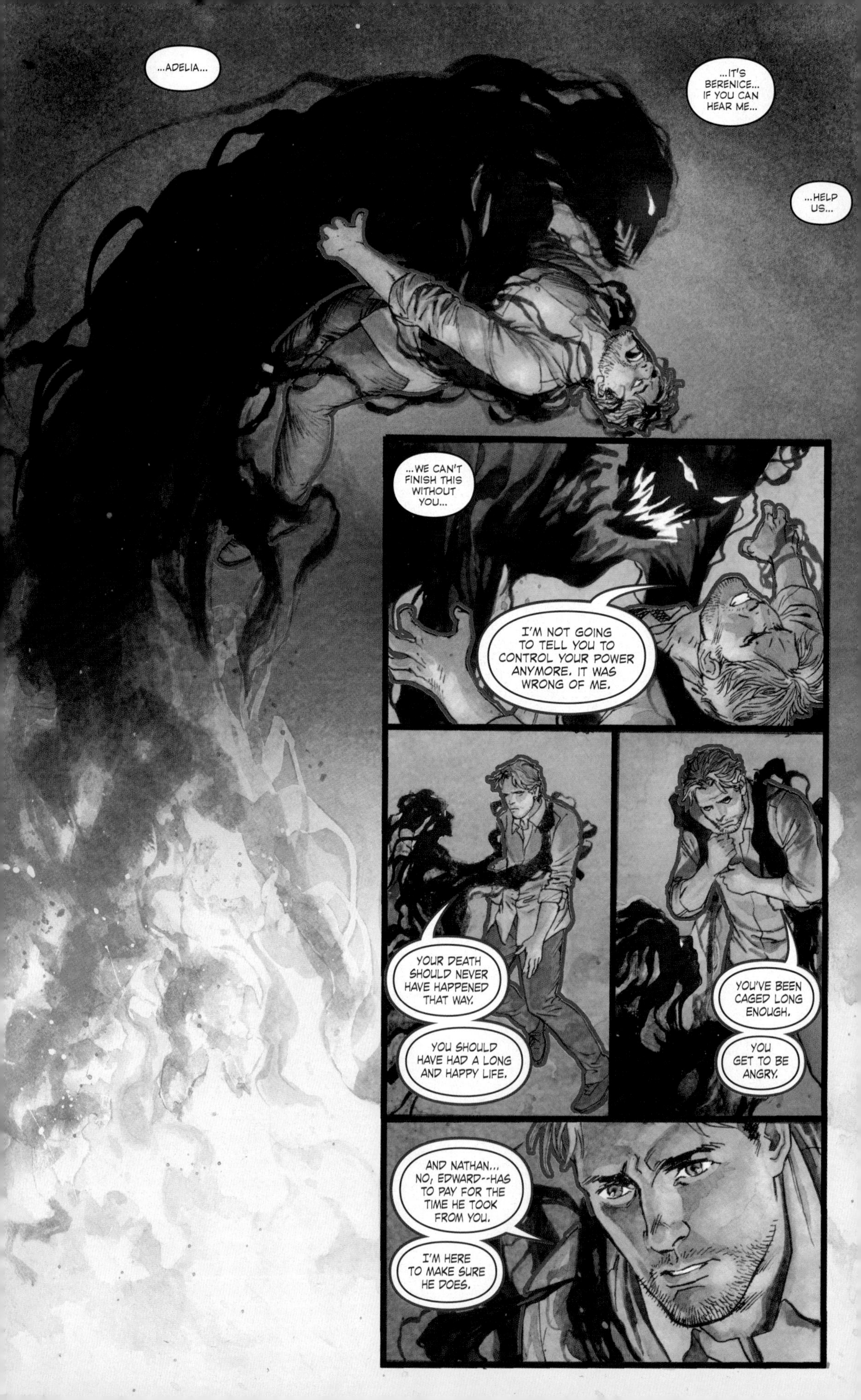
...ADELIA...
...IT'S BERENICE... IF YOU CAN HEAR ME...
...HELP US...
...WE CAN'T FINISH THIS WITHOUT YOU...
I'M NOT GOING TO TELL YOU TO CONTROL YOUR POWER ANYMORE. IT WAS WRONG OF ME.
YOUR DEATH SHOULD NEVER HAVE HAPPENED THAT WAY.
YOU SHOULD HAVE HAD A LONG AND HAPPY LIFE.
YOU'VE BEEN CAGED LONG ENOUGH.
YOU GET TO BE ANGRY.
AND NATHAN... NO, EDWARD--HAS TO PAY FOR THE TIME HE TOOK FROM YOU.
I'M HERE TO MAKE SURE HE DOES.

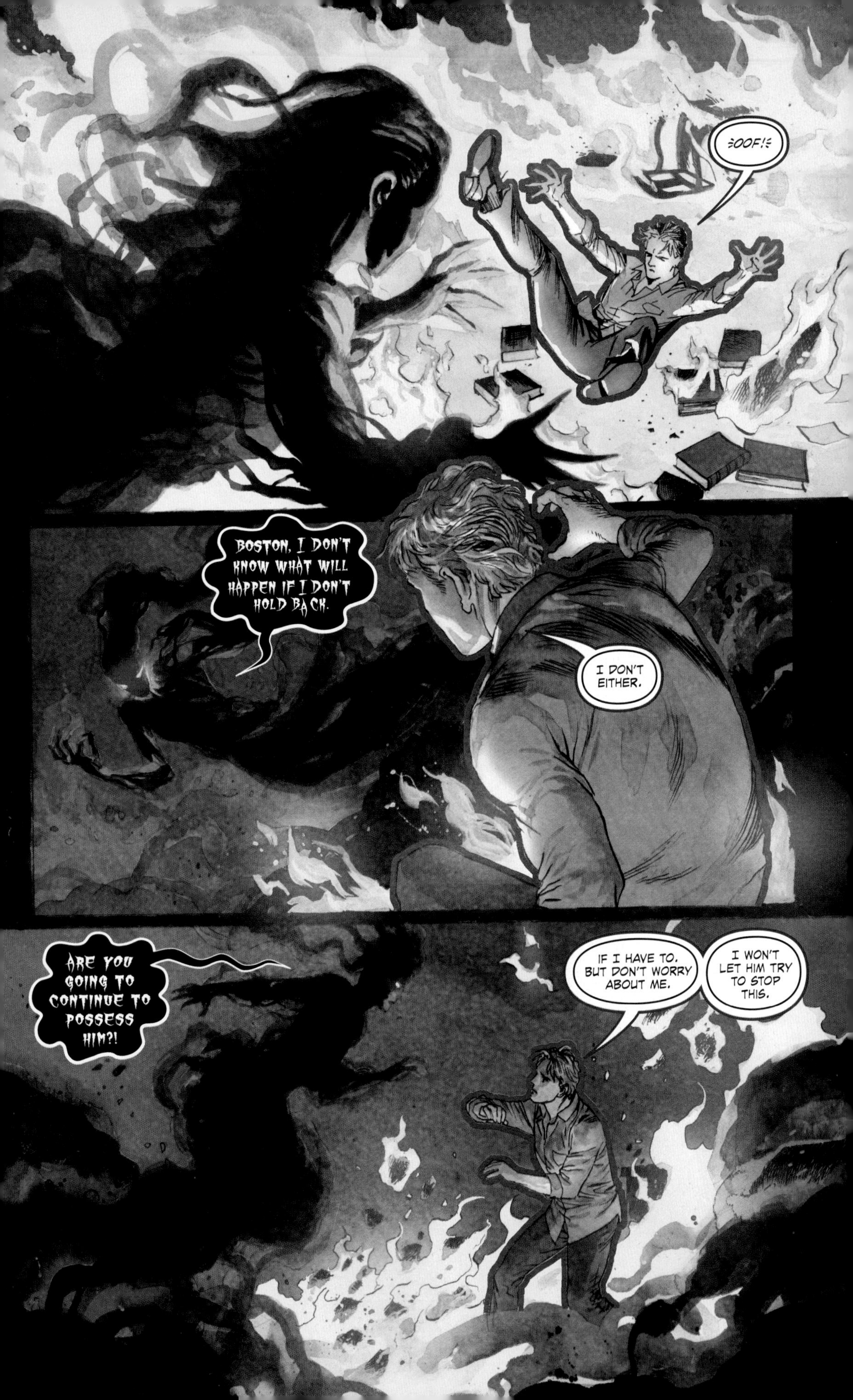
OOF!
BOSTON, I DON'T KNOW WHAT WILL HAPPEN IF I DON'T HOLD BACK.
I DON'T EITHER.
ARE YOU GOING TO CONTINUE TO POSSESS HIM?!
IF I HAVE TO. BUT DON'T WORRY ABOUT ME.
I WON'T LET HIM TRY TO STOP THIS.

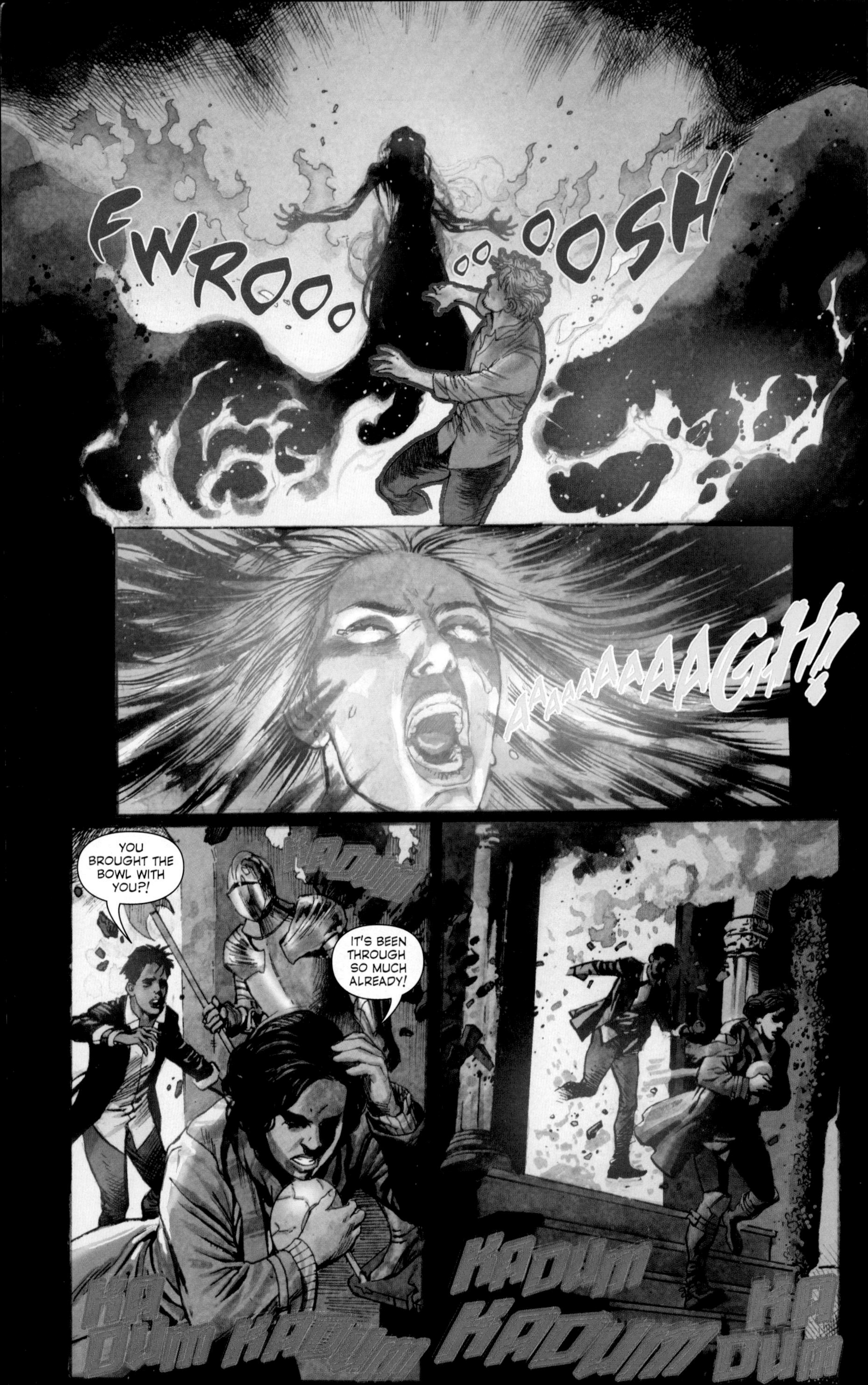
FWROOOOOOOOSH
AAAAAAAAAAGH!!
YOU BROUGHT THE BOWL WITH YOU?!
KADUM
IT'S BEEN THROUGH SO MUCH ALREADY!
KA DUM KADUM
KADUM KADUM KA DUM

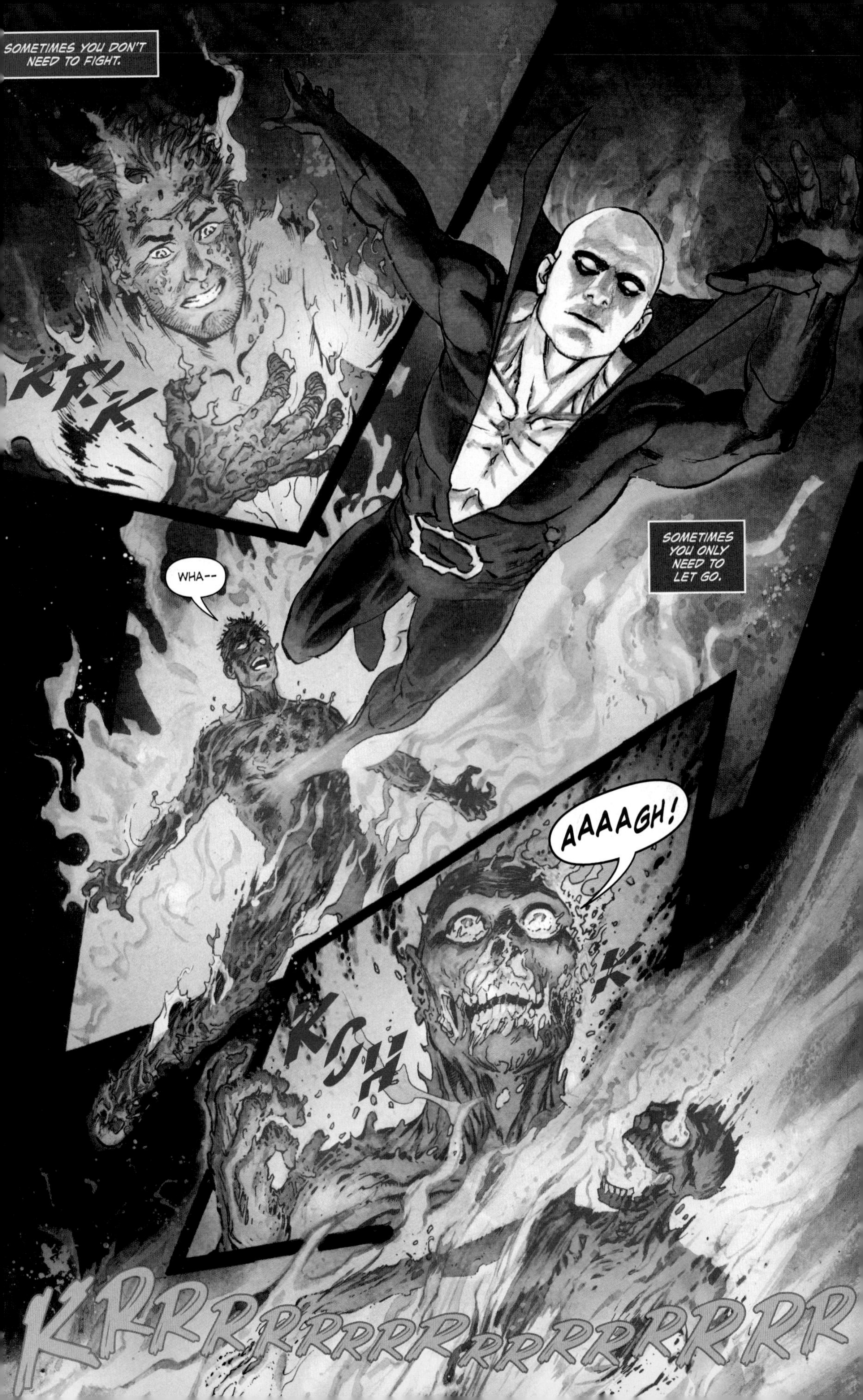
SOMETIMES YOU DON'T NEED TO FIGHT.
KRIK
SOMETIMES YOU ONLY NEED TO LET GO.
WHA--
AAAAGH!
KCH
K
KRRRRRRRRRRRRRRRRRRR

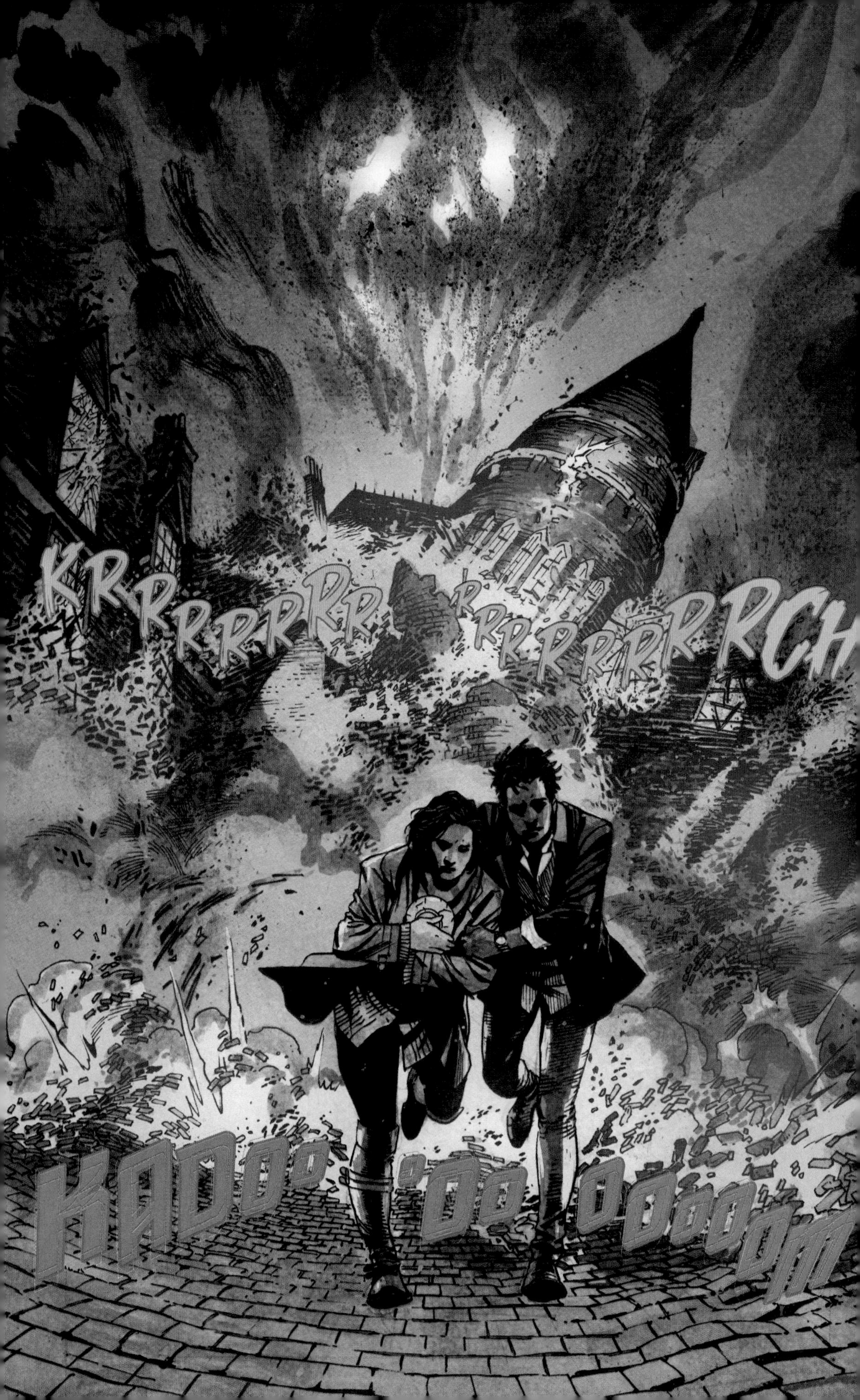
KRRRRRRRR RRRRRRRRCH
KADOOOO OOO OOOOOOM

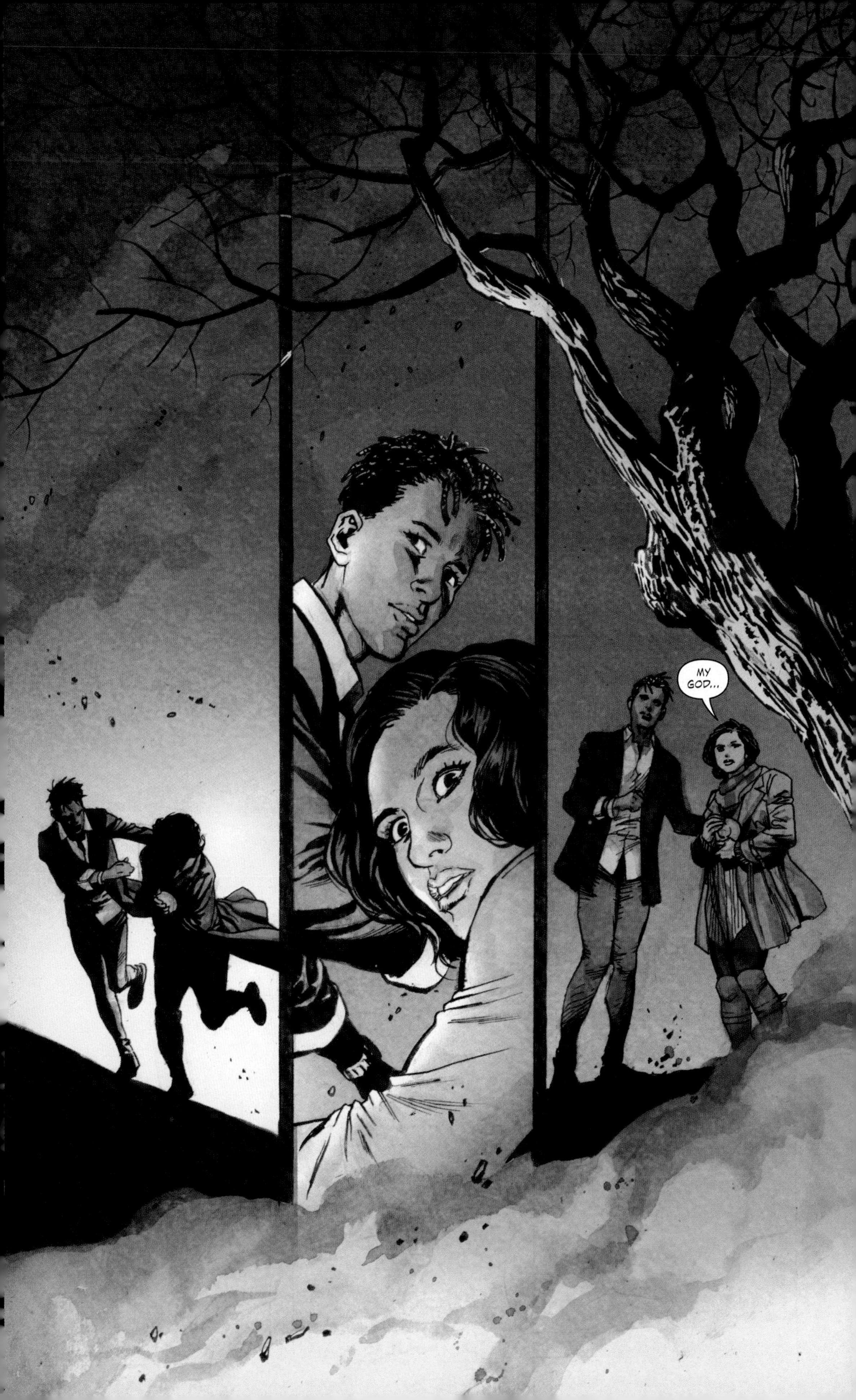
MY GOD...

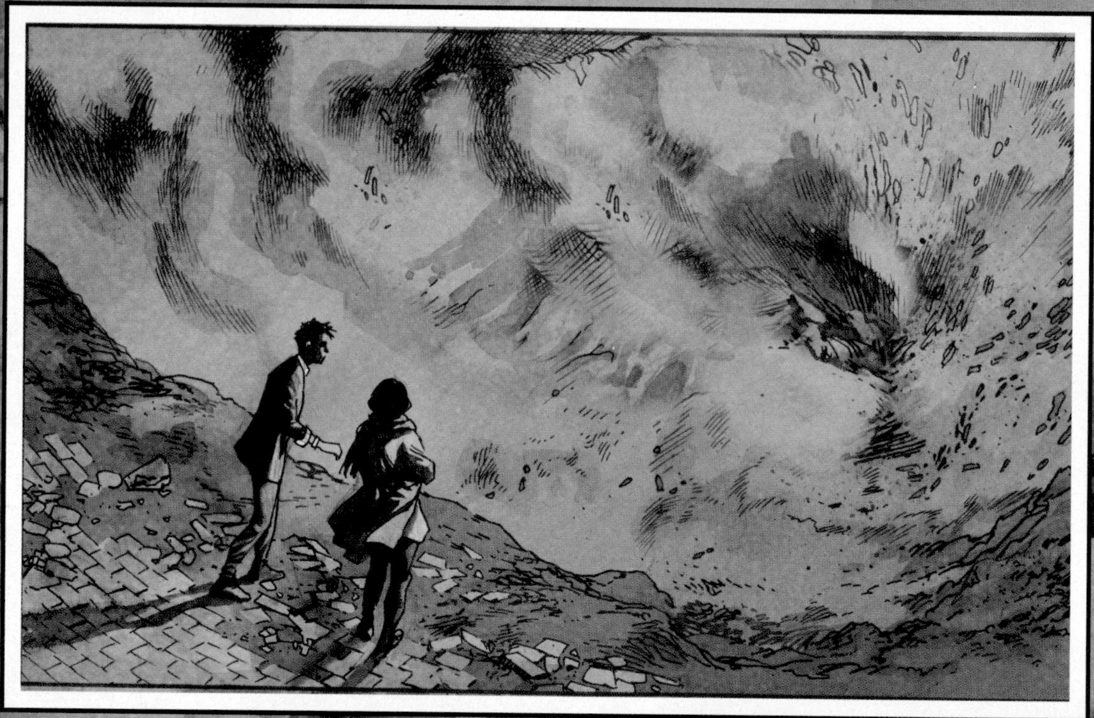
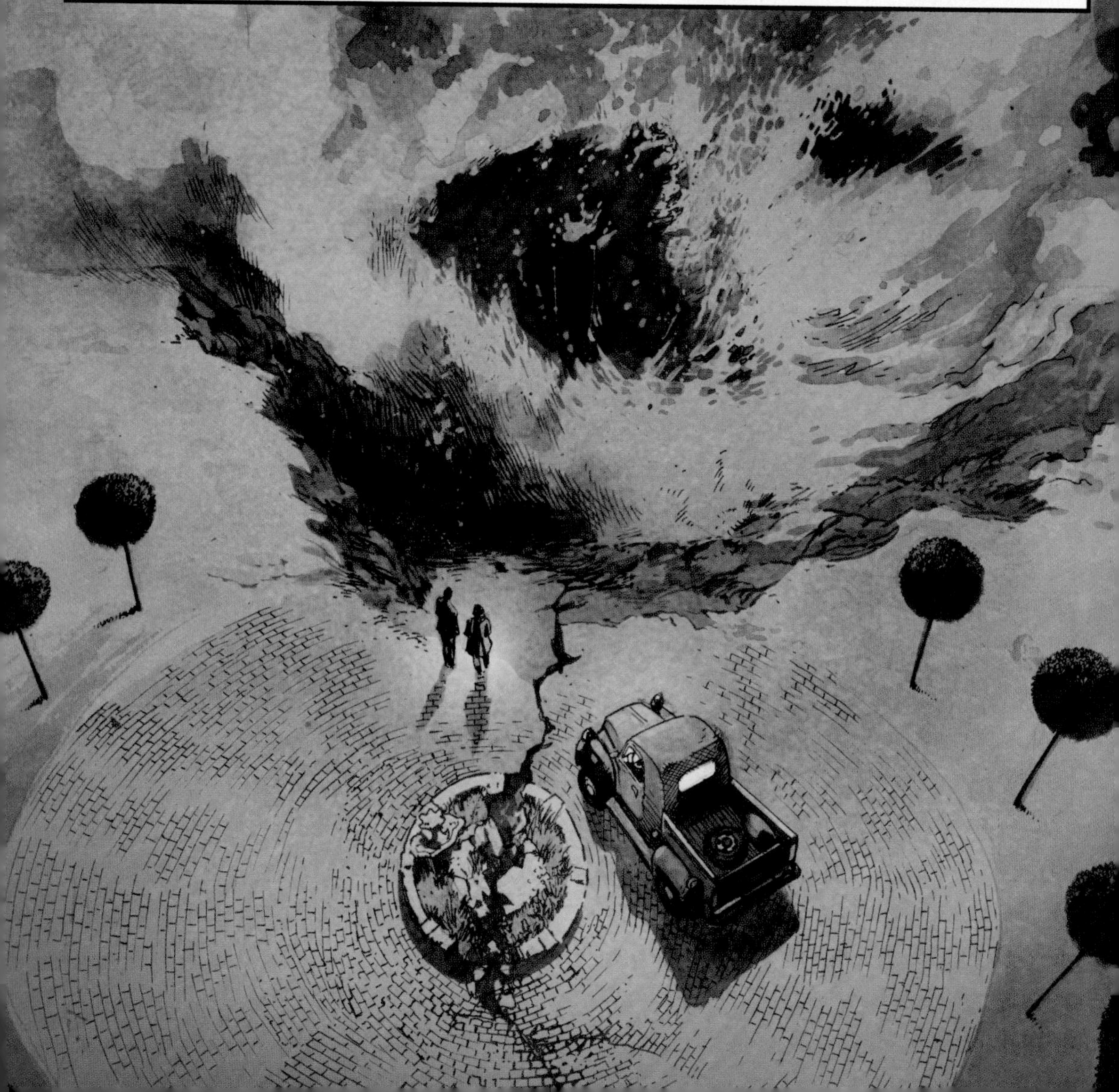

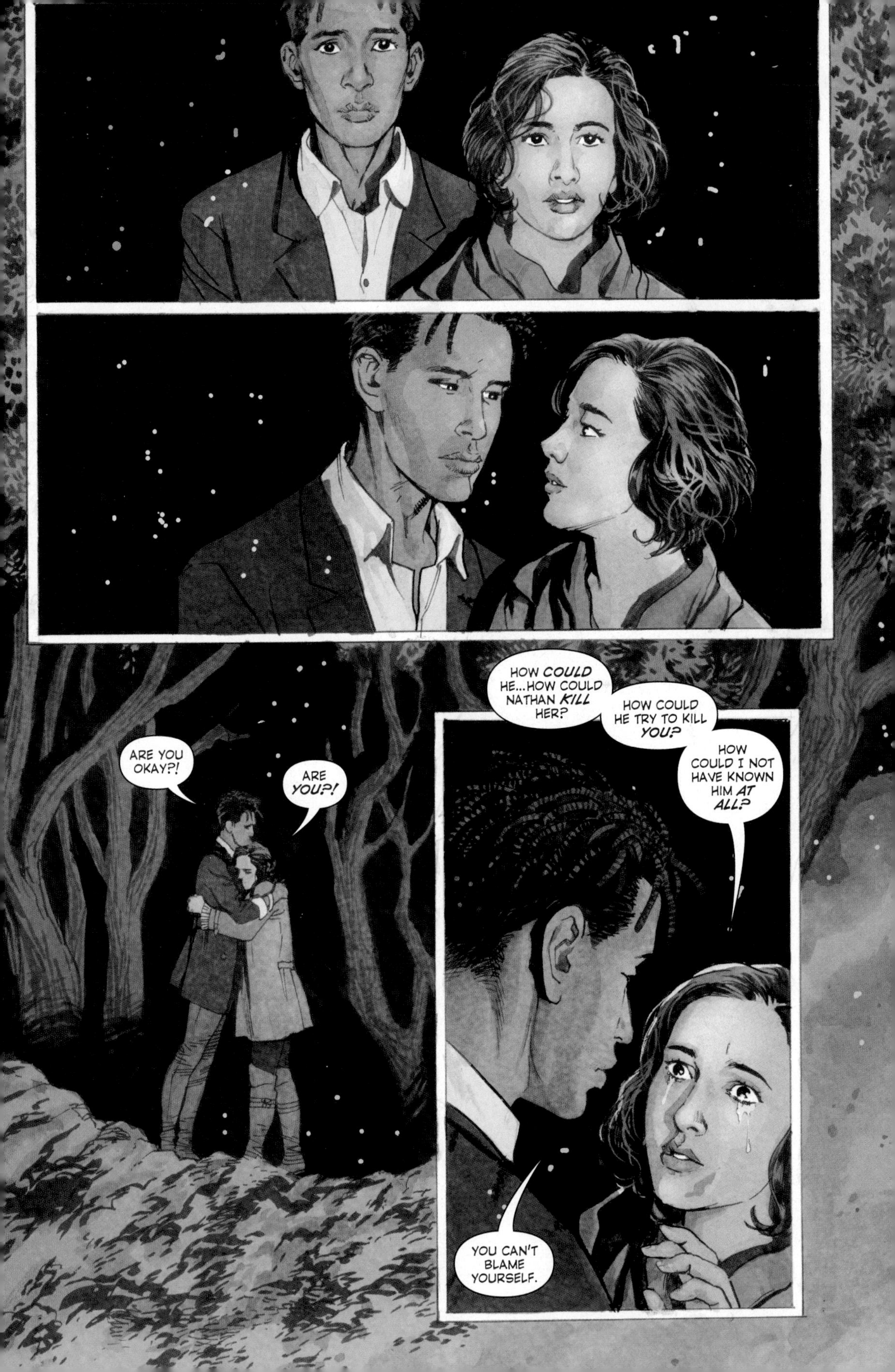
ARE YOU OKAY?!
ARE YOU?!
HOW COULD HE...HOW COULD NATHAN KILL HER?
HOW COULD HE TRY TO KILL YOU?
HOW COULD I NOT HAVE KNOWN HIM AT ALL?
YOU CAN'T BLAME YOURSELF.

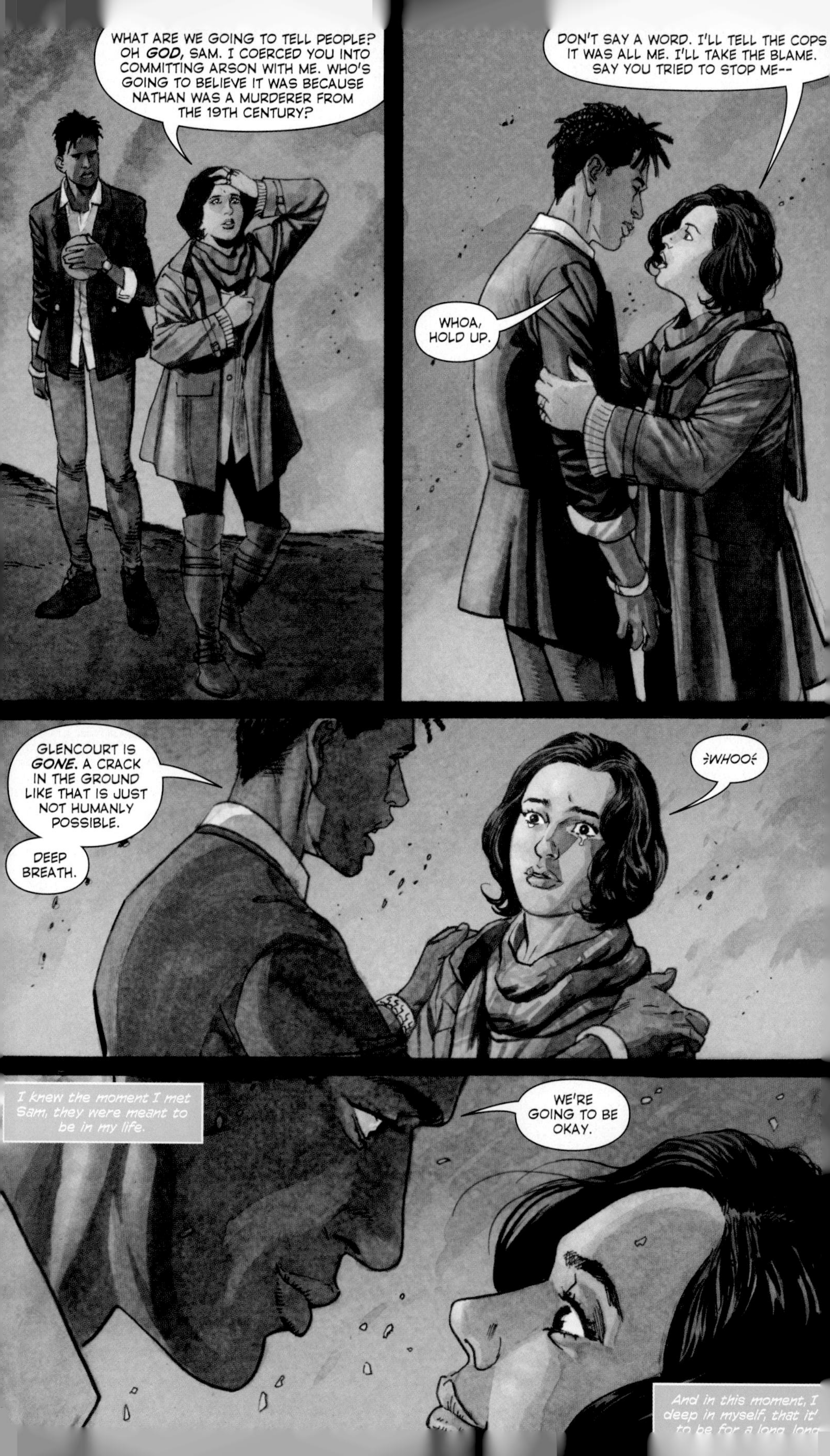
WHAT ARE WE GOING TO TELL PEOPLE? OH *GOD*, SAM. I COERCED YOU INTO COMMITTING ARSON WITH ME. WHO'S GOING TO BELIEVE IT WAS BECAUSE NATHAN WAS A MURDERER FROM THE 19TH CENTURY?
DON'T SAY A WORD. I'LL TELL THE COPS IT WAS ALL ME. I'LL TAKE THE BLAME. SAY YOU TRIED TO STOP ME--
WHOA, HOLD UP.
GLENCOURT IS *GONE*. A CRACK IN THE GROUND LIKE THAT IS JUST NOT HUMANLY POSSIBLE.
DEEP BREATH.
WHOO
I knew the moment I met Sam, they were meant to be in my life.
WE'RE GOING TO BE OKAY.
And in this moment, I
deep in myself, that it'

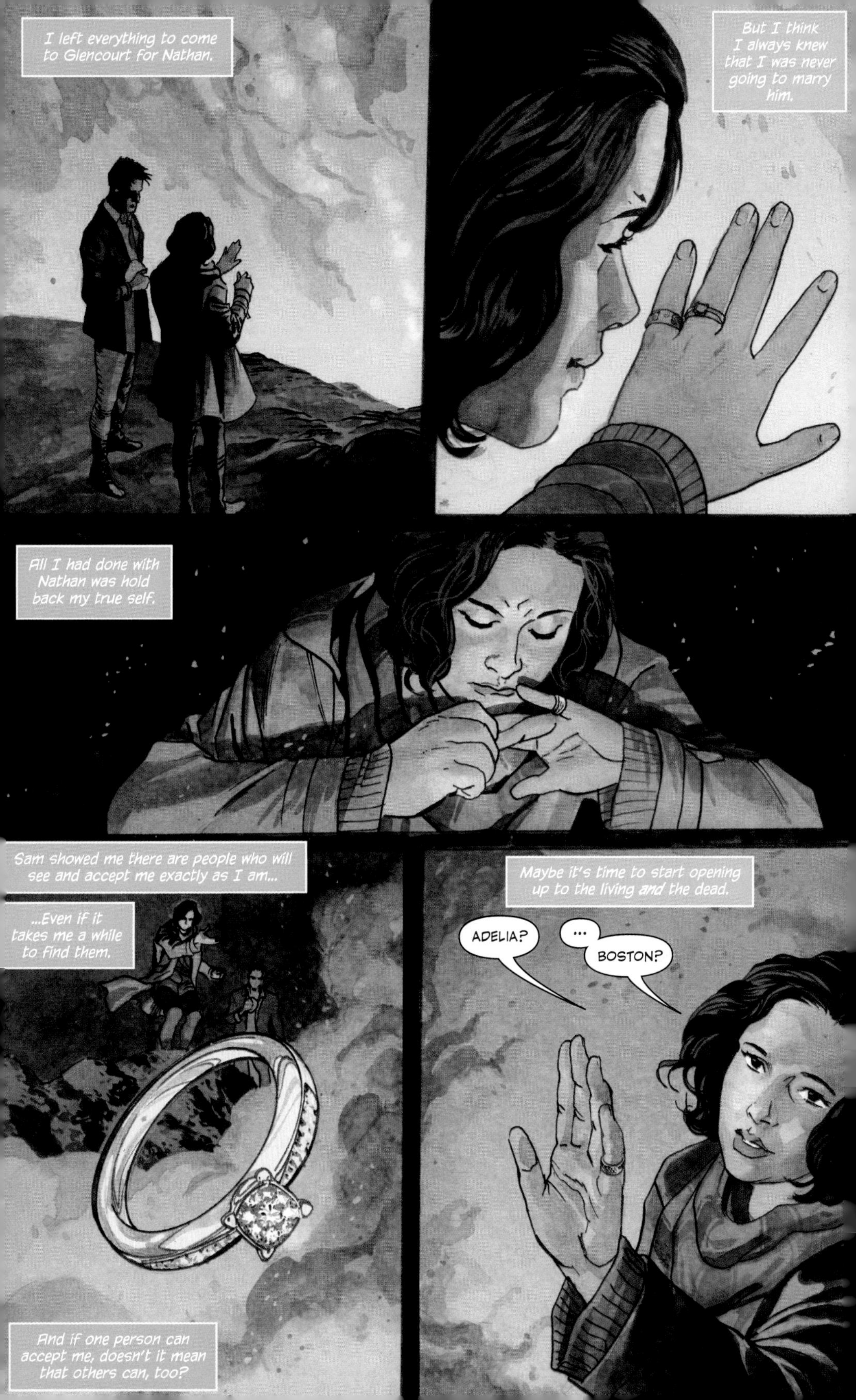
I left everything to come to Glencourt for Nathan.
But I think I always knew that I was never going to marry him.
All I had done with Nathan was hold back my true self.
Sam showed me there are people who will see and accept me exactly as I am...
...Even if it takes me a while to find them.
And if one person can accept me, doesn't it mean that others can, too?
Maybe it's time to start opening up to the living and the dead.
ADELIA?
...
BOSTON?

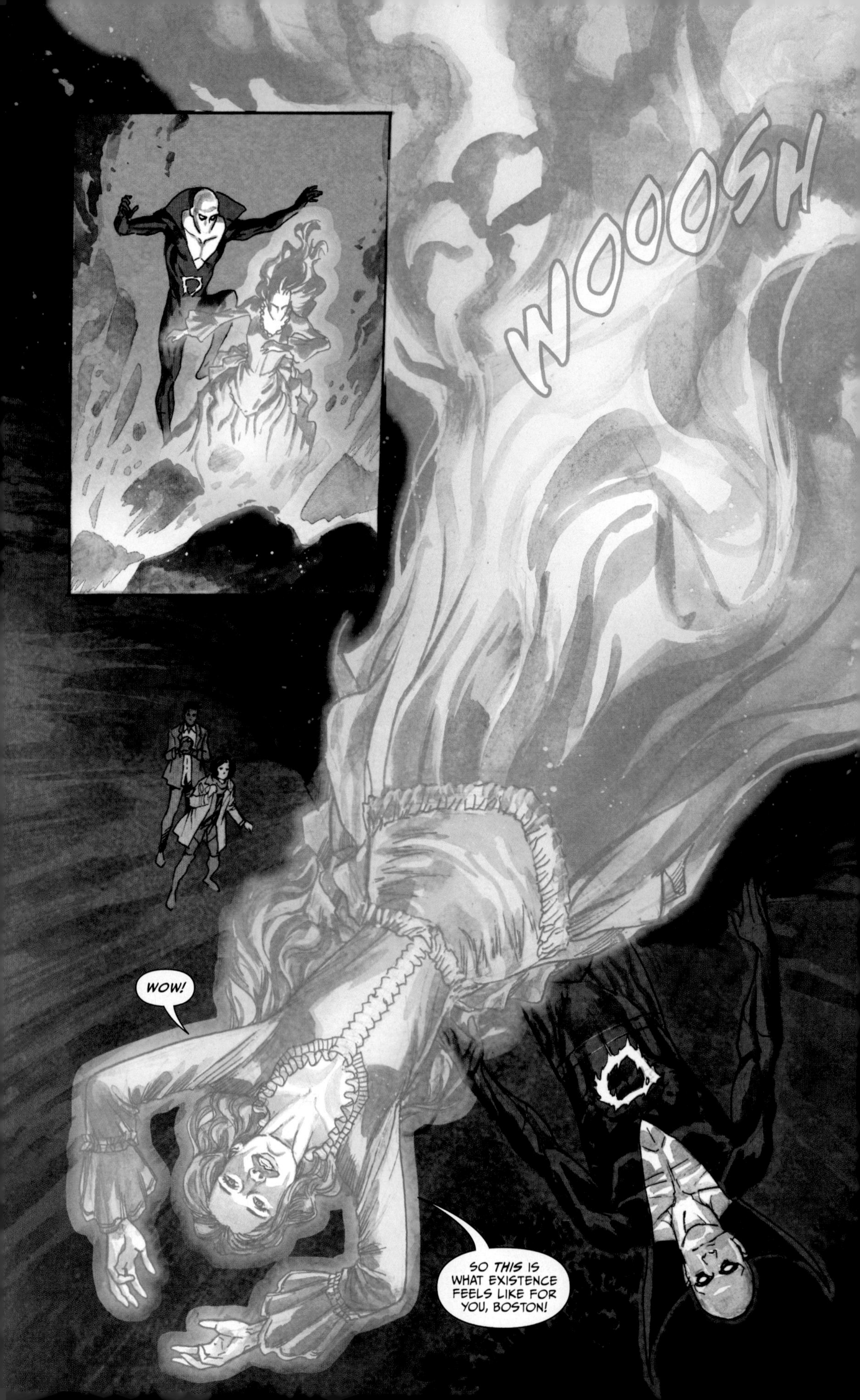
WOOOSH
WOW!
SO THIS IS WHAT EXISTENCE FEELS LIKE FOR YOU, BOSTON!

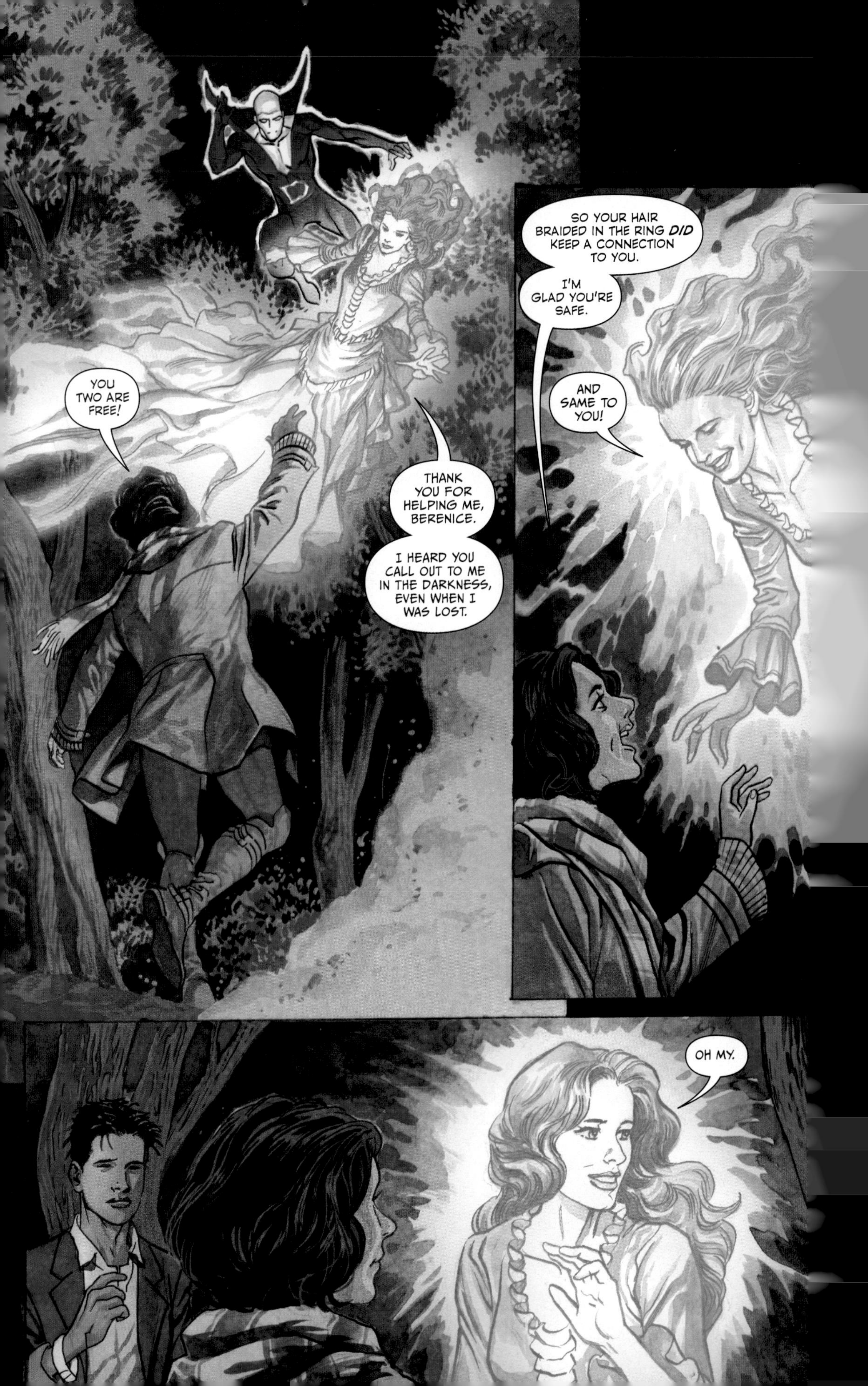
YOU TWO ARE FREE!
THANK YOU FOR HELPING ME, BERENICE.
I HEARD YOU CALL OUT TO ME IN THE DARKNESS, EVEN WHEN I WAS LOST.
SO YOUR HAIR BRAIDED IN THE RING *DID* KEEP A CONNECTION TO YOU.
I'M GLAD YOU'RE SAFE.
AND SAME TO YOU!
OH MY.

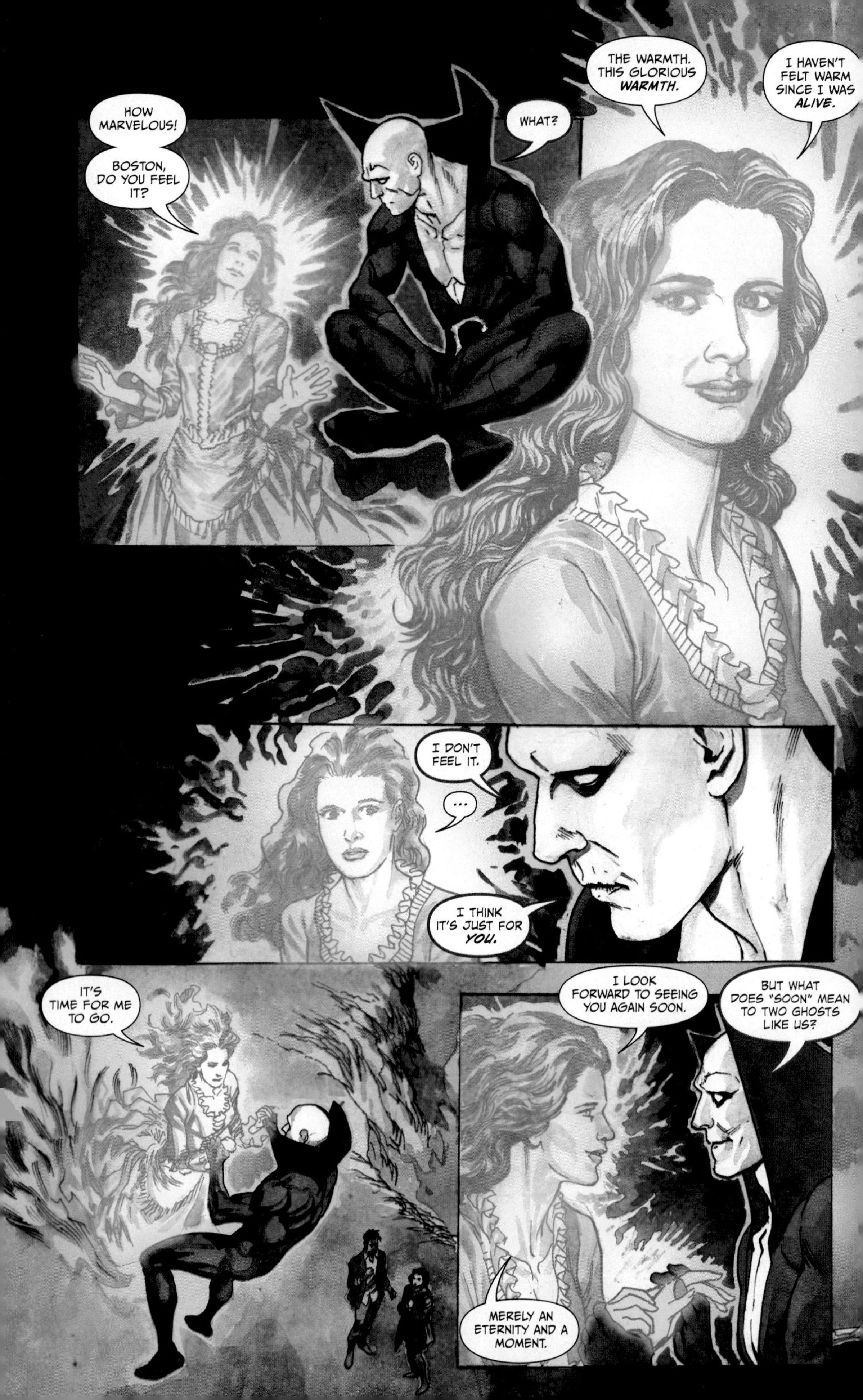
HOW MARVELOUS!
BOSTON, DO YOU FEEL IT?
WHAT?
THE WARMTH. THIS GLORIOUS WARMTH.
I HAVEN'T FELT WARM SINCE I WAS ALIVE.
I DON'T FEEL IT.
...
I THINK IT'S JUST FOR YOU.
IT'S TIME FOR ME TO GO.
I LOOK FORWARD TO SEEING YOU AGAIN SOON.
BUT WHAT DOES "SOON" MEAN TO TWO GHOSTS LIKE US?
MERELY AN ETERNITY AND A MOMENT.

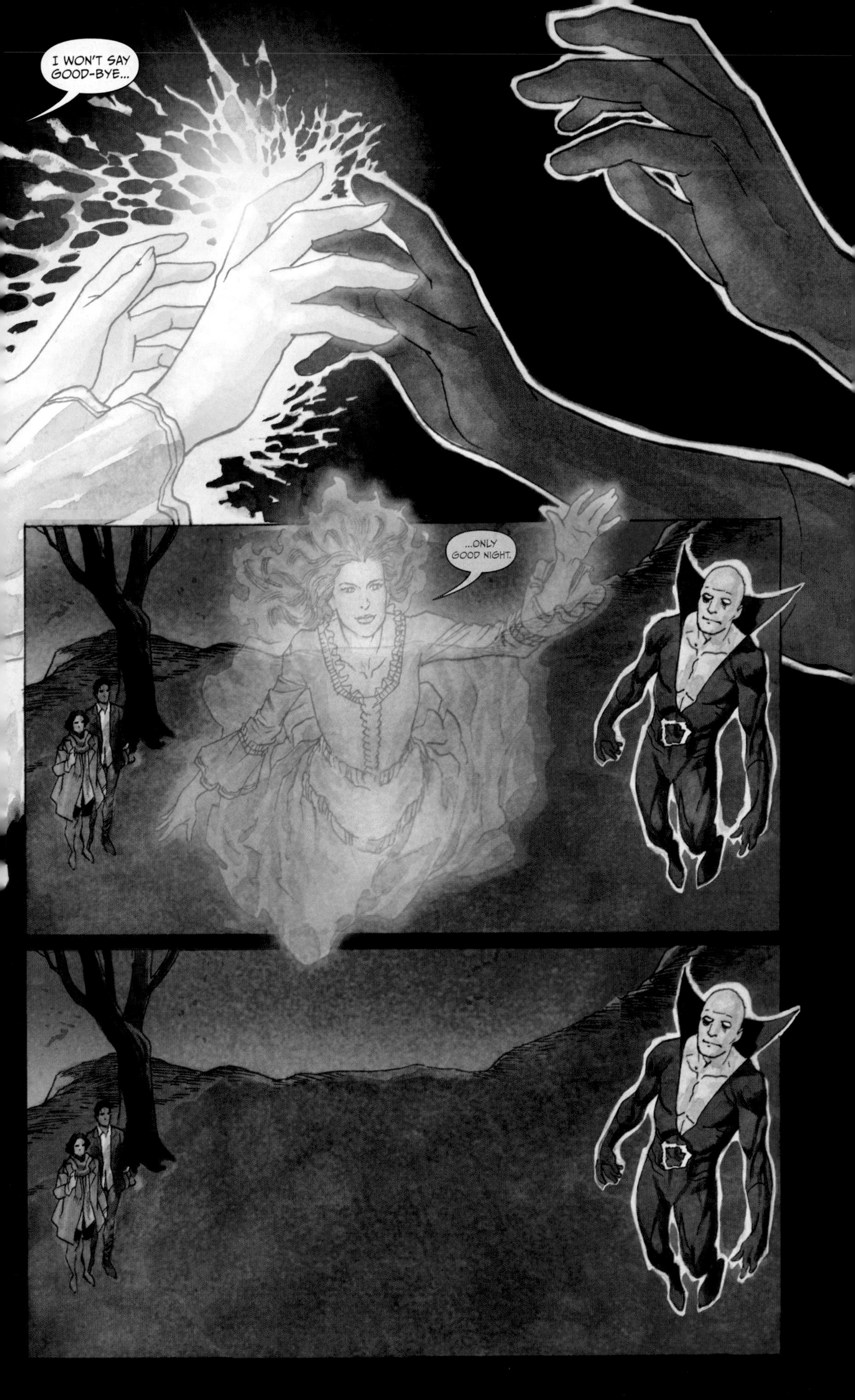
I WON'T SAY GOOD-BYE...
...ONLY GOOD NIGHT.

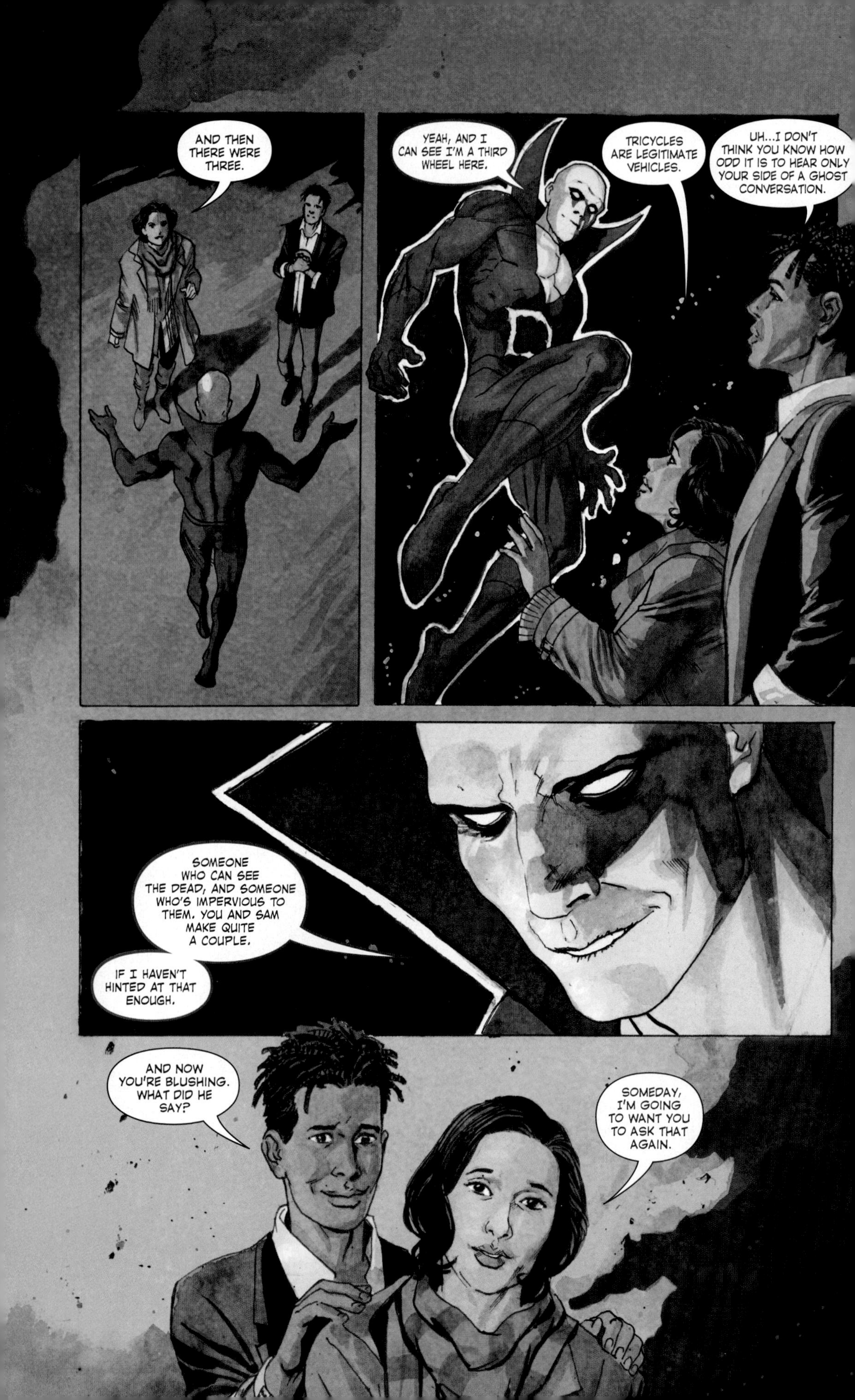
AND THEN THERE WERE THREE.
YEAH, AND I CAN SEE I'M A THIRD WHEEL HERE.
TRICYCLES ARE LEGITIMATE VEHICLES.
UH...I DON'T THINK YOU KNOW HOW ODD IT IS TO HEAR ONLY YOUR SIDE OF A GHOST CONVERSATION.
SOMEONE WHO CAN SEE THE DEAD, AND SOMEONE WHO'S IMPERVIOUS TO THEM. YOU AND SAM MAKE QUITE A COUPLE.
IF I HAVEN'T HINTED AT THAT ENOUGH.
AND NOW YOU'RE BLUSHING. WHAT DID HE SAY?
SOMEDAY, I'M GOING TO WANT YOU TO ASK THAT AGAIN.

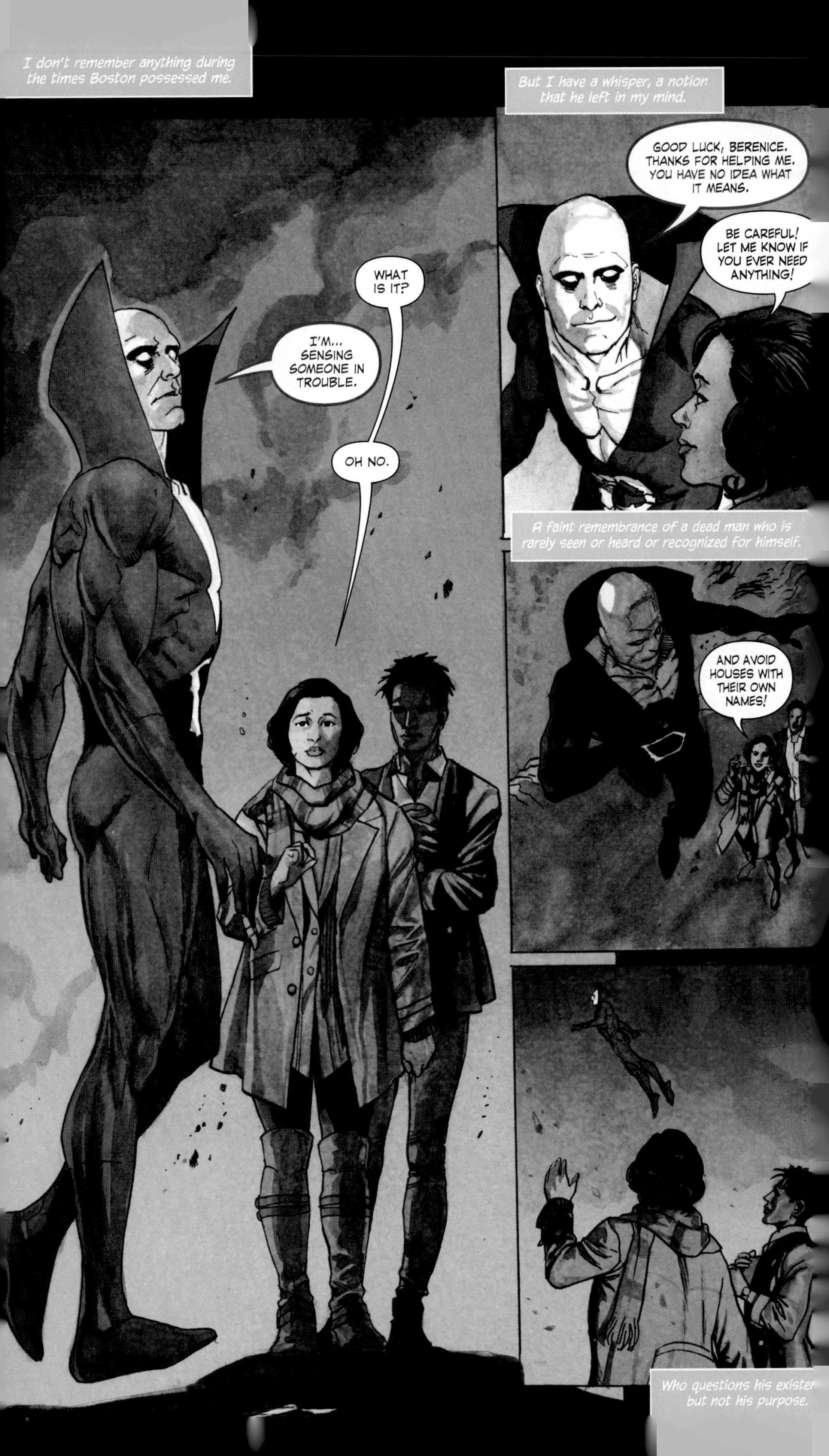
I don't remember anything during the times Boston possessed me.
I'M... SENSING SOMEONE IN TROUBLE.
WHAT IS IT?
OH NO.
But I have a whisper, a notion that he left in my mind.
GOOD LUCK, BERENICE. THANKS FOR HELPING ME. YOU HAVE NO IDEA WHAT IT MEANS.
BE CAREFUL! LET ME KNOW IF YOU EVER NEED ANYTHING!
A faint remembrance of a dead man who is rarely seen or heard or recognized for himself.
AND AVOID HOUSES WITH THEIR OWN NAMES!
but not his purpose.

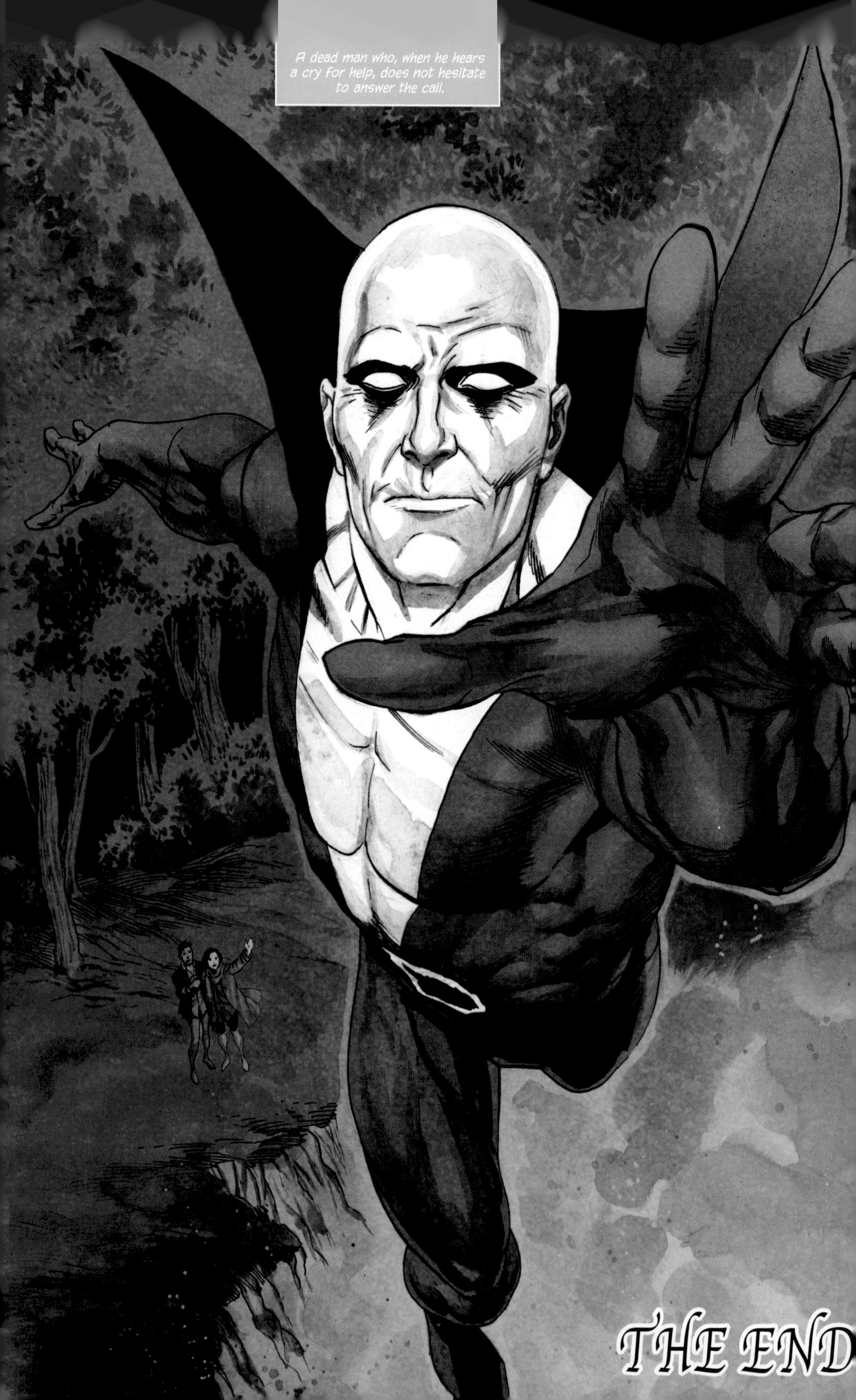
A dead man who, when he hears a cry for help, does not hesitate to answer the call.
THE END

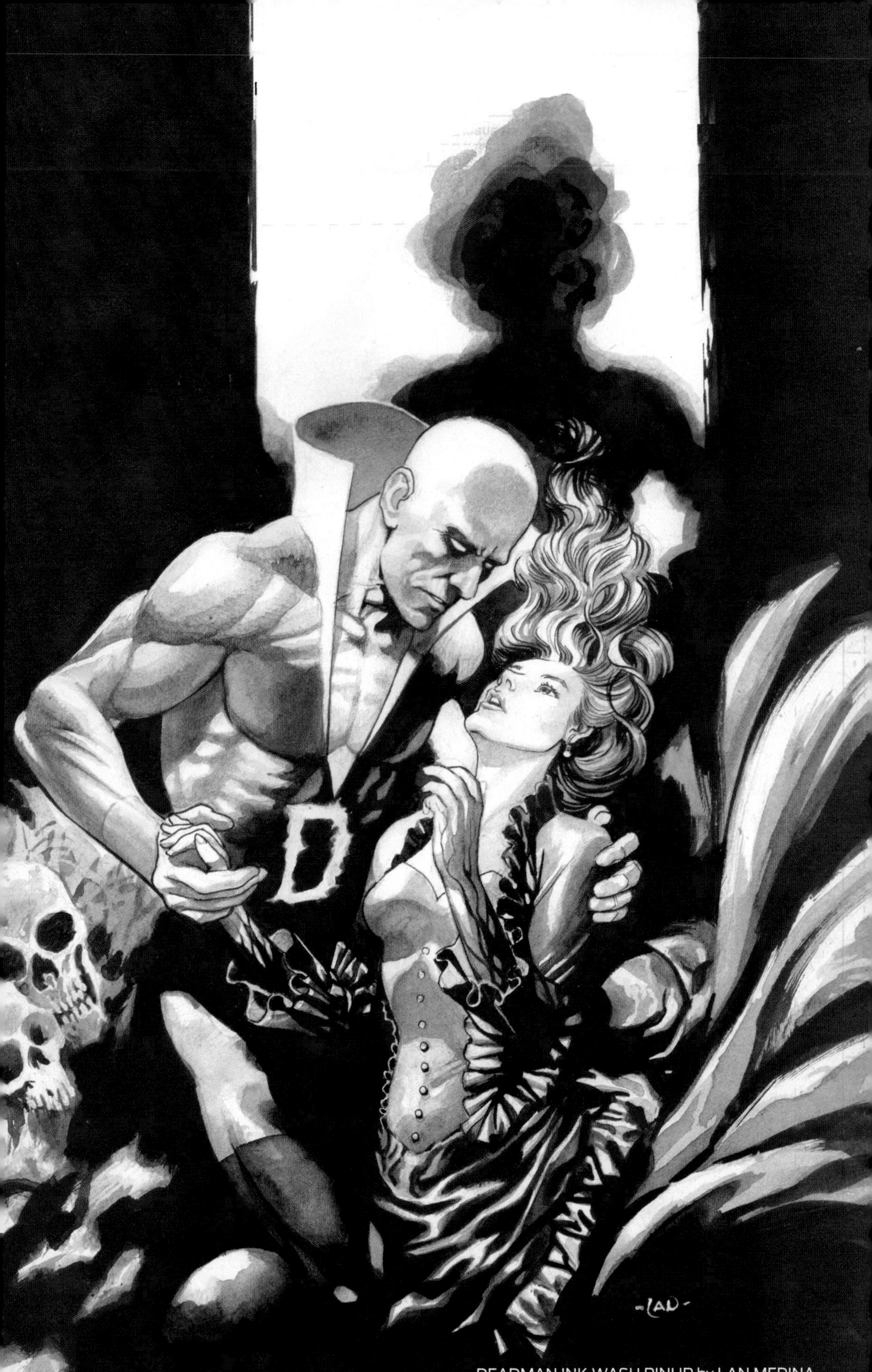
-LAN-

DEADMAN INK WASH PINUP by LAN MEDINA

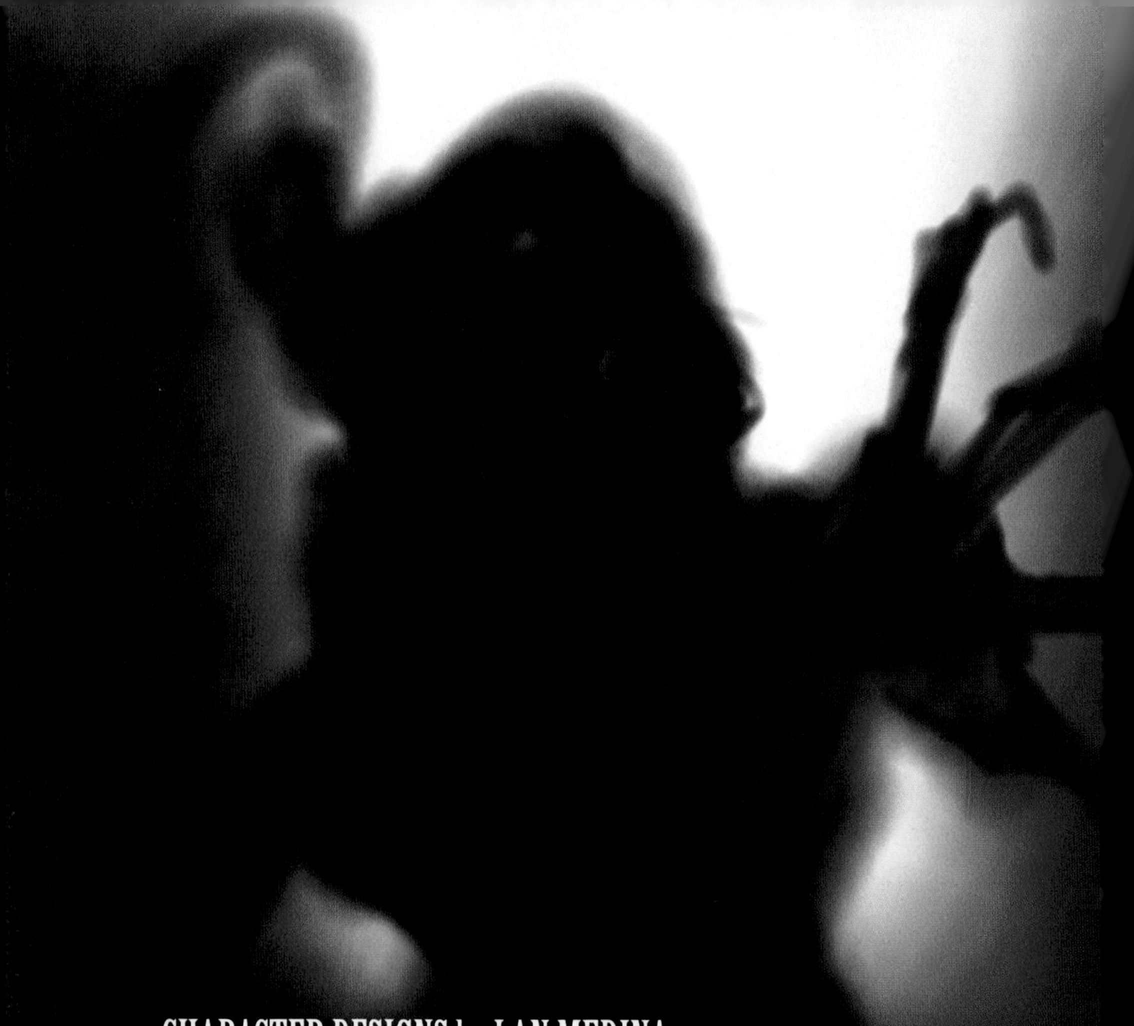

CHARACTER DESIGNS by LAN MEDINA

ADELIA RUSKIN

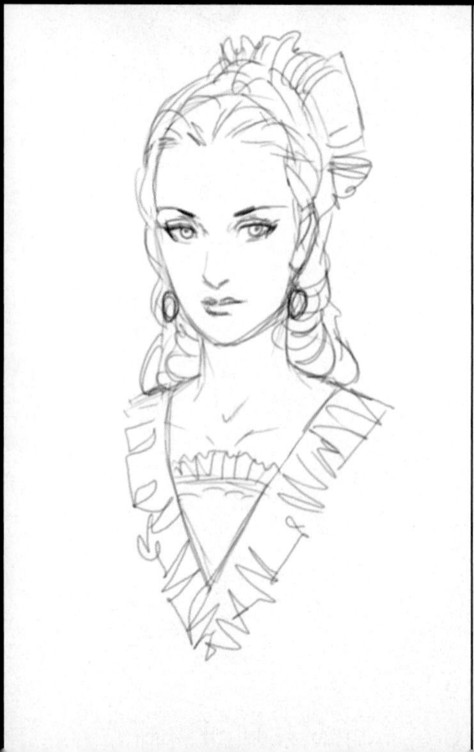

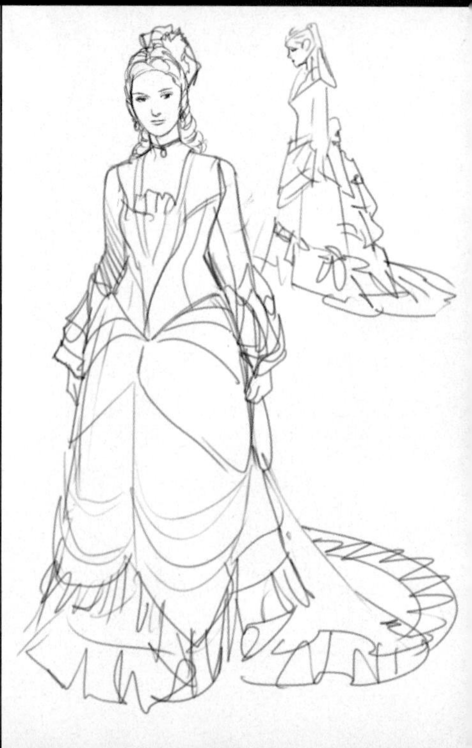

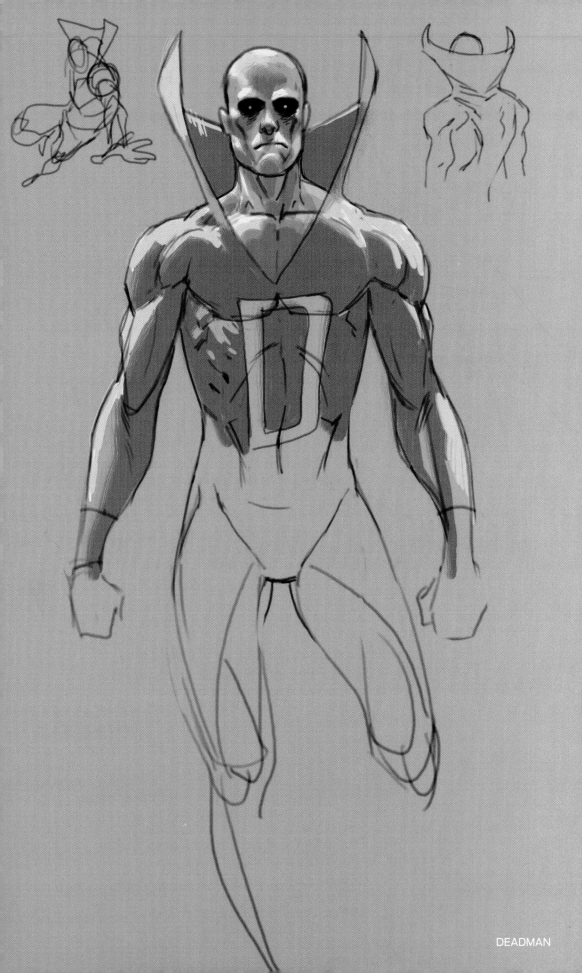

DEADMAN

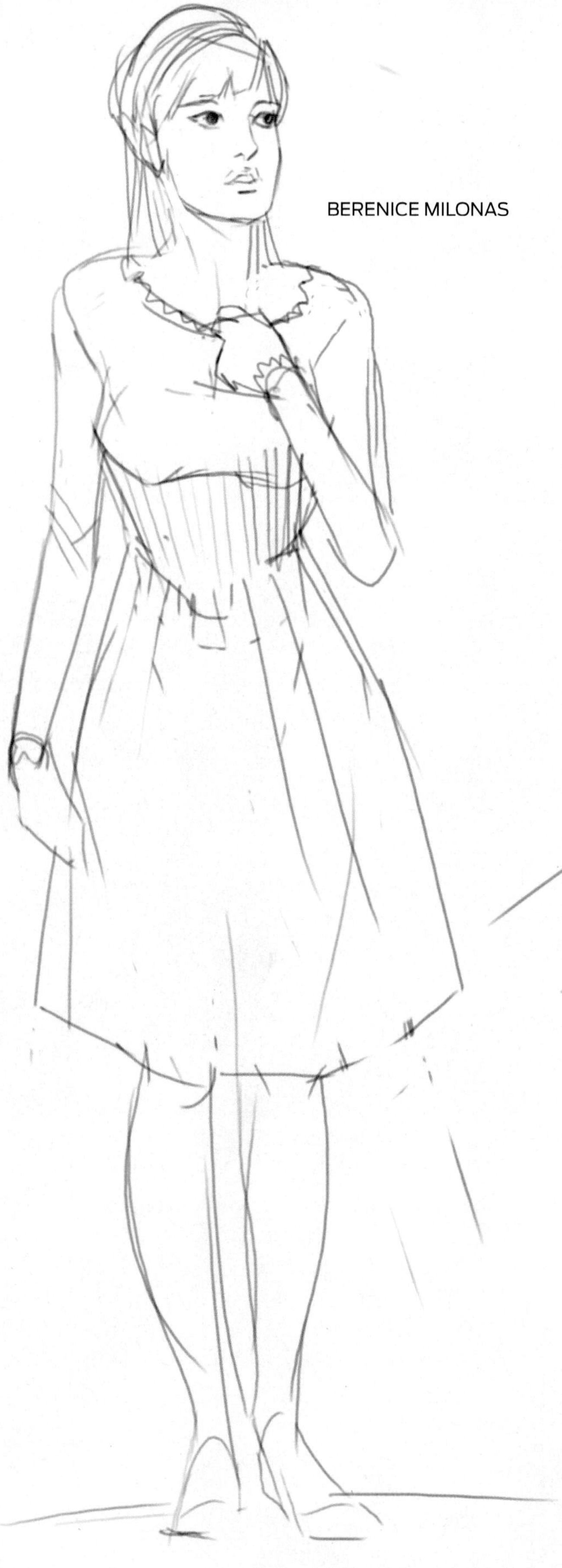

BERENICE MILONAS

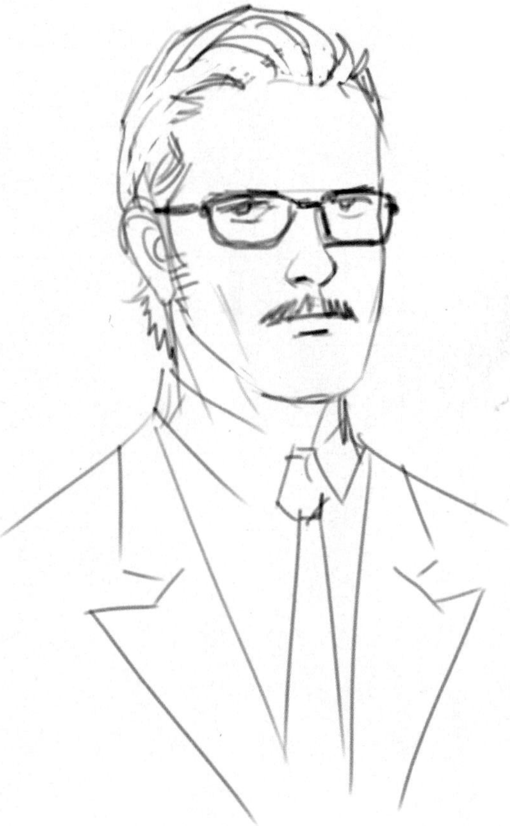

NATHAN DELAMERE

INKS by LAN MEDINA

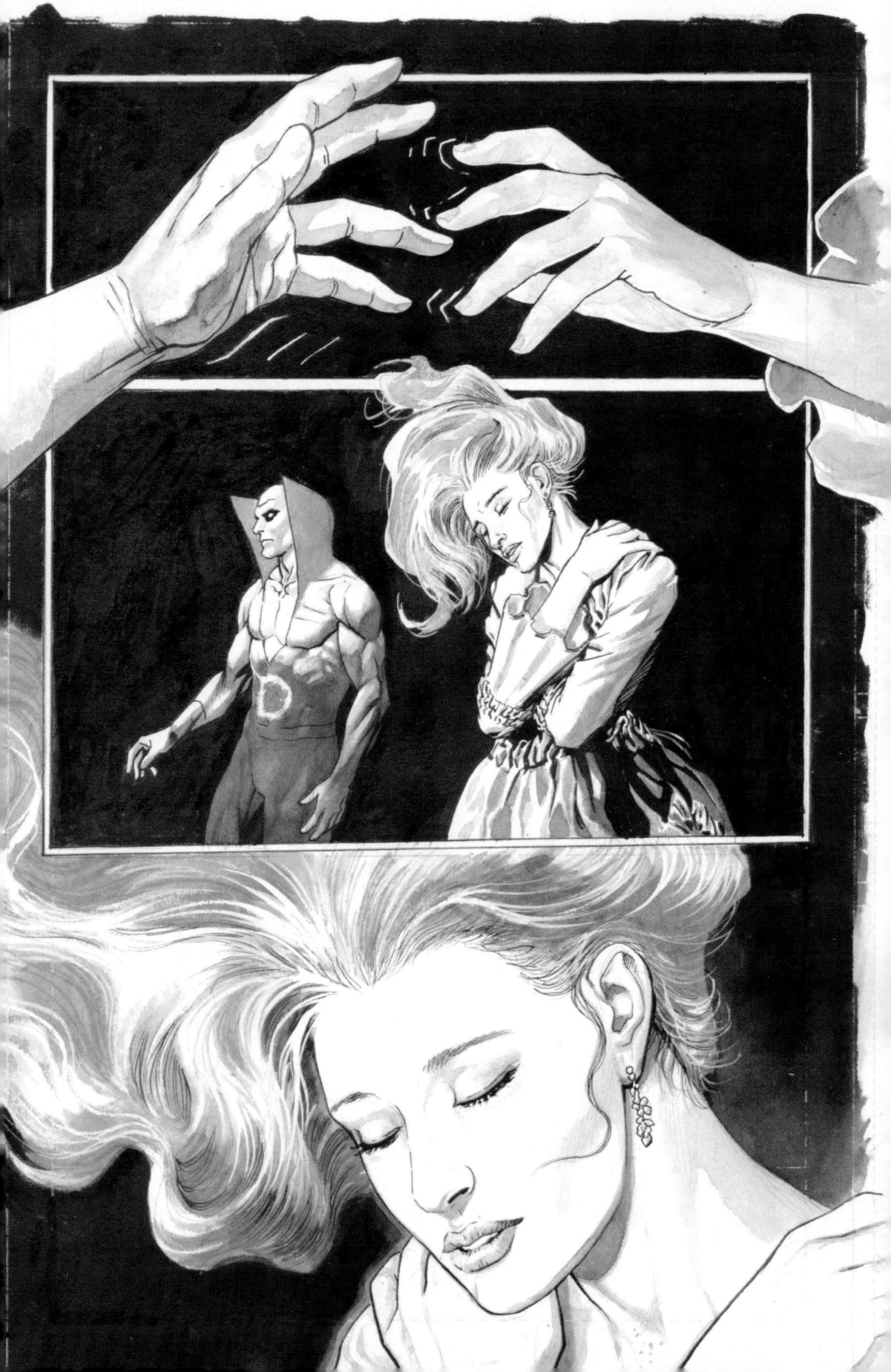

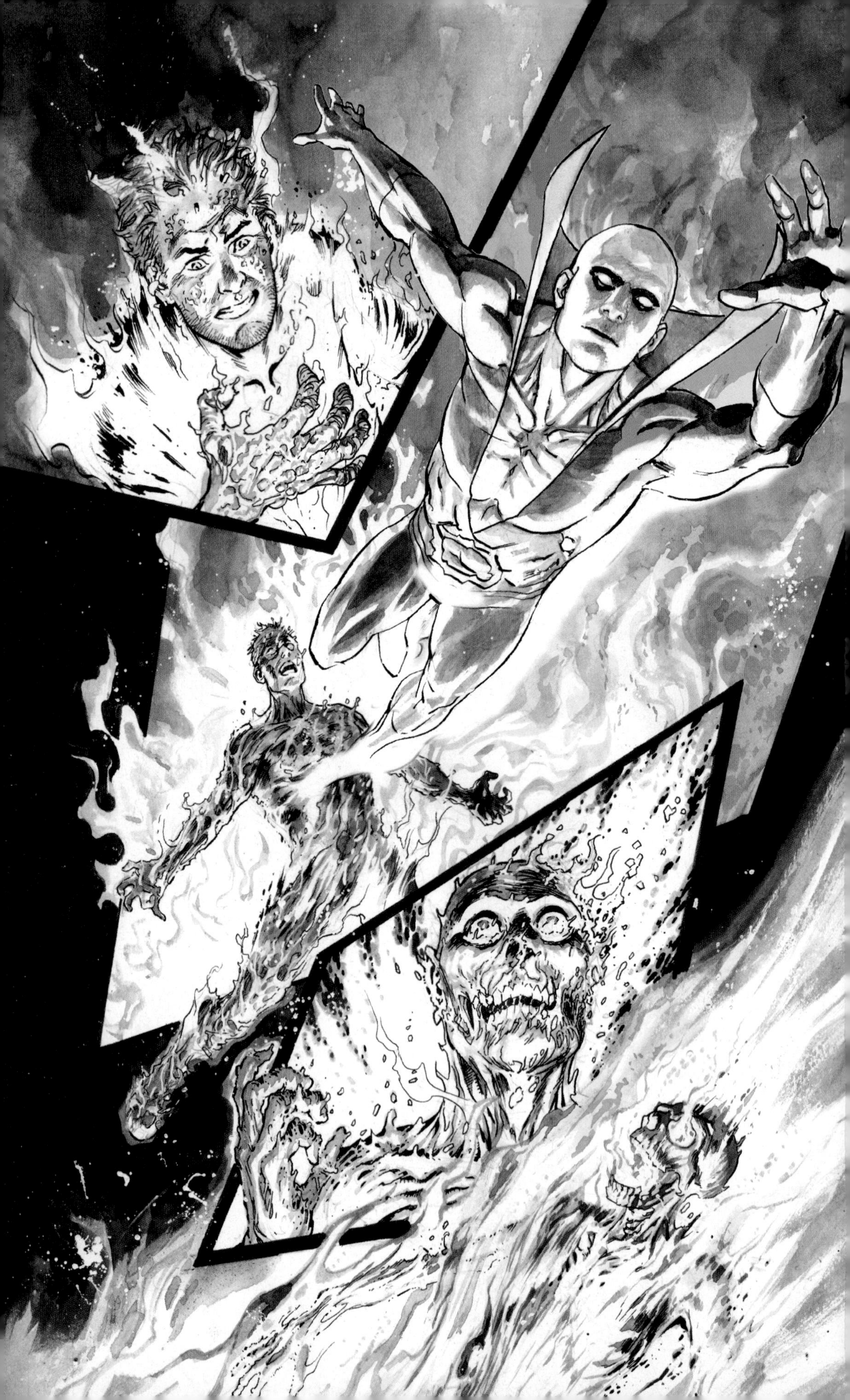